Aircraft
Carriers
at War

Aircraft Carriers At War

A Personal
Retrospective of
Korea, Vietnam,
and the Soviet
Confrontation

By Admiral

JAMES L. HOLLOWAY III

United States Navy (Ret.)

NAVAL INSTITUTE PRESS
Annapolis, Maryland

Naval Institute Press
291 Wood Road
Annapolis, MD 21402

Library of Congress Cataloging-in-Publication Data

Holloway, James L., 1922–
  Aircraft carriers at war : a personal retrospective of Korea, Vietnam, and the
Soviet confrontation / James L. Holloway.
    p. cm.
  Includes index.
  ISBN 978-1-59114-391-8 (alk. paper)
  1. United States—History, Naval—20th century. 2. Cold War. 3. Holloway, James
L., 1922– 4. Admirals—United States—Biography. 5. United States. Navy—
Biography. 6. United States. Navy—History—20th century. 7. United States.
Navy—Aviation—History—20th century. 8. Aircraft carriers—United States—
History— 20th century. 9. Korean War, 1950–1953—Naval operations, American.
10. Vietnam War, 1961–1975—Naval operations, American. I. Title.
E746.H65 2007
359.00973—dc22   2007004061

Printed in the United States of America on acid-free paper

14 13 12 11 10 09 08 07   9 8 7 6 5 4 3 2
First printing

*This book is dedicated
to the carrier aviators of the
United States Navy*

CONTENTS

FOREWORD

George H. W. Bush

There are few people as well qualified as Admiral Holloway to write this special book about the Cold War, one of the most fascinating chapters in our country's relatively young history. Drawing upon examples from his personal experience, Admiral Holloway gives his readers a front-row seat to many of the dramatic and strategic decisions made by our political and military leaders that held the Communists in check and led to the collapse of the Soviet Union in 1991.

From ensign to admiral, through World War II, Korea, Vietnam, and the nasty little skirmishes of the Cold War, Admiral Holloway served in the front lines in both operational and policy positions. It has been said of Jim Holloway that his destroyer was shot up by the Japanese in World War II, his plane shot down by the Chinese in Korea, and his flagship shot at by the North Vietnamese.

I was long an admirer of Jim's from afar but had a chance to work with him personally when, in 1985, he served as executive director of the president's Task Force on Combating Terrorism. In 1986, I appointed him special envoy to the Middle East to resolve a territorial dispute between Bahrain and Qatar. Long before anyone had ever heard of Al Qaeda, Jim knew and understood the terrorist threat and was working behind the scenes to keep our country safe.

His lucid views of the grand scheme of things are enlivened by firsthand accounts of combat and tactics. The breadth of Jim's experience, and the depth of his wisdom, gives the reader a remarkably broad perspective of naval warfare from cockpits to capitals. It's an incredible journey through a period of history that scholars and academics have barely begun to examine. Admiral Holloway's book gives all of us a head start on understanding how and why the Cold War was won.

PREFACE

"Where are the carriers?" That question, the essence of this retrospective, was made memorable during the Cold War by Henry Kissinger, national security advisor to President Richard Nixon and, later, secretary of state under both Nixon and President Gerald Ford. "Where are the carriers?" were Henry Kissinger's customary opening words to his staff and colleagues upon joining an emergency session of the National Security Council during the Cold War. The purpose of Kissinger's query was to pinpoint the location of the nearest source of U.S. military power, ready and available to serve as an effective first response to the crisis at hand.

It was the aircraft carrier and its battle group that offered a full set of options, from mere military presence to warfare on arrival, either showing the American flag or operating clandestinely. The carrier was able to use conventional weapons or employ nuclear arms and always had access to the crisis area without needing permission from another sovereign nation to enter it. Designed to be powerful enough to establish U.S. military dominance immediately upon arrival, it had the staying power to remain in the theater until reinforced or relieved.

These assets were the diplomatic and military options the National Command Authority would have as its alternatives with the closure of the Navy's carrier battle group. This was the portfolio of capabilities within the role of the U.S. Navy's carriers throughout the Cold War and as employed in all of its phases—Korea, Vietnam, and the Soviet confrontation. In the early days, the Cold War was the test bed for the genesis of the post–World War II carrier force, from which evolved the tactical structure of the U.S. Navy as it transitioned into the twenty-first century.

The confrontation with the USSR was the first global crisis, and the Korean War was the first military conflict to be faced by our country after the creation of the U.S. Air Force by the 1946 Defense Reorganization

Act. There was, as would be expected, substantial involvement on the part of the Department of Defense and interest among the American public as to how the changes would affect the operations of the air combat components of the war, especially regarding cooperation among the services and support of the ground forces.

With the advent of the U.S. Air Force, air power advocates had pushed to have the new service absorb virtually all airborne missions, including those in the maritime environment that the U.S. Navy had expected to retain and exploit. These issues transfixed Congress in the 1948 B-36 hearings, during which the relative capabilities and merits of carrier aircraft versus land-based heavy bombers and whether naval aviation should have a future role in carrying nuclear weapons were debated. An outcome of these hearings was the cancellation of the Navy's first postwar carrier, the *United States*, and the so-called revolt of the admirals, which culminated in 1949 with the chief of naval operations, Adm. Louis Denfeld, resigning in protest.

By 1950 the Navy was facing a reduction in its 1951 force levels to five fleet carriers—that is, carriers that could operate first-line jet aircraft. Then, with the remobilization that took place after the start of the Korean War and the overwhelming need for tactical aviation, a total of nineteen *Essex*-class carriers were taken out of mothballs, put back into commission, equipped with air groups, and deployed to the operating fleets. A total of twenty-one carriers of all types ultimately served in the conflict, and carrier aircraft flew more than 30 percent of all combat sorties during the Korean War.

In retrospect, historians generally now agree that the Korean War could not have been won by air power alone. There is also consensus that without tactical aviation as a component of the combined-arms support for the ground forces, the enemy could not have been stopped. Without complete air superiority, the UN would have lost the war to the Chinese.

The Korean experience demonstrated the continued viability of carrier-based air power. Carrier force levels remained at about twenty-five large carriers until the post–Vietnam War drawdown. However, this resurgence of the fleet aircraft carrier would not have occurred unless it had been possible to modernize these ships to handle the new jet aircraft that were transforming military aviation. When the first jet squadrons were deployed aboard the fleet carriers in the early post–World War II years, the results were not impressive. Naval aviation worked hard at the task, and in spite of seemingly insurmountable technical obstacles and daunting operational problems, the introduction of jet operations into the postwar carrier fleet was successful.

By July 1950, when the *Valley Forge* launched the first carrier strikes into Korea, each fleet carrier had been equipped with two squadrons of jet fighters. The first jets were the Grumman F9F-2 Panthers, soon followed by the McDonnell F2H-2 Banshee. These early Navy fighters were not as capable as the Air Force F86-E, which was able to match the Communist MiGs to ensure that air superiority would reside with the United States and its allies. Yet by the time the Navy's fleet carriers were deploying regularly in the Cold War, in the late summer of 1950, all of the embarked aircraft—Panthers, Banshees, and Corsairs—had proved capable for their mission, and the Douglas AD-2 Skyraider had no equal in any air force for close support of ground forces.

The U.S. Navy was able to build on these foundations to achieve the very pinnacle of success for the future. The McDonnell-Douglas F-4 Phantom II, a Navy carrier fighter, became the standard tactical fighter for all of the free-world air forces. Today there are nine 85,000-ton large-deck nuclear-powered carriers operating in the fleet, and a tenth, the *George Herbert Walker Bush*, launched in 2006.

This book is a largely contemporary perspective of the events, decisions, and outcomes in the history of the Cold War—Korea, Vietnam, and the Soviet confrontation—that shaped today's Navy and its principal ships-of-the-line, the large-deck nuclear-powered aircraft carriers, the unique trademark of this country's sea power, now and into the future.

ACKNOWLEDGMENTS

I would like to acknowledge the following individuals whose support and assistance were invaluable to me in the preparation of this book: John Tucker, who convinced me I should undertake the project; Beau Puryear, who got me started on my oral history; Frank Arre, who transcribed the hours of dictation and disciplined my handwritten edits; Capt. Todd Creekman, who brought order to the process; Dr. Dave Winkler, whose understanding of the history of the Cold War years kept me on track; John Reilly, whose research and proofreading made the first drafts respectable; Vice Adm. Bob Dunn and Capt. Tim Wooldridge, whose knowledge of aircraft carriers and their operations lent credibility to the details; and my faithful wife Dabney, who, having endured the experience of a Navy wife throughout the Cold War, stood by me as I tried to derive some meaning and order from those decades.

1

The End of an Era

Shortly after 0300 on 25 October 1944, the USS *Bennion* (DD-662) made its first visual contact with the Japanese heavies. I was standing up through the hatch in the Mark 37 gun director, scanning the horizon with binoculars. The rumble of heavy gunfire was now continuous, and the lower quadrant of the southern sky was aglow from the muzzle flashes. The patrol torpedo (PT) boats in the strait had sprung their ambush on the Japanese column and triggered a fierce firefight.

There was a tug on my trouser leg. The sailor at the pointer's station next to me motioned to my eyepiece, and I lowered myself into the director control seat. I looked through the magnification of the director's optics and the scene to the south became clearer: The crosshairs were fixed at the base of the jumbo "pagoda" superstructure of a Japanese battleship. The flashes from her main turret salvos and the rapid fire of the secondary battery were lighting up the entire ship. Judging by her clearly visible bow wake, she was making at least twenty-five knots.

The radar operator sitting behind me tersely reported that he had picked up the target out of the land mass return and was getting good ranges. I pushed down the bridge switch on the intercom, called that we were tracking a Japanese battleship, and locked on with the fire-control radar. The captain, Cdr. Joshua Cooper, replied that the "Martinis"—the radio call for the PT boats—were reporting that two enemy battleships, a cruiser, and at least three destroyers had passed through Surigao Strait, the narrows between Leyte and Mindanao in the southern Philippines. Our target was to be the second battleship. "Let me know when you have a fire-control solution on the Big Boy," the captain said. "Have the gun battery ready, but don't shoot unless I specifically tell you to. We have been directed to make a torpedo attack with five fish." His voice was clear and businesslike. In the background noise of the intercom I could hear on the TBS (talk-between-ships) radio the excited chatter of the Martinis as they maneuvered to launch their torpedoes. Going back to the optics, I could now see the two battleships in column. I moved the crosshairs to the second Big Boy, got a confirmation from the radar operator that he was locked on, and called the plotting room, telling them to let me know when they had a firing solution on the new target.

Now that the battleship had emerged from the strait, the image on the radarscope was clear of ground clutter and the fire-control radar was ranging consistently. In minutes, the plotting room talker reported, "Tracking in automatic." I passed this to the bridge, and the captain acknowledged, "Very well. Train out the tubes but don't launch or shoot until I give the order." I switched the 5-inch guns and both quintuple torpedo mounts to director control and again, standing up in the hatch, looked aft to see the torpedo mounts trained out on the beam.

The ship was running in and out of rainsqualls and it was very dark. The gunfire was still well to our south. I could barely make out the other two destroyers in our division; both were, like the *Bennion*, *Fletcher*-class ships. We were keeping a three-hundred-foot interval between ships in a loose column. The division was loitering at five knots, close to the western coastline of Leyte Gulf, using land clutter to hide from enemy radars. The only sounds were the popping of safeties as the engineers kept up a full head of steam for the run into the target. It was quiet in the gun director as each member of the crew was absorbed in his partic- ular duties. Our small talk had been used up long ago. For the past seven months the five of us had been together eight hours a day in this hot, cramped steel box, standing watches or at general quarters (GQ), shooting at the Japanese. We had fought together at Saipan, Tinian, Guam, and Palau, and at Peleliu, we had emptied the magazines three times in a single week. We considered ourselves experienced veterans.

There was one new member of the director crew this night. The regular pointer had been hit by shrapnel from a Japanese shore battery on Leyte. This young fire controlman, and the assistant gunnery officer standing by my side, had been wounded the day before. The assistant, Lieutenant (j.g.) Robertson, had been terribly torn up and was now wrapped in a blanket, strapped to the dining room table in the officers' wardroom (at GQ this becomes the ship's main battle dressing station). The war was over for him, but he didn't know it. He was full of morphine. Easing the pain and stopping the bleeding was about all that could be done for him. Robbie survived, but he lost an arm at the shoulder.

I had been momentarily diverted while checking the readiness of the gun mounts and torpedo stations over the sound-powered battle phones, and I was startled when I looked through the director optics again and saw how much larger the image of the Japanese battleship had grown. The enemy column was headed in our direction at twenty-five knots, and the range was closing fast.

The soft purr of the idling fire-room blowers suddenly rose to a high-pitched whine. The bridge had rung up full power. The director began to tremble, and the deck plates vibrated from the propellers' cavitation as the ship accelerated, our column of destroyers swinging southward. Suddenly, and almost simultaneously, the *Bennion*'s general announcing system and a sound-powered phone talker announced, "Starting the run-in for the attack."

Tactics had been planned to take advantage of the geography of Leyte Gulf. Our nine-ship destroyer squadron was organized into a trio of three-ship divisions that would operate individually but in coordination. From our initial positions lying in wait along the coastline of the northern gulf, the divisions would initiate a simultaneous attack on the order of the commodore, Capt. Roland Smoot. the column of nine destroyers running at full speed for the ten-mile approach to the torpedo launch point. Meanwhile, the Japanese column continued its own attack, rushing north at twenty-seven knots. It was the commodore's intention that we would meet the Japanese head on before they got within torpedo range of our own cruisers and battleships.

With the signal to commence the attack, the division turned in column to a southerly course to intercept the enemy, maintaining the three-hundred-foot interval between the ships. As we increased to flank speed, the fire rooms were ordered to make black smoke to screen our force. At darken ship (a security measure that reduces visibility of the ship by extinguishing all types of light) there was only the dim blue light from the battle lanterns for illumination. Standing in the hatch of the director, I could watch the entire panorama of the two converging fleets. Through the high-powered lenses of the Mark 37 director, the enemy could be seen in detail. As our destroyers broke out of the shadow of the shoreline, we were immediately taken under fire by the Japanese battleships and cruisers. It was strange to be rushing through the dark, closing on the enemy at a relative speed of more than fifty knots, not firing our own guns but seeing the steady gunfire of the Japanese ships and observing the explosions of their shots falling around us. The towering splashes of their 14-inch shells were close enough to wet our weather decks. Both sides were firing star shells for illumination, which added to the eerie character of the scene.

As the Japanese came into range, Rear Adm. Jesse B. Olendorf's battleships and cruisers, deployed in an east-west line to cross the "T" of the Japanese column, opened up with their main batteries. All along the northern horizon, enormous billows of flame from their 16- and 14-inch guns lit up the battle line. Directly over our heads stretched a procession of tracers converging on the Japanese column. The apparent slowness of the projectiles was surprising. Taking fifteen to twenty seconds in their trajectory before reaching their target, they seemed to hang in the sky. Through the gun director's optics, I could clearly see the shells exploding as they hit the Japanese ships, sending up cascades of flame as they ripped away topside gun mounts and erupting into fiery sheets of molten steel as they tore into the heavy armor plate.

Our division, still in column, headed directly for the Japanese battleship *Yamashiro*. At a range of seven thousand yards, the destroyer leading our division, almost obscured by shell splashes and black smoke, turned right, and I could see its five torpedoes splash as they hit the water. Following in the ship's wake, the *Bennion* heeled hard to port in a tight right turn to bring the torpedo tubes to bear. As the bridge called on the intercom and the sound-powered phones to "Launch torpedoes," the *Yamashiro* completely filled the viewing glass of my range finder. The crosshairs were stabilized on the waterline just below the pagoda mast. The plotting room computer operator down below was repeating, "We have a good solution." Glowing dials showed that the torpedo tubes were trained clear and the gyros set. I pushed the "fire torpedo" button on the console and stood up through the hatch to see our five fish shoot out of their tubes. I could hear them slap the water, running hot and straight.

As each destroyer adjusted its turn at the launch point to have the target at beam at the moment of launch, the formation became ragged, and the ships began maneuvering independently to avoid the enemy gunfire. As the *Bennion* retired to the north at thirty knots, still making black smoke, explosions erupted close off the port beam. A destroyer of our squadron, the *Albert W. Grant*, was taking hits from large-caliber shells. The scene of action was now one of growing confusion. The Japanese formation had disintegrated, with ships circling out of control, dead in the water, on fire, and shuddering from massive explosions, unrecognizable with bows gone, sterns blown away, and topsides mangled. Our own destroyers were intermixed in this melee, and on the *Bennion* we were trying to match up radar contacts with visual sightings to distinguish friend from foe. Then, unexpectedly, large-caliber tracers came in our direction from a major warship only several thousand yards on our starboard side. The rounds were passing over us, directed toward our destroyers retiring up the western side of the strait. It was quickly decided that this was not a friendly ship because the main battery was using ripple fire rather than the salvos characteristic of U.S. warships. As the warship and *Bennion* inadvertently closed, we could make out the lines of a *Mogami*-class cruiser and suddenly found ourselves ideally positioned for a torpedo shot. Captain Cooper immediately decided to launch the remaining five torpedoes at this target of opportunity. Slewing the director around to enable the fire-control radar to get a quick range and bearing, I gave the plotting room an estimated target angle. By the time the torpedo mount reported ready to fire, plot reported the computer had a firing solution with a good target course and speed. The captain ordered, "Launch torpedoes," the dials were in sync, the firing button pushed, and again it was five fish away.

The destroyer squadron had re-formed north of the strait by about 0430, and as first evidence of morning light appeared, the destroyers were ordered to proceed south at high speed to engage and destroy the remnants of the Japanese force. The scene in the lower gulf, viewed in the predawn light, was appalling. I counted four distinct fires, and the oily surface of the water was littered with debris. Japanese sailors were clinging to bits of floating wreckage and calling out to us as we raced by, but there was no time to pick up survivors. We had sighted a Japanese destroyer, the *Asagumo*, limping south, badly damaged and on fire. It had been severely pounded by the cruisers and battleships. If the *Asagumo* still had torpedoes aboard, it remained a real and deadly threat. Changing course to close on the *Asagumo*, the *Bennion* opened fire with its 5-inch battery at ten thousand yards and began to hit on the third salvo. We shifted to rapid continuous fire at six thousand yards, and as our rounds penetrated and exploded, flames burst from her hatches. At about two thousand yards, the *Asagumo* blew apart and slid beneath the gray, choppy waters as the *Bennion* raced by.

Just as the *Bennion* turned to rejoin the formation, a Zero broke out of the low clouds on our port beam heading directly at us. Our 5-inch battery commenced firing, and in a no-deflection head-on shot it scored a direct hit. The Zero was blown to pieces, the flaming remnants falling into the sea. It was now the early morning of the twenty-sixth. The crew of the *Bennion* was tired. We had been up at 0400 the day before, loading 5-inch ammunition from a Liberty ship anchored in Tacloban while Navy Wildcats tangled with Zeros overhead. We had been at GQ for more than twelve hours. Now, as we listened to the reports come in over the TBS and saw the survivors clinging to the smoking wreckage of a Japanese fleet, we realized a major Japanese force of battleships and cruisers had been virtually immolated and only one of our ships, the destroyer *Albert W. Grant*, had been seriously damaged.

THE BATTLE OF SAMAR

The thrill of victory was rudely interrupted. The TBS radio in the pilot house was picking up transmissions from Taffy 3, the escort carrier (CVE) task group operating east of the island of Samar. Three carrier task groups (also including Taffy 1 and Taffy 2), consisting of six CVEs each, were providing air cover for the Seventh Fleet ships in Leyte Gulf and close support to the U.S. Army invasion troops who had landed.

From what we could make out from the sometimes garbled, and often incomplete, transmissions, the CVEs were under long-range gunfire attack from a large Japanese naval surface force.

Our intercepted intelligence was shortly confirmed by a voice message from "Jehovah," the personal radio call sign of Vice Adm. Thomas Kinkaid, commander, Seventh Fleet. He was reporting that the three Taffy groups operating east of Samar were under attack by Japanese battleships, cruisers, and destroyers closing rapidly on the small carriers and their defensive screens. Planes from the CVEs, Wildcats and Avengers, had been making repeated runs on the attacking Japanese ships to force them to take evasive maneuvers and slow their rate of closure on the small carriers, but now they were having little effect. Their bomb bays were empty and their gun ammo expended. The Taffy surface escorts, destroyer escorts (DEs) and destroyers, had initiated a series of determined torpedo attacks against the enemy ships, but this heroic assault in clear daylight only served to slow the enemy temporarily before their torpedoes were expended and their short-range guns were disabled by the Japanese counterbattery fire. Three of the escorts were sunk and four were damaged, but their attacks gave all three Taffy groups time to launch aircraft. Taffy 3, closest to the enemy, was fleeing south under heavy fire from the Japanese. The *Gambier Bay*, bringing up the rear, was sunk, and most of the other five CVEs had been hit and damaged.

Admiral Kinkaid was ordering his Seventh Fleet battleships inside Leyte Gulf to form in a column, proceed to the eastern exit of the gulf, and, at best speed, sortie from Leyte and engage the Japanese surface force. The cruisers and destroyers were to form up on the battleship column as promptly as possible. A first concern, however, was to inventory the stocks of armor-piercing (AP) projectiles on hand. The battleships and cruisers had expended most of their AP ammunition during the night action at Surigao, and the rounds remaining in their magazines were primarily high-capacity (HC) projectiles intended for shore bombardment fire in support of the troops ashore. HC rounds, even in the 14- and 16-inch calibers of the battleships, would cause mainly external damage to the larger Japanese warships. AP projectiles were needed to pierce their armor and detonate in their magazines and engineering spaces. Listening to the reports going back to Kinkaid on the TBS, I could appreciate the admiral's concern. The count of AP projectiles remaining in the force's magazines seemed well below what might be required for the heavy engagement Kinkaid anticipated.

As the *Bennion* steamed north at thirty knots to rejoin the battleships, we gathered the other destroyers in our division. The crew was at partial battle stations, with one-third of the men at a time going to the mess decks for a ration of flapjacks and black coffee.

Before the first battleship had sortied from the gulf, Jehovah announced on the TBS that Rear Admiral Sprague, the Taffy Force commander, was reporting that the Japanese force had disengaged, turned 180 degrees, and was now headed north at flank speed for San Bernadino Strait, apparently to depart the Leyte area. Why, we wondered, when they were so close to destroying the CVE groups? They had to be concerned with getting caught by Admiral Halsey's Fast Carrier Task Force. With no air cover of their own, they could face disaster if Halsey's dive bombers and torpedo planes attacked them in the confines of the Philippine archipelago with limited room for evasion. Further, the destroyer torpedo attacks had broken up their tactical cohesion and three Japanese heavy cruisers had been fatally damaged by combined air and surface attacks from the CVE Taffy groups. Our carriers had been largely spared. One CVE and three escorts had been sunk. But apparently, the threat of the imminent arrival of Halsey's Fast Carrier Task Force had driven off the Japanese heavies. The Taffy units had been saved from almost certain annihilation off Samar.

Samuel Eliot Morison was later to write that Leyte Gulf, with the Battle of Surigao Strait, the action with the Taffy groups off Samar, the landing of a U.S. Army invasion force on Leyte, and the repulse of the Japanese air attacks on the exposed transports and supply ships of the invasion force anchored in Tacloban Harbor, was the greatest battle in naval history. The Battle of Surigao Strait would be the last major engagement of U.S. naval surface ships in which aircraft did not play a part. It was the end of an era.

It was a milestone in my career as well. A week later, during an intense air attack in Tacloban Harbor on Leyte, I transferred by whaleboat from the *Bennion* to a departing cargo ship to begin a long, slow hitchhike across the Pacific. I had orders to attend flight training. As I was saying good-bye to my skipper, Cdr. Joshua Cooper, a splendid gentleman and a great destroyer captain, he said he was sorry to see me leave the destroyer navy. I thought for a moment before I replied. I told him it was a great temptation to stay in tin cans. I particularly liked the *Bennion*, with its congenial wardroom and happy crew. But I had gone to the United States Naval Academy with the purpose of eventually becoming a carrier pilot and this was my last chance. I added only half seriously, "In the past forty-eight hours we have silenced two shore batteries, shot down three Zeros, battled a Japanese cruiser, sunk a destroyer by gunfire, and torpedoed a Japanese battleship. I think I'm ready to try something new."

Commander Cooper thanked me for my service as his commissioning gunnery officer in the *Bennion* and, gripping my hand firmly, wished me the best in my new Navy career. As I went over the side, he said, "By the time you get your wings, the war will be over. Exciting days like these will be a thing of the past." He proved to be a better destroyer skipper than a seer.

An unspoken reason for my going into aviation was that I had become convinced that the carrier had replaced the battleship as the capital ship of U.S. naval sea power. My experiences on board the *Bennion* over the last three months had impressed upon me that surface ships at war cannot survive in a hostile air environment without fighter cover. Although the *Bennion* was to win a Presidential Unit Citation for its prowess in shooting down Japanese aircraft, the carrier fighter planes, under the *Bennion*'s control, shot down ten Japanese planes for every one that our ship's guns got.

THE AIRCRAFT CARRIER EMERGES

It was in the first days of World War II that the aircraft carrier replaced the battleship as the capital ship of the U.S. Navy. The Japanese carrier attack on Pearl Harbor on 7 December 1941 had conclusively demonstrated the effectiveness of carrier-based aviation as the new fulcrum of power in naval warfare. All eight of the battleships that had been moored at Pearl were sunk or damaged in the Japanese attack. That was tangible evidence of the range and lethality of carrier aviation. When the British battleship *Repulse* and battle cruiser *Prince of Wales* were sunk at sea off Malaya just two weeks later by Japanese horizontal bombers and torpedo planes, it drove home a new axiom of modern naval warfare: the vulnerability of surface ships to air attack during daylight hours. The requirement for protective air cover for surface ships venturing into harm's way had been established. Surface ships in wartime could not operate safely during daylight hours in areas where there was probability of hostile aircraft unless local air cover was provided. Because of the need for this defensive air cover, and to exploit the striking range and power of the carrier's planes, it became U.S. Navy doctrine that the carriers would be the centerpiece of the fleet's offensive fighting dispositions, designated as fast carrier striking groups or fast carrier task forces. Carriers, battleships, cruisers, and destroyers were now to be integrated into these task forces (TFs) for mutual support. Carrier aircraft would provide the air cover and deliver the offensive punch at long range.

Surface forces continued to operate without air cover at night, when Japanese air attacks were not effective. Adm. Arleigh Burke, chief of naval operations (CNO) from 1952 to 1958, had served in the Pacific as a destroyer squadron commander in World War II. His success with the "Little Beavers" of Destroyer Squadron 23, eight *Fletcher*-class destroyers, was legendary. His operations consisted primarily of night maneuvers against Japanese surface forces in the "Slot," the channel between the eastern and western Solomon Islands, between Guadalcanal and the Japanese naval bases to the west and the U.S. supply points to the east.

THE FAST CARRIER TASK FORCE

In the first months of World War II in the Pacific, the only major battles in which the American task forces achieved some degree of success were all carrier-versus-carrier engagements in which the two carrier forces, Japanese and American, never made visual contact. These were the Battles of the Coral Sea, Midway, Eastern Solomons, and Santa Cruz. During the Battle of Midway, the American fast carrier task forces achieved a singular victory that today has come to be viewed by many historians as the turning point of World War II. The U.S. carrier aircraft inflicted heavy losses on the Japanese carrier fleet, sinking four of their carriers and decimating the experienced corps of Japanese carrier aviators, whose skill and leadership would be critically absent in future carrier-to-carrier battles, such as the Battle of the Philippine Sea. There, U.S. Navy fighters took a staggering toll on the inexperienced Japanese carrier pilots.

The Battle of Midway, America's first clear-cut victory in the Pacific in World War II, was won by U.S. carriers and so crippled the Japanese carrier fleet that major Japanese offensives in the Pacific came to a halt. As the war went on, the shipyards and aircraft factories of U.S. industry delivered modern carriers and superior carrier fighting aircraft to the fleets to replace the earlier losses and build up the force levels. The fleet carriers (CVs) were of the *Essex* class, thirty-four-thousand-ton ships designed from the keel up to be the capital ships of the U.S. Navy. The light carriers (CVLs) of the *Independence* class, displacing about ten thousand tons and capable of speeds of more than thirty knots, were a remarkably useful adaptation to expand the carrier force. Nine *Independence*-class and sixteen *Essex*-class carriers were delivered during the war.

It was largely with these modern carriers at Okinawa that the Pacific Fleet faced its greatest challenge, as the U.S. task forces operated within close range of the complex of Japanese bases positioned to defend the Japanese home islands. Okinawa saw the use of kamikaze aircraft for the first time on a large scale, and more than fourteen hundred kamikaze attacks were carried out on the carrier striking forces. The fleet survived in spite of this concentrated offensive by the highly effective manned "guided missiles." It is a matter of record that although a number of carriers were hit by kamikazes and by bombs, not one modern *Essex*-class fleet carrier was sunk during World War II by enemy action.

During the war, the U.S. Navy had operated 110 aircraft carriers in the fleet, of several types, designs, configurations, and missions. The fleet carriers, as exemplified by the sixteen *Essex*-class ships, carried sixty to seventy modern aircraft and were used as the nucleus of the fast carrier striking groups. The nine light carriers of the *Independence* class were converted from cruiser hulls and because of their speed assigned to the fast carrier striking groups with the CVs. Their complement of aircraft included F-6F Hellcats and TBM Avengers.

ESCORT CARRIERS

Early escort carriers were originally designed or built as tankers and cargo ships and were converted to small carriers for escort duty in the Atlantic. These CVEs launched Wildcats and Avengers in hunter-killer attacks against hostile submarines and were a major factor in defeating the German submarine threat and winning the Battle of the Atlantic.

The success of these small converted "merchantman carriers" prompted the construction of fifty "keel up" CVEs, which were known as the *Casablanca* class. Henry Kaiser, the American industrial genius, was turning out these carriers on a production line. Nineteen improved *Commencement Bay*–class CVEs were in commission or being built when World War II ended.

In the Pacific, CVEs were used to provide air support to troops ashore during and immediately after amphibious assaults, before land-based aircraft could be brought in to fly off the former Japanese airstrips. Their aircraft complement consisted principally of FM-2 Wildcat fighters and TBM Avenger bombers.

The Wildcat, produced by General Motors and designated the FM-2, was inferior to the F6F Hellcat and the F4U Corsair as a fighter against the Zero. But the Wildcat could handle Japanese bombers and torpedo planes, especially the older Japanese aircraft that had been pressed into service as kamikazes.

The *Bennion* was one of the earliest of the few destroyers to be outfitted with a fighter director team to control the CVE-based fighters on combat air patrol for the defense of naval forces operating outside of the protective cover of TF 38 and TF 58. For example, the CVEs provided fighter cover for the amphibious forces, underway replenishment vessels, shore bombardment combatants, and picket destroyers.

It had been the *Bennion*'s task, while a screening destroyer with the amphibious force, on the gun line with the shore bombardment units, and when on picket station, to control the Wildcat fighters flying from the CVEs as the fighter cover for these surface task forces, directing the fighters to intercept the raids of Japanese bombers and kamikazes, which could number as many as a hundred aircraft. There would be as many as thirty to forty Wildcats under close control of the *Bennion*'s embarked fighter director officers, and these fighter planes were able to shoot down as many as 80 percent of the aircraft in a Japanese air raid, turning back the strike or disorganizing the formations to the extent that the ship's antiaircraft (AA) guns could handle the confused remnants.

TRANSITION TO NAVAL AVIATION

In the summer of 1944 I had received a letter from my father, then a captain in the U.S. Navy and in command of the USS *Iowa*, the first of that class of battleship and at the time the largest warship afloat. When the keel had been laid in 1940, it was the most powerful ship in our Navy, capable of more than thirty-two knots, with sixteen-inch armor, nine 16-inch guns, and twelve 5-inch guns in twin mounts. My father's letter had a purpose: He recommended that I get into flight training and become a naval aviator as soon as possible. These were strange words coming from a career naval officer who had served in destroyers, cruisers, and battleships all his life. He had commanded a destroyer division and a destroyer squadron already in World War II before taking over the *Iowa*. He was assigned to TF 38, which had just taken part in the Battle of the Philippine Sea, an important victory for the U.S. Navy but a battle in which the surface ships on both sides never made contact with one another. The carrier aircraft were the principals. Although the *Iowa* was in the thick of the fight, its role was to help defend Halsey's TF 38 from the Japanese carrier planes, using her 5-inch gun batteries, 40mm rapid-fire guns, and 20mm machine guns. During World War II, the *Iowa*-class battleships' principal combat roles were in TF 38 and TF 58. As my father put it, "The war in the Pacific is being won by the carriers. The future of the U.S. Navy lies in naval aviation."

Up until then I had delayed my final decision on flight training. I was comfortable in the destroyer navy, and my commanding officer assured me that I had a future in tin cans. The letter from the *Iowa* did it. My application for flight training went off in the next mailbag headed east.

On 7 November 1944, I left the *Bennion* in Tacloban Harbor and embarked in a retrograde Lykes freighter for the first leg of the long hitchhike back to the states and a new career as a naval aviator. The *Bennion* went on to Lingayen Gulf and Okinawa, where, as one of the few destroyers to survive the kamikaze assaults, it was awarded the Presidential Unit Citation for its performance on an early warning picket station, shooting down eighteen enemy planes in a two-day period.

Although the attrition rate for washing out officer students in flight training was running as high as 25 percent, things went smoothly for me until President Truman's decision to use the second nuclear bomb on Japan. The war ended, V-J Day was declared, and the demobilization of the U.S. military began. Citizen-soldiers' reactions to the immediate and wholesale discharges were close to ecstasy, but chaos reigned for the career officers and petty officers left in place to run the Navy. Tanks, trucks, aircraft, and supplies were abandoned at overseas bases as the experienced operators and maintenance men went east in a mad but organized rush. President Truman had decreed that returning veterans go home as soon as possible; it was his highest priority. I later heard a lot about this. My father, a newly selected rear admiral, had been placed in charge of demobilization of the Navy.

I was in flight training at Corpus Christi, Texas, when the war ended. But the mean point of impact of the demobilization did not hit the continental United States (CONUS) commands until after I had received my wings in January 1946. That week, the entire syllabus for pilot carrier qualification training was cancelled. The course at Naval Air Station Fort Lauderdale (President George H. W. Bush's training base less than a year earlier), where I had been assigned for torpedo plane training in the TBM Avenger, was reduced by 30 percent in flight training hours.

To compound this elimination of essential training in the more complex and demanding fleet aircraft, when I reached the fleet I was reassigned to a dive-bomber squadron of SB2C-5 Curtis Helldivers instead of the TBM Avengers in which I had at least a truncated operational training. The SB2C was known to its pilots as the "Beast," and not for any affectionate reason. The aircraft's flight controls were sloppy, the mechs referred to it as a "flying hydraulic leak," and the quality control of the aircraft as delivered from Canadian Car and Foundry, which had been given the production contract from Curtis-Wright, was best described as awful. Yet it had destroyed more tonnage of Japanese shipping, warships and cargo vessels, than any other Allied aircraft.

Being ordered to an aircraft and mission in which I had not been trained was not atypical in the prevailing turmoil brought on by massive demobilization. And the disorder was further exacerbated by the resignation of many regular naval officers, tired of war and family separation and disillusioned by what they perceived to be a postwar navy that was going to be underfunded, undermanned, and overextended.

In July 1945, when I reported to Naval Air Station Oceana, at Virginia Beach, Virginia, the command of Bombing Squadron 3 (VB-3) had devolved upon a lieutenant, a former Reserve officer who had opted for a regular commission. Except for one or two lieutenants (junior grade), all of the other junior pilots were Reservists who were not interested in staying in the Navy or who had been turned down for a regular commission. Morale was at rock bottom and discipline was nonexistent. The week before I checked in, two young pilots had been killed in an accident involving an unauthorized cross-country flight in a squadron plane. The pilots were in civilian clothes at the time.

Because of my seniority, as third in the squadron, I was made squadron operations officer. It was a difficult position. Even the ensigns in the squadron had more flight hours than I did, and the lieutenants (junior grade) had flown SB2Cs off a carrier before the demobilization drawdown. It was something of a consolation to me that the executive officer, a lieutenant commander from the Naval Academy class of 1942, a year senior to me, had completed flight training only the month before. He had, however, been through operational training in Helldivers.

In August, a midair collision on a routine join-up and the failure of a pilot to pull out of his dive on a bombing run a week later took the lives of two more pilots. The VB-3 commanding officer was called over to fleet headquarters in Norfolk. He never returned to the squadron. In his place a more mature officer, Lt. Cdr. Heber Badger, a Naval Academy graduate from the class of 1941, reported. He had been through the carrier battles in the Pacific flying F6F Hellcats against the Japanese.

Within a week, before the new skipper could square away the squadron, disaster struck again. A carrier had become available to our air group on short notice for qualification landings. VB-3 was not ready. A landing signal officer (LSO) from another air group was borrowed to conduct field carrier landing practice ashore in preparation, but he was not really interested in us. His discharge date was coming up and he wanted out—badly.

On a blustery Monday morning in September 1946, VB-3 flew from our base at Naval Air Station Oceana to rendezvous with the carrier at sea off the Virginia capes. Those of us who had never before landed on a carrier had walked on board the day before and spent the night on the carrier. After the experienced pilots had made two successful landings each, the new boys would take their place in the cockpit. This transfer was accomplished with the plane on the flight deck, the engine turning over, thirty-five knots of wind buffeting the deck, and the air officer on the bullhorn—the flight deck announcing system—bellowing to the new pilots to speed up the exchange. It wasn't that easy. The parachute had to be buckled on, the safety belt and harness attached, the microphone and earphones plugged in, the seat adjusted for height, the rudder pedals adjusted for length, the map case stowed, and the takeoff checklist gone over. All this with the 1,800-horsepower engine turning over at 1,200 rpm, the plane captain fiddling with the pilot's harness, and the bullhorn urging him to hurry up. Under these conditions, the apprehension generated by the occasion of my first carrier takeoff and landing was almost more than I could bear.

Unfortunately, the brown-shirted plane captain was of little assistance. He had about as much experience on a carrier flight deck as I did. When he considered that I was properly buckled in, he leapt from the Helldiver's wing to the teak flight deck and disappeared behind the island with his load of chocks and tie-down chains.

By now the yellow-shirted plane director was motioning frantically to get my attention to signal me forward to the fly one (the flight deck area forward of the island) officer. I taxied into the launch spot in the middle of the flight deck adjacent to the island. There the launching signal officer, with his left hand in a clenched fist to indicate I should hold the brakes, rapidly twirled a small yellow flag in his right hand as a signal for me to add full power.

I pushed the throttle forward and the rpm needle maxed at 2,800. I had full power. There wasn't time to check the dashboard's many other dials and gauges for such secondary essentials as cylinder head temperature or oil pressure. I nodded to the fly one officer, who dropped to his right knee and pointed his little flag at the carrier's bow.

I released the brakes, and with the plane's wing passing over the kneeling launch officer, the Beast lumbered down the flight deck. Everything felt good as the plane lifted off the deck fifty feet before reaching the bow. I was flying. I retracted the landing gear and wing flaps just as primary flight control called, "Scarface six, your signal is Charlie. You are cleared to land." I punched the mike button on the throttle handle with my thumb to answer, "Roger Flapjack [USS *Kearsarge*], I have a Charlie." There were six VB-3 SB2Cs in a racetrack pattern around the carrier, and I eased my plane in behind the one that was passing the island as I took off. He extended his upwind leg to several miles ahead of the carrier and swung into a left turn. I waited until he was abeam of me to port on a reverse course—to get a proper landing interval—before making a similar left turn to the downwind course, opening the canopy and lowering the landing gear in the process. As the bow of the carrier came abeam to port, about a quarter mile distant, I dropped my hook, lowered the landing flaps, and reduced power to about 1,800 rpm as I put the propeller into low pitch for maximum thrust. The plane was at about one hundred feet of altitude and ninety-five knots in a thirty-degree banked left turn when I visually picked up the LSO. He was giving me the fast signal by banging the signal paddle on his left leg. I eased off a little power, adjusted my turn to get a one-hundred-foot straightaway before the cut, and noticed the SB2C ahead of me was still on deck. The LSO was signaling for me to keep coming. At the last moment before I rolled out for the straightaway, the LSO signaled a wave off, simultaneously calling out on the radio, "Wave off, foul deck." I jammed on full power, raised my landing gear, adjusted prop pitch, cranked the canopy closed, and eased up my flaps as the speed increased.

The entire procedure of the upwind leg turn to downwind and approach to landing was repeated. This time I cheated a bit and took a longer interval on the plane ahead. Canopy open, wheels down, hook down, flaps down, low prop pitch, and watch the LSO. After a flurry of signals to slow down, increase turn, and reduce altitude, the LSO brought me in low over the ramp and gave me the cut signal by running his right paddle across his throat. There was a mild but definite jolt and I was on the deck. A second later I was thrown against the shoulder harness as the arresting hook engaged a cross-deck pendant—the tail hook caught a wire. I kept my feet off the brakes as the deck-edge wire operator retracted the arresting cable. This pulled the plane back ten feet, over the crash barriers, which were lowered down flush with the deck. The yellow shirts, athletes that they were, were out on the deck immediately. The plane director, now visible off the plane's nose to port, signaled "Hold brakes." The hook men disengaged the now-slack wire from the arresting hook tip. The director signaled "Taxi forward," and as the SB2C rolled out of the arresting gear area, the crash barriers rose up behind me. Ahead was Fly One again with his little yellow flag. Within thirty seconds I was again airborne, with one successful carrier landing in my record.

Again I followed the landing sequence: canopy, gear, hook, flaps, props, and follow the LSO's signals. I was looking good at the cut. I yanked off the power, leveled off in a three-point altitude, and *twang*. Then sudden silence. I was in the crash barrier. The engine had stopped immediately, as the barrier cable was wrapped up in the prop. The crash yodel alarm, the worst noise in the world, was now deafening. A foam nozzle appeared over the cockpit coaming. The asbestos-suited "hot papa" was ready to spray at the first sign of smoke or fire. Then a head in a white helmet with a red cross appeared—the crash crew hospital corpsman was on the wing.

"Are you hurt?" he shouted.

"Just my ego is badly bruised," I replied.

"Your what is what?" he asked anxiously.

I told him I was fine, and he climbed down, just a little bit disappointed, I thought. As I was helped out of the cockpit, the crash crew had already cleared the prop and attached a tow tractor to pull the plane to the hangar deck. The Beast was otherwise undamaged. As I walked into the island structure, I was met by my new skipper, Lieutenant Commander Badger. He put his arm around me and said, "Don't feel bad, Jim, there are only two kinds of carrier aviators. Those who have gotten a barrier and those who are going to get one." He sent me down to the ready room for a cup of coffee. "A barrier doesn't even rate a medicinal brandy," he continued. "Besides, you've got to fly this afternoon and get your four more arrested landings. I'll see you up on vulture's row."

After a check on the aircraft—no damage except for a prop change—and a cup of coffee to decompress, I made my way topside to what is known to carrier types as vulture's row. This is a narrow space on the carrier's island aft of the primary air control station, itself a glass-enclosed perch sixty feet above the flight deck where the air officer and his two assistants control the plane handling on the flight deck. Spectators line up along the railing on vulture's row to watch, and of course critique, the carrier landings. I had just arrived on the row after climbing three sets of ladders and joined the skipper when the emergency klaxon went off with its ominous yodel and the bullhorn blared out, "Plane in the water." I asked Badger what had happened—I could just see the tail end of an SB2C-5 sticking out of the water one hundred yards astern of the carrier, going down fast. He replied, "A Helldiver just stalled out in the landing approach and the plane went in. Looks like the pilot didn't get out." No head had reappeared. By now the plane guard destroyer had arrived and was backing both engines, slowing down to put a whaleboat in the water. The air officer had waved off the following SB2Cs in the landing pattern and sent them up to one thousand feet to join up and circle the ship. The carrier never slowed down. The pilot was one of our VB-3 ensigns, a former aviation cadet who had just received his wings and reported aboard the squadron the same week I had.

Badger was working his way through the crowd forward on vulture's row to the navigation bridge, where he would report to the captain of the ship. I asked the lieutenant standing next to me what had happened. The pilot, the lieutenant said, was a little low and a bit slow. The LSO signaled him to increase his bank to avoid overshooting the groove—the landing straightaway—and to add power. The pilot answered the signals but put on the power too late. The steep bank with the nose-up attitude stalled him out before he could add power, and he spun in. Going in at ninety-five knots from a sixty-foot altitude was too much for the pilot. He must have been unconscious and unable to unhitch his seatbelt and harness to get out of the plane.

Forward of vulture's row, the air officer stuck a flag pole with a green flag in a socket and the signal bridge ran up the "Fox" flag (the letter *F* signal flag, indicating that a ship is conducting air operations) on a halyard. The bullhorn blared, "Clear deck, commence landing aircraft." With the order repeated by radio from Air Operations, four SB2Cs flew by on a parallel course to the right of the ship in a tight echelon at three hundred feet. Their hooks were down. As the first plane passed the bow of the carrier, it turned left in a steep bank to enter the landing pattern. The approach was normal until the plane rolled out on a short straightaway final. The LSO signaled the pilot at the last moment to lose altitude and turn left to line up to land. As the plane came over the ramp (the rear end of the flight deck), the LSO gave the cut signal, but the pilot was too low. When he dropped the nose at the cut—and even I could see it was too much—the left wheel hit the deck and the plane bounced back into the air in a right turn. The pilot pushed the plane's nose down again to return to the deck, the tail went up, the hook missed the wires, and the Helldiver crashed into the 5-inch gun mount on the carrier's starboard side, the nose going between the twin 5-inch gun barrels. Parts flew off, the massive propeller, turning at a thousand rpm, disintegrated, and the tank full of high-octane aviation gas ignited in a huge fireball.

The crash crew rushed to the scene, but the flames were so fierce that the hot papas in their asbestos suits were literally blown backward by the heat. Somehow the pilot, Bill Spiegel, our VB-3 executive officer, the second in command, was able to unhitch himself from the cockpit entanglements and jump from the plane's wing to the ship's deck. But even with his miraculous escape, the brief exposure to the searing flames resulted in terrible burns to his face and hands.

Ten minutes later, coming up from sick bay where he had just visited the exec, the skipper met with the rest of the VB-3 pilots in a squadron ready room. The captain of the ship had canceled air operations for the day. The mess on the flight deck had to be cleaned up, the smoking ruins pushed over the side. Badger told us, "Bill will survive. The burns are bad and he will be in the hospital for a long time. Jim Holloway will be the new exec." A quiet moment later I caught Badger, pulled him aside, and said, "I'm just a lieutenant with brand-new wings. The job calls for a lieutenant commander with flight experience." Badger replied, "Jim, what we need now are professional naval officers rather than experienced pilots. We must get discipline in our people and order in the squadron. As exec you can help me do that. At the same time, you will be building up flight hours and flying experience. You'll do okay."

I stayed on as executive officer of VB-3 and remained a lieutenant. It would not be the first time I served in a billet above my rank, and it would not be the last time I was promoted as the result of a casualty to my immediate senior in the organization. VB-3 recovered rapidly from its post-demobilization trauma. We did not lose another pilot during the rest of my time in the squadron. In 1947, VB-3 deployed aboard the USS *Kearsarge* with the Second Fleet to the North Atlantic and the Caribbean and served a six-month tour in Air Group Three on board the USS *Valley Forge* with the Sixth Fleet in the Mediterranean during 1948. The carrier deployment to the Sixth Fleet was the beginning of the pattern of strategic carrier deployments that endured for the entire period of the Cold War and beyond, up until 2002, as a global strategic policy requirement.

2

The Cold War

Reflections of a Campaigner

The United States and its Allies won World War II, and the victory could not have been more complete. Our main Axis foes, Germany and Japan, had submitted to unconditional surrender. Our Allies were exhausted, their armed forces depleted and their economies in shambles after years of war. Their homelands had been devastated by invading armies or fleets of bombers. The United States, alone of all the principal belligerents, had not been exposed to the presence of enemy troops or felt the shock of aerial bombardment within its national boundaries. And the United States, now the most powerful nation on Earth, had a monopoly on the atomic bomb.

Out of the embers of World War II rose another threat—not a new enemy but a dangerous adversary whose hostility toward the United States had been temporarily set aside to meet the common and more immediate menace of the fascist Axis. This new enemy was the Soviet Union, and the conflict, which came to be known as the Cold War, was ideological, between communism and Western democracy.

THE THREAT OF THE USSR

History is constructed on a framework of dates and events, and the nominal beginning of the Cold War is generally identified with Winston

Churchill's "Iron Curtain" speech given at Fulton, Missouri, on 5 March 1946. But most historians will agree that the seeds of the conflict originated in the decades following the Bolshevik Revolution and during the evolution of the Soviet Union. Josef Stalin, general secretary of the Communist Party and head of the Soviet Union, defined capitalism and the very culture of Western democracy as the mortal enemies of communism.

Even if 5 March 1946 was not the de facto beginning of the Cold War, it was the declaration of war and the call to arms for the Western powers. During this epic struggle between the West and the Soviet satellites, the very survival of the United States was at stake. For more than thirty years of this confrontation, the United States as a nation, and Americans as a people, were threatened with annihilation by Soviet nuclear weapons. By the 1970s the Russians were targeting the United States with an estimated twelve thousand warheads, and the Joint Chiefs of Staff (JCS) estimated that in a strategic nuclear exchange, between 80 and 130 million Americans would die.

Early on, during my deployment to Korea in 1951, it became clear to me that in the Cold War with the Soviet Union, just as during the conflict with the Axis powers in World War II, it was the United States that accepted and exercised the role of leadership for the entire free world.

In spite of what may be viewed pessimistically a stalemate in Korea and a loss in Vietnam, as a veteran of both wars I am today impressed by the fact that the United States consistently prevailed throughout these forty years of confrontation with the Soviet Union. During that time, there was no Soviet military aggression against our North Atlantic Treaty Organization (NATO) military partners or Japanese allies. The Atlantic Alliance has outlasted all multilateral peacetime treaty organizations in modern history, and all the members of NATO are still free countries. Soviet forces did not attack Western Europe, and North Korea has not again attacked South Korea.

Further, I am today fully persuaded that U.S. leadership and military power were responsible for our survival and our ultimate victory in the Cold War. I have seen the arms technology generated by these four decades of confrontation—thermonuclear weapons, intercontinental missiles, jet aircraft, and nuclear submarines are but several examples— restructure for all time the most basic concepts of warfare. I saw our military leadership effectively integrate the enormous power and global reach of these new weapons into our operating forces to constrain the spread of Soviet influence. At the same time, they were able to avoid plunging civilization into the holocaust of a general nuclear war.

In later years, after my active-duty career, I came to realize that Korea and Vietnam were successive campaigns in a larger and more desperate struggle that began with the end of World War II and lasted for more than four decades, until the disintegration of the Soviet Union in 1989. The Soviet Union was our real adversary throughout the Cold War. The USSR, with its enormous armies, had the capability to overwhelm and occupy Western Europe. The Soviets' nuclear arsenal, which soon reached an essential equivalence with ours, had the capacity to inflict one hundred million casualties on our population and literally destroy our industrial economy. Although we fought major conflicts with North Korea, China, and North Vietnam during this time, those countries did not represent direct or immediate threats to our national survival. The Soviet Union alone had the capacity to challenge the very existence of the United States.

Over the forty-plus years of the Cold War, I came to appreciate the consistency of our basic security philosophy. It was so logical and straightforward: The Russians were our primary enemy and our policy was to counter Soviet aggression, whether by threat from the USSR or military action by their Communist proxies. The military establishment in which I served was designed to defeat the Russian military across the spectrum of warfare, from limited wars to an all-out nuclear exchange. And because the Soviet Union was by far the most powerful adversary on the global horizon, a military posture that could contain the Soviets could handle any other foe.

THE STRATEGIC NUCLEAR BALANCE

In 1957, when VA-83, the A4D-2 Skyhawk squadron of which I was commanding officer (CO), was assigned the primary mission of nuclear-weapons strike, I became an integral player in the national nuclear community. As a squadron pilot, I was assigned a specific target in Europe to attack with a thermonuclear weapon, and in this capacity I became intimately familiar with the terrible destructive power of these devices and aware of our awe-inspiring arsenal of nuclear weapons and hydrogen bombs, immense in their terrible destructive capacity, con-stantly undergoing modernization, and continuing to grow in the size of the stockpile. It was a sobering exposure to the possibility of the destruction of civilization as we know it.

I lived with this doomsday potential for the rest of my military career. First as a pilot with the mission of dropping the bomb, and then with the task of training and leading other pilots in this somber undertaking. From there I went on to command ships whose magazines were config-ured to store "perhaps a hundred" nuclear bombs. Then later, as a flag officer and member of the Joint Chiefs of Staff, my duties included consulting with the secretary of defense (SecDef) on nuclear-weapons treaty agreements and, at the same time, serving as an advisor to the president of the United States on the operational decision for the release of nuclear weapons to be used against an enemy. This latter responsibil-ity included command post exercises (CPXs) with President Carter in the war room of the Pentagon, simulating crises that rehearsed the procedures and decisions for the release of nuclear and thermonuclear weapons to the armed forces for nuclear strikes against the USSR. Having several times viewed the films of the Bikini H-bomb tests and witnessed the virtual vaporization of the atoll and the fleet of warships anchored in the lagoon, I found that all aspects of our nuclear-warfare planning could not help but be depressing.

At the beginning of the Cold War, the balance of nuclear capabilities lay totally with the United States. The United States had exploded two atomic bombs against the Japanese in World War II and was producing additional and more-refined weapons before the Russians had their first nuclear device. But Stalin, determined to catch up, made development of nuclear weapons his highest priority. From their standing start, the Soviets did well. Their first atomic explosion took place four years after our successful test at Alamogordo, New Mexico, but the first Soviet hydrogen bomb followed our H-bomb tests at Bikini by only nine months. By 1964 the United States had about six thousand nuclear weapons in the stockpile and the Soviets six hundred. By the mid-1970s the Russians had caught up. Although the inventories of bombs, missiles, rockets, warheads, reentry vehicles, and delivery systems differed between the two powers, in terms of effective destructive power the USSR had achieved what we referred to at the time to as essential equivalence.

THE TRIAD

Although the U.S. nuclear strategy underwent some evolutionary changes during the Cold War, the elements of our strategic nuclear posture remained essentially the same. The strategy was based upon a triad: manned bombers, land-based intercontinental ballistic missiles (ICBMs), and submarine-launched ballistic missiles. As individual service chiefs and in our consolidated role as the JCS, we recognized the interdependent synergy of the individual triad elements. There was no service parochialism here. Each component of the triad brought to the equation a unique capability, and when combined, they constituted an enormously powerful, devastating, and invulnerable force against which the Soviets could never completely defend.

The manned bomber force, which numbered as many as seventeen wings, had as its strong points the enormous mega-tonnage the bombers could carry and the fact that the planes could be launched with nuclear weapons on board, kept on airborne alert, but still be recalled if the crisis abated. Its weaknesses were that the bomber bases were vulnerable to ballistic missile attack and the bombers themselves could be shot down en route to their target.

The land-based missile component had as its main advantage the quality of virtually instant response. With all of the silos located in the continental United States, communications between the National Command Authority (NCA) and these missile sites were principally by landline—immediate, secure, and reliable. The disadvantage of the land-based system was that, being in silos at fixed geographic locations, they were vulnerable to being targeted by enemy missiles and taken out in a surprise preemptive attack. The authorized inventory of deployed missiles stabilized at about thirteen hundred in the 1970s.

The quality of the submarine-launched ballistic missile system that made it so important to the strategic balance was its invulnerability. That is not to say that submarines are invulnerable, but neither side ever had the ability to prevent all deployed ballistic missile submarines from firing out their full loads after receiving the launch command. The critical link for the submarine-launched missile force was the relative slowness of communications. Contact with a submarine was maintained by ultra-low-frequency radio signals that can penetrate the depths of the water down to three or four hundred feet, but the transmission times are very lengthy. In order to achieve 100 percent reliability in getting the message through, a very slow send rate and a high number of iterations of the message are necessary. Although this ensures 100 percent reliability of communications, it might take minutes rather than seconds to get a firing authorization signal through to a submarine.

The fact remains that the submarine-launched segment of the triad did represent an invulnerable system, and the only invulnerable component of the triad. As such, it became the principal deterrent on both sides against the initiation of a preemptive nuclear strike. With the advance of multiple reentry vehicle technology, the submarine force gained an enormous mega-tonnage capacity. The Trident missile submarines, for example, were equipped with twenty-four Trident III missiles with a sufficient range to reach targets in the Soviet Union with the submarine in its homeport in CONUS. Furthermore, each missile had multiple warheads, each of which could be individually targeted. By the end of the Cold War, the ballistic missile submarine force of eighteen *Ohio*-class Tridents represented approximately half of the missile mega-tonnage in the nuclear arsenal of the entire triad.

In addition to the stockpile of strategic nuclear weapons that were targeted on major military objectives, industrial complexes, and population centers, both superpowers had developed smaller, more portable, but almost equally destructive weapons that were referred to as "tactical nukes." The U.S. Army's weapons inventory included nuclear land mines, artillery shells, and short-range rockets. The U.S. Air Force (USAF) arsenal was made up of a wide array of nuclear and thermonuclear bombs designed for delivery by tactical fighters. In the U.S. Navy, virtually every major combatant had a nuclear-weapons delivery capability: Attack submarines had nuclear antiship rockets, cruisers had available nuclear antiaircraft missiles, patrol planes could deliver nuclear antisubmarine depth charges, and the carrier's attack aircraft were capable of carrying nuclear and thermonuclear bombs for their embarked strike aircraft. Whether these nuclear weapons were actually in the magazines of a particular ship at a specific time was deliberately obscured by the Navy's policy of freely admitting which ships and squadrons had the capability of delivering nuclear weapons but refusing to "confirm or deny" the presence of nuclear warheads aboard any ship at any given time.

NUCLEAR SAFEGUARDS

In spite of the large number of nuclear weapons of all varieties deployed to the operating forces, those of us directly involved with their military employment had a high level of assurance in our system of safeguards for the control and release of nuclear weapons and for the provisions that were designed to prevent their inadvertent use. The system was well conceived and rigorously carried out. I can also say that we had confidence in the Soviets' system of nuclear-weapon control. Any rational person who understood the terrible power of the bomb was bound to have an abiding respect for its safeguards.

On two occasions when I was CNO I met with my opposite numbers in the Russian navy, Admiral Amelko in Oslo in 1975 and Admiral Smirnoff in Helsinki in 1977, in what were euphemistically called "international maritime conferences." Ostensibly to discuss safety at sea, the Soviet admirals at each meeting earnestly sought me out early in the proceedings to emphasize that we military leaders must keep the politicians from getting the armed forces into a nuclear war. In their words, "No one would win—except maybe the Chinese." They also evinced the strongest concern for effective nuclear safeguards.

In comparing the conventional military balance between the United States and the Soviet Union, the picture is complicated because it deals with ground, air, and naval forces. In terms of ground troops, the Soviet Union had what must be regarded as an enormous military advantage. The USSR had 174 divisions in the field and the United States never more than 19. Yet that comparison was not quite as negative as the raw data would indicate, because the U.S. divisions were in general somewhat larger, better equipped, and better trained. In addition, a number of Soviet divisions were pinned down on the Chinese border and others were committed to occupation duty in the European satellites. The addition of NATO ground forces, especially the West Germans, helped redress this imbalance. However, throughout the Cold War the USSR maintained a substantial advantage in the size of their ground forces.

U.S. forces never engaged in direct combat with Soviet flag forces, mainly because both sides were careful not to let this happen. The grave potential for such incidents expanding into a general conflict through miscalculation in the Cold War was recognized by both superpowers and was always taken into account when the commitment of military force was considered. Nevertheless, I felt it important to constantly emphasize to Congress and the Office of the Secretary of Defense (OSD) that U.S. forces would regularly encounter first-line Soviet weapons in combat— as we did in Korea and Vietnam—mainly MiG fighters and Russian surface-to-air missiles (SAMs), often surreptitiously flown or operated by Soviet military crews. These represented a level of arms technology clearly equal to our own, and our military planners had to consider the probability of U.S. forces encountering advanced weapons in the hands of Soviet clients when responding to crises in the Third World. Therefore, I was adamant that the Navy not be required to accept weapon systems of lesser capabilities than the state of the art, on an OSD premise that our most likely enemies would be Third World powers.

Soviet weaponry was in general on a par with our own in terms of its effectiveness within the Soviet warfighting concept, in which the philosophy was more brute force than finesse. Where we would plan to painstakingly clear a minefield using special armored vehicles and combat engineers, the Russians, as one of their officers explained, would simply march a platoon through it.

The Russian tanks and artillery, upon which they heavily relied, were well designed, modern, well made, and extremely durable. Their aircraft were rugged and easy to maintain, with powerful engines but minimum refinements outside of their combat equipment. The MiG-25 could fly at Mach 3 and to an altitude of sixty-seven thousand feet, faster and higher than any of our tactical fighters. The Soviets' later attack submarines were remarkably fast and could dive to unprecedented depths. They achieved this superior performance by reducing the shielding on the nuclear propulsion plants, with the result of a very high incidence of radiation sickness among their crews.

Soviet ground-to-air missiles were particularly effective and took a heavy toll on U.S. aircraft during strikes into the Hanoi-Haiphong area during the Vietnam War. The Israeli air force also experienced devastating losses during the Yom Kippur War from Soviet SAMs in the hands of the Arabs. In less than two hours after the initiation of hostilities, the Israelis had lost more than thirty first-line aircraft, mainly U.S.-made A-4 Skyhawks and F-4 Phantoms IIs, to the Russian SAMs being used by the Syrians.

I came to the conclusion, early in the Cold War, that the Soviet strategic planners understood clearly how dependent NATO, Japan, and our other allies were upon sea lines of communications, and like the Germans in both World War I and World War II, the Soviets were determined to capitalize on this vulnerability. They set out to build a modern oceangoing force that would challenge the U.S. Navy, employing the most modern weapons of advanced maritime technology: nuclear-powered submarines, underwater-launched missiles, supersonic maritime strike aircraft, and long-range antiship missiles, ship-based, air-launched, and submarine-fired, many of them supersonic. It seemed only logical to me that the modern Soviet navy was conceived, designed, built, and organized to defeat or neutralize the U.S. Navy.

It was also easy to appreciate how the character of the Soviet navy was shaped by the maritime strategy of the Soviet Union, which in turn was driven by the Soviets' own geopolitical situation. The territory of the USSR, spanning a continent, dominates Eurasia. On the Soviets' southeastern flank lies the People's Republic of China, and the Russians were, for good reason, deeply concerned about the Chinese threat. Arrayed along the Western border of their country were the buffer satellite nations of the Warsaw Pact. Farther to the west, and still on the same continent, lie the NATO nations of Western Europe, clearly coveted by the Soviets. As a military planner, I could quickly conclude that the Soviet Union could defend itself from the Chinese, support their Warsaw Pact allies, invade Western Europe, and never cross a major body of water. Yet they were building the largest navy in the world. Why? It could only be to oppose and defeat the U.S. Navy, deny its allies control of the seas, and ensure the quick collapse of the maritime strategy of the Western powers.

During my four years as CNO I argued that the Navy needed to be capable of maintaining maritime superiority in those areas of the high seas required for the execution of our war plans in support of our "forward collective strategy." Without maritime supremacy, which is what a widespread superiority amounted to, our strategy would fail.

When I retired in 1978, I wanted my farewell remarks to be a warning, a reminder of our need for an adequate navy and of the grim consequences of a failure to maintain our position of maritime supremacy. My remarks were referred to the OSD's public affairs officer for policy clearance then returned to me with the word "supremacy" deleted and "equivalence" substituted. "Supremacy" was considered too aggressive and, possibly, inflammatory. Later on, some bright young naval aide in the E ring of the Pentagon circulated a tongue-in-cheek memorandum that suggested that the Naval Academy Brigade of Midshipmen urge on its football team with cheers of "Tie Army!" at the annual Army-Navy football game. I changed my script but not my remarks.

THE NAVAL BALANCE

The naval balance represented a particularly important comparison in my mind, because it so convincingly demonstrated the Soviet determination to surpass the United States in every sector of national power. At the beginning of the Cold War in the late 1940s, the Soviet navy was little more than a coast guard, an inshore force to support the flanks of the Red Army. After the Cuban missile crisis dramatically exposed their maritime deficiencies, the Soviets embarked on an ambitious naval construction program that in less than three decades, under the leadership of Admiral Gorshkov, had produced a fleet to challenge the U.S. Navy. The U.S. chief of naval operations in 1973 went so far as to say that the Russian navy was "number one"—meaning that the USSR had in effect wrested control of the sea from the United States. Although this view was never shared by the OSD, the JCS, or subsequent CNOs, it was a topic of debate during a Navy Department appearance before Congress in 1973.

It is true that the Red Navy had come a long way in thirty years. Yet I had deduced one essential point from my days in the Pentagon as director of strike warfare in 1967: In total number of warships, the Russian fleet outnumbered the U.S. fleet, with more than a thousand combatants to our less than four hundred, but the U.S. Navy had fifteen attack aircraft carriers and the Soviets had none. The carrier force was the measure of difference that allowed the United States to maintain a definite margin of maritime superiority.

In the course of annual "posture statements" before Congress in 1978, I testified on 8 February, in response to direct questioning by the House Armed Services Committee on the Soviet naval threat, that in the case of a general war with the USSR, our Navy would be hard pressed to maintain maritime superiority in the western Pacific. At best, we were only capable of maintaining the military sea lines of communication with Japan. Ensuring the continuation of commercial shipping would probably not be possible. Supporting NATO was our first priority. With the continuing decline in our naval force levels, we had become a one-ocean navy.

This testimony raised questions, directed to the State Department, from the highest levels of the government of Japan. Secretary of Defense Harold Brown personally responded to the Japanese in a public statement that did not deny my testimony but simply stated that the Department of Defense (DoD) was transferring naval assets to the Pacific Fleet to rectify that situation.

From my perspective as CNO, the steady growth of the Soviet naval threat was always a primary concern. I had to accept the fact that if the U.S. Navy was not capable of maintaining maritime superiority sufficient to protect the essential sea lanes of communication to our allies and to our own overseas deployed forces, then the forward collective strategy would be unworkable. During much of the Cold War, the United States maintained an overseas force of four Army divisions in Germany, another in Korea, and a Marine division in Japan. In time of conflict, these forces, as well as those of our NATO allies, would have to be reinforced and resupplied. All of the remaining U.S. Army and Marine ground forces were located in the United States. Those divisions would have to be transported overseas if they were to enter the fight, and this reinforcement and resupply had to come from the United States across the oceans.

I consistently pursued this logic in my annual posture statement, which received wide distribution throughout the government. Yet it was never quoted or even acknowledged by the Office of the Secretary of Defense. I believe the OSD wanted to avoid a "roles and missions" showdown among the several services, a showdown that might have been ignited if the secretary of defense were to officially endorse the Navy-oriented title of "maritime strategy." So it was referred to officially as the "forward collective strategy."

SEALIFT

In their annual posture statements throughout the Cold War, the JCS had consistently stated that "in any major overseas deployment, sealift will have to deliver about 95 percent of all dry cargo and more than 98 percent of all petroleum products." From my own analyses of the war plans, it was apparent that the mechanization and firepower of the U.S. Army and Air Force's first-line components require such quantities of combat consumables, such as fuel and ammunition, and the heavy equipment characteristic of armored divisions and all-weather tactical aircraft, that their reinforcement and resupply must come by sea. As an example, more than one hundred thousand tons of cargo would be required to deploy a single mechanized division. When overseas, that division would need more than one thousand tons delivered per day to sustain it in operations.

AIRLIFT

Airlift was planned for the rapid movement of troops to join up with prepositioned equipment and for the fast delivery of small amounts of critical supplies and materiel, but as a member of the JCS, I felt compelled to point out that airlift is severely limited in terms of the total volume that can be lifted and in its ability to move outsized equipment. A large portion of the organic equipment of modern armies are tanks, bulldozers, portable bridges, helicopters, and tank retrievers, which will not fit in most aircraft. My calculations showed that one modern container ship could deliver the cargo equivalent of 150 C-5 aircraft—the largest plane in the Air Force—and there were never more than 75 C-5s in the Air Force's inventory during the Cold War.

Airlift is also very expensive in terms of fuel. The JCS experience in resupplying the Israeli armed forces during the 1973 Yom Kippur War showed that it required seven tons of jet fuel to airlift one ton of aviation fuel to Israel from the United States.

THE ROLE OF AIR POWER IN THE COLD WAR

In a general war with the USSR using conventional, as opposed to nuclear, weapons, the role of manned aircraft would be mainly in support of the ground forces in the land war, especially in Europe, where the two opposing powers had concentrated and massed their armies. The conventional war at sea was expected to be mainly enemy submarine interdiction of our overseas lines of communication and allied response with antisubmarine warfare conducted mainly by U.S. nuclear submarines and U.S. Navy patrol planes. It was possible there would be some carrier operations, mainly in the western Pacific, but the main battles would be in NATO Europe.

It was expected, however, that a general war between the Soviet bloc and NATO would start with a nuclear attack, probably of a preemptive nature. Even a general war with conventional weapons could be expected to escalate quickly to a nuclear conflict with one side initiating a preemptive nuclear attack because of the great advantage gained through a first strike (which would effectively disarm the enemy). In the case of a nuclear conflict the principal use of air power would be flying our SAC bombers against Russia and both sides using air-delivered tactical weapons against ground forces and air bases in the theaters of operations.

Korea is a good example of the use of air power in a limited conventional war. After the amphibious landings at Inchon, the North Korean army had been defeated and driven out of South Korea, yet the Korean War was far from over. As the United Nations (UN) troops pushed toward the Chinese border to fully occupy North Korea, the armies of the People's Republic of China crossed the Yalu River and entered the war. Outnumbered and stretched thin across the Korean peninsula, the UN forces were forced to retreat before finally being able to rally around the Americans and stabilize the front lines along the thirty-eighth parallel, the original line of demarcation between North and South Korea. It was U.S. air power that made the difference between defeat and survival for the UN forces. With near-total control of the airspace over the battlefield, it was close air support (CAS) that enabled those forces—led by the U.S. ground divisions—to stand and fight the Chinese to a standstill. The tactical air effort by the Air Force, the Navy carriers, and the land-based Marines was so effective that the Chinese armies moved only at night or in bad weather, hiding themselves from air observation by day.

Later, in Vietnam, it was again U.S. air power that was the decisive factor. This time a new capability was added. In addition to the close air support provided by Navy, Marine Corps, and Air Force tactical fighters and the use of the B-52 bomber with conventional ammunition, the U.S. Army and Marine Corps were exploiting the helicopter for fire support as well as a primary means of moving troops into the assault. It was the first use of airmobile infantry in warfare on a large scale. Of most significance, however, is the fact that air power was the single U.S. military force used in North Vietnam during the entire conflict in Southeast Asia—except for occasional ship gunfire strikes against targets on the coast—and it was the Linebacker I and II air campaigns into the North Vietnamese industrial heartland that eventually forced Hanoi to agree to a cease-fire. The North Vietnamese air force reacted with MiG-21s, an excellent Soviet fighter, against many strikes, mainly in the Hanoi area. But because of the overwhelming U.S. air superiority, the MiGs were just irritants compared to the batteries of Russian SAMs, which proved to be an effective and dangerous threat and caused major changes in U.S. tactics and aircraft electronic equipment. Although only 15 percent of the fixed-wing aircraft losses in Vietnam were the result of direct SAM hits, the enemy's capability to launch SAMs in large salvos against our tactical aircraft had the effect of disrupting the strike group's defensive formations. This made our attack planes more vulnerable to MiGs and forced our planes down to lower altitudes, where they became victims of antiaircraft artillery (AAA) and automatic-weapon fire.

WORLDWIDE CHALLENGES TO A FORWARD STRATEGY

I have found that too many Americans, even those well educated in military affairs, fail to fully appreciate the massive challenges our country faced in responding to the Communist initiatives in the Cold War. All were impediments that had to be resolved—for our survival and, ultimately, our victory.

During the Cold War, the complexity of the tasks faced by our military leadership was awesome. In Korea and Vietnam we fought major conflicts in combat theaters that, in terms of geography, were almost as far away from the Pentagon as it is possible to be and still remain on the surface of the globe. In the Far East, we not only provided major combat forces but also constructed virtually all of the logistical infrastructure to support the coalition forces. Americans fought alongside indigenous allies, and the latter provided much of the manpower, but it was the

United States that organized, armed, and trained these allies. In Korea we were able to end the war under a cease-fire that delineated national boundaries generally conforming to the antebellum artificial lines of demarcation, which had been violated by the Communist invasions from the North.

While U.S. military forces were fighting in the Pacific, U.S. soldiers and sailors in the Atlantic and Europe were deployed on the front lines to deter the Soviet armies and those of the Warsaw Pact satellites from attacking across the East German plains and rolling on to the Channel ports and to the North Sea in one massive offensive. While our conventional forces were defending and fighting in the western Pacific, the U.S. Strategic Command maintained a second-by-second, around-the-clock readiness for nuclear retaliatory strikes as an effective deterrent to any Soviet adventuring with their nuclear forces.

THE STRATEGIC IMPLICATIONS OF LIMITED WARS

Although the wars in Korea and Vietnam may not have appeared, at the time, to be decisive in clear terms of winning or losing, our commitment in those theaters was critical to the prosecution of the broader conflict of the Cold War. Both were strategically essential for the defense of our allies, the containment of communism, and the ultimate national objective of deflecting the threat of the Soviets' nuclear arsenal.

By the commitment of U.S. citizens to the battlefields of Korea and Vietnam, the United States demonstrated its resolve throughout the world and established a level of credibility for our foreign policy. There could be no more convincing demonstration that the United States would fight if its vital national interests were threatened. The Kremlin was well persuaded that the United States would go to war if the Soviets attacked our allies. There is little doubt but that without the deterrent presence of U.S. troops in NATO, what has been called the "tripwire strategy," the Russians would have moved against Western Europe. But the Soviet leadership was convinced, by the example of Korea, that the United States would honor its commitments to its allies and that Americans would fight in support of those obligations. Most of all, the Soviets were made to realize that the United States was absolutely determined not to lose to the Soviets, even if it meant resorting to nuclear weapons.

THE ANNUAL POSTURE STATEMENT

The Goldwater-Nichols legislation, passed in 1986, was intended to promote jointness among the services by strengthening the authority of the chairman of the Joint Chiefs of Staff. Among other measures, it created a vice chairman of the JCS. Prior to this, the service chiefs were viewed by the NCA as the professional experts in their respective services, responsible for the capabilities as well as the readiness of their commands. In those days, each chief of service, along with the SecDef, annually prepared a posture statement, a document setting forth the disposition, capabilities, and readiness of the forces for which he was responsible. My first posture statement in 1974 was sheer boilerplate. The deadline for its submission was only weeks after my installation as CNO. I was not prepared to launch any operational initiatives when so new to the job, and I was very busy responding to Congress, answering their questions regarding discipline and readiness problems in the fleet. So I just played it safe and stuck with the conventional template.

My first posture statement began with the roles and missions of the Navy as legislated by Congress in Title 10 of the U.S. Code and then laid out the national strategy of the United States as assembled from the various guidance papers and posture statements of the secretary of defense. Following this, I described the current force structure of the U.S. Navy and how it implemented the national strategy. The wrap up, and the most important part, was a summary of the Navy's budget for that year and how each line item was related directly to the Navy's requirements as derived from the national strategy and derivative guidance of the SecDef. In simplest terms, it was a case of establishing an audit trail from each item in the Navy's budget to the nation's security requirements—translating policy into substance.

My second posture statement, in 1975, represented my views and philosophy. Again I began with a statement of the Navy's roles and missions from Title 10 and again I related each line item in the Navy's budget, showing how it supported the Navy's roles and missions. To assist in the process of justifying the Navy's budget request, I had a version of the posture statement produced in the form of a five-by-eight-inch pamphlet—very modest, duplicated without color or slick paper, and about half an inch thick. It would fit easily in the coat pocket of a civilian suit or a blue service uniform. Many copies were made and widely distributed to our officers, Pentagon civilians, and congressional staffers. John Lehman, later secretary of the navy (SecNav), tells of attending a hearing on the Navy budget during his days on the Arms Control and Disarmament Agency (ACDA) where virtually all present, observers as well as staff and participants, pulled out their CNO posture statement booklets almost in unison. Lehman referred to the booklet as "Chairman Mao's Little Red Book."

In those days, there was not a concise statement of the national strategy. For the posture statement, I had to synthesize a strategy from what I knew of our war plans as a member of the JCS and the general thrust of the annual SecDef "draft" presidential memorandum. By my second year in the CNO's office, I had evolved a set of simple strategic principles for the Navy, statements and concepts based upon the various documents available to me and justified by the facts of the world's geography; the nature of the high seas; the disposition of the military forces, both friendly and hostile; the threat they represented; and the probabilities of various courses of actions. These became the Navy's interpretation of the national strategy, and they were repeated as often as possible in posture statements, in congressional testimony, and in my public speeches and writings. They are, in the aggregate, and as modified over time by my own experiences, the basis of my formal articulation of the strategy for the Cold War.

THE COLD WAR STRATEGY

By the time I had become CNO and was responsible for publicly articulating the U.S. Navy's roles and missions within the national security guidelines, I had concluded that the military strategy that governed our military posture, weapons systems, and operations during the Cold War was remarkably straightforward and enduring. It was an elegantly simple and coherent concept, it went virtually unchanged during the entire course of the Cold War, and it was remarkably successful. It was by my definition a maritime strategy, and it was predicated on the geographical disposition of the United States, its allies, and its enemies. In the Western Hemisphere, North America is virtually an island. The United States shares the continent with Canada, Mexico, and Central America, and we have only two international borders, neither of which threatens our basic security behind. On the other hand, one of our fifty states, all of our territories, and forty of the forty-two nations with whom we had treaties or security arrangements were overseas.

The forward collective strategy used the oceans as barriers in our defense and as avenues for extending our influence abroad to support our allies and protect our commerce. In so doing, it exploited the principle that, if we had to fight a war, we intended to engage an enemy closer to his homeland than to ours. This strategy depended upon overseas allies and forward-based military forces with the mobility to respond to crises around the world and the firepower to resolve incipient threats to our vital security interests in our favor before these minor crises could become major conflicts.

As our de facto national strategy took form, it became clear to me that for this concept of a forward strategy to be workable, the United States had to have the ability and the willingness to carry out a full range of military options, including overt armed warfare, against any forces threatening our interests and those of our allies.

In retrospect it was evident that, from the earliest days of the Cold War, the Soviet Union, through its Communist surrogates, was creating incidents to which the United States, as the leader of the free world, was obliged to respond. It was U.S. strategy to keep heavily armed sea-based forces deployed around the globe and constantly on the alert to react to an incident in virtually any part of the world outside the Soviet Union and China and their satellites. These sea-based forces were carrier task forces and Marine expeditionary units embarked in amphibious assault ships. During the Cold War the United States maintained a force requirement for a minimum of two attack carriers in the Mediterranean and three in the western Pacific and Indian Ocean. These regions came to be known as the "contingency area." The mission of these deployed forces was to respond to a crisis and resolve the issue in our favor, before it escalated into a general war. In most cases this tactical approach was successful within the overall strategy. But in Korea and Vietnam our early intervention did not produce a quick solution, and our national involvement in long, major wars ensued.

3

Korea

The Forgotten War

The Korean War is known as the "forgotten war," largely because after the war, Americans didn't want to remember the cruel toll the conflict took on the indigenous civilian population and our own military people. My personal experience as a carrier fighter pilot in Korea reflected the intensity of the war. I deployed in Air Task Group 1 as air group operations officer in the USS *Valley Forge* in the winter of 1951–52, attached to Fighter Squadron 111 (VF-111) flying F9F-2 Panthers. In the first week of operations, VF-111 lost its commanding officer, and VF-52, the other F9F-2 squadron in Air Task Group 1, in the course of the cruise lost four of its original seventeen deploying pilots, including the commanding officer. VF-653, a recalled Navy Reserve squadron flying F4U-4s, lost twelve of its twenty-eight pilots in five months of combat.

BECOMING A JET PILOT

In the spring of 1951, I was a lieutenant commander on the staff of the chief of naval air basic training in Pensacola, Florida, when I received orders transferring me to the Naval Air Force Pacific Fleet in San Diego, California, for further assignment. In accordance with the established career pattern for naval aviators in the unrestricted line, it would be my second squadron tour, and San Diego meant a carrier squadron bound for Korea. Because I had flown SB2C Helldiver dive bombers in my last squadron, I could expect to be assigned to a Douglas AD Skyraider squadron at best, or an F4U Corsair squadron, clearly second best. Of course I wanted to fly jet fighters. The F9F Panther was in the fleet, two squadrons per carrier, and the jet fighter jocks were considered the elite in naval aviation. Originally they were hand-picked on the basis of their reputation and experience—World War II fighter aces and post–World War II test pilots. The ensigns and jaygees being assigned to jet squadrons were those who stood at the top of their class in flight training. I didn't qualify in any of those categories.

When I reported to the commander, Naval Air Force, Pacific (AirPac), I was immediately picked off by the carrier air group plans officer, Capt. Lou Bauer, a former fighter squadron commander in Air Group 3 when I was executive officer (XO) of VB-3, the dive-bomber squadron. Captain Bauer wanted me to work for him temporarily on a priority project, finding a way to create additional air wings to fill out the decks of the carriers coming out of mothballs to join the operating forces. This assignment was only expected to take two weeks. The sticking point was that an air group was a commissioned unit just like a ship, and to create a new commissioned unit required authorization from Congress to increase force levels. This was considered much too time-consuming.

I suggested we finesse it by creating task groups that would not in themselves be commissioned units. A task group would be made up of existing squadrons, each squadron already being a commissioned unit authorized by Congress. There were a number of Navy Reserve squadrons that could be activated if planes could be found, as the pilots were already assigned. But four squadrons of Reserve pilots shared one squadron's worth of planes. World War II F4U Corsairs were available in mothballs on the desert, and the Douglas Aircraft plant at Segundo, California, was at peak production of AD-1 Skyraiders. The problem was to come up with the jet fighters, two fourteen-plane squadrons per air task group with pilots. We found that these additional squadrons could be made available for the air task groups by reducing the present number of squadrons within an air group from five to four. One jet squadron per carrier air group would be transferred to an air task group. Initially the carriers were deploying with a Corsair squadron, a Skyraider squadron, and three

Panther jet squadrons. But it so happened that the carriers in combat in Korea were experiencing difficulties supporting three jet squadrons. The main problem was fuel. The jets, compared to propeller planes, were voracious consumers of gasoline. The aviation fuel tanks on the *Essex*-class carrier—constructed before the jet age—couldn't carry enough fuel to operate three jet squadrons at the wartime tempo.

It was decided that the air task groups would conform as closely as possible to the commissioned air groups, but the individual squadrons would be ordered to a specific carrier, reporting directly to its commanding officer for duty. The air task group commander would also be a member of the ship's company, and the ship's commanding officer would delegate to him operational command of the air task group, requiring that he fly periodically with these units to exercise operational control and administrative oversight. Additionally, there would be ordered to one of the squadrons in the air task group two LSOs, a maintenance officer, and an operations officer to form the air task group staff. They would be attached to the squadron for administrative purposes but operationally would receive their orders from the air task group commander.

I drafted this proposal for air task groups as an AirPac directive, but the three-star admiral commanding Naval Air Forces Pacific sent it to the commander in chief, Pacific Fleet to sign it out as a fleet directive. This concept of the air task group as an augmenting asset during times of urgent mobilization endured for the next twenty years as a convenient expedient to quickly and effectively meet emergent requirements to fill carrier flight decks.

My work on the air task group project had a major personal benefit. I wanted very much to transition from a bomber pilot to a jet fighter pilot, but this was hard to do at my rank. The introduction of jets to carrier aviation had not been without its problems. The jet was substantially superior to any of the propeller fighters in any services, but it was better suited to long, straight runways than to the confines of a carrier deck. Jet blast was causing new and difficult problems. The endurance of jets was less than an hour compared to the cycle time of the Corsairs and the Bearcats it was replacing. The greatest concerns, however, involved the flight characteristics of these early jet aircraft, with their high approach speeds, lack of stall warning, and slow acceleration on takeoff. For the first jet squadrons in the U.S. Navy, the commanding officers and flight officers were carefully selected from the most experienced and aeronautically competent aviators. Some young Naval Academy graduates, like my brother-in-law Wally Schirra, finessed the system by requesting duty with the U.S. Air Force, in which all of the tactical aircraft were jets. Wally flew F-86 Sabres in Korea and bagged a MiG before returning to the U.S. Navy and the astronaut program.

As I finished up my work on the air task group project and it was time to move on to a squadron, Captain Bauer asked me if I would like to be the operations officer of the first air task group to deploy, Air Task Group 1 on the *Valley Forge*. I would be assigned to VF-111 for administrative purposes and flight duties. I knew VF-111 was flying brand new F9F-2 Panthers and I would be making the transition to jet fighter pilot. I accepted.

The commanding officer of VF-111 well understood my unique assignment to VF-111 and the considerations that went into the organizational concept of Air Task Group 1. He was, in fact, glad to have me in his squadron for this precedent-setting deployment of the first air task group. Unfortunately, this understanding was not shared by most of the other officers in the squadron, who were a tight-knit group, most of whom had made one previous deployment to combat in Korea with VF-111.

The squadron was three-quarters of the way through its training cycle and the tactical organization had been established. The division and section leaders and wingmen had all been assigned in a permanent organization. I would have to fly whenever I could wrangle a flight when a regular squadron pilot was not available because of duty or some other overriding reason. Even then my presence in the lineup would not be too welcome, because I was not an original member of the team and had not shared the previous cruise with my flight mates. I had not even gone through the bulk of the redeployment training with them.

This was not unexpected. I had seen the same thing in Bombing 3 when the landing signal officer and air group operations officer would come into our ready room to get themselves listed on our flight schedule. But I felt that this reluctance in VF-111 to include me would be overcome after a month or so of living with the squadron pilots and sharing their ready room and liberties ashore. The important thing was that I had broken the barrier. I was a qualified jet fighter jockey, and my future assignments would reflect this qualification.

In 1953 I returned to Korea as executive officer of VF-52 in the USS *Boxer*, again flying F9F-2 Panthers. On that cruise both my wingman and my commanding officer were downed in action against the Chinese. In the three-month period from May to July, eight VF52 aircraft were shot down, but most of the pilots were recovered. On two different occasions my own plane was shot up to the extent I could not return to land aboard the carrier and was forced to make an emergency landing at a South Korean air force airstrip.

The war in Korea was a bitter struggle. It took three years and thirty-seven thousand American lives. Twice the commander of U.S. forces in Korea proposed to the JCS that all U.S. troops be evacuated to avoid them being pushed into the sea. And twice the president said, "Stay and fight." In the first year of the war, Americans and their allies defeated the invading army of North Korea, driving all organized units out of South Korea. Then the Chinese Communists attacked without warning across their borders with the purpose of forcing the Americans off the Korean peninsula. Overcoming the initial surprise Chinese offensive, our troops rallied and drove back the Chinese regulars and held them near the original line of demarcation along the thirty-eighth parallel, where the fighting eventually ceased. The entire war, in which more than four million men, women, and children were killed on both sides, involved twenty-two nations and was fought entirely on the Korean peninsula, a piece of land approximately the configuration of Florida and only 25 percent larger.

UNPREPARED

The United States did not expect to fight, and had no plans for fighting, the Korean War, but it was a war the country had to win. Half a century later, viewed in the broader context of the Cold War, Korea has evolved as one of this nation's more important wars in terms of its long-term impact on world history.

The Korean War came at the beginning of a much larger and more desperate struggle that lasted for four decades: the Cold War. And during this epic conflict between the Western democracies and the Communist bloc, the very survival of the United States was at stake. For the first time the United States committed troops to combat in its armed confrontation with the Communists. Had the United States not elected to fight in Korea, and not been able to conclude the war successfully by driving the North Koreans and Chinese back to the line of original demarcation, the Cold War could have had an entirely different outcome, most probably to the gravest disadvantage to our country.

It has been argued that the United States won the war in Korea. However, it is probably more reasonable to suggest that the United States was not defeated in Korea. Obviously it was not a clear-cut victory such as was achieved in World War II, with the unconditional surrenders of Germany and Japan. It was a limited war, and Korea was concluded on limited terms, but ones entirely acceptable to the United States. We achieved a cease-fire with the national borders approximating the status quo ante. South Korea remains an independent democratic nation and has developed into an industrial powerhouse in the Far East. North Korea and China have not again attacked South Korea, which has proved to be a reliable U.S. ally.

WAR BEGINS

The Korean War began at 0400 on 25 June 1950, when seven crack divisions of North Korean troops stormed across the thirty-eighth parallel without warning. The non-Communist world was caught by surprise.

When the North Koreans attacked, the United States was enjoying the rewards of a welcome peace earned by a hard-fought victory in World War II, an all-out mobilization that touched every American. After World War II, without a military threat on the horizon, the United States had dismantled the massive armies and fleets that had contributed to the Allied victory. Armament production had been halted, material and supplies abandoned overseas, military equipment scrapped, ships and aircraft mothballed, and the citizen soldiers had returned to their jobs and families or to school. By 1950 force levels had been reduced to well below prewar totals. Of special significance was the exodus of veterans from the active-duty ranks.

The U.S. Navy, which in World War II had more than a hundred aircraft carriers in its operating forces, was programed to reduce its active inventory of fleet carriers—those capable of operating jet fighters—to five. The U.S. Army troops in the Pacific theater were untrained for combat. Recruited largely on the promise that in the Army they would learn a trade, the young and inexperienced soldiers were enjoying duty in Japan, which in 1950 remained an occupied country under General MacArthur's command. The troops were equipped with obsolescent weapons with which they were only marginally proficient. Neither the troops nor U.S. leadership expected they would be exposed to real battle. They were unprepared for combat.

In spite of the country's total lack of enthusiasm for a new war, its military unpreparedness, and the lack of any tangible threat to the American people by the North Koreans, President Truman did not hesitate to react. In quick succession after the invasion of 25 June, he committed U.S. naval and air forces to help stem the invasion of the South, then ordered U.S. ground forces into the conflict. At the same time he brought the UN, still in its infancy, into the war against the North Koreans. This was the first occasion of any international world-governing body organizing a military force and conducting warfare.

Truman had made the most difficult decision a president can make: to go to war. It was especially hard in this case, as Americans had not yet recovered from the hardships and trauma of World War II. The invaders were not threatening U.S. lives or property, nor had we any longstanding ethnic or social quarrels with North Korea. President Truman saw the true foe as communism. If a line were not drawn, the totalitarian regimes eventually would threaten most of the free world. The United States had to act before so many democracies were overrun, before it was too late for the Western powers to act collectively. President Truman and his advisors saw this as the time to react with force of arms, the sooner the better.

It was admittedly not the place the United States wanted to stage this first showdown with the forces of communism. Secretary Acheson expressed it well: "If the best minds in the world had set out to find us the worst possible location to fight a war, the unanimous choice would have to be Korea." But the United States and its allies were not offered a choice in the selection of the initial arena for this long-term struggle for the survival of the free world. The Communists had seized the initiative with their sudden and overpowering assault across the thirty-eighth parallel. Whether or not we liked it, the battleground would be the Korean peninsula. The United States and its allies had collided with the forces of the Soviet Union's surrogate, North Korea, while the whole world watched. Were the democracies willing to go to war for their principles of human rights? Would they fight at the risk of their citizens' lives? Could they hold their own in battle against the tough Communist troops, indoctrinated to shed their blood for their greater cause? At stake were the prestige of the United States and the survivability of free nations.

UNDERESTIMATING THE ENEMY

For the U.S. leadership, the difficult decision to go to war was initially eased by a general underestimation of the enemy. On hearing of the invasion, the commander of U.S. forces in the Far East, General of the Army Douglas MacArthur, observed, "This is probably just a reconnaissance in force. If Washington will not hobble me, I can handle it with one arm tied behind my back." The troops themselves, before their first encounter with the enemy, exhibited an "overconfidence bordering on arrogance," according to General Barth of the U.S. Army's 24th Division. The GIs thought the North Koreans would break and run when they first saw U.S. uniforms. The troops were not to blame. Ripped out of their noncombatant occupation duties in Japan, they were rushed to the front by airlift in a matter of hours without any preparation for combat.

The first major event of the shooting war in Korea for the United States occurred on 3 July 1950, when carrier aircraft from the *Valley Forge* struck Pyongyang in North Korea, destroying much of the small North Korean air force. Two days later, on 5 July 1950, troops from the 24th Infantry Division attempted to ambush the column of tanks and infantry leading the main invasion force at Osan, only two hundred miles from Pusan, the southernmost port of the Republic of Korea (ROK). The small U.S. Army force, its 540 soldiers averaging only twenty years of age, without tanks and with a total of eight antitank artillery rounds, faced a column of thirty Russian-made T-34 tanks and five thousand veteran soldiers. The Americans were routed. As U.S. reinforcements were poured into the port of Pusan, they were rushed to the front piecemeal in an attempt to slow the advance of the North Koreans and keep the entire Korean peninsula from being overrun before enough UN troops and equipment could be landed to engage the enemy on at least equal terms of manpower and equipment. Through the next sixty days, the outnumbered and outgunned Americans and South Koreans fell back before the North Koreans, who, driven by their leaders without regard for casualties, were determined to score a quick and total victory by pushing the Americans off the peninsula.

Exploiting the momentum of their attack and the fanaticism of their troops, the North Koreans enveloped and broke through the UN lines whenever the Americans attempted to make a stand, forcing U.S. and ROK forces into a constantly shrinking perimeter around Pusan. Air strikes by Navy and Marine Corps planes based on carriers offshore slowed enemy forces but could not stop them. By the end of August, the Americans and South Koreans still had not stopped the North Korean advance. The situation was so perilous that the Eighth Army commander, Gen. Walton Walker, asked the Joint Chiefs of Staff whether he should plan for an evacuation of all U.S. forces to Japan or still attempt to establish a secure perimeter around Pusan and depend upon continuing reinforcements to fight off the North Koreans and maintain his foothold in Korea. With President Truman's concurrence, the JCS instructed Walker to "stand and fight."

Then, in the first week of September, the UN lines around Pusan held in spite of the human wave attacks. This was the turning point. It had been a close thing, but the United States was not going to be driven off the peninsula. They were in Korea to stay.

From this inauspicious beginning of a war we didn't plan to fight, in the wrong place, at a bad time, against a determined enemy who had seized the initiative of surprise to come perilously close to driving U.S. troops into the sea in a humiliating defeat, the Americans found a remarkable resiliency. With the courage and a fortitude to justify its qualification for the mantle of leadership for the Western world, the United States stormed back from the very edge of disaster to badly bloody North Korea and defeat its armed forces, and then to throw the Chinese Communist armies out of South Korea, restore the original borders, and conclude the conflict on terms acceptable to our side. In this aspect alone, the Korean War must be viewed as an example to the world, ourselves, our enemies, and our allies of the power and integrity of the United States.

KOREA'S FIVE CAMPAIGNS

From the military standpoint, the Korean War falls into five distinct phases. The first campaign began in June 1950, when the North Koreans, without warning, crossed the thirty-eighth parallel to invade an unsuspecting South Korea, then in the sphere of the Western powers. Against the lightly armed South Koreans—more of a police force than an army—the North Koreans, one-third of them veterans of the Chinese Communist People's Liberation Army, quickly overran most of South Korea. The introduction of U.S. troops from the forces occupying Japan could at first only slow the North Korean columns of armor and infantry. In early September 1950, the UN lines stiffened and held, and the Americans poured reinforcements and supplies into the Pusan perimeter, while the North Koreans, battered and exhausted from their drive south, regrouped. Although all of the tactical military air forces in South Korea had been overrun by the enemy, there were now three aircraft carriers on station to provide air support for the beleaguered UN ground forces and attack the main supply routes of the invading North Korean troops.

The second campaign began on 15 September 1950, when the 230-ship Joint Task Force 7 landed the 1st Marine Division at Inchon. The Marines then drove east across the peninsula to link up with the U.S. Army divisions breaking out of the Pusan perimeter from the south. This bold strategic strike caught the Communists by surprise, and the bulk of the North Korean army was caught in a massive trap, surrounded and cut off from their bases of resupply. Most were killed or captured, and others, deserting their units and abandoning their weapons, infiltrated through the UN lines to flee to the North. As the North Korean army disintegrated, the UN forces quickly retook Seoul, crossed the thirty-eighth parallel, and pushed north. General MacArthur, the commander in chief, Far East Command, intended to occupy all of North Korea up to the Yalu River, the border with China. There were international murmurings that this advance would be considered a threat by China and could only result in an armed response. In Washington as well there was a growing desire to avoid any provocation for China to enter the conflict.

By mid-November, with the Communist forces in a complete rout, the Americans and ROKs were racing north and a U.S. Army column actually reached the Yalu River, at the town of Hysesanjin. As the U.S. troops paused to regroup and enjoy a hot Thanksgiving dinner in the field, General MacArthur announced that North Korea had been defeated, its armies destroyed, and that South Korea had been liberated and its borders restored. The Americans would be out of Korea and on their way home by Christmas.

The third phase of the Korean War began on 25 November 1950, when Chinese Communist armies entered the conflict with massed attacks in depth across the UN front. The Chinese offensive came as a surprise to General MacArthur and his field commanders, in spite of the fact that in Washington and other foreign capitals there had been a sober apprehension that China would not stand idle if the UN forces advanced to the Yalu. China had been able to infiltrate more than two hundred thousand regular army troops, euphemistically referred to as "volunteers," into North Korea without detection by UN intelligence and deployed them to cut off the overextended UN columns pushing toward the Chinese border. The surprise and the ferocity of this Chinese offensive overran and destroyed the most exposed UN forces—the U.S. and ROK divisions in the west and the U.S. Army task force at the Chosin Reservoir—and forced the entire UN front to fall back. For U.S. troops, the withdrawal back was rapid—twenty miles per day—but orderly. The retiring troops were able to break contact with the advancing Chinese but had to abandon and destroy huge supply dumps of equipment and ammunition. Again the question arose: Should the United States evacuate its forces from Korea rather than attempt to fight the armies of Communist China in their own backyard, ten thousand miles from home? In spite of popular polls in the United States that, by 66 percent, favored abandoning the war, President Truman said, "Stay."

For the third time in five months, the capital city of Seoul changed hands as UN forces fell back to re-form their lines at the narrow waist of Korea, where their available forces could fill the gaps left by the badly battered U.S. and ROK divisions and present a solid front to the advancing Chinese. In January 1951 the UN armies reestablished and stabilized their front on a line just south of the thirty-eighth parallel and held against the Chinese advance.

GENERAL MacARTHUR SACKED

On 15 April 1951, General of the Army Douglas MacArthur had been relieved by President Truman as supreme commander of the Pacific for being "unable to give his wholehearted support to the policies of the United States Government and of the United Nations in matters pertaining to his official duties." Gen. Matthew B. Ridgeway, USA, had been named his successor. MacArthur had continued to advocate an "all-out" war in Korea, to occupy the entire peninsula, a course that could have brought the USSR into the conflict. Washington wanted to pursue a negotiated settlement along the general lines of the original boundaries of demarcation.

Then, on 25 January, General Ridgeway, now in command of the UN forces in Korea following the death of General Walker in a jeep accident, kicked off the fourth campaign of the war with a full-scale offensive all along the front. The objective was to inflict heavy casualties on the Communists and drive them out of South Korea. Ridgeway's fresh leadership and the growing battle experience of the U.S. troops were paying off. There was a palpable upswing in morale as troops found themselves on the offensive again after a month of retreating. U.S. Navy, Marine Corps, and Air Force planes devastated enemy troop concentrations. Seoul was quickly retaken, and at the end of March UN troops were again north of the thirty-eighth parallel, in spite of determined opposition. China continued to rush fresh troops and equipment south to the front, and in late April it mounted a major offensive of its own, with the main weight of the counterattack down the historic Seoul invasion corridor. The UN lines held and the Chinese were stopped outside of Seoul. A second Chinese offensive in May was thrown back with heavy losses from U.S. air and artillery. By June the UN lines were again firmly reestablished along the thirty-eighth parallel. The key city of Chorwon in the central plains, controlling the invasion route to Seoul, was captured and held by U.S. forces. By midsummer, the two opposing armies had stalled and were dug in along the front, which generally followed the line of the original border.

On 10 July 1951, with the opposing armies facing each other in a stalemate, along a boundary heavily fortified on both sides, peace talks were initiated at Kaesong and later at a special compound in the village of Panmunjom in no-man's-land between the UN and the Communist forces. This marked the beginning of the fifth phase of the Korean War. The original dividing line between North and South Korea had been decreed by the Allied powers at Potsdam to lie drawn along the thirty-eighth parallel, an abstract geographical reference line. This was simply a matter of convenience, without any serious considerations of terrain or historical precedent. It was impractical as a defensible national border. The 10 July positions of the opposing forces followed the topography of defendable terrain close to, but not superimposed upon, the thirty-eighth parallel. The de facto line of demarcation between North and South Korea was now more realistic for purposes of a natural national boundary. The final campaign, which lasted more than two years while the peacemakers bargained with threats and boycotts, saw some of the heaviest fighting of the war as the Chinese and newly reorganized North Korean divisions mounted attacks and limited offensives to frustrate the UN negotiators and seize more real estate. In these last two years, the United States suffered more than twelve thousand killed before the cease-fire took place on 27 July 1953. It had been three years, a month, and two days since a surprisingly well-trained and -equipped North Korean army of twenty-two divisions had crossed this same border (now restored as the Demilitarized Zone, or DMZ) in a carefully planned and unanticipated attack with the intention of conquering South Korea and annexing its territory to the Communist nation of Korea.

THE END AND THE OUTCOME

Geographically, the Korean War ended just as it began, at the thirty-eighth parallel. For each combatant, the outcome of the three years of intense warfare was different. For North Korea, it was a clear defeat. Their objective of annexing South Korea had not been attained. The North Korean army had been defeated; their capital city, Pyongyang, had largely been destroyed; and more than three hundred thousand North Korean soldiers had been killed or were missing in action.

Communist China's end position can only be considered a draw. Flexing their muscles in a show to the world of their new military might, the Chinese entered the war to rescue a Communist ally, North Korea, and to demonstrate that China would not tolerate any military threat near its borders. The result was that the Chinese Communists suffered losses of more than 420,000 killed or missing, and in the end were unable to defeat the U.S.-led United Nations forces, even though fighting adjacent to their own borders. In the end, China was forced to accept an armistice that simply reflected the status quo ante. The failure of 120,000 Chinese to defeat the 25,000 Marines of the 1st Marine Division, surrounded at the Chosin Reservoir, was especially demoralizing to the Chinese leaders.

For the United States, the outcome was not unfavorable. In my view Korea was a limited victory, but, then, it was a limited war. It was certainly not a defeat. The Americans did what they intended to do: prevent the armed seizure and annexation of South Korea by the Communists. In the process, the Americans threw the North Koreans out of South Korea, decimated their army, and then drove the Chinese Communist army out of South Korea to end the conflict on terms acceptable to us.

From the prospect of the United Nations, the war in Korea was a success of historic proportions. For the first time an international peacekeeping body had organized a multinational military force, exercised its command, then successfully reversed the territorial incursions of an aggressor state. Furthermore, the results were lasting. South Korea has not since been attacked or invaded. Historically, the Korean War has become a unique chapter in the annals of modern warfare, setting precedents and providing lessons that have served to guide the formulation of foreign policy and national strategy for the United States throughout the Cold War.

Limited War Defined

The Korean War was instrumental in defining limited war as a conflict fought under its own unique sets of rules. In Korea, the United States could not fight to win unconditionally. To do so would engulf the United States in a general war with China on the Asian mainland. Nor could the United States lose the war. The nation's honor and prestige, and leadership of the free world, were at stake.

The war was limited to fighting the Asian Communists. During the entire conflict, NATO forces facing the Soviet Communists in Europe and the North Atlantic had to maintain a posture of readiness and strength to deter a Soviet invasion of Western Europe. The Soviets had available more than one hundred divisions of ground troops and were rapidly modernizing their navy, creating a formidable challenge to the United States, in which the military might and political leadership of NATO reposed.

Mobilization during Korea was limited; "guns and butter" was the policy. The American public was sensitive to casualties, and Congress was concerned about the budget. Tactical operations had to be planned with careful consideration to hold down losses. This often eliminated major operations with a high potential for significant long-term military and political success. Budget pressures limited procurement of ammunition and aviation fuel, resulting in rationing of rounds for artillery bombardments in support of the ground forces, and the marginal readiness of combat aviation units due to too few flight hours.

With the war limited to the Korean peninsula, the concept of politically defined sanctuaries was established. U.S. air operations north of the Chinese border were proscribed by the UN with the consent of the U.S. government. Although locked in combat with the Chinese Communist army, UN air strikes on airfields, logistic bases, and troop-marshaling areas north of the Yalu were forbidden. Even the hot pursuit of Communist aircraft returning to their Chinese bases after combat in Korea was forbidden beyond the Yalu. The United States also had its de facto sanctuaries, but these existed not by political denial but as the result of the air and naval superiority achieved by the United States in the theater of operations. Maritime forces operated with impunity off the coasts of Korea, launching air strikes, conducting shore bombardments, reinforcing troops, and delivering combat logistics, all in support of the UN forces ashore. UN aircraft could fly virtually without concern for hostile fire at altitudes above ten thousand feet over the terrain. This was the upper limit for effective enemy AAA fire, and there were no surface-to-air missiles in North Korea.

Conditions of War

U.S. air superiority over all Korea was virtually absolute. U.S. Air Force F-86 North American Sabre fighters flying a barrier combat air patrol in the northwest corner of Korea intercepted Chinese MiG-15s as they crossed the Yalu coming out of their sanctuary bases to provide cover for the UN aircraft conducting air-to-ground interdiction operations to the south.

Korea was the first conflict in which the United States had an operational inventory of nuclear weapons. The world, as well as the American people, were waiting to see how the U.S. policy for the employment of these weapons of mass destruction would evolve. By the time of the Korean War, tactical nuclear weapons had reached yields greater than the Hiroshima bomb. The USSR by then also had the A-bomb. Concern for escalation and the resulting mutual destruction had rendered original policy for the normalization of nuclear weapons impractical. The U.S. policy on the use of "special weapons," as they were known, hardened, and although the inventory continued to grow in numbers and effectiveness, the requirement for presidential release made it clear that their application would be reserved for those *extremis* situations in which national survival would be at stake.

There were occasions when field commanders in desperate situations may have contemplated the use of tactical nuclear weapons as an equalizer to limit U.S. casualties in the face of the seemingly inexhaustible Chinese numbers. But the employment of nuclear weapons in Korea was never seriously considered. In another sense, during the Korean War, nuclear weapons played a key role in our national survival. With the United States engaged in a full-scale war in Korea, the USSR could see this preoccupation as a weakness in NATO and an invitation to launch an attack on Western Europe. It was only the persuasion of the United States' readiness for strategic warfare, constantly displayed by ongoing SAC operations, that served as a powerful deterrent to a Soviet temptation for an invasion across the East German plains.

Conventional Warfare Capability

As the war in Korea crystallized our policy on tactical nuclear weapons, it conversely drove home the lesson that in the future, U.S. national defense planning must be as much concerned with conventional warfighting as with nuclear deterrence. Nuclear weapons did not deter the war in Korea, nor were they to be employed tactically. In the future,

U.S. national security policy would have to be prepared to fight and win conflicts by conventional arms, reserving the nuclear arsenal to deter the escalation of limited wars by the introduction of Soviet military forces. The Communists may have assumed that the United States was not prepared to fight a conventional war in Asia in 1950, but they badly underestimated the national will, the resourcefulness of the United States' military planners, and the resilience of the American character.

The Mothballed Reserve

At the end of World War II, the United States' first priority was the return of the civilian soldier to his home. Millions of tons of ammunition, supplies, and equipment had to be abandoned overseas. However, the greatest capital investment in weapon systems was in ships and aircraft, all of which were fortunately mobile. Great numbers of these modern assets were brought home and mothballed, the ships in freshwater estuaries and the aircraft on desert air bases. When the North Korean invasion caught the newly established Department of Defense at its nadir, the services turned to their mothballed equipment.

The Navy carrier force grew to nineteen fleet carriers, enough to maintain four off Korea as well as two constantly in the Mediterranean for the support of NATO. P51 Mustangs, veterans of Eisenhower's World War II campaigns through France and Germany, became the main ground attack aircraft for the U.S. Air Force and our allies. F4U Corsairs, which had fought Japanese Zeroes in the Pacific, again flew from Navy carriers and Marine shore bases in support of UN ground forces. It was this air support that achieved total air superiority over the Korean battlefield and formed the third leg of the UN's combined arms triad of infantry, artillery, and air. By the Chinese army's admission, UN air power was the equalizer that offset the Communists' vast superiority in ground forces.

Battleships, cruisers, and destroyers came out of mothballs to provide seagoing artillery to support the UN flanks. The evacuation of General Almond's X Corps, with its combat vehicles, out of Hungnam in December 1950, would not have been possible without the ring of fire delivered from these major combatants and the sealift provided by the amphibious and auxiliary ships.

TWO EPIC BATTLES

Although called the forgotten war, the Korean War nevertheless contributed two unforgettable military operations to brighten the legacy of
U.S. arms: Inchon and Chosin.

At the west coast port of Inchon, just fifteen miles southwest of Seoul,
the U.S. Navy, in an amphibious operation conducted under the most
difficult conditions of terrain and tide imaginable, put ashore fifty
thousand troops, led by twenty-five thousand Marines, on 15 September
1950. The troops drove east to link up with the Eighth Army, breaking
out of the Pusan perimeter to complete a massive rout of the North
Korean army. The 1st Marine Division made the assault landing, secured
Inchon in one day, reached Seoul on the eighteenth, and liberated the
capital of South Korea five days later. By the end of September, the
Americans had routed the North Koreans and reached the thirty-eighth
parallel. By means of the amphibious landing at Inchon, the United
Nations in just three months had accomplished what it had set out to
do: repel "armed invasion and restore peace and stability in South
Korea." In the long term, Inchon was more than a boldly conceived
operation, a masterpiece of technical execution, and a pivotal victory. It
was an essential lesson for our new Department of Defense that advancing technology would not necessarily make obsolete the proven funda-
mentals of warfare. In 1949, Gen. Omar Bradley, chairman of the Joint
Chiefs of Staff, had stated in congressional testimony that amphibious
landings were a thing of the past. Never again would it be feasible to
assemble and concentrate the shipping required for such an operation,
since it provided too inviting a target for atomic bombs. Bradley implied
that a U.S. Marine Corps was no longer needed as part of our defense
establishment.

Chosin was a different sort of campaign. On 25 November, when the
Chinese Communists People's Liberation Army first entered the Korean
conflict, catching U.S. intelligence and UN forces by surprise, the 1st
Marine Division was deployed deep in North Korea, west of the Chosin
Reservoir, at the end of a seventy-eight-mile two-lane dirt road winding
through some of the most mountainous country of the Korean peninsula.
Surrounded by 120,000 regular troops of the Chinese Communist army,
battling deep snow and temperatures down to thirty below zero, the

25,000 Marines of the 1st Marine Division fought their way out of the trap, defeating seven Chinese divisions in the process. China was so determined to destroy the Marines—and equally sure they would be able to do so—that staggering losses were accepted. Sixty percent of the 120,000 Chinese engaged became casualties, including 30,000 killed or missing in action. Marine losses were a thousand killed and missing, but the 1st Marine Division battled their way out and destroyed two Chinese armies in the fighting.

The extraction and survival of the 1st Marine Division could be characterized justifiably as a successful tactical operation for the 1st Marines and a tactical failure for the Chinese. The mission of the Chinese army was to trap and destroy the Marines, and the People's Republic of China failed to do so. The objective of the 1st Marine Division was to "advance to the South," fighting their way through the encircling Chinese army groups and linking up with UN forces in the south. The Marines were successful, bringing out their wounded, most of their dead, and all of their military equipment. It was clearly a tactical success for the UN, the United States, and the Marines and a defeat for the Chinese.

Marine Corps historians make it clear that the "advance to the south" could not have been successful without total air superiority. Maj. Gen. Field Harris, USMC, the commanding general of Marine Air Wing 1, encompassing all Marine aviation in Korea, said the withdrawal of the entire 1st Marine Division from the Chosin Reservoir area would not have been possible without close air support. Most of this support came from carriers, Marines flying from the Task Group 96.8 CVEs off the northwest coast of Korea, and Navy planes operating from the three *Essex*-class carriers in the Sea of Japan. General Harris, in an official dispatch to Rear Admiral Ewen, USN, commander, Task Force 77, stated specifically that the 5th and 7th Marine Regiments trapped by the Chinese at Yudamni on 2 December 1950 would never have made it to Hagaru-ri without the TF 77 air support.

4

Korea

Naval Operations

I t was 2 June 1953, and the USS *Boxer* was operating off Korea in the Sea of Japan. The weather was overcast with showers. As the Panther taxied up the deck and made a sharp turn to line up with the port catapult, the F9F's thin tires were skidding on the wet teak deck. The yellow-shirted plane director, who was finding it difficult to keep from slipping, leaned into the forty knots of wind as the rain buffeted the flight deck. The wind was not a problem for me. The Panther needed all it could get. Loaded with four 260-pound fragmentation bombs and two 200-pound general-purpose bombs, the F9F was at maximum weight for launching. I was leading a six-plane F9F strike against a Chinese army marshaling area at Kisong-Ni in North Korea, about fifty miles north of the front lines, and would be the first plane off on the 7:30 AM launch. I heard the clank of the catapult bridle and then felt the jet squat slightly as the cat took tension on the aircraft. The catapult officer gave the turn-up signal and I pushed the throttle hard against the forward stop. The revolutions per minute (rpm) dial showed 100 percent. I watched the gauge for three seconds to be certain the rpm reading was not just a surge, and then, bracing my hardhat against the ejection seat's padded headrest, I saluted. There was the short delay, and then *bang!* the catapult fired. In two seconds I was off the catapult, over the ocean, ahead of the carrier, and flying at 125 knots.

Going straight ahead, I climbed to four thousand feet, easing power back to 250 knots. After three minutes, time for six planes to be catapulted, I made a 180-degree turn to the left, and the rest of the flight, climbing out on the opposite heading, turned successively and joined up quickly.

As we passed by the carrier, I turned north and started a climb to ten thousand feet, checking out from ship control and switching to the Task Force 77 (TF 77) frequency on the five-channel very high frequency (VHF) radio. All of the TF 77 flights were under positive radio control from catapulting to arrestment. In the vicinity of the ship, it was the home carrier's Air Operations Center. En route over the water, it was the commander, TF 77 (CTF 77) flagship's Combat Information Center (CIC). When over Korea, the Tactical Air Control Center (TACC) in Taegu took over. The TACC was an Air Force flight-control center, colocated with the Joint Operations (JOC), which controlled, or really monitored, all air traffic over Korea, north and south of the front lines. Being under a radio controller from takeoff to landing was a good arrangement, analogous to the civilian air-control system in the United States. The pilots sometimes complained about the number of frequency changes and the check-in and checkout procedures with the daily changing code words, but the system was useful and reassuring.

Crossing the North Korean coastline at Wonsan, I switched to the TACC and checked in, giving my call sign, mission number, and type of aircraft, all in voice code. TACC acknowledged and went silent. We were now over enemy territory, and immediately the dirty gray puffs from enemy AA guns began to appear around us. The cockpits were silent except for the heavy breathing noises of the oxygen regulators. No chatter from the pilots. We were jinking, making random turns and climbs to give the enemy gunners a more difficult shot. We were working harder now and the adrenaline had kicked in.

Good navigation was essential. One wrong turn and we could be lost over this terrain, which all looked the same. There were no recognizable landmarks in this sector. I had planned to fly due north from our coast-in point, travel over four mountain ridges, and then turn northwest along the fifth valley and follow it ten miles to the confluence of the two rivers that formed the delta on which the village of Kisong-Ni was located. I had drawn this track with grease pencil on the acetate of my 1:250,000-scale chart and it required constant reference to stay on course. At the same time, I had to maneuver the formation constantly to avoid the heaviest concentration of tracers and gray AA puffs.

We made our left turn down the fifth valley. Now the clouds had lowered to mountain-top level and there was some scud below us as we jinked our way through the valley, below the hill tops at four thousand feet. We were at 98 percent full power, usually good for 450 knots, but the Panthers were only indicating about 280. The heavy external bomb load and the constant maneuvering had slowed us down. The flak had picked up and the tracers were clearly visible in the gloom of the overcast in the valley. It was uncomfortable. It was mainly 37mm and 20mm automatic fire, with some bursting rounds below us. The flak had become steady and was coming from all directions. The lighter stuff was passing through the formation between the planes.

Because of our low altitude and the scud, the target area could not be identified until we were almost over it. Then suddenly, there was Kisong-Ni. There was no time to rebrief the flight, so I simply called out, "Sealancer One commencing attack" and waggled my wings—the signal to follow me—and rolled left into a forty-degree dive. There wasn't enough altitude to go much steeper. I pulled the nose of the plane around to put the sight pipper on a large barnlike structure. Heavy tracers were now coming head on from the vicinity of my target.

I was into my dive, passing through three thousand feet, when I heard a loud *pow* and the sharp rattling impact of shrapnel striking the fuselage. My plane had been hit. Pulling hard on the stick, I got a solid response and pushed the throttle hard, but it was already all the way forward at 100 percent rpm. The left-wing tip tank had been struck by an explosive 37mm round, and I was leaving a trail of blazing fuel. I called on guard channel (the frequency set up for the radio to communicate on in an emergency, overriding whatever preset channel the pilot has selected) for the air group commander, who was leading my second section, to take over the attack, as I was hit and heading south at max speed. I wanted to be as close to the front lines as possible when the engine quit or the fire took over, and I had to eject or ditch. I called my wingman to join up on me. No answer. This was not good. He was supposed to be there.

Then a Panther pulled up alongside my plane and I recognized from the side numbers that it was John Chambers, my wingman. There was blood smeared on the inside of his cockpit canopy. He signaled that his radio was out and held up his left arm, which was covered with blood. His plane had also taken a direct 37mm hit. As it turned out, the round had struck the plane in the fuselage below the cockpit and exploded under his seat. The parachute had absorbed most of the blast, but shrapnel had torn into his arms and legs.

On guard channel I called the TACC, gave them our approximate position, and asked for a vector to the nearest available search and rescue (SAR) facility. I turned my radar beacon to emergency, to identify my plane to the friendly radar operators as the Panther with the battle damage, and almost immediately the TACC picked us up on his radar and gave me a steer to K-18, the Republic of Korea field at Kangnung, which had a single, narrow, pierced-steel (marston matting) runway. By now the fire in the wing was only intermittent, but my fuel gauge was going down alarmingly. I didn't know how badly hurt Chambers was or whether his plane would make it to the friendly lines, still twenty miles away.

TACC vectored us straight into K-18. A khaki canvas–covered ROK army ambulance and a firefighting jeep were lined up by the runway. Chambers went in first and piled up about halfway down the strip. The medics got him out right away, but the jeep had trouble clearing the wreckage off the strip, a problem with marston matting. Low on fuel, I crash-landed in the cleared paddy area alongside the runway. The plane was a mess, but I was unhurt.

I caught the crash jeep over to the medical tent where Chambers was already on the table, an ROK army doctor pulling shrapnel out of his arms and legs and cleaning up his wounds. He would be evacuated to a U.S. Army hospital an hour later by helicopter and then in a week sent to the Philadelphia Naval Hospital, which was near his home. He returned to flight status a year later but was killed in Vietnam in an F-4 Phantom II. He was a carrier air wing commander.

Later that same day, Lieutenant Hayek, operations officer for VF-52, also made an emergency landing at K-18 accompanied by his wingman. His Panther was full of holes from heavy flak shrapnel, but he was unhurt.

An AD-2N Skyraider was flown in from the *Boxer* to pick us up at K-18 that afternoon. The AD-2N was a propeller plane with two seats in the fuselage behind the pilot for a pair of radar operators. In emergencies, like this, it was used as a transport between tactical airfields and the carrier. Back on the *Boxer*, I debriefed with the intelligence people, wrote a letter to Chambers's parents, and then checked the flight schedule. I had another interdiction strike mission on a target twenty miles behind enemy lines, the next morning.

EARLY AIR OPERATIONS

In the early days of the Korean War, after the North Korean invasion and President Truman's commitment of U.S. military forces to the support of the Republic of Korea, the first significant U.S. forces to engage the enemy were the planes of Air Wing 5 flying from the USS *Valley Forge*. This *Essex*-class carrier, its construction completed too late for World War II, had deployed to the Seventh Fleet in May 1950 and arrived on scene off Korea to deliver strikes on Pyongyang, the North Korean capital, on 3 July. As the UN forces withdrew into the shrinking Pusan perimeter during July, the only advantage the beleaguered and outnumbered U.S. and ROK troops could expect was U.S. air power. But air power was limited.

The USAF tactical squadrons in the Far East at the commencement of the conflict were almost entirely F-80 Shooting Star units. The F-80 was primarily an interceptor. It had relatively light external ordnance capacity and was short on endurance, which limited time on station, an essential requirement for effective close air support.

In the first weeks of the war, all of the jet-capable airfields in South Korea had been overrun. The U.S. Air Force fighter bases in southern Japan were so distant from the objective areas in Korea that the F-80 Shooting Stars had less than five minutes on station and could carry only two 5-inch high-velocity aircraft rockets (HVARs).

Navy tactical air was the only heavy air support available to the UN ground force in those early days. Then, and throughout the war, all naval tactical air was carrier based. The principal source was Task Force 77, the fast carrier striking force of the U.S. Seventh Fleet, stationed in the western Pacific. TF 77 included only the *Essex*-class carriers. Capable of thirty knots and carrying more than seventy aircraft and a commendable combat record from World War II, the *Essex* class was the Navy's postwar fleet carrier and the first class of ship to be able to support and operate jet squadrons.

The Carrier Air Group

The nominal air group of the *Essex* class consisted of two F9F-2 Panther jet squadrons, one F4U-4 Corsair squadron, and one AD-2 Skyraider squadron. Each squadron consisted of fourteen to sixteen aircraft, depending largely upon the availability of aircraft at the time of deployment. In addition there were detachments of photo, radar search, night fighter, and night attack aircraft plus rescue helicopters, bringing the total aircraft complement up to more than seventy planes.

The F9F-2, although classified as a fighter, was really better in the fighter-bomber role. To improve its capability as a ground-attack aircraft in Korea, eight bomb pylons were added on the wings, which reduced its maximum speed by thirty knots. No longer did it have the performance needed for air-to-air combat, but it now carried eight external stores. Initially limited to about five hundred pounds of external ordnance, the F9F-2 had its bomb-load capacity further increased through the installation of stall fences, narrow fore-and-aft fins mounted on the dorsal surface of each wing to decrease a plane's stalling speed while loaded. After the installation of the wing fences in 1951, the Panther routinely carried twelve hundred pounds of bombs and rockets. A typical load for air support would be four 260-pound fragmentation bombs and two antitank aircraft rockets (ATARs).

The real heavy hitters of the air group were the propeller-driven Skyraiders, capable of lugging eight thousand pounds of bombs to any target in Korea, and delivering their armament, one bomb at a time, with precision accuracy. The World War II–vintage F4U-4 Corsairs could routinely handle three thousand pounds of ordnance on carrier-based sorties.

Carrier Force Buildup

The USS *Valley Forge*, an *Essex*-class carrier, had been instrumental in slowing the North Korean advance during the first month of the war. Its planes were in demand in all sectors and for every kind of mission from close air support of troops to far-ranging strikes on the North Korean supply routes, destroying truck convoys of war material and killing hundreds of North Korean regular troops. But its air group would have been even more effective had there been proper air-ground communications. The roles and missions agreements after World War II had made the Air Force responsible for aviation support of the Army, including tactical air support of the ground war. The air-control system was geared to a European war type of conflict with elaborate control facilities such as the Army and Air Force JOC and TACC. In NATO, these command centers were in place and operating. In Korea, both of these facilities had to be startups, with all of the associated flail. All Navy missions in support of the ground forces had to be scheduled and controlled by the Air Force, which then passed them on to the Army forward controllers. Unfortunately, the communications were totally inadequate and the system just wasn't working. With the front lines in a state of flux, pilots were often unsure of the identity of the troops on the ground under them. It was essential that close support missions be under positive control to avoid hitting friendlies.

By August, the military situation of the hard-pressed UN ground forces had become so perilous that the commanding general of the Eighth Army, General Walker, authorized the Navy to arrange missions and conduct strikes by communicating directly with the ground forces being supported. Commander, Air Force Far East, Gen. Hoyt Vandenburgh, was not pleased with this arrangement but acceded because of the desperate need for close air support.

In early August the *Valley Forge* was augmented by the arrival of the *Philippine Sea*. Later in the month, the *Leyte* and *Boxer* reported on station to substantially reinforce TF 77 and give some relief to Air Group Five.

Also in August 1950, the 1st Marine Air Wing arrived in Iwakuni, Japan, from CONUS, and two Corsair F4U-4 squadrons were immediately embarked in the escort carriers *Badoeng Straits* and *Sicily*, which constituted Task Element 96.23. The Marine squadrons were equipped with the B-versions of the F4U-4, which mounted four 20mm guns, especially effective for ground support with their explosive shells. Also, the Marines did not suffer from the impediments imposed by the roles and missions policy. The mission of the 1st Marine Air Wing was to support the 1st Marine Division, which was currently engaged in combat in Korea. There were no problems in their air support mission planning or execution. Close support for the Marines was always available from Marine aircraft, and most of the ground tactical air parties had trained in the United States with the squadrons they were now controlling. The carriers of Task Element 96.23 moved around the Korean coastal waters as needed, to be as close to the Marines' battlefield as possible, reducing reaction intervals and increasing aircraft time on station.

By September 1950, just two months after the war had begun, the Navy was sustaining a force of four carriers in the Seventh Fleet with two or three on station in TF 77, "Carrier Striking Force, Seventh Fleet," off Korea on a continuing basis. Carrier force levels were continuing to grow with the introduction of newly overhauled carriers from the mothballed reserve fleet. During the Korean War eleven *Essex*-class carriers served in combat, most of them more than once. Some, like the *Valley Forge, Philippine Sea,* and *Princeton,* made three deployments, and the *Boxer* made four.

During the Korean War a total of six escort carriers, with Marine Corsairs embarked, were deployed with Task Element 96.23. A force of never less than two, and sometimes three, escort carriers was maintained in the western Pacific. The *Bataan, Badoeng Straits,* and *Sicily* all made three seven-month deployments during the two-year conflict.

Royal Navy carriers also provided tactical air support for the UN ground forces. The HMS *Glory* was on station with Task Group (TG) 95.1 providing Sea Furies and Fireflies for the interdiction campaign. The HMS *Ocean* followed, and a total of six Commonwealth carriers served in Korean waters, including the Australian carrier *Sydney.*

THE WEEKEND WARRIORS

By the creation of the air task groups, the Navy was able to provide the aircraft to outfit the decks of the *Essex*-class carriers returning to the operational fleet out of mothballs. But the cockpits still had to be filled and the maintenance personnel had to be provided. The U.S. Naval Reserve responded in just the way it had been designed, to augment the naval aviation squadrons during mobilization in time of war.

During World War II, the Navy had invested heavily in the training of Navy pilots, a process that involved the meticulous selection of young men with aeronautical aptitude and took time and resources—bases, planes, and instructors. In the postwar demobilization, most of these pilots had left active duty to return to civilian life. Fortunately, the Navy had made plans to preserve this pool of talent for the day the Navy would again need these very special citizen-warriors to serve the country. In the most general terms, the Navy's plan was to create a system of naval reserve air stations distributed regionally throughout the country, conveniently located in the vicinity of population centers where there would be concentrations of naval aviation veterans. Using surplus World War II naval aircraft, reserve squadrons would be created and former Navy pilots and aviation ratings signed up in the Naval Reserve squadrons to maintain their skills by regular periods of drill at the Reserve's air stations or at municipal airports. The Reservists were organized into squadrons—replications of the commands in which they had flown in the war. Each squadron would drill—and that included lots of flying—one weekend a month. Hence the nickname "weekend warriors." This way, one squadron's inventory of aircraft would support four squadrons of pilots, who would maintain their flight proficiency sufficiently to be ready mobilization assets. They loved the flying and were being well paid for it. Each squadron of Reservists would also be activated for a two-week period each year to fly together on an extended and intensive schedule, usually at a Navy field well away from their home station.

During the early days of the Korean War, reserve squadrons would be called up for active duty as a unit, each unit to deploy as an organic squadron under its own commanding officer, with a full roster of Naval Reserve pilots and administrative organization. Of course, most of these pilots and sailors had well-established civilian careers that they very well might be reluctant to leave to fight in an unexpected war half a world away. Yet invariably they served with willingness, pride, and true professional competence. Their contribution was a major factor in the nation's ability to mobilize sufficient tactical air power to successfully stem the advance of the Communist armies on the Korean peninsula.

When Air Task Group 1 deployed on board the *Valley Forge* to Korea in November 1951, the F4U Corsair squadron in the task group was Fighter Squadron 653, a Navy Reserve unit from near Cleveland, Ohio. The commanding officer of VF-653 was Lt. Cdr. Cook Cleland, USNR. I got to know Cook quite well, because as the group operations officer who dealt with the squadron commanders to coordinate scheduling, I was more deeply involved with VF-653 because, as a Reserves squadron, they were short on administrative experience and lacked familiarity with the routines and requirements of current carrier operations, especially in an air group with jet aircraft. Cook and I became very close friends as the result of that cruise, and our friendship has endured to this day.

Cook Cleland was a legendary figure in naval aviation even before he embarked with VF-653 for the Korean War. During World War II, he had been a dive-bomber pilot flying the Douglas Dauntless SBD and received the Navy Cross for scoring a bomb hit on a Japanese battleship early in the war. On another occasion he had been on antisubmarine patrol around the carrier when a force of Japanese land-based aircraft attacked the task group. Cleland and his rear-seat gunner intercepted the Japanese and got credit for shooting down a "Betty" multiengine bomber.

After the war, Cleland stayed in the Naval Air Reserve and became a racing pilot. The Cleveland Air Races, indisputably the most prestigious of the prewar air races, was starting up again in 1946 after a hiatus over the war years. Cleland entered with an FG Corsair, the Chance Vought–designed F4U-4 built by Goodyear Aircraft, which he had bought as government surplus. Cleland came in sixth, badly defeated by surplus Army Air Corps Mustangs and Aircobras. He appealed to the Navy for assistance in obtaining an F2G Corsair, a better-performing Navy plane. This Goodyear Aircraft version of the F4U had been built at the war's end, and none had been delivered to operational Navy squadrons. Only a handful had been produced. It mounted an enormous radial engine with four banks of cylinders, the Pratt and Whitney R4360, nicknamed "the corncob." It was the most powerful radial aircraft engine yet built. Adm. Bull Halsey, who had known Cook Cleland as a Navy pilot, arranged to have three of these F2Gs declared surplus, and Cleland bought all of them for his racing team, all former Navy pilots. With his F2G, Cleland won the Thompson Trophy, the most coveted of the Cleveland Air Race events, in 1947 and 1949. With his three F-2Gs sweeping first, second, and third in the 1949 race, Cleland had high hopes for continuing his successful racing career. Then, in 1950, the Cleveland Air Races were again cancelled because of the Korean War, and Lt. Cdr. Cook Cleland immediately volunteered for active duty. He was given command of VF-653, which drew its complement of pilots from the Cleveland-Pittsburgh area.

As a Navy Reserve squadron, its pilot roster was made up entirely of Reserve officers, most of whom had flown during World War II. VF-653 was mobilized and ordered to active duty at the beginning of the Korean War. Of the twenty-six original officers, there were twenty-five lieutenants and one lieutenant commander, Cleland. They called themselves "Cook Cleland's Flying Circus" and developed a great squadron camaraderie. Cleland flew in Korea with the same panache he had exhibited as a civilian racing pilot. He was unabashedly admired by his squadron pilots, who tried to emulate his daring flying style. The unfortunate result was that VF-653's combat losses were staggering. During the 1951–52 tour in Korea, VF-653 lost twelve of its twenty-six pilots. All but two were combat losses.

During this period, the carriers were primarily engaged in cutting railroad lines. The accuracy required for cutting the lines required repeated passes in a single area. The Communists reacted to these tactics by a buildup of flak all along the major railroad lines and mounted automatic weapons and antiaircraft guns on flat cars in reaction to concentrations of effort by CTF 77. All of the squadrons in the rail interdiction campaign were getting shot up, but VF-653 was especially hard hit. Cook Cleland and his squadron wanted to get more rail cuts than any other outfit. It was a finite but indisputable measure of success. After each mission, photo planes took vertical pictures of the assigned track segments and the photo analyst's report went straight to commander, Seventh Fleet, where it was included in a daily damage assessment report distributed to all air units in Korea. VF-653 rolled up an impressive record, getting an average of 1.3 rail cuts per sortie. At this time the Air Force average was about 0.2 to 0.1 per sortie. This remarkable disparity was due in part to the Navy's Corsair being a better tactical bomber than the Air Force's P51, as well as to the skill and determination of Cleland's Flying Circus.

Cleland was publicly criticized by the Pittsburgh-Cleveland area press for his squadron's heavy losses. In Cook's defense I can say that he was not an irresponsible squadron commander. He flew more missions than any of his pilots. He was deeply sensitive to the loss of any one of his officers. To him the Flying Circus was more than a squadron, it was a band of compatriots who did everything together—work, play, and go to war. Cook was a fierce competitor. He wanted to win. When engaged in combat, he wanted his squadron to be better than any other squadron in doing damage to the enemy. His squadron pilots reflected his competitive spirit and desire to get results. The damage-assessment photos were proving that. They didn't have the aviation ability, or perhaps the luck, that Cleland had, but they were determined to prove their courage and combat skills. Cook counseled them to be prudent in the face of limiting weather or heavy flak. But when he wasn't leading the flight, he couldn't hold them back. No one, from the admiral on down, was going to tell the Flying Circus to take it easy on the North Koreans. VF-653 was an asset for the UN side, and its contribution to the air interdiction campaign, both in results and example, was not to be restrained.

With all of his enthusiasm and dare deviltry, Cook Cleland was a warm, friendly, serious person whose hobby was collecting and restoring Early American furniture. In his post-Navy retirement he became an acknowledged expert in that field and for years owned and operated one of the finest antique stores in Pensacola, Florida.

THE JOINT AIR CAMPAIGN IN KOREA

From its inception as a piecemeal stopgap in the summer of 1950, the tactical air campaign in Korea evolved into a pattern of operations that was designed to the specific character of the theater and adapted to the military strategy, operations, and capability of the enemy. The UN air campaign made the best use of all the forces available to the theater.

The superiority of the Navy's ADs and Corsairs over the Air Force's F-80s for tactical support of ground forces was not lost on the Air Force commanders. Far East Air Force (FEAF) commander General Stratemyer took quick action to replace the F-80s with more suitable aircraft. With the Navy taking all of the Skyraiders and Corsairs available from new production and the mothballed reserve, the Air Force drew on their large inventory of F-51 Mustangs, a fighter that had proved itself in the ground-attack role in Europe during World War II. On 23 July 1950, less than one month after the war had started, the USS *Boxer* delivered to Japan 145 F-51 Mustangs pulled from Air National Guard squadrons. By 11 August 1950, six fighter squadrons of the Fifth Air Force in Korea (FAFIK) had converted from the jet F-80s to the propeller-driven F-51s for the air-ground war in Korea.

About that same time, U.S. Air Force headquarters in Washington decided to deploy two wings of F-84 Thunderjets, previously earmarked for NATO, to the Korean theater. The F-84 was not up to F-86 performance for air-to-air combat but was far superior to the F-80 as a fighter-bomber and was considered more survivable than the F-51. The F-84s were transported to Japan on U.S. Navy aircraft training transports (CVT), which were converted from World War II escort carriers.

Both the F-51 and F-84 shipments suffered some aircraft corrosion en route. This is a problem almost universally misunderstood outside of naval aviation. Over the years it has plagued foreign air forces attempting to create a sea-based air arm. As recently as 1972 a number of U.S. Navy helicopters were severely damaged by corrosion as the result of efforts to reduce costs and procure "off the shelf" helicopters for cruisers and destroyers.

It had become accepted early in the Korean War that the only fighter in the UN inventory that could successfully take on the Soviet MiG-15 in air-to-air combat was the "E" model of the North American F-86 Sabre. When this became apparent, the Air Force deployed a wing of these first-line fighters from Langley Air Force Base to Kimpo Air Base (K-14) in the vicinity of Seoul in December 1950. It became the mission of the F-86s to maintain a barrier patrol in the northwest corner of North Korea on the south side of the Yalu River, opposite the airfields on which the Chinese MiG-15s were based. The F-86s were controlled by the UN radar site on Yodo-ri, an island off the west coast of North Korea. This radar, manned by U.S. Air Force personnel, was able to track the MiGs virtually from takeoff at the Chinese airfields and as they flew south over the Yalu. The F-86s, flying from the airfields at Kimpo and Suwon, both in the vicinity of Seoul, were controlled by the Yodo-Ri radar. They flew a barrier patrol in the northwest corner of Korea known as "MiG Alley," where they could intercept and shoot down any MiGs crossing the Yalu. It was the objective of the Chinese MiGs, on the other hand, to get by this F-86 barrier to attack the slower and less maneuverable tactical fighters providing support to the UN ground forces. Any MiGs that got through the F-86s protective screen could create havoc with the slower and heavily loaded attack planes.

THE MIG-15

The MiG-15 was a surprisingly good fighter, thought by some analysts to be superior to the F-86E. It climbed faster, turned more quickly, and in general was more maneuverable. The Sabre could dive faster and had a better gunsight and cabin-defrosting system. The MiG-15 was Russian designed and produced, and furnished to the Chinese. They flew from Chinese airfields north of the Yalu. According to the F-86 pilots, who were the best fighter jocks in the Air Force, the MiG pilots were very, very good in air-to-air combat. There was always a suspicion that the pilots were European or Russian, but that was not confirmed until about 1995, when an article appeared in the Soviet press describing the MiG pilots as Soviet air force officers, most of whom had World War II experience flying against German pilots in first-line Messerschmits and Focke-Wolfs. One Russian pilot was said to have a record of close to one hundred air-to-air kills. It is no wonder that the U.S. Air Force F-86 pilots considered the Chinese MiGs a formidable adversary.

Although aviation assets were being committed to the war in the Pacific—F-51s from the National Guard, F-84s from NATO, and F-86s from CONUS—basing these forces in South Korea was taking time. Except for the airfields inside the Pusan perimeter, the air bases in South Korea remained in danger of being overrun by enemy ground forces during the Communist offensives of August 1950 and January 1951. It was not until the Chinese Spring Offensive of 1951 had been thrown back and the front lines stabilized north of Seoul that the airfields in the Seoul and Taegu areas could be considered secure.

Then much work had to be accomplished by the engineers to repair the extensive damage to the runways and facilities caused by artillery, bombing, and even tank treads. All of these fields had been taken by the enemy at least once, and those around Seoul had been seized twice by the Communists.

The Republic of Korea air force (ROKAF) operated a small squadron of F-51s from a strip at Kangnung on the east coast of South Korea, about twenty miles below the DMZ. There was an advisory group of Americans at Kangnung. Commander, Naval Forces Japan had also furnished a small fleet aircraft service squadron (FASRon) detachment at Kangnung. They were there to take care of TF 77 aircraft unable to make it back to the carriers for reasons such as mechanical trouble, flak damage, or weather conditions. It was the closest friendly airfield to TF 77's operating area; many Navy planes, and probably a few pilots, were saved by its ready availability. Kangnung was a primitive installation with pierced-metal (Marston matting) runways, and Quonsets, Butler huts, and tents for the support facilities.

Tactical air support for the UN ground forces was provided by two commands, the ground-based squadrons in South Korea under the Fifth Air Force, and the carrier air groups under commander, Seventh Fleet, specifically, commander, Task Force 77. To minimize interference and delineate clear lines of responsibility and authority, Korea was divided by a longitude line running down the approximate center of the peninsula. The area east of the line was the Navy's responsibility; that to the west belonged to the Air Force, which had control of all land-based aircraft in Korea, regardless of nationality or service. This system worked well, without any significant interference in operations or problems in authority and responsibility.

NAVAL CARRIER DEPLOYMENTS

Carrier-based air was one of the two major components of the tactical aviation forces in Korea. The other component air force was FAFIK. The Navy squadrons flew from carriers attached to Task Force 77, the fast carrier striking force of the Seventh Fleet. Commander, Seventh Fleet and commander, Fifth Air Force were under the direct operational control of General MacArthur. TF 77 nominally included two *Essex*-class carriers, each with a standard air wing of two jet fighter squadrons of F9F-2 Panthers, an F4U-4 Corsair squadron, and a squadron of AD Skyraiders. Occasionally the air group would include F2H-2 Banshees instead of Panthers, but this was an exception (usually occurring when an Atlantic Fleet carrier was deployed to the western Pacific).

Shortly after the outbreak of the war, Adm. Forrest Sherman, the chief of naval operations, was determined to commit the maximum possible number of carriers to the Korean theater. Already the United States had agreed to the full commitment of two attack carriers (CVAs) in the Sixth Fleet in the Mediterranean in support of NATO. The difficulties of maintaining two CVAs forward deployed in the Sixth Fleet, in addition to supporting a force of carriers in the western Pacific conducting combat operations, were formidable. Carrier force levels were still in the building stage. Ships were being reactivated from the mothballed fleet and planes were being transferred from the Navy Reserves and coming out of mothballs in the desert. The buildup was beginning to exceed the Navy's capacity to man the additional ships and squadrons.

In balancing the Navy's carrier assets, the decision was made to keep four CVAs in the western Pacific assigned to Seventh Fleet. This would allow two carriers to be in TF 77 at all times. Each carrier would have thirty days at sea on the line conducting combat operations. Then after a two-day transit to the U.S. Naval Base at Sasebo or Yokosuka, nine days in port would be available for maintenance and repair and for rest and recreation (R&R) for the crew. Then two days of transit back to TF 77 and another line-period cycle would begin.

To keep four CVAs deployed forward in the western Pacific required a total force of twelve carriers, based upon the three-to-one ratio that was the planning thumb rule at that time: Only one-third of the total carrier force in the active fleet can be kept forward deployed in the standard peacetime cycle of repair and maintenance, training, CONUS operations, transit, and forward deployment. There were not enough CVAs in the national inventory to assign twelve to the Pacific Fleet and at the same time satisfy the mandatory NATO commitments. There was to be no backing down on NATO; the Soviets remained the real threat to the United States and its allies. The Korean War, in fact, was seen by the NATO leadership as a machination by the Kremlin to squeeze the Western powers. The allocation of four CVAs to the Seventh Fleet would have to be sustained by getting some help from the Atlantic Fleet and cutting short on the carriers' maintenance and training schedules.

Some difficult measures were employed. One of these was cross-decking, the only solution to critical shortages in certain key ratings. When a carrier departed the western Pacific for CONUS at the end of its deployment, some of its crew were transferred in Japan and assigned to an incoming CVA. These were ratings that were in short supply, mainly ship engineers and flight-deck personnel: catapult crews and plane directors. Without these experienced petty officers on board, the carrier couldn't steam or conduct flight operations. Whenever possible, the necessary cross-decking was done in CONUS. After a carrier returned from deployment in the western Pacific, critical ratings would be given one or two weeks leave, depending upon how much time was available until the next carrier sailed, and then ordered to the next deploying CVA. Cross-decking was a serious blow to morale. Two seven-month cruises, back to back, with only the break of a week's leave was terribly hard on the overworked ratings. It was not as bad for morale as the 1st

Marine Division being sent back into action immediately following their breakout from the Chosin Reservoir, however, or the thousands of soldiers killed in action by the Chinese who would never come home. But the sailors didn't see this. There were no televisions or newsreels in the carriers. They only saw their civilian neighbors in San Diego and Alameda bringing home fat paychecks from the aircraft factory or the shipyard and enjoying life in California with their families. The war was being fought on a guns-and-butter economy. As morale in these particular ratings suffered, so did reenlistments. When experienced petty officers left the Navy in large numbers, the situation became even worse. Eventually the shortages corrected themselves, thanks to the quality of the American bluejacket. The new sailors and petty officers learned the skills of their ratings quickly and within their first enlistment were beginning to fill the petty officer leadership positions on the flight decks and in the ships' engine rooms.

Task Force 77's operations continued without a diminution of performance as the newly recommissioned carriers joined the force and the old ones returned with fresh air groups. A total of eleven different CVAs served in TF 77 during the war and all performed up to fleet standards.

After the first year of the war, when the front lines had become stabilized, TF 77 developed a standard pattern of operations, highly effective for their current mission. The two carriers conducted flight operations from 0500 to 2100, a sixteen-hour day. Every hour and a half, aircraft would be launched and then recovered following launch. The first and last cycles—from 0500 to 0630 and 1930 to 2100—were flown by the night fighters and night-attack detachments in F4U-4N and AD-2N aircraft. The flight and hanger deck crews had a long day. Flight quarters was sounded at 0400 and secured at 2200. Men were given half-hour breaks for meals and personal needs but no time off for rest.

Task Force 77 air operations were conducted in a localized area around a geographical reference point called Point Oboe, about 125 miles due east of Wonsan Harbor. Oboe was conveniently located to cover most targets in northeast Korea from Wonsan to Chongjin. It was far enough at sea to not be visible to the highest flying enemy planes over the Korean and Asian landmass. The task force would depart Point Oboe as necessary, whenever the carriers were needed to concentrate on a single target area, or to conduct special operations. Although the carriers tried to remain in the vicinity of Oboe, flight operations could cause TF 77 to move some distance from this reference point. A light prevailing wind and a long, drawn-out launch and recovery cycle could have the carriers steaming at thirty knots for three hours—away from Point Oboe. The carriers then had to make high speed between subsequent launch and recovery cycles to close Point Oboe. Sometimes TF 77 would not be able to return to Oboe until nighttime, after flight operations were completed.

The carriers operated in formation about four thousand yards apart on an axis ninety degrees to the wind. A cruiser or battleship was stationed between them as fleet guide, and the destroyers formed a bent line screen on the wind line axis. During actual flight operations, the guide shifted to the carrier operating aircraft and a destroyer would detach from the screen to take up plane guard position one thousand yards in the carrier's wake. Usually the carriers launched and recovered aircraft together (the senior captain had the guide, but the junior carrier had all the leeway needed to keep the proper relative wind over its deck). Often the carriers would alternate launch and recovery times, one going every forty-five minutes. Then the entire task force guided on the operating CVA. This system of carrier task force operations was a holdover from World War II, and it was expensive in terms of fuel. The escorting ships were required to maintain station in the formation even when the carriers accelerated to thirty knots to launch or recover aircraft.

It was important that the carriers not stray too far from Point Oboe. Returning pilots based their navigation, and their fuel state, on their carrier being at or near Oboe. In June 1953 three F9F-2s from VF-653 off the USS *Boxer* ditched in the vicinity of TF 77 from fuel exhaustion. Not only had the task force moved far to the east chasing a light easterly breeze, but a flight deck mishap had delayed the launch and, hence, the recovery. When the Panthers returned to the carriers, there was no deck ready to receive them.

LOGISTICS AND CARRIER LANDINGS

After three days of flying, TF 77 would take the fourth day off for replenishment, retiring fifty miles to the east to rendezvous with the underway replenishment group (URG). The URG consisted of fleet oilers, ammunition ships, and general stores ships. On this day off from flying, the air groups worked on aircraft, the ship's crew loaded ammunition and stores, and the flight-deck crew repaired their equipment. It was not a "rope-yarn Sunday" or holiday routine.

The air group pilots did get a break. Drinking any alcohol on board ship is prohibited by Navy regulations, but there is one exception: Alcohol may be prescribed for medicinal purposes. At 1700 on the eve of a replenishment day, the air group flight surgeon went to each of the four squadron ready rooms (each squadron also hosted a detachment of specialized aircraft such as photo planes or night fighters) and provided one bottle of bourbon and one bottle of scotch to each. The pilots relaxed with the medicinal alcohol, ate popcorn, and watched old movies on a 16mm projector. Some got pretty stewed, but never outside the ready room.

All resupply of fuel, ammunition, support parts, personnel, and provisions was transferred at sea from URG ships. Virtually no logistic support was supplied during the carrier's port visits to Yokosuka or Sasebo, both former Imperial Japanese navy fleet bases. Nonflyable aircraft were transferred in port and offloaded onto barges, which then moved the duds to the nearest naval station for repair and reassignment to a fleet squadron. It is an interesting bit of folklore that the 7 December 1941 attack on Pearl Harbor was planned in a private dining room at the Officer's Club of the Sasebo Naval Base. In 1950 Sasebo had been turned over to the U.S. Navy, and the Japanese club became an allied officer's mess. That private dining room was a favorite for ship and squadron parties.

By 1950, carriers were completing the sometimes difficult transition of changing their flight deck procedures and air operation to accommodate jet aircraft. By 1951, there were two jet squadrons regularly assigned to each fleet carrier—the *Essex* and subsequent carriers. With its full air group complement of about seventy aircraft embarked, planes filled the carrier's hangar deck and a third of the flight deck. The teak flight deck was equipped with six to eight arresting wires stretched taut across the after half. At the center of the flight deck were the crash barriers, which, like the arresting wires, were rigged perpendicular to the carrier's fore and aft axis.

Their purpose was to stop a landing aircraft from crashing into the pack in the case when a tailhook failed to catch a wire. "Pack" was the term applied to the dense mass of closely parked aircraft on the flight deck that had just landed on this recovery cycle and been taxied up to the forward end of the flight deck for rearming and refueling. If an aircraft that had just landed had a mechanical problem that needed to be fixed before the next flight, the pilot signaled a thumbs-down to the yellow-shirted plane director on the flight deck as the plane taxied out of the arresting-gear area. This plane was immediately shunted aside to the deck-edge elevator and taken down to the hangar deck, where the squadron maintenance crews were standing by to make repairs and get the plane ready for the next launch.

If there were no gripes on the aircraft that had to be fixed before its next flight, the pilot signaled thumbs-up and was directed to taxi into the pack for fueling and rearming for the next mission. All the planes in the pack were surrounded by gasoline hoses, bomb carts, missile gurneys, and the electric power carts for starting aircraft. Purple-shirted fuel gangs pumped gasoline; red-jerseyed ordnancemen hung bombs and rockets, plugged in pigtails, and installed fuses; green shirts topped off the pilots' oxygen bottles and made minor repairs; and brown-shirted plane captains inspected their assigned plane from nose-tip to tail-cone to ensure that the aircraft was ready for the next flight, checking for loose access panels, low tires, leaking oleos, popped rivets, or unreported flak damage. All of this was going on as thirty-five knots of relative wind whistled over the deck, with crosscurrents of prop wash and jet blast. Just aft of the pack was the constant roar of engines as the arrested planes jammed on full power to blast clear of the landing area quickly so the next plane could land.

A landing interval of thirty seconds was the fleet standard. Toward the end of a deployment an experienced carrier and its air group would get the interval down to twenty-five seconds. Proper interval was the pilot's responsibility, one of the more difficult judgments in the carrier pilot's inventory of special skills. Too short an interval will not allow the aircraft ahead to clear the landing area and the approaching pilot must be waved off and take his place at the end of the circle of landing aircraft and go around again. A wave-off extends the recovery time and adds to the average interval. Dragging out the carrier's recovery time will reduce the time available for refueling and rearming. When those functions are rushed, mistakes become more likely.

A pilot will be waved off for a poor landing approach as well as for a fouled deck. About halfway through the final landing approach, the pilot is committed. Major corrections in altitude, speed, or lineup cannot be applied in the last ten seconds without excessive last-second maneuvering, which usually results in a bad landing. It is the function of the landing signal officer on the aft end of the flight deck to indicate to the approaching pilot any deviations from the optimum approach. The LSO does not literally control the plane; the pilot must fly his own pass. But the LSO's signals are intended to keep the plane from getting into dangerous altitudes close to landing. If it appears the pilot is exceeding the allowable envelope of speed and altitude, the LSO will wave him off, sending the plane around for another try. Wave-offs not only slow down the recovery but also add to the pilot's tension factor. Every wave-off wastes an inordinate amount of the limited fuel remaining. Especially in jets, this creates a potentially dangerous situation. High power at low altitude imposes a very high rate of fuel consumption on a jet, and seldom can a pilot return to the ship after a combat hop with enough fuel for more than two or three landing passes.

On the straight deck carrier, as opposed to the modern angled deck, there were frequent accidents on landing. These were usually due to pilot aberrations, too late for the LSO to detect and wave off. Being too fast at touchdown can cause the plane to bounce and the hook to skip the arresting wires. That's where the barriers come into play. As their name implies, the barriers prevent a plane, which failed to catch a wire for any reason—poor landing, broken hook, or a parted crossdeck cable—from plowing into the pack.

Easing power in the groove (the final straightaway) in an effort to reduce speed, can cause the plane to sink and strike the rounddown, the aft end of the flight deck. This normally resulted in the plane breaking in half aft of the cockpit and the two pieces of the fuselage tumbling down the deck in flames at better than one hundred miles per hour.

During World War II, there was a single type of deck barrier, a simple arrangement of wires that engaged the plane's prop to stop the aircraft in a matter of feet with little damage. A propeller change would usually have the aircraft back on the flight schedule in a day. The prop type barrier would stop a jet aircraft, but not without major structural damage. A new type barrier had to be designed and installed. The barrier operator in the flight-deck catwalk was responsible for raising the correct barrier for the type of aircraft about to land. This was always a potential hazard, but very few errors were made by the deck-edge flight deck crew in selecting the wrong barrier.

Then another jet-induced problem arose, a new kind of carrier landing accident with catastrophic consequences. When a prop pilot cut his power on the signal from the LSO, the aircraft literally stalled. It quit flying and glided to the deck to stay and simply rolled forward. Fully retarding the throttle on a jet, however, reduces the engine power slowly as the turbine has to unwind. The jet is still flying and the pilot must fly it onto the deck and hold it down as it rolls ahead. With their high landing-approach speeds, up to forty knots higher than the prop planes, a jet on a bad landing could bounce over the jet barriers and plunge into the pack at more than one hundred knots, tearing through the parked planes and servicing crews. The presence of high-octane gasoline being pumped under pressure and live ammunition exposed on deck and on the aircraft was guaranteed to set off explosions, and fires would spread quickly through the pack.

By 1950, after several years of jet carrier operations with fleet units, there had been enough of these incidents that a third barrier was added to the carrier's flight deck just forward of the first two. This was called the "barricade" but referred to by the crew as the "tennis net." It consisted of a taut wire rigged about eighteen feet high across the deck, with heavy nylon straps attached to a parallel wire cable at deck level. The crashing jet would poke its nose between the vertical nylon straps and be arrested as the straps engaged the jet's wings. It stopped the runaway jets with little damage to the aircraft. But in an accident when a Banshee jet engaged the barricade, the vertical straps pulled the top wire into the cockpit, killing the pilot. So all jets from then on landed on board the carrier with the cockpit canopy closed.

The Navy moved with alacrity to backfit all of the fleet carriers with the barricade. I was flying in Fighter Squadron 111 in the *Valley Forge* during its first Korean War deployment. The *Valley Force* had no barricade installed. So en route to Korea in November 1951, the carrier was diverted to the naval base at Yokosuka. A crew of more than one hundred Japanese shipyard workers (who had worked on the carriers of the Imperial Japanese navy in World War II) accomplished the installation of the barricade under the supervision of U.S. Navy engineers and technicians flown out from the Naval Air Station at Lakehurst, New Jersey, in two days. Under normal conditions in a U.S. shipyard we would have been tied up for at least a week.

Unfortunately, there were still occasions when planes actually bounced—or flew—over this barricade to crash on deck. In 1953, in preparation for deploying to Korea on board the USS *Boxer*, a replacement pilot in Fighter Squadron 52, of which I was then executive officer, went out of control on touchdown, bounced over the barricade, and crashed his F9F-2 Panther on the forward flight deck. The pilot was a lieutenant and had flown prop fighters from carriers in World War II. He had been recalled from the Reserves for active duty in Korea.

CATAPULTS

A second major change in carrier operations in the Korean War was also the result of the addition of jets to the air group. In World War II, almost the entire air group could become airborne during the launch cycle by taking off from the flight deck under their own power. The carrier would turn into the wind and make the speed necessary to create a relative wind of thirty to thirty-five knots over the deck. This was enough to allow the propeller aircraft to take off with a full load of fuel and ordnance under the power of their own engines.

With jet aircraft this was not possible. Jets accelerate more slowly and can not attain flying speed without the additional push provided by a catapult. Deck launching for the early carrier jets with a combat load was not feasible, even if the full length of the flight deck could be made available. So all of the jet squadrons in the carrier air wing had to rely on catapulting. The *Essex*-class carrier had two catapults mounted in the forward flight deck all the way forward. These monsters used a hydraulic-powered piston to move a shuttle along a track in the flight deck through a system of cables and pulleys. There were several different models in the carrier fleet, the more improved version being longer as well as more powerful. The catapult had to accelerate ten tons or more of aircraft from a standstill to one hundred knots in a distance of a hundred feet.

Catapulting demanded a careful line-up and hook-up of the aircraft to the shuttle, and this required forty-five seconds to more than a minute, depending on the experience of the pilots, the proficiency of the catapult crews, and the type of aircraft. With two catapults, this meant a carrier launch rate of one plane every half minute. A deck launch could put a prop plane in the air every ten seconds.

As the case in all mechanical devices, catapults could break down. With one catapult out of commission, the carrier's launch rate for jets was cut in half. If both cats went down, the jet squadrons were grounded. The care and maintenance of cats was a high priority on board the carrier. The catapult maintenance crews on board were kept fully up to their authorized manning level and well supplied with spare parts. A catapult was seldom out of commission for more than one launch and recovery cycle. If a catapult developed a serious problem, expert assistance was available. The Navy maintained a special troubleshooting and repair team of civil service technicians on both coasts and in Japan. These teams were ready to fly out in six to twelve hours to any carrier anywhere in the world. It was very seldom that an operating carrier would ever have all of its cats (in later years carriers had three and four catapults) out of commission at one time.

This emphasis on the reliability of the carrier's catapults was rough on the cat crews. Their only time for tear-down, inspection, and preventive maintenance of the machinery was in port, when no air operations were scheduled. Port visits for a deployed, operating carrier were never more than ten days, and the cat crews seldom got more than a day or two of liberty during a port visit.

Pilots were concerned about the catapults. A pilot put his life in the hands of the catapult operator and maintenance crews. If the catapult didn't work properly, the result was a fatal accident. In the early days of the Korean War, with the tremendous expansion of the jet-capable carrier force from ten ships to nineteen in three years, experience levels dropped dangerously low at times for some ships. The catapult operator at the deck-edge control panel was usually a nineteen-year-old third-class petty officer. Although bright and fully aware of his critical responsibility, he was exposed to the weather elements and jet blast, and with the noise and continually changing situation before him on the flight deck, he could become rattled and misread hand signals. Modern carriers have an enclosed catapult control station in the middle of the forward flight deck, and all catapult crew members have short-range radio receivers with earphones built into their flight deck helmets, referred to as the "mickey mouse" because of the big earphones.

The pilot's main concern was that the plane would be launched before he was ready. Instruments and power had to be checked and control settings adjusted. A premature shot was usually fatal. The plane was full of fuel and ammo and had no buoyancy; it immediately sank. These were categorically known as "cold shots," because usually the engine had not come up to power enough to sustain flight at the end of the cat shot. Some cold shots were due to mechanical malfunction rather than operator error. The plane was held back by a disposable holdback link and pulled forward by a steel cable bridle, also disposable. If either of these were mechanically faulty or not properly adjusted, the plane would not have flying speed at the end of the catapult run.

In May 1953, during the final months of Korea, I was piloting a Panther of VF-52 on a CAS mission. As I taxied up to the port cat of the *Boxer*, the Panther ahead of me was launched and immediately disappeared below the flight deck and plunged into the sea. There was a short pause by the port cat crew, and after a flurry of hand signals and shouting among them, the yellow-shirted plane director signaled me to taxi onto the cat for hook up to the shuttle. I shook my head. I was not about to ride that cat for another shot until I was assured that my predecessor's accident had not been a cold shot. I called the ship's flight control on the very-high-frequency (VHF) radio and told the ship's air officer (a senior commander) that I wasn't hooking up until he personally cleared the cat for use. In less than a minute he called back to say that the crash had been due to pilot error. The squadron commander had been with him in primary flight control and agreed that the pilot had overrotated the plane at the end of the cat shot and stalled out. The catapult crew had checked the instruments and gauges and reported all indications were normal. But I also knew the air officer was under pressure from the ship's captain to keep the launch on schedule. So reluctantly I eased onto the port catapult, and after double-checking all instruments, setting my controls, retightening my seat belt, and freeing the inflation tabs on my Mae West (the bright yellow life vest that was a trademark of the U.S. Navy), I saluted—the signal that the pilot is ready. Before I could change my mind, I was airborne and en route to Korea.

PATTERN OF OPERATIONS

The pattern of operations for the carriers in Korea was substantially different from that in World War II. In the last war, the fast carrier task forces, such as TF 38 and TF 58, commanded by Admirals Halsey and Spruance, consisted of several carrier task groups. Each group had three to five carriers (CVs and CVLs) to provide the striking force, and battleships, cruisers, and destroyers to furnish defense against Japanese ships, aircraft, and submarines. The aircraft carriers in these task forces were fleet carriers with decks big enough to handle large numbers of the latest production combat planes and could make a speed of thirty knots. This thirty-knot speed was a requirement for all of the combatants assigned to the fast carrier task force, including the battleships, cruisers, and destroyers. Task groups were organized so as to be capable of a high-speed run into an objective area. They used this speed, and the striking range of their aircraft, to achieve surprise and flexibility, which became major advantages for the U.S. Navy during the drive across the western Pacific in 1944 and 1945.

For the World War II carrier squadrons, the fast carrier operations translated into a schedule of two months of training, refit, and planning, a week for the fast run to the objective area, and then four or five days of intense combat, dogfighting with Zeros, attacking Japanese warships and shipping, and raiding enemy targets ashore—airfields, naval bases, and arms-production centers. The group then moved on to a second objective, perhaps one thousand miles away, for a similar series of fighter sweeps, attacks on fleet units, and strikes on military shore installations. After hitting two or more of these target areas, the task force withdrew to a forward staging area for refit and rest, while the other fleet, the Third or Fifth, went into action with its own fast carrier task force (TF 38 or TF 58) taking over the rapid, long-range strikes deep in Japanese territory. For the pilots this meant relatively long periods of preparation followed by brief and intense weeks of combat in different, widely separated areas against a fresh array of targets with each strike. These operations were characterized by the great carrier air battles of the Marianas Turkey Shoot, the strikes on Formosa, and the raids against the Japanese home islands.

In Korea it was a different kind of war for the carriers. During the first year, the front lines were fluid. The UN forces pushed to the Yalu, were repulsed by the Chinese, and then stiffened and counterattacked. In these campaigns the target objectives for the tactical aircraft were varied and covered a wide range of areas over the Korean peninsula. Then, in 1951, as the front became static along the eventual lines of the DMZ, the missions for the pilots remained essentially unchanged for the next two years until the cease-fire in July 1953.

Although the missions fell into a fixed pattern, this is not to be criticized. Our commanders were employing their available forces in the most effective fashion against the now routine tactics of the enemy and limitations imposed by Washington. Both of these factors, Chinese tactics and Washington rules of engagement, were, on the other hand, reasonable and prudent policies, given the unique circumstances of this limited war.

Lt. (j.g.) James Holloway Jr., executive officer of the USS *Truxtun*, holds James III on the deck of his ship as she departs Cavite, Philippines, for China in 1923. *Admiral Holloway collection*

Mid. James L. Holloway III in August 1941. Originally a member of the United States Naval Academy's class of 1943, he graduated in 1942 as a member of the academy's first three-year class, his education accelerated to meet the urgent needs of World War II. *Naval Historical Center-NH 103828*

Midshipman Holloway in 1942 as a member of the Naval Academy's varsity wrestling team. He has long maintained his interest in wrestling and, in 1998, was elected to the National Amateur Wrestling Hall of Fame. *Naval Historical Center-NH 103824*

The destroyer *Bennion* "crosses the line," September 1944, as shellbacks and pollywogs, following a time-honored initiation ceremony, assemble on the forecastle as the ship approaches the equator. Lieutenant Holloway, the ship's gunnery officer, was a pollywog and had to wear an overcoat and carry a shotgun and a simulated radar antenna all day. *Admiral Holloway collection*

The *Bennion*, a *Fletcher*-class destroyer, in 1944 pattern camouflage. Called "one of the most successful destroyer classes ever built for the Navy," the *Fletcher*-class ships proved their worth in Pacific combat and served around the world into the 1970s, seeing combat in Korea and Vietnam. *National Archives*

Lieutenant Commander Holloway during the Korean War. He served as executive officer and commanding officer of VF-52 on board the USS *Boxer* in 1952–53 while operating off Korea. *Naval Historical Center-NH 103825*

An F9F Panther of Fighter Squadron 52 prepares for takeoff from the USS *Valley Forge*, 1952. *National Archives 80-G-428122*

Lieutenant Commander Holloway climbs into the cockpit of a Grumman F9F-2 Panther jet fighter while serving as acting commanding officer of VF-52 in the USS *Boxer*. *Naval Historical Center-NH 103852*

Commander Holloway, commanding officer of Attack Squadron 83, in front of the squadron's A4D-2 attack jets on the flight deck of the USS *Essex* with pilots of his division (*left to right*): Ens. Jackie Adams; Commander Holloway; Lt. (j.g.) Charlie Hunter, winner of a Navy Cross for gallantry in Vietnam; and Ens. Henry Strong, awarded a Distinguished Flying Cross and killed in action as an A-4 squadron commander in Vietnam. *Admiral Holloway collection*

Some of the thousands who visited the *Enterprise* at Pearl Harbor after its first Vietnam deployment, June 1966. *Admiral Holloway collection*

The *Enterprise* passes under the Golden Gate Bridge on 20 June 1966, welcomed by fireboats and small craft. Its arrival at its new home port in Alameda was a festive occasion for the San Francisco Bay area. *Admiral Holloway collection*

5

Korea

Air Combat Tactics

In making their decision to go to war with the UN forces in Korea, the Chinese Communist leadership had understood and accepted the fact that total naval and air supremacy would reside with the United States. But the Chinese armies were prepared to fight under these circumstances and clearly believed that they would prevail. In their judgment, tempered by years of conflict with the non-Communist world, they had developed the most suitable military tactics in consideration of the UN's areas of clear superiority. The Chinese and their North Korean allies tried to constrain their movements to periods when darkness or low visibility limited U.S. air operations. By day they hid from air observation in villages or through camouflage, in which they became consummate experts. They knew that any troops or vehicles spotted by UN forces would be attacked immediately.

The U.S. military commanders in Korea were equally confident that complete air and maritime superiority in the theater could be established quickly as U.S. military forces were deployed. But the problem remained: How to utilize this air and sea power to defeat a semiguerrilla army operating in a relatively primitive industrial state. There were no sea lanes to interdict, no important industrial centers to demolish. The war against the Chinese in Korea would have to be fought with air and sea tactics different in many ways from those used in the past. Korea would be a conflict of opposing ground troops. The role of the Air Force and Navy would be as the supporting arms for the troops on the ground. There would be differences from the targeting and tactics used against Germany and Japan in World War II and the operations planned in case of a NATO war against the Soviet bloc.

This was not considered a major problem. Aircraft are easily adaptable to new tactics, and the carriers would be the principal naval forces employed against the enemy, their mission almost entirely in the role of supporting the ground forces. Surface warfare and antisubmarine operations would be essentially irrelevant except to maintain proficiency in those areas. The enemy presented no actual threat from submarines or major surface combatants. Even gunfire support, so important in the island-hopping campaigns in the Pacific in World War II, was limited in that so much of the critical land battle would be fought in the center of the Korean peninsula.

Of the four basic types of air-to-ground tactics for carrier strike aircraft—close air support, strikes against fixed installations, road reconnaissance, and main supply route (MSR) interdiction—only the first two (close air support and coordinated strikes) were routinely practiced by the carrier squadrons before Korea.

When the carriers commenced persistent combat operations in Korea, it became evident that close support of ground troops would always be a high priority in a land campaign but that strikes on large, identifiable targets such as bridges, factories, and airfields could only be useful in the early days of the campaign before the limited numbers of these targets were all destroyed. With the Chinese and North Korean troops relying on camouflage and evading detection, it was the reconnaissance-type missions that became important—scouting the roadways for traffic and then pouncing on any discovered troops or vehicles or, in the case of interdiction, attacking areas in which friendly intelligence suspected troop dispersal areas or supply depots.

The tactics for road reconnaissance were developed on the spot by the first Navy pilots to be assigned those missions after the *Valley Forge* arrived on station in July 1950. Those pilots passed on the tactics that had proved most effective, and the fleet air gunnery unit (FAGU) at the Naval Auxiliary Air Station at El Centro, California, became the coordinator of these evolving doctrines, teaching them to the carrier squadrons during their two-week live-weapons training deployment prior to going overseas.

WEATHER AS A FACTOR

Regardless of the ingenuity of our tactics and the skill with which we flew, an entire mission of a half a dozen sorties could be wiped out if the weather turned bad.

On 5 July 1953 I was launched at 0615 from the USS *Boxer* to lead a VF-52 four-plane Panther flight on an interdiction mission against a supply dump and billeting area near Ipo-ri, about twenty miles north of the front lines. The weather during July in Korea was generally not too favorable for these kinds of missions. There was usually a low layer of clouds over the peninsula that went down to below a thousand feet in the valleys where the targets were located, with cloud tops at two or three thousand feet, often with a couple of higher layers as well. The low stuff in the valleys would also sock in the Air Force bases, and for the first week in July, the Fifth Air Force in Korea had been unable to get any tactical sorties off the ground.

At Point Oboe, the reference center in the Sea of Japan for TF 77 carrier operations, the weather was flyable with the ceiling at three hundred feet. The layer was not thick and there were enough holes or thin spots in the overcast where a division of planes in tight formation could let down. Panthers were minimally equipped for instrument flying, having only a barometric altimeter, airspeed indicator, needle-ball instrumentation, and artificial horizon. The low-frequency direction finder was the pilot's best friend in the cockpit. When manually tuned to a prescribed frequency, it would reliably home on the emitting station. It provided direction only, no distance. Flying blind, the pilot knew when he had arrived at the homer's emitter only when the needle reversed itself as the plane flew over. The carriers all operated their homers on a frequency of 414 kHz, so it was doctrine that only one carrier or ship in the formation had a low-frequency homer activated.

After takeoff, I checked my instruments and found that the artificial horizon was not working. Fortunately, the indicator wings were stuck directly on the instrument's horizon, so I would not intuitively be correcting for a bank that wasn't there. With all other engine and flight instruments okay, I didn't feel I should abort. The Eighth Army was pleading for all the air support available. The Chinese were engaged in what would turn out to be their final major offensive. Climbing out, my plane entered the low overcast at three hundred feet, and flying on the needle-ball, airspeed, and altimeter, I popped out at eight hundred feet with clear blue skies above the solid white blanket of stratus. The visibility above the cloud layer was unlimited, and to the west the mountains of Korea rose up, standing out in clear contrast to the bright white layer of clouds covering their bases.

Looking aft through the cockpit mirrors, I could see the rest of the flight breaking out of the clouds behind me. At fifteen hundred feet I leveled off and throttled back to 250 knots for a running rendezvous. Checking plane-side numbers, I could see that the entire flight had gotten off without the need of a spare. We climbed to ten thousand feet and went "feet dry"—crossed the coast line—just north of Wonsan. I was able to recognize the mountains easily by now. After checking out on the radio with commander, TF 77 and reporting to the TACC at Seoul, we switched to the squadron tactical frequency and I took a heading for our target area. We were now only about two to three thousand feet above the mountain tops, and the valleys and low areas were packed solid with a thick layer of fog and clouds. Navigating by dead reckoning, we arrived in the general area of Ipo-ri in about ten minutes, and the only ground visible as far as the eye could see from ten thousand feet was the tops of mountains. Not a chance of getting through this solid overcast.

We turned south, throttling back to conserve fuel, and I again called TACC to ask for an alternative target. The center reported that all of Korea was reported to be socked in and told us to call "Heat Stroke," the call sign of the Tactical Air Direction Center (TADC) located near Kumhwa, on button (channel) 4. There were two TADCs on the ground in Korea, both located just south of the forward edge of the battle area (FEBA) or front lines, where they had reliable VHF communications with the troops in contact with the enemy and could further assign incoming close-support sorties to the tactical air control parties (TACPs) that were embedded with the ground forces at the battalion level. Then TACP would "hand off" the inbound flight leader to the forward air controller (FAC), in either a spotter aircraft or foxhole, who would have the intended enemy target in visual contact. Surprisingly, there was very little chatter on the VHF, probably because so few tactical aircraft were in the air. I reported in to the TADC with four jets, each with four 250-pound and two 100-pound bombs, and was immediately passed to a TACP, who requested a radar drop under MPQ, a radar-controlled bombing system. The MPQ was a Marine Corps development for using tactical aircraft in controlled radar bombing near the front lines when bad weather obscured visual targets. The procedure was much like ground-controlled approach, or GCA, for an instrument landing. The MPQ takes over control of the flight, which remains in formation, issuing headings, speeds, and altitudes.

We were vectored to an initial point near the front lines and turned to a southerly heading as we set our altimeters to the MPQ's prescribed barometric pressure. As we were brought north in a 180-degree turn, we tightened up the formation and stabilized our speed at three hundred knots, carefully maintaining an altitude of ten thousand feet. The controller was by now giving almost constant heading changes to keep the formation on a precise radar vector that would head the flight for the target. The run-in course had been adjusted for a the release point to compensate for the prevailing wind at release altitude. Once on the final course, every ten seconds we were given time to go to release. At ten seconds to go, we were told to set up our armament panel. These switches controlled which racks would release their bombs and would select nose or tail fusing. The nose fuses were set for instantaneous, which was most effective against troops, vehicles, and billeting areas. As an alternative, tail fusing was available for a one-second delay, which was more suitable for bunkers, buildings, and artillery emplacements. We were instructed to select instantaneous, and at zero countdown, the four planes released their six bombs simultaneously.

The controller reported that his radar indicated all bombs fell in the target area. This MPQ drop could have been extremely effective. The enemy troops would have had no warning of the attack. With the low ceiling and lack of visible aircraft, they would have been out of their bunkers and foxholes, doing their necessary housekeeping and chores, fully vulnerable and without any apprehension of impending attack. On the other hand, the bombs could have missed the billeting area completely and fallen on the barren slopes of a mountain. For an MPQ drop, there was no way of getting a bomb-damage assessment (BDA), which was a standard requirement in all of our visual missions.

With the MPQ drop accomplished, we checked out with the FAC and turned east. I wanted to get back to the carrier well before scheduled landing time, conserving as much fuel as possible in case the recovery process was protracted due to the bad weather. Both the ship's captain and the pilots wanted to get the planes on board before the weather really closed in and visibility was reduced to the point where planes had trouble seeing the carrier, and orienting the downwind leg and adjusting the landing approach. Under these conditions the whole operation got very tense and the chance for mishap sharply increased.

I had not yet gotten to the coastline to report "feet wet" and check in with commander, TF 77, when "Jehovah" (the voice call of commander, Seventh Fleet) blared out over guard channel, "All CTF 77 aircraft in the air are instructed to land at any available field in South Korea. All launches and recoveries for TF 77 are cancelled. Ceiling and visibility at the task force is zero-zero in fog. Task Force 77 is departing Point Oboe and heading east."

I immediately put the flight into a port orbit, throttled back to maximum endurance power, loosened up the formation to reduce the need for throttle jockeying to maintain position, and started calling, first to the *Boxer* to confirm Jehovah's instructions. The flight operations officer confirmed the orders emphatically. The carrier did not want any planes to return to the task force in the hope of a break in the weather to get on board. The conditions at the ship were thick fog, and the aerologist expected it would stay that way for the next twenty-four hours, the limit of his ability to forecast.

I next called the TACC at Seoul to get a steer to the nearest available field in Korea for landing. The center responded that all the fields in South Korea were closed. Just to make sure, I requested weather conditions at all of the fields that could handle jets: K-18 at Kangnung, K-2 at Taegu, K-3 at Pohang, and K-16 at Kimpo. All were reported closed due to fog.

When I asked if the TACC had any recommendations, the controller replied they had nothing to offer. All of the Air Force and Marine Corps planes were parked at their home fields. Weather had prevented any air operations from South Korean bases for the past week. When I added that our situation looked pretty grim, he agreed, sounding sympathetic but without any further comment.

The pilots in the flight had heard the complete exchange on VHF. And apparently, so had other Navy pilots over Korea who also were tuned in on the TACC channel. This became obvious when I saw the formation had grown to six, with the addition of two more Navy Panthers, which, according to their tail markings, were from the USS *Princeton*. With hand signals they indicated their wish to join our flight, and with a responding thumbs up, they were welcomed on board. No radio transmissions. No need to clutter up the air with the obvious.

Now six of us had the same problem, no place to land. To let down through the overcast and hope to break out underneath was unthinkable. All of the airfields were reporting clouds down to the deck. With the mountainous nature of Korea, our chances of putting the plane down in a flat spot were about one in ten. The reverse odds were that we would run into a mountainside. At 150 knots that would be a crash, not a crash landing.

I instructed the flight that we would continue to look for a hole to let down through, but after the first plane hit a fuel state of five hundred pounds, the pilots, on my orders, would eject in rapid succession from a six-plane echelon, last man in the formation first. I wanted to keep the parachuting pilots as close as possible so we could quickly get together after hitting the ground. On the other hand, I didn't want to chance an ejecting pilot being struck by a following jet.

In one of our squadron bull sessions some time ago, the pilots had discussed the possibility of ejecting over Korea. So our pilots registered no surprise and there were no questions when they were asked to acknowledge the instructions. The two *Princeton* Panther pilots must have thought this was a VF-52 SOP (standard operating procedure).

Now the main concern was to parachute into safe territory. In the periodic general-situation briefings by the intelligence officers, several sizable areas were highlighted on the map of South Korea as being under the nominal control of guerrillas. These were North Korean troops who had been trapped by the Inchon landing, had escaped capture, and gone to the hills. The area was not precisely defined but was in the rugged mountainous terrain toward the center of the peninsula north of

Andong. The ROK had opened some of the important roads in the area but had not undertaken to hunt down the well-armed guerrillas. Also, I wanted the flight to be under the control of Tactical Air Control (TAC) when we bailed out so that the Joint Operations Center would know where we had gone down and get a ground force to our position as soon as possible to recover the group.

While these details were being arranged over the voice radio, we were in a wide left-hand orbit. I switched the flight to the TACC frequency and asked the controller to take us under positive control for a controlled ejection into a safe area. The controller had given us the initial vector when I sighted a dark spot in the undercast, just a thin rift in the clouds. I could tell from the mountaintops it was near the coastline. It might be a hole we could sneak through. Breaking off from the TAC vector, I headed for the spot in a sixty-degree diving turn. Unbelievably, there were water, coastline, and about two thousand feet of pierced-steel runway. I immediately recognized K-18, the ROK strip at Kangnung. There were too few fields in Korea for me to be mistaken. I switched to guard channel and told the K-18 tower that six F-9Fs were on a steep approach for an immediate landing. The tower came back with a negative—repeated twice for emphasis—the field was closed due to zero visibility. I replied that I could see two thousand feet of runway, the east end, and that we were going to touch down there and make our landing run-out in the soup.

The control tower's transmission was understandable. They were in the fog. The tower was in the middle of a seven-thousand-foot runway, and only two thousand feet at the approach end was in the clear. I repeated that we had the field in sight from five thousand feet altitude and were low on fuel with no alternative but to crash into the sea or eject. The tower's comeback was that if we were going to land, that was our responsibility, but that the runway was clear. Finally a positive note. Somebody on the ground was being helpful.

I motioned the rest of the flight to ease back to take a good interval for landing. They all had been listening to the VHF traffic and like the real pros they were, didn't have to be told twice what to do when time was so important. How long the hole in the undercast would remain open was unpredictable. It was probably the result of the local coastal configuration. The mountains, a river valley, a delta, and the ocean all came together at that point and must have caused unusual air currents and temperatures.

Each pilot made a steep approach to final, touching down close to the end of the runway at minimum flying speed in order to have the plane on the deck and well under control when we entered the fog bank. The transition from clear skies to a half-mile visibility was sudden. The runway lights were on and truck and jeep headlights outlined the single taxiway at the west end of the runway. All six F9Fs landed safely and parked on the apron generally reserved for TF 77 aircraft. A detachment of a dozen sailors from a Japan-based FASRon worked out of a Quonset hut to provide line maintenance services in this area.

K-18 was crowded but orderly. Our six Panthers were the only planes from the carriers. The leader of the two *Princeton* fighters said that after he and his wingman were catapulted, the rest of the launch was cancelled. Jehovah had decided the forecast weather was too bad for carrier operations and the JOC had reported all target areas in Korea were obscured. By the time the decision to cancel TF 77 air operations had gotten to the carriers, the six of us were already on our way. K-18 had been open briefly earlier in the week because there were a number of Army, Air Force, and Marine administrative and light aircraft on the tarmac that normally would not have been there. Kangnung was a ROK air force field.

Our six pilots spent two nights in a Quonset hut bunk room, and the FASRon provided us with blankets. The U.S. Army advisory group detachment at the airfield had set up a consolidated mess and "club" in a quonset hut. Although we lacked a toothbrush and a change of clothes, we were not only comfortable but also able to socialize with our FASRon hosts in their modest club. This is how things worked on the front lines. The thunder of artillery to the north and west was constant and not too far away. The local ROK were concerned they might be overrun by the Chinese at any time and were nervous. We Americans just depended upon being evacuated before that happened.

Two days later the weather improved, and commander, TF 77 sent us a recall through the FASRon communications. As we taxied out for takeoff, all of the other transients were leaving at the same time. With the single taxiway, the line of departing aircraft was moving very slowly. Because of the jets' high fuel consumption on the deck, I called for takeoff priority and got it. The other prop planes didn't like it, but it was SOP for the jets to go to the head of the line. This especially irritated the Corsair and AD pilots, who thought jet pilots were spoiled kids. We accepted our perks gladly and attributed the prop pilots' attitude to envy.

As I made the turn from the taxiway to the runway, my left wheel hit a hole in the Marston matting. Marston matting was essentially six-by-twelve-foot interlocking rectangles of steel pierced with one-inch holes and placed over packed earth to form runways, taxiways, and aprons. When a steel plate broke or became loose, the taxiway in that spot became a mud hole. My left wheel was stuck. Nothing else to do but add enough engine power so the jet blast would kick me free. As I was adding power, and lots of it, to get moving, a figure in Air Force flight coveralls ran in front of my plane waving his arms. As I continued to blast, he was joined by a second, more portly figure also very agitated. By then I had gotten out of the mud hole, the Panther was moving ahead smartly, and I was turning onto the runway for takeoff. I looked back briefly to see what was the cause of the excitement. It was immediately apparent. Just behind the mud hole and the spot where I had turned onto the runway was an olive drab C-47 transport, identical to the hundreds of other C-47s in Korea except in one respect. This had two blue stars in a large white flag displayed on the fuselage aft of the cargo door. Its tail had been toward my jet blast, and now the C-47's rudder was dangling from the plane's vertical fin. Obviously, the jet blast hitting the rudder surface from the wrong direction—astern—had broken the hinges. The C-47 was not flyable, nor easily fixable. I jammed the throttle full open, roared down the runway, headed for the *Boxer*, and didn't look back until Kangnung and K-18 were lost in the haze.

AIR GROUP STRIKES

Air group strikes were scheduled for major fixed objectives such as bridges, dams, or large industrial areas. These missions were composed of planes from each of the group's squadrons with the propeller planes carrying the heavy bombs and the jets providing air cover from hostile fighters and conducting flak suppression at the target with 20mm gunfire and rockets. The thirty to fifty aircraft in the group would make a simultaneous attack on the target, coming in from different directions, the

Skyraiders in near vertical dives, the Corsairs in sixty-degree glides, and the jet fighters strafing and rocketing the defenses at low level before, during, and after the bombing passes. The Skyraiders and Corsairs might be assigned different aim points within the target complex, but all ordnance was dropped on a single pass.

These missions were also known to the planners as deckload strikes, as every plane that could fit on the flight deck for a single launch was included. To the pilots they were familiarly referred to as group gropes. This term also came to be applied at the squadron pilots' muster at the Officers' Club (O Club) happy hour. A well-executed strike was a source of personal professional satisfaction to the pilots. A less-than-perfect operation, usually due to faulty timing or bad weather over the target, might get the job done but provided lots of fuel for ready room arguments for the next week. These pilot sessions were a natural way to improve the coordination among the squadrons and the effectiveness of the combined group operations without too much senior finger pointing. In the heat of battle it is often difficult to accurately determine just what happened.

By 1951 there were very few group gropes, primarily because all of the major target complexes in Korea had been obliterated or were on the prohibited list.

INTERDICTION

Deep interdiction missions were made against military targets twenty to forty miles behind the front lines. These usually were areas of troop concentrations, staging areas for Chinese army units headed for the front or suspected fuel and supply dumps. Our targets were generated by the photo interpreters in the Intelligence Center on board the carriers from photography taken by the air group's photo planes. The photo planes were F9F Panther fighters with the four nose 20mm guns removed and equipped with a stabilized camera system. The photo missions were flown by specially trained and designated photo pilots.

Deep interdiction missions were assigned to a particular squadron on the group's daily flight plan, and four to eight planes were committed to the strike. The armament load was prescribed by the task group staff, Air Operations Section.

Sometimes these deep interdiction targets were large visible targets, easily identifiable by the strike leader. One such objective was the North Korean airstrip at Hyesanjin on the Yalu. Once every two weeks, a flight of eight Panthers would be scheduled to crater the runway with 250-pound GP bombs to keep it unusable by enemy aircraft. It was always an interesting flight, penetrating to the limits of enemy territory and striking a real target under the noses of the Chinese MiGs. A hard left turn on pullout from the bombing run was necessary to avoid overflying Manchuria. My main recollection from these flights was the forbidding barrenness of that vast expanse of land north of the Yalu.

Often, though, these deep interdiction missions were directed against strategic areas, where we seldom saw the actual targets that were the objectives of our mission. The enemy troops or equipment were obscured from observation by terrain, forests, or camouflage.

In the fall of 1952 a special deep interdiction campaign nicknamed "Cherokee" was initiated in a major effort to attack Chinese Communist troops as their armies were shifted behind the front lines to exploit weaknesses in the UN front. Cherokee was named for the commander, Seventh Fleet, Vice Adm. Jocko Clark, an energetic and aggressive flag officer in the Halsey mold who became a very personally engaged leader in the air campaign. Clark, a native of Oklahoma, proudly claimed to be a full-blooded Cherokee.

The targets in these Cherokee strikes were difficult to pick up by armed reconnaissance flights because of the excellent camouflage that effectively hid men and equipment. So the photo interpreters back at the intelligence centers at the fleet headquarters were doing most of the Cherokee targeting.

CLOSE AIR SUPPORT

One of the most profitable uses of tactical air, especially during the last two years of the war, was close air support. On these missions, the carrier planes were under the positive radio control of a FAC and ordnance could be delivered against enemy targets within one hundred yards of our own men. Close support involved strict operating procedures to make the most efficient use of the planes and weapons on hand as well as to minimize the danger to our own troops on the ground.

In the early days of the war, close air support of the troops on the ground by Navy and Air Force tactical aircraft was totally unsatisfactory. Although the aircraft were generally available, our troops were desperate, and the enemy were in the open and vulnerable, there was unfortunately no reliable control system in place, and our troops on the ground could not communicate with the pilots in the planes. The frustrations with this very bad situation extended from General MacArthur in Tokyo to the private in the foxhole.

The root cause was that the interservice arrangements and doctrines for CAS had never been agreed upon, much less rehearsed, since the Reorganization Act of 1946, which established the services' roles and missions and governed the joint and combined operations in Korea. Compounding the lack of procedures for command and control of tactical air assets were technical communication problems so basic that the radios of the Air Force, Navy, and Army were not compatible. The situation was in such disarray that it became a primary concern of the senior officers to the extent that they were persuaded to be more flexible in their perceived command prerogatives. They were virtually shamed into making the concessions necessary to create a workable system for tactical air support for the ground forces under the conditions existing in Korea. By 1951 an effective system was in place and working well.

In essence, the organization consisted of a JOC in Taegu and, later, Seoul in which the Air Force, Navy, and Army were all represented by flag officers, whose joint staff allocated the resources of the supporting arms, such as strategic aircraft, tactical air, and naval gunfire, in response to requests from ground force commanders—the Army, Marines, ROK, and other UN allies. Colocated with the JOC in Seoul was the TACC, which processed all requests for tactical air support as sorted out and passed down by the JOC. The TACC would also receive requests for air support from the two TADCs, which were responsible for managing the air support requirements and assignments for the ground forces engaged with the enemy. One TADC handled all units in the eastern half of Korea, and the other was responsible for the western sector. Each TADC was networked with a total of sixteen TACPs embedded with the troops at the regimented or battalion level. It was these TACPs, located with the ground forces in contact with the enemy, that ultimately assigned a close air support mission—a flight of Air Force, Marine, or carrier aircraft—to a forward air controller. It was this FAC, in either a mosquito (a light liaison aircraft) or a foxhole, who was in visual contact with the enemy and radio control of the CAS mission aircraft.

The procedures sound complicated, but they were as simple as possible considering the circumstances of aircraft from Air Force bases, Marine fields, and aircraft carriers at sea providing support to ground units from the U.S. Army, ROK army, U.S. Marines, and various UN allies. And it worked, in spite of the limitations of the radios in the UN tactical aircraft. These provided only four channels of VHF voice plus a guard, or emergency, channel. As a result, communications discipline was an absolute necessity. It was usually pretty good until a plane got hit, and then there could be brief moments of panic.

All of the carrier's squadrons flew CAS missions. The AD Skyraiders were the controllers' favorites because of their ability to endure one and a half hours on station and the seven-ton mix of bombs and rockets they carried. The Corsairs also had good endurance and sizable bomb loads, not equal to the ADs, but superior in both respects to the jets. The Panthers were usually limited to about fifteen minutes on station and carried a nominal load of four 260-pound fragmentation bombs or four to six 5-inch rockets. All three types of planes also had machine guns. The Skyraiders and Panthers had 20mm cannons, a devastating anti-troop weapon as each round was an explosive shell comparable to a hand grenade but with a rate of fire of two hundred rounds per minute.

During the relatively static warfare of 1952 and 1953, the ground commanders sent their daily requests for close air support to the TACC, the joint Air Force–Navy facility in Taegu and later in Seoul. These CAS requirements would usually be enough to fill all of the airspace over the front lines. Every ground commander in contact with the enemy wanted his dedicated air support available in the event of a firefight. Even if the sector was quiet, there were plenty of bunkers and trenches to pound.

The practical limit to the amount of effective close air support that could be accommodated was the finite number of communication channels available on the planes' VHF radios. There were only four, and each mission had to have its own discrete channel to avoid interference.

At the TACC, the combined ground commanders' requirements were allocated to the Air Force and the Navy, with the Seventh Fleet getting about 60 percent of the CAS missions. The Air Force was already heavily committed to the F-86E anti-MiG-15 barrier mission in northwestern Korea. Commander, Seventh Fleet then assigned the CAS missions to the available carriers to fill out the Navy's allocation. This was an efficient arrangement. The Army sent their requirements to Seoul in the early evening for the next day, and the carriers had their assignments by 2000, in time for the squadrons to publish the next day's flight schedules by 2100, before the pilots turned in for the evening. It was the intelligence officers who worked late into the night, researching the targets so they could fully brief the pilots scheduled for the 0700 takeoff.

Even after a flight was launched, there was a lot of flexibility in the mission's objective. The weather over the scheduled target could be unsatisfactory. A four-thousand-foot ceiling and three miles visibility were minimums under routine circumstances. The bomb and rocket attacks were made from dive or glide (shallow-dive) runs, and a minimum release altitude of a thousand feet was mandatory to avoid damage from bomb blast. Also, if there was a situation on any part of the front where friendly troops were in trouble—such as a difficult retraction of a recce platoon probing into the enemy's front lines—flights scheduled for CAS in a quieter sector would be reassigned to provide the weight of air effort where it was most needed.

The jet squadrons flew a large share of the CAS missions. Although their endurance was limited, the Panthers had four 20mm cannons in the nose, a lethal concentration of fire when used against troops. Then, too, the jets' speed and agility (the ability to climb rapidly in a zoom after weapons release, minimizing exposure to hostile fire) allowed the Panthers to approach CAS targets such as troops, trenches, and bunkers, at flatter angles, and using the 20mm cannon, they pressed the attacks to very close ranges—one or two hundred yards. There was minimum danger of blast damage from the cannon fire. This ability to select the best direction for the attack—along a line of trenches, for example—and bore into minimum range gave the jet squadrons a high priority with the FAC requests.

But even with their speed and agility the Panthers were not immune to flak. In fact, it was on these close support missions that enemy fire was most visible. Because of the low-altitude approach and close-in recovery, the jets were vulnerable to automatic-weapons fire from Chinese heavy and light machine guns, which could not reach the Skyraiders and

Corsairs at an altitude of two thousand feet or more. In June 1953 two pilots from VF-52 were downed by enemy fire on close air support missions. In both cases the pilots survived by crash landing in a flat paddy area behind the front lines. The forward air controllers took this "safe zone" into consideration when controlling strikes, trying whenever possible to orient the direction of attack from north to south so a plane, if hit, could recover over friendly territory.

Close air support missions almost always yielded positive results. There was little chance for failure. The FAC knew where the enemy troops were, and usually, during the 20mm strafing runs, the troops could be clearly seen, firing their heavy weapons from sandbagged positions and running down the trench lines to bunkers. As the jets pulled off the target after the final pass and began a running rendezvous toward the coast, checking out successively with the FAC, the TACC and the TAC, the Skyraiders and Corsairs would be called back to deliver the balance of their load of 1,000-pound and 500-pound bombs precisely where the FAC wanted.

Close air support in Korea worked well, and the U.S. tactical air forces was the greatest single advantage the UN had over the Communists. During the bitterly fought withdrawal of the 1st Marine Division from the Chosin Reservoir, flights of Navy and Marine carrier aircraft loaded with rockets, bombs, and napalm circled over the Marine column throughout the daylight hours without a break, ready on short notice to provide close air support where needed. This closely coordinated use of tactical air as a supporting arm of the infantry was instrumental in the success of the Marines' breakout.

INTERDICTING SUPPLY LINES AND CUTTING RAILS

The purpose of air interdiction was to interrupt the flow of war material moving from the supply bases north of the Yalu, safe from UN attack by the sanctuary status of China, through North Korea on the primitive road network and limited railway system. The Chinese and North Korean troops, although less demanding than their U.S. and allied counterparts, still required substantial quantities of logistic support: fuel for tanks and vehicles, ammunition for the infantry, shells for the mortars and artillery, and medical support, food, and replacements for the troops. The Communists may have been classified as light divisions, but they were nevertheless modern armies, using up combat consumables, especially ammunition, at a great rate. It was doctrine that every Chinese attack would be preceded by heavy preparatory bombardments from their supporting arms—mortars and artillery—and the direct fire from individual arms and automatic weapons was always intense. Many Chinese soldiers carried submachine guns, "tommy guns," with a high rate of automatic fire. All of this logistic support had to come overland from China. The U.S. Navy controlled the seas to the extent that even the remote coastline could not be used for resupply, much less major ports such as Wonsan, Hungnam, and Chongjin, which were regularly shelled and bombed by the U.S. Navy.

The supply routes from the Chinese depots to the front lines consisted of a railroad system and a road network, much of it primitive and unimproved. The railroads were a primary objective of the UN air campaign in Korea. During the winter of 1951–52, the majority of strike sorties from TF 77 were directed against the railroad system. Priority targets were the locomotives, then the rolling stock, followed by bridges and then the tracks themselves.

After some initial successes by TF 77 aircraft against operating locomotives, referred to as "loco busting," the North Koreans, whenever possible, kept their trains in long, deep mountain tunnels by day and moved them only at night. Occasionally during a night mission, an F4U-4N or AD-1N would immobilize a locomotive in an open area by rockets or strafing, and the next day a large-scale commitment of sorties from the Task Force 77 carriers would be scheduled in an all-out effort to destroy the engine in daylight precision attacks by Skyraiders and Corsairs with heavy bombs. The Communists quickly countered by moving in batteries of 37mm automatic weapons and heavy machine guns on flatbed cars along the tracks adjacent to the stalled locomotive. This didn't deter the carrier strikes, but the missions became more complicated, with jets added for flak suppression, attacking the antiaircraft cars with 20mm automatic cannons, rockets, and 260-pound frag bombs. This increased level of effort diverted sorties from other tactical missions and resulted in a sharp increase in friendly losses. Nevertheless, a stalled locomotive was a big event, relished by the pilots as an exciting target to be destroyed with skillfully coordinated tactics. It was much more satisfying than cutting rails.

In the dedicated campaign to interdict the railroad system, lucrative targets soon became scarce. Tunnels proved effective in protecting the trains. Squadrons developed various tactics to toss bombs inside the tunnels, such as skip bombing. A 1,000-pound bomb with delayed fusing was released at minimum altitude over the track leading into the tunnel. The 1,000-pounder would hit the tracks with a flat trajectory, skip into the tunnel entrance, and explode deep inside. There were many problems with this tactic, however. There had to be a straight run of track leading into the tunnel, and there had to be maneuvering room for the attacking plane, usually an AD, to make the low-level approach and pull up after release to get over the mountain through which the tunnel penetrated. In pursuing these tactics, planes were lost, crashing into the terrain during the approach and postdelivery recovery. On occasions when this tactic was successful, the results were said to be spectacular. The detonating bomb was, in effect, an exploding cartridge blowing everything in the tube of the tunnel out the far end like the muzzle of a gun. The North Koreans emplaced heavy automatic weapons along the tracks at the tunnel approaches, however, so the flat, low-level skip-bombing approach finally became lethal for the attacking aircraft.

Railroad bridges were prime targets in the interdiction effort. Early in the campaign most of the substantial concrete and steel spans were knocked out by major carrier deckload strikes. The North Koreans rebuilt those bridges that were on the MSR and surrounded the sites with flak positions in depth and in a variety of calibers.

ARMED RECONNAISSANCE

The most important interdiction missions flown by Task Force 77 jets were armed reconnaissance missions covering the road networks in Northern Korea. Because of the speed and agility of the jets, virtually all of the route recces were conducted by Panthers. Most of these lines of communications (LOCs) and MSRs were one-lane dirt-and-gravel roads that wound through the valleys and mountain passes of the rugged mountainous territory that made up most of North Korea. The curves and slopes in these roads limited the ahead visibility of low-flying aircraft to no more than a couple of miles. The mountainous terrain made armed reconnaissance missions especially tricky and often difficult, because the aircraft usually could not see potential targets until the last minute. On the other hand, those on the ground could not see approaching aircraft until they were virtually overhead. If the aircraft overran the target, the pilot could circle and attack on the second pass. On the mountain roads, the trucks usually had nowhere to go but over a precipice.

In the flat coastal plain areas of Korea such as Hungnam and Wonsan, vehicle movement along the MSR was visible for miles and consequently vulnerable to artillery and naval gunfire. So the Communists avoided moving any traffic along these exposed routes except at night or during low visibility. But those routes that wound through the mountains could only be reconnoitered by aircraft and then only attacked effectively by air. The defilade of the terrain prevented artillery or naval gunfire interdiction.

During the final two years of the war, with the Communists and UN forces engaged across the relatively static east-west front, route recces, along with railroad interdiction, became especially relied upon to slow the flow of logistics and combat consumables to the enemy's combatant troops. Normally each carrier jet squadron would be scheduled for two road recce missions each flying day. A mission consisted of four jets armed with six HVAR rockets or four 260-pound frag bombs and full 20mm ammunition. All of the main roads comprising the LOCs and MSRs in North Korea were organized into numbered recce routes by the JOC. Each designated route consisted of an MSR segment of fifty to seventy-five miles. This was the maximum distance that could be covered by a division of jets, as flying at low altitudes and high speed with external munitions resulted in high rates of fuel consumption.

The tactical formation for road recces was unique for that mission had evolved with experience. Different squadrons employed variations of the basic techniques. After launch, the four planes would join up in a standard two section close tactical formation and cross the beach at ten thousand feet, checking in with the TAC. At the initial point of the route, the jets would make a rapid letdown from ten thousand feet with the pilots moving into the recce formation. The lead plane would descend to three hundred feet above the road. Initially the airspeed would be about 300 knots, but with the weaving and turning to stay over the road, airspeed was soon reduced to about 250 knots. The number two pilot maintained an altitude of about one thousand feet above and on the quarter of the low jet. Pilots three and four maintained a loose-section formation three thousand feet higher, where they could provide air cover against MiGs and keep a lookout ahead to assist in navigation and warn of flak.

The number one pilot served as the spotter. At his low altitude he could discern whether an object in the road was an ox cart, truck, or military vehicle and whether it was active or abandoned. As he flew over the object, the spotter would call out his evaluation, such as, "Over a truck now, attack with rockets" or "Over an abandoned ox cart, no target." The number two pilot at one thousand feet would be watching the low plane's position closely and at the spotter's call would know exactly where to look for the target. Then from his perch position he could select and arm his weapons and make a precision attack. If bombs were used, a minimum pullout altitude of five hundred feet was required to avoid bomb blast. With rockets, a flat run could be made, firing as close in as fifty yards followed by a sharp pull-up. The 5-inch HVAR was powerful enough to cause blast fragment damage to the firing aircraft unless a sharp break-away was made. This use of a spotter plane on the deck and the attacker at one thousand feet allowed a precision attack with any weapon without having to circle around to gain position for the attack.

The second section leader at three thousand feet was responsible for navigation, such as advising the low man, "Be ready to turn in about a mile" or telling him, "Around the next bend are two reported AAA positions." The low man would be jinking at 250 to 300 knots below three hundred feet, to both avoid enemy fire and be able to observe the road directly below the Panther's nose. He had his hands full. After pilot number two had made his attack and expended his ordnance, the flight positions would rotate, number one and two trading positions. After a second attack the formation would rotate again, but this time by sections, with the second section taking the two low positions and the first section with ammunition expended—except for a reserve of 20mm for use in case of a MiG engagement—climbing to three thousand feet for lookout and navigation.

That is how it should work, but circumstances seldom were ideal. Weather could make it difficult to keep the low section in sight, often resulting in all four planes down on the deck looking out for targets and maneuvering to avoid a collision with a wingman. When flak was encountered, as it usually was, the situation became more complicated and the tactics more exciting. The Communists would often move overnight in tactical vehicles mounting 37-mm automatic weapons or multiple heavy-caliber machine guns. These would be camouflaged and placed in a draw or around a bend. Then a vehicle would be placed in the road. If the spotter did not recognize, at a mile or so, that the target was a decoy—no people, not moving, or obviously a derelict—the whole flight would be drawn through the shooting gallery. With a little experience most pilots got to recognize a flak trap. They could "smell it."

All of this activity would take place at less than one thousand feet above the ground at a speed of 250 to 300 knots—in a narrow valley with the mountains rising to six thousand feet on both sides. In spite of the difficulties, most jet pilots preferred armed reconnaissance over other missions. Route recces offered the best chances for visible targets, moving vehicles, and real people. Route recce also demanded, with the exception of air-to-air combat, the highest level of pilot skill and gave pilots the opportunity to demonstrate their flying ability, marksmanship, and daring. Spotter pilots would often turn off their planes pressurization system (which produces a noisy rush of air in the cockpit) so that the sound of gunfire from the ground could be heard clearly. This could sometimes be the best indication of enemy activity along the route, troops taking cover along the side of the road and firing their rifles. The heavier flak showed up as tracers, which were clearly visible in the shadow of the valleys. It was difficult, though, to follow the tracers to their source and actually spot the gun positions. This had to be done by looking for muzzle flashes.

Typical of the rugged character of the road recce routes on the east coast of Korea—TF 77's area of responsibility—was Recce Route Red Five. The entry point for a division of jets—four fighters deployed in the recce formation—was at the island of Kojo on the coast just south of Wonsan. The route initially ran south for four miles through the village of Tongychon,. passing a 37mm AAA site about a mile east of the road. From there, the route turned southwest for four miles through a deep valley to Sinjon-ni, with the thirty-three-hundred-foot mountain, Udong-san, a mile to the west. Then there was a hard jog to the west for a mile through Chingon-ni and past a 37mm installation on the slopes of four-thousand-foot Koyun-san, a mile to the east. Three miles and another sharp turn to the southwest. The valley widened slightly and there was a prominent lake—a useful landmark—to the west. The trail made a turn to the south again for a five-mile straightaway down a deep narrow valley between two four-thousand-foot mountains, Koyum-san and Paegaw-san, to the town of Hwachon-ni, with two camouflaged 37mms. Then there was a four-mile stretch of road along a streambed with precipitous banks. Another 37mm position marked the sharp turn to the south following the valley between Koyum-san and Hill 2699. From there the trail ran south-southeast for ten miles in a valley between hills of twenty-six hundred to three thousand feet. The recce route jogged around to avoid Sinamoung-ri, a medium-sized village with three or four 37mms. The MSR was picked up again at the entry of a steep canyon running south between 2,923- and 2,549-foot hills and went on for ten miles before hooking hard right over a bridge crossing a river feeding into the Kunsang-ni River. The next five miles were through an open valley to Changdo-ri, just east of the mountain Platok-san, a steep 3,600-foot rise. The gloomy valley had at least one 37mm and opened up to pass through the large village of Changdo-ri, which contained a 57mm, several 37mms, and a number of machine guns arrayed near the road to protect a small factory building. After running the gauntlet here, the road ran for thirteen miles through less-mountainous country without permanent AAA installations before ending at Changyong-ni in the no-man's-land of the Iron Triangle. This was the end of the route, and here the planes could pull up over friendly territory. If the aircraft had any ammo left, the leader would check into "Heat Stroke," the Chorwon sector TADC, which usually could provide an enemy position nearby, upon which the flight could dump any onboard ordnance.

Considering that the low man was flying at four to five miles per minute at an altitude between one hundred and three hundred feet, these missions could be very physical for the pilot, who was constantly pulling Gs while turning in a forty- to sixty-degree bank, jinking, and changing course. There was, on average, a turn in the road once every minute. It was important that navigation be accurate. Missing a turn might mean flying directly over a 37mm at two hundred feet.

Yet it was not uncommon to get lost on a route recce mission. Maps were not entirely accurate, weather could hide navigational checkpoints, or flak evasion could disorient the flight. The spotter had his hands full, looking for targets, watching for flak, avoiding the terrain, communicating with his high element, and checking his navigation chart. The danger was to fly down the wrong road, entering unknown territory for which the flight had not been briefed by the air intelligence officer and possibly encountering unexpected AAA positions. The MSRs that carried the heaviest traffic and fed into ammunition dumps and troop staging areas were heavily defended by multiple AAA positions and would normally only be attacked by a large, coordinated strike with preplanned and dedicated flak suppression aircraft. More often, complications arose from the rapidity with which the tactical situation could develop. All could be routine until, rounding a bend, the flight would come suddenly upon a convoy of trucks, so close that there was barely time to arm the weapons and get the pipper on a target.

In April 1953 I was leading a four-plane recce mission on Recce Route Red Twelve, which ran north from Hamhung through the mountains to the Chosin Reservoir. It had been a 0615 launch, and ours was the first flight off the deck. With a light north wind, our carrier was well north of Point Option, and with a running rendezvous and going "feet dry" at Hungnam, we arrived at the initial point of the route in such a short time that my wingtip tanks were not empty. I had to blow them clear before starting the letdown because it was standard operating procedure in the Panther not to have a partial load of aviation gas in the external tanks when exposed to enemy fire. The fuel-air mix would cause a much more severe explosion if the tank was hit by flak. The jet squadrons on the *Boxer* were using the more-volatile aviation gas instead of a safer jet fuel, such as JP-3, because the *Boxer*'s fuel system had not been modified when it was taken out of mothballs, and the props could use only AvGas.

The flight had just gotten into the recce formation and I was the low man at about three hundred feet as we got to Kodo-ri, where the road climbs through a mountain pass. As I came around the first tight bend in the road, there ahead of me was a column of trucks. I was going fast and a little bit high, but I was in an ideal position for a rocket attack. I shoved the stick forward to get the nose down and get the pipper on the lead truck, at the same time reaching forward with my left hand to select rockets on the armament panel and to flip up the master arm switch. All this took a second or two, and I was closing the target very quickly. I still had to make a final adjustment to get the sight on the first truck with the proper amount of lead to compensate for my angle of dive and the distance to the target—the mil-allowance for HVAR. (We had lead computing sights, but only for air-to-air gunnery.) By now I was much closer than I intended to be, or should have been. I could see the drivers scrambling out of the cabs. With a three-thousand-foot precipice on their right and a two-thousand-foot cliff on their left, they had nowhere to go. I had a clear image of the lead truck. It was a U.S. Army Studebaker of the type we had seen so frequently in Japan and South Korea. This far into North Korea, though, I had no concern that it might be a friendly. I fired off two rockets and pulled back on the stick. Nothing happened. Or at least nothing much happened. I could tell from the intense pressure of my G-suit that I was pulling lots of Gs, maybe over nine. I didn't look at the accelerometer. My eyes were fixed on the ridge line ahead, which I was going to have to get over unless I wanted to end up as a flaming monument to pilot error. The plane's response was unusually sluggish.

I did clear the ridge, but just barely. The high section as well as the number two pilot had spotted the truck column and, in accordance with the doctrine of section initiative, the second section leader had come down to join in the attack. As I circled and climbed for a second pass, I could see the bombs of my wingman missing the target by only ten feet in deflection to the left, but they missed the road entirely and exploded at the bottom of the precipice three thousand feet below. They second section did better. With more time to select their weapons, they set up their runs carefully and were boring in with rockets and scoring hits. I came around a second time in a much more conservative approach for a strafing pass, breaking off early enough to clear the ridge comfortably. After a third run to assure ourselves that the trucks and their cargo were completely destroyed, we continued our recce north to Hagaru-ri without encountering any other targets. Then we made a strafing pass at the AAA positions in Hungnam before going "feet wet" and returning to the carrier.

I was shaken from my close call in clearing the ridge. The reason was simple: I was making my run with a full load of internal fuel and at an altitude of about five thousand feet. Normally road recce attacks are made at much lower altitudes and with about half of the fuel load depleted, reducing the weight of the aircraft by three thousand pounds. That's what I was used to. At Koto-ri I had not taken into account my full internal load and the altitude, as a prudent pilot should have done. But in the rest of my flying days, in F9Fs and A-4s, I never made that particular mistake again.

6

Korea

Grand Finale

By the third week in July 1953, the massive Chinese offensive had torn holes in the eastern front of the UN line, shattering entire ROK divisions and sending others reeling. The 103rd U.S. Army Division had fallen back to avoid being outflanked with the collapse of the ROKs but was able to regroup in a supporting position behind the 1st ROK Army. But on the Chinese side, the requirement for logistics, the resupply of fuel, small-arms ammunition and artillery shells, as well as the need to bring up replacements, was finally slowing down Gen. The-Huai Peng's advance.

On 13 July my F9F had taken a hit from a piece of shrapnel during a strike on the North Korean airstrip at Hyesanjin, just south of the Yalu. The skin on the horizontal stabilizer had been pierced and torn near the elevator hinge, and I was reluctant to attempt a carrier landing with this damage of an unknown extent to the plane's control surfaces. So I elected to divert to K-18 at Kangnung. This airfield, a single, six-thousand-foot runway of Marston matting, served as the divert field for TF 77 carrier aircraft that had suffered battle damage or were low on fuel.

By the thirteenth, the Chinese salient was approaching Kangnung and the steady rumble of Chinese heavy artillery and disorganized stream of ROK troops and army equipment moving south along the main supply routes were sobering if not alarming. I would feel much more secure when

I returned to the carrier. I was relieved when I was picked up late that afternoon by an AD Skyraider from the *Shangri-La*; it delivered me home, landing on the *Boxer* en route to the "*Shang*." The pilot, by chance, was a United States Naval Academy classmate with whom I later served at the Naval Aviation Ordnance Test Station at Chincoteague, Virginia.

Four *Essex*-class carriers were continuously on station at Point Oboe, conducting coordinated and overlapping operations in support of the UN ground forces, providing close air support to engaged ground units, and striking the main supply routes north of the front lines to interdict the flow of fuel, munitions, and replacement manpower. Although weather was a problem, the *Boxer* was making every scheduled launch, its aircraft going to secondary weather-divert targets when the primary objective was obscured. On almost every sortie, enemy elements were heavily engaged, the evidence being the heavy flak that our planes were encountering on every mission.

Then, on 19 July, another one of our VF-52 F9Fs was hit while on a CAS mission. With fire in the after fuselage and his engine losing power, Lt. (j.g.) Al Brunner managed to stick his Panther into a seven-hundred-foot L strip, a dark brown gash in the rice paddies bulldozed as a forward landing facility for the light aircraft of the forward air controllers. These were L-3 and L-4 liaison aircraft and T-6 trainers that flew along the front lines and provided spotting for the artillery and air support of the ground forces. Brunner went in wheels up and the plane was demolished, but he was uninjured and returned to the ship the next day. His was the seventh VF-52 F9F-2 that had been lost to enemy ground fire in July.

VF-52 pilots were now regularly flying two hops per day, and on the morning of 20 July, I was scheduled to lead a four-plane mission of F9F-2 Panthers for close support of U.S. Army troops in the vicinity of the village of Kumhwa, one of the points of the Iron Triangle. The tasking had been posted the evening before, and prior to turning in on the nineteenth, I had looked over the available intelligence and discussed the tactics with my section leader. There was not too much we could plan on. We would simply check in with the TACC then be passed down the line to the TADC and then to the FAC, who would designate our targets for us.

Our bomb load had been specified as four 260-pound fragmentation bombs, fused instantaneous, and two HVARs. I asked the schedulers to eliminate the HVARs, as the winds were forecast to be light and variable. I doubted very much that there would be sufficient wind over the deck to get us off with that full load. It would save time if the rockets were deleted from the armament plan now, rather than having to take them off with the planes on the catapult, as the carrier struggled to get a couple more knots of wind over the deck. None of the pilots really liked to leave it to the judgment of the catapult or flight deck officer whether there was enough wind to fly or not. We preferred to make that decision ourselves. It was always uncomfortable being on the borderline of maximum weight and drag for a cat shot. The staff armament planners had no problem with my request to cancel the HVARs. Four frag bombs plus full 20mm ammo was a good load for CAS.

MISSION PREFLIGHT

On the morning of the twentieth, there was the unwelcome rap on the stateroom door and the call, "5:45, Sir." I answered with "Roger." My roommate, Jim Kinsella, the squadron CO, groaned and rolled over. He had a later launch time and was going to sleep in until 0730. I put on my flight gear, less helmet and anti-G torso harness, and arrived for an à la carte breakfast of eggs and bacon in the ship's wardroom at 0630. Our ready room was just forward of the ship's wardroom, and the pilots straggled in with cups of coffee in hand, but all were in their seats and ready for the 0700 briefing.

First the aerologist went over the weather situation in the Sea of Japan and the central Korean peninsula, and we heard that the conditions were not at all favorable for what we were expected to accomplish. It was typical summer weather for Korea, with unstable masses of moist air resulting in low cloud layers from three hundred to one thousand feet with large cumulus buildups on top, particularly in the mountainous terrain. It was not bad enough for a weather abort, but the chances were that the weather in the objective area would be inadequate for close support. It would be prudent to anticipate the possibility of a weather divert to a secondary target.

Next followed the second part of the briefing, given by the squadron intelligence officer, a bright young lieutenant who summarized the tactical situation on the ground, with the locations, as best we knew, of the friendly front lines and the general disposition of the Chinese forces. There had been some sharp fighting during the night, and the Chinese had again broken through the ROK lines on the eastern side of the peninsula, posing repeated threats to the right flank of the adjacent U.S. army group. The Chinese had not disengaged with daylight, and U.S. and ROK forces were flooding the TACC with requests for close support. All four of the Task Force 77 carriers at Point Oboe were committing the maximum number of their available sorties to CAS assignments. I dog-eared my charts of the areas north and east of Chorwon and the Iron Triangle, in case we were diverted to a secondary target. Those chart sections covered the front lines where most of the Chinese attacks were now taking place.

The final part of our briefing covered several new Chinese flak positions in the Iron Triangle, the current emergency procedures, the day's rescue call signs, and the availability of a rescue helicopter on a tank landing ship (LST) operating off of the coast just south of Wonsan.

Although we went through the ritual of the preflight briefings twice a day, before every combat mission, all of the pilots for good reason paid special attention and demanded of the intelligence officers the most up-to-date information. There was nothing peremptory about these sessions, even after three weeks on the line.

At 0740, primary flight control called over the squawk box directing the pilots to man aircraft. We picked up our helmets, pistols, lifejackets, and book bags containing navigation charts and filed out of the ready room for the short ladder leading up to the hangar deck. We crossed the hangar deck as a group. Six pilots were assigned to the flight, including the two spare pilots who would be available in case one of the primary aircraft was mechanically grounded before the launch, and we walked out on the deck-edge elevator. Normally, aircrews were supposed to wait for an aircraft to be placed on the elevator to catch a ride up to the flight deck, but by now the elevator operators were resigned to the pilots' determination to ride free. So our flight, plus other flight-deck personnel and ordnancemen with boxes of fuses for aircraft arming, rode up to the flight deck on the deck-edge aircraft elevator. Our assigned planes were located just forward of the island, convenient to the catapults. We would be the first to launch.

My plane was parked on the starboard catapult, and after a careful inspection of the aircraft and an even more detailed inspection of the bombs and the integrity of their arming wires, I climbed in and the plane captain passed up my chart bag and helmet. Then the plane captain, an eighteen-year-old sailor with six months of carrier warfare experience behind him, helped me buckle up my seatbelt and harness while I attended to making the radio, oxygen, and G-suit connections. For both of us, the timing had become instinctive, and just as we completed our cockpit check, the flight deck bullhorn announced, "Pilots start your engines. All personnel stand clear of prop wash and jet blast." With a growing roar the two dozen aircraft scheduled for this deck-load launch fired up their power plants.

I could feel the ship noticeably heel as it turned into the wind. This was an indication that the *Boxer* was making maximum speed, a sure sign that the winds were light. I felt better about having dropped the two HVARs. As the carrier settled down on a straight course—easy for me to tell by looking out my cockpit down the track of the catapult—the catapult officer stepped into my view and began rapidly twirling the first two fingers of his right hand. This was my signal to go to full power. I eased the throttle up and jammed it against the forward stop, waiting for the rpm indicator to hit 100. I gave the needle two seconds against the 100 percent peg before saluting the catapult officer with my left hand and pushing my helmeted head back against the headrest. *Bang!*

The catapult, an old H4B model having a shorter stroke than the newer catapults on the later carriers, had to accelerate more rapidly, and the cat shot was so abrupt that the first thing I was conscious of, after raising my hand in the salute, was that I was airborne off the forward rounddown of the carrier deck. I instinctively checked my altitude, which looked good, and the plane's flight attitude, which was correct. With my left hand I reached over and flipped up the wheel lever to retract the landing gear. The plane was so sensitive at this juncture that it was necessary to concentrate on not applying any forward pressure on the stick while leaning forward to reach the wheel controls. The plane was just a couple of knots above stalling speed with less than one hundred feet of altitude. In about ten seconds the plane's speed had increased to 190 knots, and I hit the flaps-up switch and could feel the plane accelerate as I maintained 100 percent power and the flaps came up. I checked my flight instruments and eased back on the stick. I was immediately in the soup. The ceiling was about three hundred feet. Now, flying on instruments at zero visibility, I maintained 100 percent power but held the aircraft's speed at about 230 knots for an optimum rate of climb. In less than ten seconds I had popped through on top of the cloud layer (an experience that never ceased to excite me). Below the overcast it had been misty and dreary with a sprinkling of rain; on top of the clouds, a July sun was blazing in a brilliantly blue sky.

But now was not the time for aesthetic contemplation. I switched from the launch frequency to the ship's traffic control to report I was airborne and rendezvousing my flight. When I got to five thousand feet, I leveled off and reduced power to maintain 250 knots and checked the clock so that exactly three minutes after takeoff I would make a 180-degree turn to the left. By then the last of the planes in my flight had become airborne—the launch interval was thirty seconds per plane—and would see me as I headed toward them so they could make an easy rendezvous.

Luck was with us. All four of the primary aircraft had become airborne and Air Operations Center decided to launch the spares because of the urgency of the request for air support for the troops. By the time my radio direction finder showed that I was abeam of the carrier—which I could not see because it was below the overcast—the six-plane flight had rendezvoused. I added power to 97 percent, made a sweeping turn to a course of 265 degrees magnetic, which would take us to the designated coast-in point, and commenced climbing to our ingress altitude of ten thousand feet. The carrier was about sixty miles off of the coast, and although the cloud level was solid under us, the rugged mountains of Korea were clearly visible, poking their tops up through the cloud layer ahead. Even from this distance I could see the cumulus building in between the mountain ranges, an indication that finding our way into the assigned target was going to be tricky.

During the run in to the beach, there was no radio conversation among the members of our flight. We had been flying together for almost a year, with the same pilots in each section and division. The only change was my wingman, Lt. (j.g.) Pete Lebuski, who was replacing Lt. (j.g.) John Chambers, my original wingman, who had been shot down and wounded the previous month during a strike on a Chinese troop-marshaling area.

As we crossed the coastline, I called the carrier to report "feet dry" and that I was shifting to the TACC control. Going to button three on my VHF, I called up the TACC and reported inbound with six Panthers loaded with four 260-pound fragmentation bombs each and scheduled for close support. From the amount of chatter on this already-overworked circuit, it was apparent that there were a lot of requests for air support and that the weather over the front lines was not conducive to the tactical aircraft getting together with the FACs. I had been on the TACC circuit less than a minute when the controller told me to switch to button 4 and contact the flight leader of a flight from the USS *Lake Champlain*, who had been departing his target area when he had spotted a lucrative target. His flight was low on fuel and out of ammunition and had to go home. The controller then directed our six planes to divert from the CAS mission—all of the FACs were saturated, anyway—and attempt to follow through on the sighting reported by the *Lake Champlain* jets.

The *Lake Champlain* flight leader reported that on a diversion from his assigned CAS mission he had spotted a column of trucks and tanks headed south on the main supply route leading into Kumsong. At this point, I was flying over the Hwachon Reservoir, which because of its very distinctive shape was easy to recognize and provided a solid navigational fix. There were enough breaks in the clouds that there was a promising chance we could find our way to Kumhwa, a good-sized town, and then head up the relatively wide and flat valley running to the northeast to Kumsong.

I called up TACC and requested permission to divert from the preplanned CAS mission and proceed to this target of opportunity. The controller had been on the net and listened to my conversation with the *Lake Champlain* flight leader and right away called back with an okay. Rogering the instructions from the TACC, I reported "going button 4." With the complexity of the chain of command and the paucity of radio channels, meticulous radio discipline was essential. With hand signals I moved my flight into a modified trail formation, presuming that each pilot had been listening in on the conversations between the *Lake Champlain* flight and the TACC.

The loose trail formation was almost a tail chase, but each pilot alternately moved out far enough to the right or left of the flight line of the leader, which made for easy station keeping and allowed every pilot to maintain a lookout of both the air and ground picture. We had gotten a good fix over the Hwachon Reservoir, and from the gridlines on the

50,000-scale chart, I estimated a course that would put us over Kumhwa in about three minutes. Kumhwa appeared on schedule through a break in the overcast, and from ten thousand feet we could clearly see the artillery bursts north of the city but had no idea which side was under fire. It was evident that there was heavy fighting going on around Kumhwa and the truck convoy that had been spotted on the main supply route from the north was bringing down ammunition for the enemy troops and mortars. A heavy firefight such as we were witnessing could not go on long without ammo replenishment. As our flight crossed over Kumhwa, I changed course to about 020 and nosed over to lose altitude and get down to the level of the tops of the cumulus, which were at about seven thousand feet. As our flight moved north toward Yodo, the northern terminus of the route on which the convoy had been sighted, the broad valley narrowed to a virtual mountain ravine and the mountain peaks and the cloud bottoms were blending together at about four thousand feet.

Now some hard decisions had to be made. Should we pull up and proceed on top and hope for a break in the overcast? Or should we go under the low cumulus, which appeared to bottom out at about four thousand feet, and hope we weren't heading up a dead end valley? To compound our difficulties, we had begun to pick up flak after leaving Kumhwa, and at five thousand feet were running into some bursting stuff and a whole mess of tracers coming from all directions and passing between the planes in the formation. It was at this point, just north of Kumsong, that I picked up the convoy. It was not hard to find, just a case of following the road north. The weather had given us a break. The ceiling in the vicinity appeared to be between three and five thousand feet but very irregular, with patches of scud and rain under the base of the cumulus.

I called to the flight on our tactical channel that the column of trucks was at one o'clock and that I would swing around the target in an arc so that each plane could peel off and take separation in order to avoid the preceding aircraft's bomb blast. We would make only a single pass, dropping all four bombs on that run. The decision to drop everything on the first pass was a judgment call. If we attempted to drop one bomb on each of four runs, we stood a good chance of either losing the target in the very changeable weather or losing a couple of planes. Each plane was going to have to come down the same chute because of the low ceiling and the steepness of the mountains on both sides of the road. That would ease the problem for the Chinese gunners, unfortunately.

In order to get more separation between each of the aircraft in our trail formation, I pulled out hard to the right and then broke back left again in an S-maneuver, letting down all the time. It must have been a wild ride for the rest of the flight, because it was certainly an exciting one for me. I was doing about four hundred knots and pulling over three Gs, trying to keep the plane at a high speed and also within the very confined area of the mountainous valley.

It was only about a mile from the lead truck in the column that I was able to get the wings level over the road at about three thousand feet. I nosed over and put my pipper on the first vehicle. I reached up with my left hand and hit the master armament switch on and selected "guns" in the same motion. Then I pulled the trigger. All four of the 20mms grouped in the nose of the F9F opened up. I shifted my eyes from the pipper to the tracers and saw that I was hitting about fifty feet short and some ricochets were going over the truck column. I nudged the stick back a hair and squeezed off another burst, and it was satisfying to see this very tight pattern of 20mm shells impacting on the first three trucks of the column. But at 350 knots, the range was closing so rapidly that I had already reached my minimum release height. So in that instinctive reaction I had developed on the bombing ranges at El Centro in California and sharpened in the mountains of Korea, I pulled my nose up enough to get the proper mil lead on my illuminated gunsight, jam my thumb on the bomb pickle (the projecting button on the pilot's control stick that releases the bombs), and pull back on the stick until the hardening pressure from my anti–G-suit on my legs and stomach told me that I was pulling more than four Gs.

I had to keep my plane wrapped up in a tight turn in order to stay out of the low-lying clouds. I wasn't about to fly through them; I didn't know what mountain might be inside. There was a patch of blue that I was chasing, and at about six thousand feet I broke clear of the clouds. So I eased off on the turn and throttled back to about 85 percent to allow my wingman to find me and join up.

I looked over my left shoulder to see if I could assess the damage we had done on the truck column, but the target area was blocked by the clouds. However, I was pleased to see one, then two, then three, Panthers coming up through the hole in the overcast, their dark blue silhouettes very clearly defined against the whiteness of the cumulus tops. I was still in a gentle climb at about 85 percent power when Pete Lebuski joined up. As he did, he flew above and slightly to the forward of me, as I was in a left-hand turn, so that I could check his ordnance stations. The purpose of this post-attack procedure was, first, to determine if all the ordnance had indeed been released, and, second, if a weapon had hung up, to see whether it still had its arming wire in place. A bomb hung up on a rack without an arming wire was a worrisome hazard. The arming propeller on the fuse had probably completely unwound and the bomb was not safe. That is, it would detonate with virtually any shock that the fuse would sense to be striking the target, including the plane's deceleration due to an arrested carrier landing. I was able to tell Pete that his racks were clear. Then he dropped back and down to perform that same function for my aircraft. I was shocked when Pete gave me a thumbs-down signal and held up two fingers. That meant that I still had two bombs aboard. The other planes were now joining us and I was swinging around to a southerly course to head for friendly territory. But first, before departing the objective area, I had to determine what our overall ordnance situation was.

After we had reached an altitude of eight thousand feet and I had settled down on a course of south, I stuck my head down in the cockpit to check my armament switches and saw that they were all properly set up, so the failure of the bombs to release was not a pilot problem. Unfortunately, what I also saw as my eyes swept the instrument panel was a fire warning light. In the F9F-2 there was a warning light that glowed bright red when it sensed a fire in the engine compartment of the aircraft.

At this point I felt the ordnance problem had to be resolved before I could make a further decision on the next evolution, and did not want to go through the uncertainty of trying to do this by hand signals. So I called up Lebuski on the squadron tactical circuit and asked for a report. He said that two 260-pound frag bombs were hung up, one on each side, on the wing bomb racks. He added that the arming wires appeared to be in place. The other two section leaders, hearing this report on the radio, chimed in to report that there were no hung bombs in their sections.

Now I had to make a tough decision. This was too important a target to abandon without dropping our full bomb load, so I was going to have to make another run. At the same time, I had to decide whether I had a serious fire in the after section of the aircraft. Third, I really didn't want to take all five of the other pilots through that valley again with the low clouds and the hornet's nest of flak that we had stirred up. I told Lebuski that I had a fire warning light and asked him to drop back and check for signs of battle damage in the after section of the aircraft and to look for any smoke or flames in the tail section. Lebuski slid back and gave my plane the complete once-over. He called up saying there were no visible signs of flak damage or fire.

There was no time for debate with myself or the other pilots. I called the flight and told them that I had a fire warning light but Lebuski had failed to find any indications of damage and that I had two hung frags and was going to go back and get rid of them on the truck column. I told Lt. Paul Hayek, the next senior pilot on the flight, to rendezvous the other four aircraft, get out of the flak zone, but remain in the vicinity to pick up Lebuski and me as we climbed out after making this final pass. I then instructed Lebuski to drop back half a mile as we approached the target and told him I would make a thirty-degree bombing run. I wanted him to come in flat on the deck, where he probably would not be detected, and fire his 20mms in a strafing run to enfilade the entire column. Lebuski acknowledged with two clicks of his mike switch.

I swung around to the north again and was able to quickly establish my position with relationship to the truck column by the proximity of the target area to a prominent mountain sticking up through the clouds. Finding a hole in the broken ceiling, I wrapped up my plane in a four-G corkscrew letdown at 350 knots, pulling the turn tight to stay within the cloud opening. I almost immediately picked up the road again, and I knew that the weather in the vicinity of the trucks was at least three thousand feet because the truck column had been immobilized and the weather wasn't moving much. I was going so fast when I hit the undercast that I overshot the road, and there was no way at my speed I was going to be able to get lined up on the target, which I could now spot—by the smoke, bursting shells, and gasoline fires—only a mile away. So I did what I did not want to do: throttled back and popped open my speed brakes in order to get the plane slowed down and under control in this narrow valley with the mountains on both sides and the clouds above me. I figured that with the 260-pound fragmentation bomb I had to have at least twenty-five hundred feet of altitude at release point in order to avoid being damaged by my own bomb blast. That didn't give me a hell of a lot of room for setting up my bombing run. So this final pass was a real makeshift affair.

I sucked up my speed brakes, added full power, pushed the nose over to level off at about three thousand feet, and headed up the highway toward the leading trucks of the column, which was now burning fiercely with most of the vehicles smoking and exploding. As I approached the trucks, I dipped my nose and, using a lot of mil lead, put my pipper on the center of the column. At this point the flak and tracers were very thick, although it was hard to differentiate them from what could have been exploding ammunition. I released both bombs using the manual handle, which required ducking my head into the cockpit, reaching for the T-handle, and yanking with all my might. I popped my head back up, broke into a very hard left climbing turn, and was able by looking over my left shoulder—a particularly hard exercise with four Gs on the plane—to see the explosions of my bombs. I couldn't tell whether I had made a direct hit or not, but I knew that a 260-pound frag in the vicinity of that truck column loaded with gasoline and ammunition was not going to go unnoticed.

As I was about to pull my eyes away, there was Pete Lebuski flying over the column in his strafing run, and I could see his tracers going into the trucks all through the column. He pulled up hard in a climbing left turn, and at this point I dove for the deck and followed the road south at five hundred feet and four hundred knots. As I passed the four-hundred-knot mark on the airspeed gauge, I pulled back on the stick and climbed straight up until I was on top of the cloud layer at seven thousand feet. I looked around for the rest of my flight, who were to be waiting for me, and there was no one in sight. That upset me. Then I started a left-hand turn to clear my six o'clock and there, strung out behind me, were the other five airplanes of my flight. Disregarding my instructions, they had all come down to follow me and shoot up the remnants of the column with their remaining 20mm ammunition. They wanted every pilot in the attack to be covered by a wingman's fire.

As we returned south, I continued the climb to ten thousand feet at 90 percent power with lazy S-turns, which gave the flight an easy opportunity to rendezvous. A quick check from the section leaders on the tactical frequency indicated that all external weapons had been expended and no aircraft had suffered any damage. It seemed like a miracle.

We headed for the nearest point on the front lines, just to get us over friendly territory. We had had enough excitement for the day. Meanwhile, I advised the TACC of our success with an estimate that there were between fifteen and twenty trucks in the column with some "flak wagons" interspersed with them mounting machine guns and 37mms. I recommended that the next available flight of jets go back in on the target and tear up the remnants of the reinforcing column. About that time we were over the coastline and I checked out with the TACC and called the Task Force 77 control, announcing that *Boxer* Flight 2201 was feet wet, with six Panthers, mission successful, with no battle damage to our own aircraft.

THE IRON TRIANGLE

On 21 July, the next day, I was scheduled for a CAS mission in the vicinity of Kumhwa, where the 103rd Division GIs were under heavy pressure from the Chinese. My flight was armed with four 260-pound frag bombs fused instantaneous, two HVARs, and full 20mm ammo. We were fortunate in being in the day's earliest launch, and we were the first planes off the catapults, arriving on station ready to go, without waiting for an earlier flight to complete its mission. We also had the benefit of both an airborne FAC in an L-4 orbiting at three thousand feet just behind the front lines and a FAC on the ground within fifty yards of the closet Chinese positions. The weather over the target was a five-thousand-foot overcast, and we were able to conduct very accurate thirty-degree glide-bombing runs. With ample fuel, we were able to make individual runs for each item of ordnance being delivered. The frag bombs could not achieve pinpoint accuracy on a bunker or a machine-gun nest, but the shrapnel did raise hell with the troops, even in their foxholes. By the time we commenced our passes with the rockets, we had become familiar enough with the Chinese positions that we were able to spot the machine-gun locations and the mortars. The HVARs, fired one per pass from a very low altitude at exceedingly short range, were almost all direct hits. At the end of our six passes, the flight still had enough fuel for another ten minutes on station, so I offered to conduct two more firing passes with the 20mm guns, strafing the trenches and the foxhole areas. The controllers were delighted. The 20mms in the Panthers were a very formidable weapon. With the four guns bunched in the nose, they were capable of great accuracy. The pilot could place his pipper on the target and then adjust his fire by watching the tracers, without shifting his line of sight. The fighters would always prefer not to fire all their machine-gun ammunition because it was their self-defense in the event that MiGs strayed into our sector or because the jets did not often have sufficient fuel to make the strafing runs.

After completing our second strafing pass, we checked out with the FAC. He was lavish in his praise for the damage we had inflicted on the Chinese. We pilots knew that the ground observers tended to go over-board with their damage assessments and kudos to the pilots, to bolster our morale and give us a sense of accomplishment that would incline us to put a high priority on future CAS missions. Nevertheless, we were pleased by the reports that substantial damage had been inflicted on the Chinese unit. As we headed east to the coastline, effecting a running rendezvous, we climbed slowly to ten thousand feet. At the water's edge I checked out with the TACC, switched to button 3, and called up the Task Force 77 net to report that we were feet wet at Chang Sung, return-ing to the carrier with our assigned mission completed.

At this point I heard the TACC announce on guard channel that a Navy Panther was down in the sector we had just left. Because there were four carriers, each operating two squadrons of F9Fs, this downed aircraft could be from any of eight squadrons; all of the carriers were overlap-ping in their missions over the beach. Nevertheless, I was apprehensive. I knew our squadron was scheduled to have a flight in that area. When we got to the carrier, the weather was squally, with the winds strong but variable and the deck wet. Our signal was Charlie on arrival—land immediately—and each of our pilots got aboard with minimum interval and without a wave-off. As I taxied my plane to its parking spot ahead of the island, where it would be rearmed and refueled for the next launch in forty-five minutes, I had that nice feeling of having returned safely from a flight that had gone well in all respects. We had found our primary target, been successful in achieving a commendable level of damage to the enemy, and gotten back on board ship easily in spite of some nasty weather. Then came a shock. Unbuckling my seatbelt and unplugging my oxygen and G-suit connections, I passed my helmet to the plane captain standing on the ladder alongside the cockpit, and he said to me, "Too bad about the Skipper getting shot down." That confirmed my worst fears. The Navy Panther down was Jim Kinsella.

I made my way down to the squadron ready room as quickly as I could against that heavy traffic that clogs the ladders, hangar deck, and passageways between launch and recovery cycles. As I came through the watertight door of the ready room, the squadron duty officer, whose desk was at the far end of the compartment, was just putting down his phone and called out in a loud voice, "Well, Triple Sticks [a squadron nickname from the "III" at the end of my name], it looks like now you're the Skipper of VF-52!" That was his rather tasteless way of confirming that it was Jim Kinsella's F9F that had just gone down. I suppose that was excusable, because the younger officers in the squadron—in all squadrons—generally took the loss of a pilot with little evident emotion, a protective device that was helpful in maintaining their morale over a long deployment fraught with all kinds of hazards.

I joined him at his desk and he told me what he knew based upon communications from the TACC ashore and intercepts of the conversations of the other pilots on his flight. Kinsella's aircraft had been hit in the vicinity of Kumhwa, and his plane, on fire, had crashed some miles to the south in no-man's-land. Lt. (j.g.) Bill Brooke, his section leader, had just flown over the crash site and reported no survivors. I stood there while the duty officer dialed the phone and punched buttons on the squawk box in an effort to get more information.

About ten minutes later a call from the ship's Operations Center reported that the pilot of the crashed Panther apparently had survived and been picked up in no-man's-land by an armed patrol from the Second Infantry Division. What a remarkable change in the situation.

When Kinsella's flight landed back on board the *Boxer*, Bill Brook told us what had happened. "The flight was normal, with a quick rendezvous after takeoff and a high-speed run into the beach, where we were rapidly cleared by the TACC to a FAC in the vicinity of Kumhwa. We were quickly briefed on the target, and Kinsella identified it and made one dummy run to ensure both the FAC and ourselves we had the right spot. The FAC called for a rocket firing pass on the first run, and as we strung out in single file, Kinsella was first and I saw him go in flat and very low, and then there was a tremendous explosion, which was either his plane being hit by heavy antiaircraft fire or his bombs going off right beneath him. As he pulled off the target, I could see that he was in trouble. Fire was streaming from the engine compartment and the tailpipe. He immediately commenced a turn to the south, calling on the VHF that he was in trouble. He knew he was on fire, but he was not going to eject over enemy territory. He would ditch as soon as he got over friendly lines. He did not attempt to climb for altitude but remained pretty much on the deck, flying at the maximum speed he could get out of his aircraft. This was consistent with what he had briefed us on before other flights. He did not want to be taken prisoner, and if his plane was damaged, he would stay low so that when his plane was no longer flyable, he would be able to make a crash landing with some control of the aircraft remaining."

It was always apparent to pilots when we got to the friendly side of the front lines because of the open activity of the ground forces, which were not subject to hostile air surveillance. "Jim knew where he was," Brook continued, "and when he saw a reasonably good spot, he put the plane in and it disintegrated on impact. The fuselage broke at the cockpit, and the engine and the after part of the fuselage went hurtling along in a flaming mass. The cockpit and nose section was rolled up in a ball tumbling after it. I was convinced nobody could have survived a crash like that because of the fire and the disintegration. But as we came around for one final low pass, I looked over the section of the cockpit and I could see Kinsella unstrapping himself from his ejection seat and walking away from the wreckage. We made one more pass to make sure he'd safely gotten out, and by then Kinsella was fifty yards south of the wreckage and he waved to us. We could see an infantry patrol with some armored vehicles coming out to meet him, and we knew there was no more that we could do so we headed for home, except for my wingman, who had some suspected flak damage and went into K-18. We still had enough fuel and the time to make our landing cycle, so I opted to return to the ship rather than take all three planes into King 18."

At that point, in my capacity as the senior officer in the squadron, I appointed a board to start on the necessary paperwork. At the same time I told Brooke he would now lead the skipper's division and we would use spare pilots to fill in the flights as necessary for the rest of the day's schedule. It was time to get back to business. Paul Hayek's division had arrived in the ready room to prepare for the next launch, and Lt. Bob Hayes was preparing his section for their combat air patrol, launching at the same time. I wanted to write Dotty Kinsella, Jim's wife, right away, but I decided to defer my letter until I knew more.

I had another flight that afternoon, a CAS mission, again on the central front. According to the FACs, we were successful in inflicting casualties on the enemy. I landed back on board the *Boxer* at about 1600. The squadron duty officer had a message from commander, Seventh Fleet's representative at the TACC to the effect that Lieutenant Commander Kinsella had crashed north of the front lines in the Second Infantry Division's sector and had been brought in by an armed patrol. He was evacuated to a mobile army surgical hospital (MASH) unit for immediate medical attention and assessment. Kinsella had suffered serious burns on his face and hands and had been taken by ambulance to Seoul. He would be evacuated that evening to Japan for hospitalization and further evacuation to CONUS. There were no broken bones or internal injuries.

What a remarkable outcome of what had appeared to his flight to be a fatal crash. His F9F, in flames, had disintegrated upon hitting the ground. Jim Kinsella was the eighth pilot in the squadron to have his plane brought down during hostile fire. All had survived, although some had been wounded.

NEW SKIPPER

I did not have much time to reflect over the report on Kinsella. The squadron duty officer said that the *Boxer*'s skipper, Captain Gurney, wanted to see me on the bridge as soon as I had landed and been debriefed. I dropped off my helmet and navigation kit and walked up the four levels of ladders to the navigation bridge. Captain Gurney was sitting in his CO's perch overlooking the flight deck as the last of the Skyraiders on this recovery were landing on board. He motioned me over and asked if I had seen the message on Kinsella. I told him I had and that we all considered Kinsella a very lucky pilot. Capt. Marsh Gurney, who was a very fine naval officer, a good carrier skipper, and a very thoughtful and friendly individual, then said to me that he was preparing to send a message to the Bureau of Personnel (BuPers) recommending that I be given command of Fighter Squadron 52 as of that date. I thanked him very much for his consideration in recommending me. He said he would send a copy of the message to the squadron and that I should immediately assume all the responsibilities and prerogatives of the CO. A very thoughtful gesture. He was busy running the recovery and I had things to do, so I excused myself and was leaving the bridge when he called me back and said, "Jim, I know you'll do a good job. That's a fine squadron and you certainly showed that you can fill the shoes of Jim Kinsella." Again, a thoughtful senior officer. That brief comment was a substantial boost to my morale. I went back to the cabin that I shared with Kinsella and broke out a sheet of Navy-issue lined paper and wrote a quick note to Dotty Kinsella, his wife, who was a close friend of Dabney, my wife, and told her just what had happened as far as we knew and that we were all grateful that Jim was going home all in one piece, with the prognosis of a full and complete recovery. I knew that we would be getting a mail plane off first thing the next morning and I wanted her to hear personally from someone on the ship close to Jim. I then went through the onerous task of packing up Jim's clothes and belongings. It was not nearly as depressing as it had been for me on the previous cruise, when Tom Pugh, the XO of the Skyraider squadron, a Naval Academy classmate, and my next-door neighbor in quarters at the Naval Air Station Pensacola, had been killed in action and I was packing up his worldly possessions, which ultimately would be opened by his widow and children.

The next day, VF-52 was at it again as if nothing had happened. Except that the pilots made a great point of calling me Skipper and generally laughing and scratching about the change in command. There is a great deal of black humor among naval aviators because of the losses they sustain among their close friends and their leaders. I had been with this squadron for almost three years and been XO for twelve months. They knew me well and were confident that there would be no surprises with me as CO. I had been running the squadron under Jim Kinsella since coming on board. Jim was essentially an air combat tactician and spent minimum time dealing with the pilots or the enlisted men. He left that up to his XO while he pondered new tactics and strategies for more effective ways to kill the enemy.

Years later, at a squadron reunion in San Diego, Jim Kinsella and I were reminiscing about our Korean War days and he told me this story. When he had crashed and saw the infantry patrol coming out of their lines into no-man's-land, he had run forward to meet them in his pleasure at realizing they were friendly troops. When he reached the group, grateful and breathless, the patrol leader, a sergeant, said, "Mister, the CO of the 217th Engineers is going to be very mad at you." In response to Jim's "Why?" the sergeant said, "He had told us that mine-field you just ran through was impenetrable."

We went to work the next day with the same kind of schedule, but now the spares were being launched with every flight, just to get the maximum weight of effort over the target. At the end of that day the squadron received a copy of a message from commander, Seventh Fleet reporting that the carriers in Task Force 77 had flown the highest total of combat sorties up to that time in a single day in the Korean War. This was in response to the appeals from the ground commanders. The Chinese were battering the UN strongpoints all along the eastern front— Pork Chop Hill, Little Berlin, Sniper's Ridge—using human-wave attacks preceded by the heaviest heavy artillery bombardments of the war.

TRUCE

Then suddenly silence. A truce had been declared, and we flew our last mission on the afternoon of 27 July. I had suspected something was up, because my last mission had taken me to a target northwest of Hungnam, and although the city was devastated, none of us had ever seen as much flak coming up at us as we did that afternoon. My guess was that the people on the ground knew that the truce was imminent, so there were no constraints on their expenditure of ammunition. They probably didn't care whether we were within reasonable range before they let go with barrages of heavy artillery and automatic-weapons fire. It was colorful, to say the least.

The next day, with no flight operations scheduled, seemed very strange. The carriers retired to the east about thirty miles to join up with a replenishment group to take on board black oil for ships' propulsion, aviation gasoline for the aircraft, and food and general supplies to keep the people and machines going. That afternoon, we were told we could exercise on the flight deck, and so our squadron took up a couple of blankets and we sat around, relaxing in the sun and wondering when we would be going home.

Two of the carriers in Task Force 77 immediately departed from Point Oboe for Sasebo, where one, the *Princeton*, would then head for home. The second carrier would have a brief period of R&R and return to the line to relieve the *Lake Champlain*, which would in turn go to Sasebo to prepare for her homeward trip to CONUS. There was no mention of the *Boxer* going anywhere. There was much disappointment on board, but had we been reasonable, we would have understood that we had been one of the most recent arrivals, not getting to the western Pacific until April. So the chances were that we would not head home until fall.

THE BRIDGES AT TOKO-RI

The James Michener novella *The Bridges at Toko-Ri* is a fact-based but fictional account of a carrier air group attacking a key bridge in North Korea. It drew upon the operational experience of Air Group 5 while embarked in the USS *Essex* in their 1951–52 deployment to Korea. Michener had spent several weeks on board the *Essex* that winter. The story first appeared in *Life* magazine and was then published in book form. It immediately became a best seller. The book was then made into a movie, produced by Paramount and starring Grace Kelly, William Holden, Mickey Rooney, and Frederick March. The film was acclaimed by Admiral Burke, who was CNO when it premiered in Washington, D.C., in 1955, as a meticulously accurate depiction of the air war in Korea and, in his experience, the best Navy war film ever. Burke had been deputy commander in chief, U.S. Naval Forces, Japan in 1951 and 1952 and largely responsible for running the Navy's war in Korea. Vice Adm. Turner Joy, the CinC, had been ill with cancer.

I had the memorable experience of flying in the movie version of *The Bridges at Toko-Ri*. In early 1954, my squadron, Fighter Squadron 52, flying Grumman F9F-2 Panthers, had just returned to the Naval Air Station Miramar outside of San Diego from a combat deployment during the Korean War. Commander, Naval Air Forces Pacific Fleet had been designated by the CNO to supervise the Navy's participation in the production of the film. VF-52 was designated as the squadron to provide air services, virtually working full time for the producer. The secretary of the Navy had ruled that the Navy Department would cooperate to the fullest extent with Paramount.

The most prominent aviation cinematographer at the time, Paul Mantz, had been engaged by Paramount to do the aerial photography. Mantz had rigged a World War II B-25—the light bomber used by Gen. Jimmy Doolittle in the Tokyo raid of 1942—for this purpose. The guns and plexiglass had been removed from the tail turret and replaced with a large camera mounting. During the filming of the air action, which included our Panthers joining up, dive-bombing, strafing, and even crashing, Paul Mantz himself was manning the camera rig. Standing waist high in the plane's slipstream, he wore a leather jacket and cloth helmet with World War II–era aviator's goggles as he manhandled his enormous cameras as if they were machine guns.

The maximum speed for the B-25 while filming was 175 knots, close to the minimum air speed for the Panthers in a clean landing (flaps-up) configuration, the condition required for the combat simulation. During most of the filming, the Panthers were flying just above the stalling airspeed with flaps up. With flaps down for landing, the stall speed was under 120 knots. However, all of the pilots were combat veterans with extensive flying time in the Panther under all conditions of flight, and performing the simulated combat maneuvers after having done the real thing was just pure fun. As the senior pilot in the squadron, I had the distinction of flying in the role of Lieutenant Brubaker, played in that film by William Holden, and it was a source of deep satisfaction to have my Korean experience, which had been similar to *The Bridges* in so many ways, memorialized in this fashion.

The kindest flourish to the episode was Paramount's invitation to the eight pilots who flew in the film, together with our wives, to spend a weekend in Hollywood as their guests. A private railroad car picked us up in Del Mar, California, near the Miramar Naval Air Station, where VF-52 was based, and took us to Hollywood. We had a full day of visiting the sets where the movie was being filmed, meeting the stars, and watching the production. That night, with the major actors in attendance, we were treated to a formal dinner at an elegant nightclub. It was, in retrospect, a very generous gesture to the military, something that did not have to be done but was offered with the most genuine appreciation and thoughtfulness.

7

Tactical Nukes

I t was 0415 on 14 January 1958. I was sitting in the pilots' ready room on board the USS *Essex*. Because I was the commander of Attack Squadron 83, my assigned seat was in the front row and the message that blared from the intercom was loud and clear: "Pilots, man your aircraft for the 0500 launch." The squadron duty officer, a sleepy lieutenant (j.g.), responded with "Roger" then said to me, "Skipper, since you are the only sortie on this launch, I guess that means you."

I slipped on my bandolier with the holstered Police Special .38, Navy issue, grabbed my helmet and map case, and headed topside. As I walked out on the flight deck through the control station hatch, I could see my plane, a single A4D-2 Skyhawk, parked on the port catapult. It was strange to see it all alone. All of the other aircraft were pulled aft on the flight deck. The weather was nice: sixty degrees, five-tenths cloud coverage, a setting half moon, and about ten knots of breeze. The *Essex* had not yet turned into the wind.

The Skyhawk, side number 301, was surrounded by a small group of flight deck crewmen—a brown-shirted plane captain, a green-shirted troubleshooter, a red-shirted ordnanceman, and a yellow shirt in a starter jeep to provide the air to start the plane's engine. Standing guard over the group was a Marine in combat fatigues cradling a Thompson submachine gun. As I came up to the plane for my preflight inspection, the red shirt approached with his clipboard. "Sir, please sign this receipt for custody of the weapon," he said. The sheet read: "One (1) Mark 28 Mod 0 Thermonuclear Gravity Bomb." I signed off without a word and went over to the centerline pylon where the weapon was suspended. The chief ordnanceman pointed out the umbilical connections that would allow the bomb to be armed from the portable console in the cockpit. It all looked familiar, just like pictures in the handbooks and lectures. As I ran my hand over the bomb to ensure the proper adjustment of the pylon braces and the attachment to the bomb rack, I could not help but reflect on its deceptively graceful appearance. It packed the equivalent explosive power of 350,000 tons of TNT into its twenty-inch-diameter streamlined form. As I climbed in the cockpit, the wind caught my large, flat map case like an airfoil, whipping it around, and the plane captain helped me put it into the cockpit. I said, "Thanks, I'm going to need that."

As the sweep second hand on my cockpit clock went by 0500, I turned on my exterior running lights for the catapult officer to let him know I was ready for launch and in three seconds, the A4D was airborne. I flipped the wheels-up lever and eased up the wing flaps. The power stayed at 100 percent as I swung to my departure course, turned off my lights, and commenced the long climb to thirty-five thousand feet. Not even a good-bye from the carrier. We were in radio silence. The entire launch had been done without a radio transmission.

At altitude I felt really alone in the cockpit. No crew, no wingman, and seven miles from the nearest fish. The A4D did not have an autopilot, and at this altitude, with two 250-gallon tanks on the wing pylons and the centerline weapon, the little plane was wallowing and required constant pilot attention. At 0542 I throttled back to 85 percent and commenced to let down according to my preplanned flight profile. Leveling off at ten thousand feet would get me under the coastal search radar, but not for long. Ten minutes later another descent would be required. I had planned to wait until sunrise at 0617 before dropping down to my two-hundred-foot ingress altitude, after I had gotten a visual check on the coastline to verify my position at the start of the overland leg. With the rising sun behind me and just a trace of morning mist, I was able to easily confirm my landfall position, the confluence of two rivers on an otherwise unbroken coastline. Leaving the coast, the navigation would be harder: four hundred miles of flying at two hundred feet altitude and

360 knots. I had selected a series of geographically prominent features as my navigation checkpoints, and they all turned up on schedule. I had a time on target (TOT) of 0748. At 0700 I pushed the power up to 100 percent to squeeze five hundred knots out of the A4D. I had jettisoned both of the 250-gallon drop tanks as they had emptied, and now the Skyhawk was cleaner and lighter. At 0747 I was over my initial position but still three minutes out. I was going to be two minutes late—more headwind than I had expected—and it was not possible to make it up. I concentrated on getting a good hit on the target. Dropping down to fifty feet, I eased off a percent of power to give me exactly five hundred knots, set the armament switches on the weapons console to arm the Mark-28 bomb on the centerline rack, and selected it for automatic release. And then I concentrated on flying the final maneuver.

Suddenly there it was. A whitewashed, pyramid-shaped building, just like the intelligence photos. As I crossed the target, I pulled back the stick firmly but smoothly to about four Gs, and as the G forces jammed me down in the ejection seat, the anti-G suit pressure, squeezing on my legs and abdomen, forced the blood to my head to prevent me from blacking out. I concentrated on keeping my wings horizontal. As I pulled up into the half Cuban eight maneuver, I was flying entirely by reference to the instruments of the low-altitude bombing system (LABS). As the nose of the plane went through the vertical straight up, I felt a slight jar as the MK-28 weapon was kicked loose. The bomb would continue in its vertical trajectory up to thirteen thousand feet, then it would fall straight down as gravity overcame the upward velocity imparted by the airplane. As the A-4 completed a full half-circle of a loop and reversed direction in a vertical turn, I shifted my eyes from the cockpit instruments to outside the canopy. The plane was on its back with the nose falling through the horizon. At this point I rolled the plane right side up. I was in a thirty-degree dive with the engine at full power. This was the escape maneuver—a half Cuban eight—to put the maximum distance between the delivery aircraft and the MK-28 bomb. It had been set for a five-hundred-foot airburst, an altitude that would maximize the blast effect of the 350-kiloton thermonuclear warhead—more than twenty times the explosive power of the A-bomb that destroyed Hiroshima in World War II.

As the A4 streaked away on the deck from the bomb's trajectory, I watched in the rearview mirrors on each side of the cockpit plexiglass canopy for the explosion. And there it was. Not the blinding flash of a thermonuclear detonation in this case, but the dirty brown smoke from the TNT "trigger" that would have set off the charge of plutonium if the thermonuclear warhead had been installed. This had been an operational test of a war reserve weapon, selected at random from the nuclear-weapons stockpile. These operational tests, which were conducted periodically to ensure the reliability of the stockpile, attempted to duplicate as closely as possible all the conditions of a war shot. In this case, the carrier had been off the coast of Florida, and the bomb was dropped on a ground-zero target at the specially instrumented bombing range at the Eglin Air Force Base Proving Grounds just east of Pensacola, Florida, on the Gulf Coast. Theodolites on the range had tracked both my delivery aircraft and then the bomb through its trajectory to the detonation to measure every parameter in the delivery sequence.

The exercise was not over. To get back to the carrier, I had to rendezvous with a tanker aircraft from the *Essex* that should be waiting in a port orbit at ten thousand feet over the Gulf of Mexico, twenty miles south of the eastern tip of Padre Island. Still climbing to thirty thousand feet to conserve fuel, I spotted the twin-engined AJ-1 "Savage" tanker below me in a port orbit at ten thousand feet. He was trailing a refueling drogue, a large funnel at the end of a fifty-foot fuel line. Because we were still in radio silence, I joined up on his wing and we exchanged hand signals. The tanker straightened out on a steady course at 250 knots and I plugged the A4D-2's refueling probe into the drogue and took aboard seven thousand pounds of fuel, three and a half tons of JP-5. Then breaking away, I began the long flight back to the carrier. When the carrier was finally in sight, the landing signal officer was flashing the Morse code letter "Charlie," which meant that I had a ready deck on arrival and was to land immediately. The task group was still in radio silence.

Within an hour, Eglin Proving Ground had followed up with a message to the *Essex* reporting the results of the exercise. The weapon had detonated within three hundred yards of ground zero, which was not as good as a direct hit but was within a radius that would have achieved the desired amount of damage at the constructive target, a Soviet fighter strip in Hungary.

The operational test had been part of a three-day exercise in which the *Essex* had participated, simulating a conflict in the Mediterranean that had escalated from an incident in Berlin to all-out nuclear war. The flight flown for the test of the war reserve weapon had been the replication of a profile from a launch point in the Tyrrhenian Sea to strike an airfield in the Balkans from which Soviet fighter aircraft would operate to intercept Strategic Air Command (SAC) bombers en route to targets in the Soviet Union. The U.S. Navy was committed to maintain, at all times, two carriers in the Mediterranean, each of which had an embarked squadron with the mission of special-weapons delivery, "special weapons" being the euphemism for nuclear bombs. These were tactical nukes that could be targeted against "tactical" targets, as opposed to strategic targets, which were a responsibility of the SAC.

FIGHTER SQUADRON 83

I had assumed command of Fighter Squadron 83 at the Naval Air Station Oceana, just outside Virginia Beach, Virginia, in September 1956. At that time the squadron was equipped with the Chance Vought F7U-3M Cutlass, a supersonic carrier fighter, the first to be armed with missiles only—no guns. The Cutlass was a disaster, but an ambitious disaster. It was a giant step forward in aircraft capability, but a little too long a stride. The technology of a supersonic, after-burning, tailless plane was too much for the carrier squadrons to maintain and the pilots to fly. The carrier landing-accident rate was out of sight. On VF-83's previous cruise to the Mediterranean in the Sixth Fleet, the carrier's commanding officer had gotten fed up with the Cutlass's poor maintenance availability and deck crashes its first month on board and put the whole squadron ashore for the rest of the deployment at the French Naval Air Base at Port Lyautey in Morocco, where the U.S. Navy kept a small fleet air support facility.

The one useful aspect of this tour in the F7U was the experience of flying supersonic jets whose armament consisted solely of missiles. The F7U-3M was equipped to carry four radar-guided Sparrow I air intercept missiles. For the pilots, including myself, it was an introduction to the new tactics that would prevail in the future, as all naval fighter aircraft became equipped with air-to-air missiles as their primary offensive armament.

All of this changed in the spring of 1957, when VF-83 was changed over to a new mission of nuclear and conventional attack and equipped with the A4D-1 Skyhawk, a remarkable new production aircraft built by Douglas that had been specially designed to carry nuclear weapons. The designation of the squadron would also be changed to Attack Squadron 83, or VA-83. The primary mission of the squadron would be the delivery of tactical nuclear and thermonuclear weapons of up to 1.1 megatons yield.

This new mission required first a background security check for all of the pilots and a number of the enlisted men in the squadron, and then the successful completion of nuclear weapons training school on the part of the pilots. This was a three-week course in the design, operational use, and delivery techniques of nuclear weapons. It was a very practical course. The pilots learned everything they needed to know to deliver an atomic weapon or a small hydrogen bomb, but no more. They were not told so much that if they were captured—as they could expect to be in the real event—they would be able to help the enemy. This was not very comforting to the pilots, but it was better than flying the F7U.

When the first Skyhawk was delivered, it turned out to be an absolute delight to fly. My reaction was that the fun in flying had been returned to the pilot. The mission of special-weapons delivery required the plane to fly long distances at altitudes below five hundred feet, which would enable the planes to penetrate target areas by flying under the radar. Until this became a special-weapons delivery technique, it had been known as "flat-hatting," a popular term for forbidden low-altitude flying, which was punishable by court-martial. Now it was not only authorized, but also prescribed for the A-4s as a primary tactic for day-to-day training.

Second, the principal method of attacking a target with a nuclear bomb from an A-4 was the "over the shoulder" technique, called by the pilots an "idiot loop." In this maneuver, the plane flew over the target at a fifty-foot altitude at five hundred knots and immediately pulled into a four-G loop. As the plane passed through the vertical, a computer released the bomb, which went up to thirteen thousand feet and then fell back down on the target the pilot had just overflown. The purpose of this maneuver was to allow the delivery airplane to escape the blast effects of the nuclear weapon. After the bomb was released, and when the plane had passed through the top of the loop, the pilot completed the maneuver as a half Cuban eight, turning the plane right side up and diving for the earth to gain maximum speed and low altitude to escape. These were, in fact, low-altitude aerobatics, and engaging in them had been a court-martial offense. Now they were not only legal, but also practiced for hours on end as the idiot loop became the primary mode of A-4 special-weapons delivery.

The squadron also was capable of using conventional weapons: virtually every bomb in the inventory, forward-firing air-to-ground rockets, and guided missiles. With these dual missions, the squadron pilots were kept busy practicing their weapon techniques while at the same time maintaining the skills required for landing on a carrier. The A-4 was a light and nimble aircraft. Empty, its weight was thirteen thousand pounds. Filled with fuel and loaded with weapons, it could weigh almost twenty thousand pounds on the catapult ready for launch on a combat mission.

In the winter of 1958, the squadron flew down to the Leeward Point Naval Air Station at Guantánamo Bay, Cuba, where the Navy maintained an extensive target complex with the bombing ranges instrumented with theodolites. The range observers would triangulate the puff of smoke from the bomb impact and send it to the range-plotting station. The radio talker would then call the pilot within ten seconds, giving the exact impact spot of the practice bomb in distance and direction from the bull's eye. Direct hits on the bull's eye were not unusual as the pilots became proficient through practice, especially on windless days.

The daily flight schedule was rigorous. All pilots flew two bombing flights lasting an hour each in the morning and two in the afternoon. Each bombing flight consisted of eight idiot loops with the pilot pulling four Gs on each maneuver. These training missions carried eight 6-pound miniature bombs with a shape aerodynamically designed to give them a trajectory similar to that of a full-sized bomb. The miniature bomb had a shotgun shell, loaded with black powder, in its nose. This fired on hitting the ground, marking the bomb impact point for the theodolite operators on the bombing range.

SIXTH FLEET DEPLOYMENT

On 31 January 1958, Attack Squadron 83 embarked in the USS *Essex* and deployed to the Mediterranean for a six-month tour of duty with the Sixth Fleet. The squadron had exchanged our original A4D-1 aircraft for a new model, the A4D-2, which had an in-flight refueling capability.

This upgrade was necessary for the A4Ds to reach all of the programmed general war targets in central Europe from a larger number of launch points in the Mediterranean.

The squadron's aircraft were factory-new, and VA-83 was the first squadron to deploy to the Sixth Fleet with an in-flight refueling capability. The A4D-2 had a long probe projecting from the nose of the aircraft to receive fuel from a tanker. It also had the capability of carrying a three-hundred-gallon fuel tank that could reel out a trailing drogue to refuel other probe-equipped squadron aircraft.

The nicest aspect of the cruise, though, was the carrier's angled deck and mirror landing system. In my last squadron deployment in F9F-2 Panthers on board the *Boxer,* I had flown from a straight deck—a real nightmare, especially for jets. We got used to it, but only because we had no choice; there was nothing else. On the straight deck, the plane landed on the aft end of the carrier with all of the previously landed planes—the pack—on the forward end. There was a wire barrier that was raised and lowered to stop the landing plane from crashing into the pack if the landing pilot's hook failed to catch a wire. Often a jet that failed to catch a wire would bounce all the way over the barrier fence and crash into the pack with predictably horrible consequences. It was part of the problem of flying jets from carriers.

The angled deck changed all that. This innovative design was invented by a British carrier pilot, Rear Admiral Cunningham, Royal Navy, but was first installed on the U.S. carrier *Antietam* in 1952. The angled deck had a major influence on carrier air operations from then on. It eliminated all of the bad features of the straight deck design. The angled deck was aligned ten degrees to the left of the ship's centerline, and equipped with transverse arresting wires, it was the landing area for the carrier's planes. Landing aircraft followed a mirror beam glide path to a touchdown on the angle where its hook caught a wire. If the hook failed to engage a wire, the pilot added power and continued down the angled deck to take off and circle for another landing approach. To miss a wire and go around again was to "bolter." The axial deck became the parking area for the planes that had just landed, keeping the angled deck clear. The forward end of the straight deck was also the aircraft launching area, using the installed catapults. The angled deck had been installed on the *Essex* in 1955, a project that took almost a year in the shipyard. It was worth it, however, and all of the Navy's carriers were being converted to the angled deck at the highest priority.

Weather conditions in the Mediterranean during the winter were generally nasty, with high winds and heavy seas. In February, the commanding officer of the Essex AD Skyraider squadron crashed into the sea during an approach to a night carrier landing under stormy conditions. He was lost in the rough seas and dark night before the plane guard destroyer was able to recover him. Night air operations from carriers in the late 1950s were primitive, with inadequate ship's radars for aircraft control and a deck lighting system little better than a row of flashlights down each deck edge.

Most of VA-83's flying during the work-up phase, land-based at Oceana before going on board the carrier, concentrated on the special-weapons delivery mission. In the event of general war with the Soviet Union, SAC bombers from British bases, and SAC fields in the United States would head for their main targets inside the Soviet Union. B-52 bombers were also launched from SAC bases in the United States to orbit in the Atlantic. This put them closer to their targets in case war was declared and reduced their vulnerability to a preemptive Soviet nuclear strike on their air bases. The bombers' route to their targets overflew the Warsaw Pact countries of central Europe. The military airfields in the satellite nations were used to base Soviet and Warsaw Pact fighter planes and surface-to-air missiles to engage the strategic bombers along their penetration route. The Sixth Fleet special-weapons delivery squadrons—there were two on each carrier, one jet squadron and one propeller squadron—were responsible for neutralizing these satellite air defense bases with nuclear weapons. Each VA-83 pilot had an assigned nuclear weapon stored in the *Valley Forge's* magazines and a specific target in the satellites. The information on each target was contained in a top secret dossier available only to the specified pilot and one assigned air intelligence officer.

My target in the Rollback Campaign, as it was called, was a fighter strip in Bulgaria. My flight profile was to climb to thirty-eight thousand feet over the northern Tyrrhenian Sea and then let down to five hundred feet north of the Carpathian Mountains and penetrate the target area underneath the radar coverage. Upon reaching my assigned airdrome, I would pull up in an idiot loop, and my bomb, a tactical thermonuclear weapon, would be released over the center of the field. After delivering my bomb, I would then fly to a designated geographic location near Bari on the coast of Italy, trusting that the SAC computers at Omaha had provided me an exit route that kept me clear of a friendly bomber's ground zero.

At this rendezvous point would be a Navy AJ-2 Savage tanker from the *Valley Forge*, circling at ten thousand feet as the pilot waited to transfer sufficient fuel to get us back to the carrier. The flight planning provided the A4 pilots with only ten minutes of fuel remaining as we arrived at the rendezvous point.

The *Essex*, with its embarked aircraft, was scheduled to complete its Sixth Fleet deployment in July 1958 and return to Norfolk. That was not to be. The CNO was then Adm. Arleigh Burke, and Burke had astutely foreseen problems in the Middle East and wanted to have naval forces in the theater to provide whatever presence and military capability the national command authority thought appropriate. Therefore, when the carrier that was to relieve the *Essex* on station sailed into the western Mediterranean, the *Essex* was retained in the eastern Med so that the Navy would have three ready carriers in the Mediterranean should trouble erupt. Admiral Burke similarly extended the Marine infantry battalion embarked in the amphibious ready group deployed to the Sixth Fleet. When White House orders came to land Marines in Lebanon, there were two battalions of U.S. Marines, rather then the normal one, available for the operation.

LEBANON

In September 1958 the situation in Lebanon was coming to a boil. A full-sized Middle East conflict was possible unless immediate steps were taken to stabilize the situation. The president ordered the Sixth Fleet to land Marines at Beirut under the cover of air support from the three carriers. The Marine landings were unopposed, and the show of force on the ground and in the air quickly calmed down the belligerents, preempting a major conflagration in the area.

The joint commander of the Navy, Army, and Air Force components in the landing force was my father, Adm. James L. Holloway Jr., USN, who was regularly assigned as commander in chief, Eastern Atlantic and Mediterranean, a JCS theater command, with the additional contingency responsibility as "commander, Specified Command, Middle East," another and separate JCS force. This specified command by designation was to be activated when required to conduct military operations in the Middle East, which at that time was on the eastern boundary of CinCLAnt and the western boundary of CinCPac. That was before Central Command (CentCom) was created.

The Marine landings and U.S. occupation of the Beirut area provoked a strong and unpleasant reaction from the Soviet Union. Within seventy-two hours after the Marines had hit the beach, Khrushchev made a statement from the Kremlin that the USSR "viewed this American adventuring with alarm, and that the Soviet Union was very capable of turning the Sixth Fleet aircraft carriers into flaming coffins for the American sailors." Meanwhile, the Sixth Fleet carriers' fighters and attack planes were maintaining a constant air presence over Lebanon loaded with conventional bombs and forward-firing rockets. But with the belligerent statements from the Kremlin, the nuclear capability of the Sixth Fleet was placed in a higher readiness condition.

VA-83 was ordered to have two planes on nuclear strike alert. The first A4D-2 was on the port catapult with a 300-kiloton nuclear weapon in its centerline station, the pilot in the cockpit, and a starter cart alongside and plugged in. A Marine with an automatic weapon stood guard over the bomb. Behind the port catapult was a second VA-83 A4D-2, also with a thermonuclear weapon hung on the center station. This pilot was not in the cockpit but allowed to relax next to his aircraft. Otherwise he was ready to go, fully briefed with his plane fully preflighted. These were designated the ready aircraft, and they gave rise to an alarming incident.

I was just entering the squadron ready room to get ready for my next hop over Lebanon when I heard the intercom from the ship's operation center tersely order, "Launch the ready standby aircraft." It was like being hit in the solar plexus. Once an A4D-2 with a nuclear weapon was launched, the plane with the weapon attached could not land back on the carrier, so this could not be a practice takeoff. When the nuclear-ready planes went, we could expect them to go all the way.

I ran up to the flight deck as quickly as I could and headed for the port catapult to find out what was going on. When I got to the forward end of the carrier's flight deck, an A4D was just being launched, but it was on the starboard catapult. What had not registered with me was that VA-83 was also maintaining two Skyhawks loaded with forward firing aircraft rockets (FFARs), to be on call if the Marines on the ground in

Lebanon encountered trouble from hostile forces and asked for close-air support. That was the ready plane that had been launched, not the nuclear-ready bird. I had been badly shaken for a moment.

Within a week after the landings, the fiery rhetoric of the Kremlin had subsided and the nuclear bombs were returned to the carrier's magazines. VA-83 settled down to flying daily patrols along the borders of Lebanon to detect and dissuade unfriendly Arabs from entering the country. Several of our pilots asked how to identify an unfriendly Arab. The best answer that could be provided by the air intelligence officer was that "an unfriendly Arab shoots at you." The Lebanon affair was good experience for the task group pilots. Each aircrew was flying three flights every two days, and these were interesting sorties with a real mission. Although few planes were fired at, one of our Skyhawks was hit in the wing by what appeared to be rounds from a muzzle-loading gun. This was the first occasion a Skyhawk was damaged by hostile fire, and it was a modest precursor of things to come. More than 280 A-4 Skyhawks were to be shot down by enemy fire during the Vietnam War. The A-4 was the principal light attack plane in the Navy from 1954 to 1970.

These operations, conducting border patrols around Lebanon and maintaining station over Beirut for on-call missions to support the Marines, continued for thirty days without a break. Then, on 15 September, the *Essex* was ordered to proceed to Athens and prepare to end her deployment with Sixth Fleet, depart the Mediterranean, and to return to Norfolk. At this point, the *Essex* was in the ninth month of what had been scheduled as a six-month tour of duty with the Sixth Fleet.

At about 1700 on the first day of liberty in Athens, a large contingent of uniformed sailors with Shore Patrol arm brassards arrived ashore with instructions to round up all *Essex* personnel and instruct them to return to the ship immediately. This sweep through the better bars and restaurants of Athens during the dining hour was successful in making sure that all but two or three of the ship's and air wing's people were back on board at 0600 the next morning when the *Essex* weighed anchor and steamed off toward the Suez Canal.

PACIFIC BOUND

There were no announcements from the ship's captain as to the future plans of the ship, but the crew observed a wooden platform being erected on the centerline of the flight deck, sixty feet tall, with a walkway from the platform to the ship's island structure, which was on the starboard side. One old-timer said that meant the ship was going through the Suez Canal. This was to allow a local pilot to con the ship using the carrier's jack staff as the directional reference line. If so, it would be the first time in history that a U.S. aircraft carrier had made a transit of this waterway. The concern, of course, was that it made the warship vulnerable to being bottled up in the canal as had been many commercial ships in the aftermath of the Yom Kippur War. It was not until the carrier was entering the canal that the crew was informed that the *Essex* would go through Suez and then proceed through the Indian Ocean to the Taiwan Strait. Our mission was to reinforce the carrier force of the Pacific Fleet in facing down a Chinese Communist threat to invade Quemoy and Matsu, two islands belonging to the Republic of China on the island of Taiwan.

The transit of the Suez Canal proved uneventful for the *Essex*. The carrier was part of a thirty-ship convoy. The canal runs traffic north and south on alternate days. The carrier positioned photo planes, which were indistinguishable from the fighters onboard, on both port and starboard catapults, where they took pictures with their side-looking cameras all the way through the canal for intelligence purposes.

From Suez, the *Essex* proceeded at twenty-seven knots, her maximum sustained speed, on the most direct route to the Taiwan Straits. Because of the need to make the best progress, the carrier did not attempt to fly aircraft, which would have involved turning into the wind for protracted periods of time to launch and recover her air wing. After a six-day sprint, the *Essex* joined Task Force 77, the Seventh Fleet carrier task force, operating off the coast of mainland China within the claimed territorial waters of the People's Republic of China (PRC) but not flying any military aircraft closer to the landmass than the three-mile territorial waters limit the United States recognized at that time.

VA-83's pilots were immediately launched with the air wing's fighters upon arrival in the Task Force 77 operating area to conduct "training" operations at an altitude and a proximity to the landmass to ensure they would be seen clearly on the Chinese early warning radars. The carrier aircraft formations were to proceed up to the three-mile limit. There was an obvious absence of any Chinese fighter reaction to the presence of the U.S. Navy's aircraft.

A week before the *Essex*'s arrival, several Chinese fighters had ventured into the airspace protected by Task Force 77's planes and were immediately shot down. There had been no Chinese Communist air activity offshore since that time. There were seven *Essex*-class carriers operating in the Taiwan Straits at this time. Never less than four in the Task Force 77 carrier disposition actually operating their aircraft in the vicinity of the offshore islands.

After two weeks on station with Task Force 77 conducting the show-of-force operations, the *Essex* was sent to Subic Bay in the Philippines for upkeep maintenance and R&R for the crew. At this juncture, one of the Pacific Fleet carriers was detached to return to its homeport after only seven months' deployment, a circumstance that annoyed the *Essex*'s crew, who had now been away from home ten months.

In talking to my counterpart commanders of A4D squadrons on the Pacific Fleet carriers, I learned that they were not flying their A4Ds at night from the carriers. Because of the unsuitability of the A4D models in the fleet at that time for night or all-weather flying, due to the plane's inherent instability and its lack of suitable cockpit instrumentation, there had been a succession of accidents at night in which several experienced and senior squadron pilots were lost. In one A4D squadron both the CO and the operations officer were killed in accidents during the same night carrier recovery. The morale in the A4D squadrons deployed to the Seventh Fleet was so troubled that several distinguished aviators commanding Skyhawk squadrons prevailed upon the admirals commanding the deployed carrier divisions in TF 77 to limit the Skyhawks to daylight flights. Unfortunately, the captain of *Essex* did not consider that the Pacific Fleet directives restricting A4Ds at night applied to Air Task Group 1. VF-83 continued to fly their share of night operations.

At about this time the commanding officer of the F2H-2 Banshee night fighter squadron, a close friend and classmate, Cdr. Bill Allen, was killed when making a night approach for landing on the *Valley Forge*, as his plane flew into the water several miles in the wake of the ship. This was a blow to Air Task Group 2 and to me. Bill Allen was well liked, and he was considered to have a promising future in the Navy.

In mid-November, the *Essex* received orders detaching the carrier from the Seventh Fleet and directing her to return to Norfolk, Virginia, via the Cape of Good Hope around the southern tip of South America.

After a brief stop at Subic Bay to offload certain equipment and supplies in short supply in the western Pacific, the carrier bent on twenty-seven knots for her maximum sustained speed for the voyage home. As in the case with oil-fired ships, the carrier would have to make three refuelings en route. The first was in Ceylon, the second at Capetown, and the third at Rio de Janeiro. In each case, two nights were spent in these seaports to allow the crew to experience a liberty in these exotic places. The carrier arrived in its homeport of Jacksonville, Florida, on 15 December 1958, and VA-83 flew to NAS Oceana, having been away from home for a total of eleven months on what had started out to be a six-month cruise.

On this cruise, two of the four original squadron commanders had been killed in aircraft accidents involving landing on a carrier at night. VA-83 had been called upon to step into the breach, flying night fighter missions when the Banshees were grounded and continuing to fly at night in spite of the inadequacies of their aircraft and the primitive nature of electronic facilities aboard ship. This kind of experience was not atypical of the carrier cruises during the Cold War. The carriers were essential to the success of the forward strategy, and our potential adversaries had to be convinced of the carriers' full capabilities. So the limits of both people and equipment were pushed to the extremes. Experienced leaders were lost to the pressures of the Cold War, but VA-83 was fortunate on this cruise. We brought everyone home.

8

The Pentagon, a Seaplane Tender, and Typhoons

In 1959 Washington, D.C., was the capital of the free world and the Pentagon was headquarters for the free-world military forces that were confronting the USSR and its Communist bloc allies in the Cold War. Within the Pentagon were the secretary of defense, the Office of the Secretary of Defense, the Department of Defense, the chairman of the Joint Chiefs of Staff, the Joint Staff (JS), and the four services, the Army, Navy, Air Force, and Marine Corps. In those days, the commandant of the Marine Corps was not a full-fledged member of the JCS but attended all meetings and could vote only on matters directly affecting the Corps (in 2005 a Marine Corps general was appointed chairman of the JCS). In 1959, the chief of naval operations, the uniformed head of the Navy, was Adm. Arleigh Burke. Burke was CNO for three successive two-year terms, the only service chief to have been reappointed twice. His wisdom, energy, and accomplishments set him apart as an inspirational military leader.

Washington, D.C., is considered a required tour of duty for every aspiring naval officer. It was deemed almost impossible to be selected for flag rank without a tour of duty in the Pentagon or the Washington Navy Bureaus. The time to go was as a commander or fresh-caught captain. So in 1959, I was pleased to receive orders detaching me from command of Attack Squadron 83 after two years and sending me to the Pentagon. I was a commander at the time, with a wife and three children, and my father, Adm. James L. Holloway Jr., had retired as a four-star and was living quietly in Philadelphia. I make a point of this because there has often been a tacit presumption that my father was in a position to advance my career as I gained seniority in the Navy. On the contrary, as a retired officer he had little or no influence over his own future, much less mine.

I was detached from my squadron in May and ordered to report for duty in the Pentagon on the Air Weapon System Analysis Staff of Vice Adm. Robert B. Pirie, the deputy chief of naval operations for air warfare, or DCNO (Air). My first assignment was as all weather flight coordinator, developing improved equipment, tactics, and procedures for operating aircraft off carriers at night and in all weather conditions. Although I served in this position for only four months before being drafted as executive assistant to the deputy chief of naval operations for air, I did leave a modest legacy to naval aviation. At the annual All Weather Flight Conference at the Naval Air Test Center, Patuxent River, in 1959, I introduced a proposal that would influence the way carrier air operations would be conducted in the future. It was a concept based upon my experiences flying A4Ds at night in the fleet.

During and since World War II, aircraft returning to a carrier for landing would rendezvous over the ship in orbits at different altitudes depending upon aircraft type—fighters, dive bombers, torpedo planes— awaiting the signal for recovery. This signal would not occur until all of the planes scheduled to land had joined up in a mass formation over the carrier and all aircraft were accounted for. This seemed like a waste of time and fuel in the jet age. I remembered my own experience as a flight leader in Bombing Squadron 3 in the USS *Kearsarge* in 1947. Being the last squadron in the landing order, the SB2Cs had to circle the ship for as long as half an hour before commencing the letdown for landing. This was time that could have been more profitably used by conducting mission training rather than boring holes in the sky.

The proposed system gave each aircraft scheduled for the next recovery a specific time to be at the ramp, that is, a landing time. Then it was up to the pilot and the ship's air controllers, working together, to have that plane at the ramp at the required time. Furthermore, instead of having one landing procedure for daylight operations and then an entirely separate procedure for night or bad weather, the doctrine called for all carrier recoveries to use the same flight procedures both night and day and under all conditions of weather. The purpose of this latter provision was to familiarize the pilots with the procedures that they would be using during the more difficult flying conditions. They would not be changing to a different procedure when landing conditions were unfavorable but would practice low-visibility procedures on every flight, without loss of flight time available for primary mission training. This procedure was adopted for standard use in the fleet but was replaced several years later to better adapt to the characteristics of the jet aircraft that were then entering the fleet in numbers.

DEPUTY CHIEF OF NAVAL OPERATIONS
FOR AIR WARFARE

In the late 1950s the DCNO (Air) was a very powerful position in the Office of the Chief of Naval Operations (OpNav). Located in the Pentagon, DCNO (Air) had the responsibility for all of the aviation programs of the Navy: carriers, aircraft, people, and weapons. Management of aviation personnel in the Navy was something of a unique responsibility for a DCNO, as that responsibility had been assigned as a specific task of the Bureau of Naval Personnel. At that time virtually half of all personnel in the Navy were concerned with aviation in one capacity or another. The position of DCNO (Air) appeared on the Pentagon organization charts as OP-05, and that is how the office was familiarly referred to.

In 1958 the incumbent OP-05 was Adm. Robert Pirie. He was what was popularly known as one of the "Barons" because of the territory and the people in the Navy that he controlled. The other Barons were in charge of the submarine forces and the surface warfare component of the Navy. At this time, the aviators and the submariners were the only two branches of line officers who wore a warfare distinguishing insignia above the ribbons on their working and dress uniforms. The aviators wore gold wings and the submariners had their treasured dolphins. Later I had the pleasure and distinction of introducing the comparable surface warfare officer pin when I was CNO.

Of all the Pentagon Barons, DCNO (Air) was probably the most powerful and independent. He was the only warfare deputy who controlled his own people in spite of the charter of the chief of naval personnel, which gave BuPers the responsibility for complete Navy personnel management. The Office of Aviation Personnel was located in the BuPers office spaces, but the rear admiral in charge was a naval aviator and reported to Admiral Pirie as well as to BuPers. Through aviation officer detailing, Pirie exercised a very tight control over all aviation matters in the Navy. He supervised the office that detailed all officers, from students to rear admirals to aviation billets, within the Navy, including the aviation flight surgeons.

As a frequent briefer to the admiral on matters relating to the Air Weapon System Analysis Staff, I had established something of a rapport with Pirie. In January 1959 I was ordered into the DCNO (Air) front office as Pirie's executive assistant, OP-05A, a captain's billet. The OP-05A was privy to all of the DCNO (Air)'s business, sitting in on the admiral's conferences as a note taker and listening in on his telephone calls in order to prepare memos, aide-memoirs, and drafting action taking directives for signature by the DCNO (Air).

NAVAL AIR TRAINING AND OPERATING PROCEDURES

Pirie at that time had four rear admirals reporting directly to him and exercised a strong influence over the vice admiral who was chief of the Bureau of Aeronautics, the technical command responsible for the design, acquisition, production, and maintenance of all naval aircraft. DCNO (Air) also had the responsibility—as the CNO's deputy—for developing and drafting the military requirements for the design of naval aircraft and for budgeting their acquisition. Although the executive assistant's ostensible duties might have been largely administrative, Pirie was collegial in his management style and sought the views of all of his staff officers, especially those with recent fleet experience. I was close to Pirie and still fresh from the fleet, and as such I frequently was asked for my private opinions after a conference when the others had left Pirie's office. I was careful not to abuse this confidence by pushing my own views, but my relationship was responsible for a seminal development that affected a major change in naval aviation operational standardization.

Up until 1959, pilots' handbooks were much like owner's manuals for new automobiles. They described the mechanics of how to operate an aircraft but not how to employ it as a carrier-based weapon system. The handbook might describe how to lower the landing gear, but it didn't tell you how to land—the proper airspeeds, altitudes, and techniques.

Pirie overheard me one day in his outer office discussing carrier landing techniques in the A4D aircraft with several fellow Skyhawk pilots. The question was whether to make the carrier approach with speed brakes extended or speed brakes closed, the regular position for normal flight. Speed brakes on the A4D were large, rectangular flat panels that were hydraulically extended from the plane's fuselage by a cockpit control lever to slow the aircraft to controllable speeds in steep dives. With brakes extended, the pilot would need more engine rpm to maintain his approach speed of 128 knots. Then if the pilot was given a wave-off—instructed to go around again for another pass—his engine was already turning up at high rpm and would reach maximum power more quickly. A characteristic of jet engines is their slow acceleration to full power because of the need for the turbine to overcome inertia when increasing rpm. Reciprocating engines, on the other hand, have almost instantaneous reaction to full throttle. The other school of thought was to leave the speed brakes in and the plane in a clean configuration, where it inherently was more aerodynamically responsive. Pirie asked the two pilots, both former A-4 Skyhawk squadron commanders, which technique their squadron used. One said brakes in and the other said brakes out; a third former CO said it was the individual pilot's choice.

Pirie seemed surprised at this apparent lack of uniformity and asked me to see him privately. I was gratified to have this invitation to talk to him about a subject to which I had given much thought as a pilot. I explained to Pirie what I saw as the shortcomings of the existing pilots' handbooks: They didn't cover operational flying, and there were no other documents that took up where the handbook left off, at least none that were published for compliance on a fleet-wide basis. I proposed that one of the Navy's experimental squadrons, Development Squadron 4 or the Service Test Division at the Naval Air Test Center, Patuxent River, evaluate all operational aircraft to establish the optimum parameters for configuration, power, weight, altitude, and airspeeds for each naval aircraft in all standard maneuvers. This would include takeoff, landing, carrier procedures, weapons delivery, air-to-air refueling—in fact, everything.

Then these optimum procedures would be published to the fleet and the training command as mandatory standard operating procedures for all pilots in all squadrons. This would standardize training and greatly improve the interoperability of flight operations among squadrons.

Pirie agreed and immediately decided to set up an office in OP-05 to get the project going. He called a meeting of his branch heads, rear admirals and senior captains, all men of extensive aviation experience. Surprisingly enough, there were some strong objections. In fact, the head of the Air Weapons Systems Analysis Staff, a World War II ace with a dozen Zeros to his credit, took the position that such standardization would stifle the initiative of individual pilots and hamper squadron commanders from developing innovative tactics. I suggested that there had to be an optimum or best technique for each aircraft type conducting standard maneuvers, and that would be determined by trained and expert test pilots. As for tactics, the proposed standardization process would stop short of prescribing tactics but would formalize the best aeronautical flight maneuvering techniques upon which to build multiaircraft formation tactics.

Vice Admiral Pirie's ad hoc jury gave the go-ahead to the concept and it was given the title Naval Air Training and Operating Procedures Standardization, NATOPS for short (it subsequently has always been referred to by this acronym). Pirie requested from the CNO authority to establish a new office branch in OP-05 to move ahead on this project. But at the CNO Executive Panel, with all of the Barons present, the DCNO for fleet operations and readiness insisted that the project fell under his charter and the new branch should be established in his directorate (OP-03). Arleigh Burke, the CNO, agreed with OP-03, and when Pirie saw that the decision had been made, he simply asked if his officers could participate, and the arrangement was accepted without objection or rancor.

NATOPS took a year or so to get to the fleet and another year to become full-blown dogma. When I reported to command of the carrier *Enterprise*, I found that all ten squadrons and aviation units on board were operating in accordance with their individual NATOPS manuals. This was especially useful, considering that the carrier's embarked air wing included four squadrons of A-4 Skyhawks.

CARRIER COMMAND

I was one of four early selectees for captain on the 1961 promotion list. One of the others was Cdr. Elmo R. Zumwalt Jr., a classmate and friend who later became the CNO immediately preceding me. I had hoped to be assigned to an air group command upon leaving the Pentagon, but now I would be too senior. Instead, my most promising assignment would be to a "deep-draft" logistics ship that I would have to command successfully to qualify for selection to command a carrier.

Command of an aircraft carrier is the *sine qua non* of a naval aviator's career. A naval aviator could not hope for selection to flag rank without a successful tour of carrier command duty. The importance of carrier command, in terms of both an officer's career chances and ensuring that these complex ships would receive the most talented commanding officers available, had resulted in a unique selection system, the "carrier list." When a naval aviator reached the rank of captain, his record of duty assignments and fitness reports was reviewed by a special panel of senior aviators convened by the Bureau of Naval Personnel's Aviation Detailing Section. Then each aviation captain was given an overall grade by the panel as to his qualification to command a carrier based upon his professional performance. These aviation captains were then placed on a lineal list, ranked according to their grade. This was clearly a competitive process. There were in the fleet at that time sixteen CVAs and nine antisubmarine warfare (ASW) carriers. The first sixteen captains on the carrier list were earmarked for attack carrier command, the next nine were programmed for an ASW carrier, and those below the cut, at twenty-seven, could hope to be ordered to command a naval air station or one of the many other captain assignments in the Navy. The highest on the carrier list would be assigned particularly desirable commands, such as a large-deck *Forrestal*-class carrier or as the commissioning commanding officer of a newly constructed carrier. When an aviation captain made the cut of the carrier list, he was first ordered to his "deep draft." This was a service force ship such as a supply vessel, an oiler, or an amphibious transport. For most aviators, it would be their first experience on the bridge of a large—ten thousand tons or more—steam-powered, twin-screw naval vessel. This one year's experience, plus their time on board carriers as a pilot, would prepare them for command of an aircraft carrier on their subsequent sea duty assignment.

Several months after selection for captain, Pirie informed me that I was ranked number one on the 1961 edition of the carrier list. He asked me if I was interested in the USS *Enterprise*, the Navy's only nuclear-powered aircraft carrier, then under construction at Newport News Shipbuilding and Dry Dock Company. The first and second commanding officers had already been chosen and were undergoing their nuclear training with Vice Adm. Hyman G. Rickover. If I was interested and Rickover approved of me, I would be the third CO. If rejected by Rickover—as was the case with more than half of the captains nominated for the *Enterprise* to Rickover—I would still get command of a *Forrestal*-class carrier.

The selection process for nuclear-powered vessels, which up to recently had applied only to submarines, began with a panel of line officers convened in BuPers to select those officers best fitted for command of the type of nuclear-powered ship under consideration. Then that list was submitted to Admiral Rickover. Next, Rickover and his staff would interview the candidates and screen out those officers not considered technically capable of completing the rigorous nuclear-power training course or judged to be lacking the sense of commitment Rickover demanded of the people in his program. Finally, the Rickover-approved list would be sent to BuPers, where the prospective commanding officers would be picked from the Rickover-approved names after some further consultation with the OpNav deputy in charge of the appropriate warfare community. Not having gone to postgraduate training after graduating from the Naval Academy, I didn't have a technical specialty, and a nuclear-power qualification seemed to be advantageous for the future Navy. So I told Pirie I was willing to put in the hours of study and training required to qualify for a nuclear ship command.

Pirie nominated me to Rickover for the *Enterprise* on the basis of my number-one ranking on the carrier list. Then, within a month, Adm. George Anderson, a naval aviator who had relieved Admiral Burke as CNO, told Pirie that the procedure for selecting the captain of the *Enterprise* would be changed. Admiral Anderson said that he, the CNO, would select the nuclear carrier skippers and simply tell Rickover to see that they were adequately trained. Furthermore, George Anderson had his own candidate in mind, another naval aviator with a brilliant record as a carrier aviator and a test pilot.

AIDE TO PRESIDENT KENNEDY

Another perturbation intruded to confuse the direction of my career. Rear Adm. Evan "Pete" Aurand was a legendary Navy fighter pilot, an ace in World War II who flew F6Fs against the Japanese. After the war he had been selected to command the Navy's first operational carrier jet fighter squadron, equipped with F6U Pirates. The importance of this command and how well the squadron performed would have a signifi- cant influence on the future of naval aviation. Pete had done well in this assignment and upon leaving the squadron was selected to be naval aide to President Eisenhower. The three military aides to the president in those days were extremely influential. There was no national security advisor to the president, the SecDef was not technically fluent in military equipment and operations, and the military aides who traveled with the president were always on hand and available to respond to questions from the president on military matters. Pete Aurand was said to have sold Eisenhower on the importance of aircraft carriers.

After his stint in the White House, Pete had come to the Pentagon for duty in OpNav, the CNO head quarters staff. One morning in November 1960, after John F. Kennedy's election but before his inaugu- ration, Pete barged into Admiral Pirie's outer office—as was his style— and motioned for me to follow him into the DCNO's inner sanctum. With a minimum of prelude except to remind Pirie that he had been naval aide to President Eisenhower, Pete made his pitch: Jim Holloway should be nominated to serve as naval aide to President John F. Kennedy, who at this time would just be putting together his White House staff. Pete rattled off what he considered to be my qualifications: not too old or too young, a combat veteran decorated in both World War II and Korea, recent fleet experience, and a solid background in Navy plans and policy as the result of my current assignment in the E ring of the Pentagon. Moreover, he said, Jim is shorter than Kennedy and that is important for an aide who accompanies his senior to ceremonial affairs!

Pirie thought it was a great idea, and the two of them went to see the CNO, Adm. Arleigh Burke, who also agreed, although he hadn't given it any previous thought. So the nomination, drafted by the chief of naval personnel and signed by the CNO, went to the White House. Up to this point, I had barely been consulted. When I asked, "What about the deep draft and carrier?" the answer was, "Jim, you have to make this sacrifice for the Navy. Once the tour as aide is over, you can name your next assignment." Well, I thought, I can't dream up a comeback comment for that.

So with my future up in the air, I went back to my desk outside the office for the deputy chief of naval operations for air warfare, arranging appointments, screening messages, and editing drafts of correspondence from 0715 to 2000 and waited for the decision.

The selection of Kennedy's aide was a surprise, and it happened fast. A Naval Academy classmate of mine, Cdr. Tazwell T. Shepherd, USN, was chosen for the job by the White House. He had not been nominated by the Navy or the DoD. Taz, as he was known, had been a friend of mine since we had roomed together in an Annapolis boarding house as callow youths, seventeen years old, waiting to take our physical exams to get into the Naval Academy in 1939. Taz had been nominated by Senator Sparkman of Alabama, the senate majority leader, directly to JFK. The senator was Tazwell T. Shepherd's father-in-law. It turned out to be a great assignment. Taz was perfect for what the president wanted in his naval aide, and he did a great job.

NATIONAL WAR COLLEGE

In June 1971 my tour in the Pentagon was up and I was detached from OP-05 and ordered to the National War College (NWC) at Fort McNair, the Department of Defense's senior educational service school. I had entered the War College in the summer of 1961 in the class of 1962. My classmates included captains and colonels from the Navy, Marines, Army, and Air Force as well as employees of the State Department, CIA, and NSA, all of which had quotas to be filled by career officers at the executive level. It was a watershed experience in my professional career and served me well in later flag-level dealings at top government assignments. The NWC class of 1962 also included several of my Naval Academy classmates who later rose to distinction. Jim Calvert had been one of the earlier nuclear submariners and had surfaced his submarine at the North Pole, a feat that made headlines and gained him membership in the exclusive Explorer's Club. Calvert, along with Bill Anderson, another early nuclear submariner classmate, had been selected for captain two years early.

Another classmate attending NWC with me was Cdr. Elmo Zumwalt, the nineteenth CNO. Captain Calvert was voted the outstanding member of the NWC in our class of 1962.

Meanwhile, back in the Pentagon, two names had been submitted to the Division of Naval Reactors as prospective commanding officers for the *Enterprise* and one was mine. Rickover, in his authority under the Atomic Energy Commission (AEC), had pointed out to CNO Admiral Anderson that the CNO had the authority to order an officer to command of a nuclear-powered ship but the law gave Rickover the responsibility of determining whether or not an officer was qualified to actually operate such a vessel. So he, Rickover, would make that determination only if and when the officer completed Rickover's training. Rickover alone had the authority to select officers for nuclear training, based upon his evaluation of their engineering ability. He still insisted that the process would be for the CNO to nominate qualified aviation line captains until Rickover found one he considered also qualified by his own technical standards. Adm. George Anderson was furious, but it did him little good. The law was on Rickover's side, and so was Congress. After all, Congress had written into the law just what Rickover considered necessary to ensure that adequate nuclear safeguards for the Naval Reactor Program would remain in place through the selection of those, and only those, whom Rickover considered smart enough and sufficiently dedicated.

SEAPLANE TENDER

After graduating from the NWC and having been promoted to captain, I was ordered to command of the USS *Salisbury Sound*, a fourteen-thousand-ton seaplane tender operating out of Okinawa as flagship of the Taiwan Patrol Forces. The *Salisbury Sound*'s mission was to support a squadron of sea-based patrol planes, Martin P5M Mariners. These were large flying boats capable of long-range ocean reconnaissance. The operating concept was for the seaplane tender to move forward to a remote location such as the Ryukyus and set up a buoyed seadrome in a sheltered atoll or bay, complete with runway lights and aircraft mooring buoys for the seaplanes. The planes would be fully serviced with the seaplane tender's aircraft rearming boats and refueling craft. Then, with its personnel boats, the tender would pick up the flight crews, bring them back to the tender, and provide messing in a wardroom and berthing in comfortable staterooms, and deliver freshly rested and fed crews to fully fueled and rearmed patrol planes for their next day's missions. The *Salisbury Sound* was fully prepared to provide the complete range of operations support, even nuclear depth-charge capability in its magazine, to be fully ready for action, even in the event of the balloon going up in a nuclear war with the USSR.

The *Salisbury Sound*, known affectionately to her crew as the *Sally Maru*, was one of the *Compass* class of seaplane tenders. The ship was typical of a naval auxiliary, displacing fourteen thousand tons with a crew of about 260, not counting the additional people, such as pilots, crews, maintenance men, and an embarked admiral and his staff, who would be on board when the ship was actually tending seaplanes. These vessels had considerable capabilities. From amidships forward, the class had the superstructure of a fleet tender, with staterooms, flag spaces, and the wardroom mess above the main deck. Above the bridge was a Mark 37 director to control two single, enclosed, 5-inch dual-purpose gun mounts installed on the foredeck. Below the navigation bridge level were the flag bridge and the flag plotting room for the embarked admiral and his staff. The after half of the ship was taken up by a commodious aircraft hangar and a large, unobstructed aircraft parking deck served by two massive cranes, one on each side, capable of lifting on board the P5M seaplane.

The *Salisbury Sound* was homeported in Alameda, California, and deployed six months out of an eighteen-month cycle to White Beach on the Japanese island of Okinawa to serve as flagship for the commander, Taiwan Patrol Force. The staff was homeported at White Beach, a very pleasant piece of real estate located on the shores of Buckner Bay. The installations were minimal but included quarters for the staff dependents, bachelor's quarters, a pleasant officer's club, a chief petty officer's club, and an enlisted recreation center. The beach itself was a spectacular strip of sparkling white sand on Buckner Bay, protected by extensive coral reefs. A special pier at White Beach had been constructed for mooring the flagship of the commander, Patrol Force, and a rock breakwater had been built to protect the pier.

When the tender was deployed to Okinawa as the flagship, it went to sea every six weeks for a cruise to visit such exotic ports on the Pacific Rim as Sasebo, Japan; Kaoshung, Taiwan; Hong Kong, and Singapore. Although these visits were officially to show the flag and remind the nations in the Pacific that the United States had a commitment for their defense, they were also opportunities for the crew to visit foreign ports.

The commander of Patrol Force Formosa Straits, to whom I reported upon taking command of the *Salisbury Sound*, was a rear admiral, Naval Academy class of 1937, who had been a fighter squadron commander in the Pacific, flying off carriers against the Japanese in World War II. He was an ace and considered a topnotch naval officer. On the afternoon of the day I had assumed command, "Smoke," as he was known, called me down to his cabin. He was not a glad-hander; to the contrary, he was a man of few words, most of them carrying substantial weight. As I stood in front of his desk—he had not invited me to sit down—he said, "Holloway, I know that you have been sent out here to *Salisbury Sound* as your deep-draft command prior to assignment to command an aircraft carrier. As such, there are lots of things you will want to do with this ship. But I want to tell you right now that this tender is primarily my flagship as commander, Taiwan Defense Force. It is not here for you to play with. Consequently, when you prepare the ship's schedule, please keep this guidance in mind. I do not wish to be inconvenienced or have my staff's job made more difficult by your scheduling the ship to be underway any more than the minimum required to get your sea legs and to keep the crew qualified." That was very clear guidance.

In the fall of 1962, a major typhoon, with winds of up to sixty knots, was forecast to pass within one hundred miles of Okinawa. I did not want to ride out sixty-knot winds tied up to a pier. The ship would take a lot of hull banging and could not manuever to keep its bow into the wind to avoid damage to antennas and light topside equipment. The admiral suggested the ship remain at the pier and simply ride it out, using anchor chain as supplementary spring lines fore and aft. But I had been through a typhoon on the destroyer *Bennion* twenty years earlier and had an appreciation for the problems encountered with high winds even if only approaching typhoon velocities. Consequently, I replied that I believed it would be a dereliction of duty to fail to get the ship underway. I suggesting anchoring in Buckner Bay, putting out two anchors ninety degrees apart with lots of chain and riding to this arrangement with the ship manned as for underway at sea, with the engines turning over and a senior officer on the bridge at all times. The ship would be maneuvered to minimize the strain on the two anchor chains. The admiral snorted and said okay, but he knew I was right to play it safe. He ordered his staff to come on board at eight o'clock in the morning. We spent two nights at anchor before the blow subsided and the ship returned to its berth at White Beach. That experience made it clear to me that if the winds exceeded sixty knots, I would not want to be in Buckner Bay either at the pier or anchored out. I would only feel safe with plenty of sea room to avoid the high-wind areas of the typhoon and stay within its "safe" quadrant.

Two weeks later, the Fleet Weather Central in Okinawa forecast a typhoon to move directly over northern Okinawa. White Beach could expect winds of well over one hundred knots. I told the admiral I intended to get underway before the winds in Buckner Bay got over thirty knots. The admiral again suggested that perhaps I look at the possibility of remaining at the pier with the ship's anchor chain as bow and stern springs with the weight of their catenary to absorb the shock of the gusting winds. I told him that on the basis of our last conversation I had looked very carefully at this arrangement and could only conclude that it could result in severe damage to the ship.

On the morning when the forecast for the following day showed winds of thirty knots in Buckner Bay, I told the chief of staff that I would embark the admiral and his staff—if he wanted to be onboard for typhoon evasion—by nine o'clock the next morning. I wanted to be underway by eleven, before the winds had built up to dangerous velocities. He passed that information to the admiral, who said that his staff would be on board at nine and he would follow shortly afterward.

His two dozen or so staff members were on board on schedule, and the ship was at sea detail by nine o'clock. The admiral did not show up for an hour. The winds had by then increased to forty knots and it was raining hard. I was getting more upset by the minute. The wind would be on the *Salisbury Sound*'s beam as we were passing through the narrow entrance at the breakwater, the worst possible combination of wind and tide. The admiral came on board with his aide at about ten o'clock and the aide explained that there had been problems in taking care of the dependents. There were no structures on that part of Okinawa that would withstand a hurricane of the forecast intensity. The Army had sent a number of armored personnel carriers (APCs) to be parked in the quarters area for the dependents to use as a refuge during the height of the storm. The admiral had delayed his departure from his quarters until he was satisfied that the personnel carriers were in place and were satisfactory for their intended purpose.

An assortment of last-minute line handlers on the pier threw off our lines and the *Salisbury Sound* got underway with the winds gusting to forty knots and the rain horizontal. Once out of Buckner Bay we took a course southwest for the safe quadrant. As the storm approached Okinawa, we were proceeding away from the low-pressure center, and the wind and the seas remained constant. About 1900 the weather began to improve as the wind showed a definite abating trend and the seas were flattening. I had moved to the sea cabin and was spending most of my time on the bridge, with the regular officers of the deck exercising the con.

At about 2100, after the movie in the flag plot, the admiral appeared on the bridge and asked me why I was heading southwest. I told him that I wanted to be well clear of the typhoon. I would reverse course and head back when the typhoon center had crossed to the other side of Okinawa and was definitely no longer a threat. "You're being overly cautious," the admiral said. "You've evaded the eye of the storm and are in the safe quadrant. The center of the storm has moved to the northeast at twenty knots. If you follow a course of northeast, it will take you to Buckner Bay and at ten knots you'll continue to open the distance on the storm center." I was very uncomfortable with this advice. I had been on the bridge virtually full time since we first encountered the heavy weather, and there appeared to be many cells of severe weather within the overall mass of the typhoon. We had not really been able to anticipate what sort of weather we would encounter as we were evading. I started to explain this again to the admiral and he said, "No, I think you're okay to return to homeport. Go northeast and return to White Beach." The admiral turned and departed the bridge. It was with strong misgivings that I gave the orders to the helm to come to 045 degrees and asked the navigator to give me a course for the entrance to Buckner Bay. I rang up turns for ten knots on the engine room annunciator and we plodded into the blackness of the night and what appeared to me to be the renewed fury of the typhoon. In the next two hours the weather deteriorated markedly. The wind was gusting over one hundred knots and the seas were fifty feet. I was especially uncomfortable with the ship's roll. We had the wind and the sea on the port beam, and the *Salisbury Sound* was rolling as much as forty degrees. On the more extreme rolls, she seemed to hesitate before starting a recovery back to the vertical. Anyone who has experienced this phenomenon on large ships at sea in very heavy weather knows how uncomfortable it can be.

At about two in the morning we seemed to hit an especially severe spot. The seas became confused and the wind was shifting unpredictably. At this moment the ship's whistle started blowing. This added to the perception of confusion on the bridge. Three or four inches of water covered the deck in the pilothouse, trapped by the hatch coamings. Sloshing in this were pencils, paper trash, and cardboard coffee cups, among other things. At this point, the admiral appeared on the bridge in his pajamas and bathrobe. In contrast, I was a mess. I had been soaked to the skin for hours. The one consolation was that the weather was warm. It was not like some of the arctic storms that I had encountered in the USS *Ringold* in World War II in the North Atlantic. But the entire bridge crew was supporting themselves by clinging to the vertical stanchions in the pilothouse, slipping and sliding from one to another as we moved from the chart table to the radar and the helm. Often three of us would be hanging onto the same stanchion or each other as the ship rolled. The admiral said to me, "I had always understood that a steady blowing the ship's whistle indicated an emergency situation or that the vessel was going down and all hands should abandon ship." He said this half jokingly but asked if we were having real problems. I told him that we suspected that the rope lanyard to the whistle actuating arm on the smokestack had parted and the engineers down on the greasy and heaving gratings were trying to find the valve that would shut off steam to the ship's whistle. Other than that, the ship was not in immediate danger. I told him that I was planning to come around to a course that would allow us to ride more easily with the prevailing wind and swell and that it would probably not be toward Buckner Bay. The admiral replied, "You do what you think best in your judgment. You need to get us out of this bad weather."

We did turn southeast again, and by daylight the foul weather had largely dissipated. The wind was now gusting to only thirty-five knots, the seas had dramatically flattened out, and there were patches of blue sky on the southeast horizon. At this point I shaped a course for Buckner Bay and instructed the XO to take a survey of the ship to determine the damage. In a half an hour the XO returned with the ship's master-at-arms to report that most of the damage had been superficial. Ventilators had been ripped off and gone over the side, hatch covers had been blown loose and lost, some watertight doors were leaking and on the mess decks there were dishes and stores that had broken free from their moorings and had crashed to the floor. The broken crockery and loose gear could be taken care of in a day's work by the crew, but of real concern was that an aircraft rearming boat (ARB)—a one-of-a-kind small craft with special gear to handle bombs and depth charges for the seaplanes—had been lost, disappearing sometime during the storm, having torn the lines right out of their padeyes. Also an aircraft refueling boat—another specialized craft with pumps, filters, and tanks installed to provide clean-filtered aviation gasoline to the seaplanes—had its bow stove in and its gunwalls splintered. These boats were made of wood in order to minimize the possibility of sparking when in contact with the metal hulls of the ship and the seaplanes. This boat would have to be completely refitted in a boat yard.

This was not good news. Navy regulations are fairly specific in the responsibility of a commanding officer for taking proper precautions to secure boats and equipment in bad weather. In our case it was particularly serious, because these boats were essential to the *Salisbury Sound*'s primary mission of supporting seaplanes in a seadrome.

We arrived at our pier at White Beach at about 1400 the next day, and the staff departed the ship while the ship's company turned to restoring the damage. The admiral had come up to me on the bridge while I was tying the ship up, and said that he understood our aircraft rearming and refueling boats had been lost or damaged. He added that he would take care of having replacements located and delivered to the ship. His staff would be responsible for getting that done as soon as possible and would keep me informed. I thanked him very much for his offer of help. Then he turned, saluted the quarterdeck to leave the ship, and said, "You did a very nice job of minimizing the damage from the typhoon during our little trip to sea." With an impassive face, masking what was probably a wink and a smile, he crossed the gangway to his waiting staff car to return to his home and find out what damage had been done to his own quarters.

9

Nuclear Propulsion

Vice Adm. Hyman G. Rickover

In December 1963 the *Salisbury Sound* returned to San Francisco to undergo a major overhaul in the Bay Area, and I was ordered to report to Washington, D.C., to be interviewed by Admiral Rickover for the *Enterprise* job. It turned out to be a special experience for me, as it was for all officers who underwent Rickover's oral examination.

The offices of the Naval Reactors branch of the Bureau of Naval Ships (BuShips) were located in the Navy Department's ancient, "temporary" World War I wallboard-and-plywood office buildings on the Mall along Constitution Avenue. Arriving at 0730, I was first interviewed by three of Admiral Rickover's top civilian technical assistants. These were a group of engineers who had been with Rickover since his earliest days at the naval nuclear site in Oak Ridge, Tennessee. They had stuck with Rickover because of their intellectual admiration of his style and technical respect for his accomplishments. These interviews were tough, designed to test the depth of a candidate's technical knowledge and aptitude for nuclear engineering. The sessions lasted throughout the morning. The meeting with Rickover himself would take place that afternoon, after the admiral had reviewed the notes provided by his interviewers in the morning session.

I was summoned to Rickover's office at about 1330 and seated on a hard wooden bench in the hall outside his door. At about 1430, Rickover's secretary showed up from her office—Rickover had no anteroom—and she took in a file of papers. When she came out after several minutes, I was ushered in and offered a seat in an uncomfortable wooden armchair with one short leg. Rickover was sitting at his desk behind piles of papers in a cluttered office and in front of a dirty window that placed him in silhouette so that I had difficulty in seeing his facial expressions. He was courteous, his voice soft, and he started with the expected questions. What were my favorite duty assignments? Why did I want command of the *Enterprise*? Did I think I could handle the academics of the course? What books had I read recently? Which ones had I liked, and why? Rickover then read from a copy of my academic transcript of grades as a midshipman at the U.S. Naval Academy. This report showed that I had received good grades—a B average—as a plebe, but for the next two years my grades steadily declined right up to graduation. Rickover asked why had my academic performance been so poor in the last two years. I replied, trying to be scrupulously honest, that with the prospect of going off to war, I had decided to enjoy life at the academy as much as possible and study as little as necessary to get by without failing. Rickover said firmly but positively that was not a good answer and sent me into an unoccupied office next door to think of a better reasoned reply.

I was called back in half an hour after mentally struggling to determine what Rickover was really after. So I explained that I had been on the wrestling team and that took up much of my time and quite a bit of my energy. Again, Rickover calmly but firmly said that was not a good answer and sent me back to the empty office. Rickover added that I would get one more chance to come up with an answer that made sense. In our conversation, I had observed that Rickover expressed himself with a minimum of words and extraneous explanations. Rickover was direct and bluntly to the point.

When I returned, Rickover, without any preliminaries, asked me point blank, "Why were your grades so poor your final two years?" I answered directly with an equally short, but firm statement: "Because I wasn't very smart." By this I meant that I was pretty dumb to let my grades decline when I could have done much better (it was a double entendre in a way). Rickover understood exactly what I meant and it was the answer he wanted. "You are absolutely right," he said. "I will arrange to have you report to me for duty next month to start your nuclear training."

So in February of 1964, I was detached from the *Salisbury Sound* in Oakland, California, and returned to Washington for duty in the Naval Reactors Division of BuShips under Admiral Rickover. A half a dozen carrels had been installed in Rickover's office spaces, and that is where four of us senior officers undergoing study with Rickover's staff would make our headquarters for the next year. It was full immersion. Study, lectures, and meetings with Rickover from 0800 in the morning to 1800 in the evening, when Naval Reactors closed down shop. Then a minimum of three more hours of homework every night, with problems to be solved and papers to be turned in the next morning for grading. Our instructors were the senior staff members of Rickover's organization, who had to take this on as an additional duty, consistent with Rickover's idea of exercising the greatest possible economies, including manpower. The routine at "Rickover's College of Nuclear Knowledge" was especially rough for us senior officers attending the course. There were formal classroom training courses set up for the junior officers in the program, which were conducted in an academic environment at the Naval Reactors School in Newport, Rhode Island, by trained and experienced instructors. Rickover considered that these formal training courses were fine for the junior officers coming in at the entry level of his program, just out of the Naval Academy and NROTC colleges, but he wanted to personally oversee the training of his future carrier commanding officers. In 1963 the senior group consisted of myself, a prospective CO of the *Enterprise*; Cdr. Forest Peterson, a test pilot, and astronaut and prospective Enterpirse XO; Cdr. Walt Schwartz, the prospective XO of the nuclear cruiser *Long Beach*; and Cdr. Kent Lee, a fighter pilot and a prospective CO of the *Enterprise* who had received his master's degree in nuclear physics from the Naval Postgraduate School in Monterey just three years earlier. It was a professionally distinguished group, and everyone but me had gained strong academic credentials at the graduate level in recent years.

For me it was a difficult experience. The entire course consumed eight months, including three one-month periods on the site at Arco, Idaho, the shore-based reactor plant that fully replicated one-fourth of the *Enterprise*'s propulsion unit. This consisted of two nuclear reactors powering two steam turbine engines driving a single propeller shaft through a reduction gear to produce 35,000 shaft horsepower (shp). It was a precise duplicate of the *Enterprise* installation. Rickover had set up this land-based prototype using components acquired on the justification that they could be used as spares for the *Enterprise* power plant in the event of an emergency.

Our prospective commanding officer (PCO) group studied thermodynamics, electricity, nuclear physics, and reactor engineering from textbooks under the tutelage of Rickover's engineers and scientists at the headquarters. At the prototype installation in Idaho, we would actually operate the reactors and the steam plant. The senior officers were required to double-shift at the Arco site, working two eight-hour watches per day. As Rickover had told us, "The town is sixty miles from the site and there is nothing there when you get there. That leaves you eight hours a day to study, eat, sleep, shave, and do your calisthenics." These were difficult times for me. Academics had not been a problem at the Naval Academy. Once I was confident I could pass the midshipman courses, I only did enough studying to keep a safe margin above a failing grade. In the Rickover program, however, an A average was required.

In Washington, the Holloways had no social life during that year with Rickover. I had several hours of homework every night, worked for Rickover on special projects on Saturdays, and used Sundays to catch up. On at least two occasions, Rickover called me in to express concern over my academic performance. Then, at about the eighth month, the dawning came, and all of the pieces of reactor technology came together for me. My last two months were actually enjoyable. Rickover assigned his senior students fascinating projects such as designing an inherently "unsafe" reactor. I received a grade of 97 percent on my finals, by one point the highest grade in our group.

The senior active duty naval officer permanently attached to Admiral Rickover's staff was Bill Wegner, a Navy commander and a very bright and especially dedicated nuclear-trained officer who had been with Rickover from the beginning of Naval Reactors and would stick with "the kindly old gentleman," or KOG, as Rickover was privately referred to by his staff to the very end. Although he was Rickover's "chief of staff" in Rickover's naval organization, I never saw him in uniform. Incidentally, nor did I ever see Admiral Rickover in uniform; he preferred the anonymity of civil clothes. The chief of staff ultimately retired without making captain and became very influential in the field of nuclear power at the policy level.

The gap between the three stars of Rickover and the three stripes of his next senior officer was pretty large, and Rickover called upon his PCOs for administrative help when he had large numbers of officer candidates from the Naval Academy and ROTC schools for interviews. These were midshipmen in the fall semester of their senior year of undergraduate work who had volunteered for nuclear-power training with the guarantee of further assignment to submarine school (by then all new submarines were nuclear powered) or to nuclear-powered surface ships—cruisers, missile frigates, or aircraft carriers.

The candidates from the Naval Academy were delivered to Rickover from Annapolis by the busload. Arriving at his drab office spaces with its spot-patched industrial-quality linoleum floors, the midshipmen went through a series of three interviews with members of Rickover's technical staff before their visit with the KOG. No officer or senior civilian was ever ordered to an assignment in the U.S. Navy's Naval Reactor Program without a personal interview and approval by Admiral Rickover. Some might have as many as three sessions before Rickover was assured that the candidate would commit to hard work expected in any job working for Rickover.

The staff engineers in their interviews would probe the levels of intellect and technical potential of each interviewee and then prepare a written summary report on the candidate. Rickover himself reviewed these evaluations before his private meeting for the final interview. He would see as many as twenty midshipmen a day, beginning at 0900 and running until 1800 if necessary to complete the entire busload. All of this took a lot of organization—briefing the candidates, getting them to the preliminary interviews, and ensuring that the entire process ran smoothly with no delays and absolutely no gaps in the interviewers' schedules. Rickover relied on our PCO group to run this process. He didn't tell us how to do it, he just said what he wanted done.

As the senior officer among those under instruction, the job of running the interview process became my responsibility whenever I was not at the site in Arco. This also meant I had the additional duty of being present in Rickover's office for every interview. This was the admiral's

decision because, in a previous year, one of the candidates—who incidentally had been turned down—told his congressman that Rickover had
called him "a dumb shit." Rickover probably did, and the midshipman
probably deserved it. But the admiral wanted an officer present as a
witness to deny future accusation of coarse language. At times I found it
convenient to be out of earshot.

The other senior PCOs shared the duty as "the hot shell man" waiting
to snag the usually bewildered candidate as he was ejected from the
admiral's office at the completion of the interview. The overall reaction
of the PCOs who sat in on the interviews was unanimous: Rickover's
interview process was remarkably effective in selecting the people he
considered suitable for his program. True, cognitive skills were a large
part of the criteria, but Rickover was looking beyond that—for common
sense, commitment, and, especially, integrity. I recall an incident that
occurred when I was the inside man. A Navy medical corps doctor, a
lieutenant, was being interviewed to be the medical officer on board a
nuclear-powered submarine. He seemed to me to be a likely candidate
until I witnessed the following exchange.

"Were you married going through medical school?" Rickover asked.

"Yes," the lieutenant answered.

"Are you still married?"

"Yes."

"To the same woman?"

"No."

"Did your first wife pay your way through medical school?" Rickover
asked.

"Yes," said the lieutenant.

"That's all, you are excused."

After the doctor left, Rickover looked over at me and said, "Mark
him down as unacceptable. Bring in the next candidate."

At Naval Reactors in Washington, the staff and students worked six
days a week. Rickover worked seven. He used Saturdays and Sundays to
visit the shipyards where nuclear ships were being constructed and to go
to sea on preacceptance trials for the new construction submarines. These
sea trials were always scheduled for a Sunday to accommodate Rickover's
schedule. Rickover liked to take a nonsubmarine PCO with him on these
trial runs. He wanted to expose the aviators and surface officers to the

horrendous squeaks and groans emitted by the submarine's steel hull as it approached test depth—just above the calculated crush point for the particular class of submarine.

The admiral would depart Washington on Saturday afternoon and fly to the shipyard. Embarking late Saturday, he would spend the night on board, going through the boat to ensure it was ready for sea trials. Then early Sunday morning the submarine would get underway to proceed to deep water. There the submarine crew would conduct tests and drills, including a dive to test depth and a crew demonstration of their ability to recover power after Rickover, in a surprise drill at an unannounced time, shut down the power plant. This was scary to me, but the crew knew it was part of their qualification and had practiced diligently. (Still, the nuclear submarine *Thresher* was lost at sea with all hands when the crew failed to recover the reactor plant properly following an inadvertent emergency shutdown, or SCRAM, of the reactors while underway submerged). Sunday afternoon the sub would return to its homeport, and Rickover would get back to Washington late Sunday night. Obviously, the senior students did not like being tapped for this escort duty, especially since the Naval Reactors offices were abandoned on Saturday as soon as the KOG had gotten out of sight en route to his inspection of the construction yards.

One particular experience I had while arranging Rickover's itinerary gives an insight into the KOG's character and personality. Rickover had scheduled a weekend visit to the Pascagoula shipyard to ride a new attack submarine. He asked if I could arrange a Navy plane, preferably a fast jet for transportation; otherwise it would be a tedious trip by commercial air because of the limited airline service to the remote location of the shipyard. The Naval Air Facility at Andrews Air Force Base, which served Washington, did have available for VIP transportation a converted Navy bomber, an A-3D Douglas Skywarrior. This was a twin-engine carrier-based long-range nuclear bomber that had been remodeled to carry one or two passengers. With Rickover's three stars he was eligible to use it on business. He asked me to schedule the A-3 for his weekend trip.

Then Rickover became nervous. The main reason he traveled commercial air was that he was totally unfamiliar with naval aviation—just as he was totally comfortable in the milieu of submarines, surface ships, and nuclear plants. He preferred to be the greatest living expert when in the company of other Navy professionals and this was not the case on a Navy plane. A sailor would tell him where to sit and when he could get up. Rickover didn't know how to use the toilet. His inferiority complex really became apparent under these unfamiliar circumstances, and he hated that.

The trip was ill-fated from the start. Rickover asked me to pick him up at 0800 Saturday morning at the Naval Reactors offices. No official car, please. That would be a symbol of privilege. The Holloways then owned two cars, a four-door Chevy for my wife and two daughters and a Triumph TR-3, a British roadster with two bucket seats that was mine alone. It was the ultimate sports car with chrome wire-spoke wheels, a soft top, and a leather belt over the bonnet—or hood. I had planned, of course, to use the Chevy. But my daughters had left the windows down when the car was parked in the driveway on Friday night and the next morning the interior was sopping wet due to a passing thunderstorm. It couldn't be dried out. The TR-3B would have to be used.

When I pulled up at Naval Reactors fifteen minutes early, Rickover was already impatiently waiting. He was nervous about flying in a converted Navy carrier jet atomic bomber. Then he absolutely could not believe I was going to drive him through Washington and onto Andrews Air Force Base riding in a bucket seat. At first he refused to get in. But Rickover still had his pride and he wanted no one to say he wouldn't ride in such an outlandish vehicle.

The A-3 was sitting on the tarmac in front of the operations building at the Naval Air Facility with various Navy duty officers nervously hovering on the sidelines. Rickover asked, "How do I get in?" It was a reasonable question as there was no ladder, platform, or steps. Rickover had also noted, immediately, that there was no door or window for an internal compartment. The crew chief explained that he should climb into the cockpit through the nose wheel well and then squeeze into the seat in the converted bomb bay, where he would strap on a parachute. Rickover's face fell, and then he turned to me and said, "Why don't you come along with me?" I said I had an exam that day at the Naval Reactors office, the only excuse I knew that Rickover would accept. The crew chief had Rickover put on a one-piece suit of coveralls over his civvies, explaining that they were nomex and in case of a crash would not catch on fire. The sleeves and the pant-legs had to be rolled up in order to fit Rickover, who weighed less than 120 pounds. The crowning blow, though, was the hardhat. Rickover was required to wear a standard Navy plastic flight helmet, complete with boom mike and earphones. The crew chief foolishly explained that Rickover had to have the communications in case the plane got into trouble and he had to be told to bail out. At this point I had more than a twinge of guilt and compassion as I watched Rickover, in his ridiculous rolled-up flight suit and enormous helmet, being led away like a prisoner with a resigned compliance that I had never seen before.

Monday morning, Rickover called me into his office at 0800 to tell me how successful the submarine's trials had been. He didn't mention the flight down to Pascagoula, or the return, until the conversation was ending. Then Rickover said in the most matter-of-fact, almost casual manner, "That was a good flight down and back. I'd like to do it again sometime." But he never did.

Rickover had a custom—perhaps a habit born out of the loneliness of his misogynism—of calling his subordinates on the telephone in the evening, just to chat. I remember that during the periods I was studying at the Washington office and residing at my home in Arlington, Rickover would call three or four nights a week, invariably getting me up from the dinner table. At first it was flattering to be called by this great man just to philosophize, but my wife Dabney grew tired of it quickly, seeing her home-cooked meal turn cold while she and the two girls were left on their own at the one time of the day the family got together. I will admit that I nevertheless continued to enjoy these conversations with Rickover. They were a rare opportunity to gain a candid insight into that unusual personality. The conversation was all one-sided—Rickover—and always philosophical. There were no taskings or admonishments. Rickover would start with a recitation of the advantages of nuclear power, then describe how much he had contributed to the Navy and the nation, and end on a note of exasperation at how much he was unappreciated. All of it was true. But in these calls that could last half an hour to forty-five minutes, Rickover inadvertently demonstrated his insecurity, and perhaps something of a persecution complex. Yet all told, I would consider my relationship with Rickover always a pleasant one. When I got chewed out, I deserved it.

Rickover had his detractors—or, really, mortal enemies—as well as supporters. Much later, in the fall of 1974, when I had been in OpNav for about five months, Capt. Powell Carter, the CNO executive assistant, informed me that he would like to put a Mr. Thomas Corcoran on my schedule at a request coming through the OSD. I observed that I did not know who Thomas Corcoran was, nor had I even heard of him or what it was that he wished to discuss with the CNO. I also considered myself quite busy and explained that I did not have the time to meet with everyone who asked for an appointment. I suggested that Powell send word back that I would not be available to Corcoran. Captain Carter replied that I had better see Corcoran, because there was political pressure to get him in to see me. Rather than make it an official request from SecDef's office, it would be wise if I agreed to allow Corcoran to call. I trusted Powell Carter implicitly in these matters, because his judgment was superior in reading the intent of instructions that came down from Secretary Schlesinger's very competent executive assistant, Brig. Gen. Wickham, who later became chief of staff of the Army.

A little research showed that Thomas Corcoran was known as "Tommy the Cork," and he had the reputation of being the premier lobbyist—in any and all matters—in Washington, D.C. There was no indication of what he wished to discuss, but I guessed it was to do someone a favor. Several days later Tommy the Cork appeared on time for his ten o'clock appointment, bustling into the office in a very officious but friendly way, accepted a cup of coffee, and sat in the guest's place of honor, a comfortable divan at the opposite end of the CNO's office from the large working desk that was the CNO's command post.

Tommy the Cork got right to the point. He said, "Admiral, I want you to send Admiral Rickover to Annapolis to be the superintendent of the academy. We all know how interested he is in education and this would give him an opportunity to exercise this very special preoccupation of his." I was frankly surprised and I'm sure I showed it when I said, "But Rickover is now the director of Naval Reactors and an assistant secretary of energy on the Atomic Energy Commission. He has an enormous span of responsibilities in his position, and although he may be interested in education, he is not the man to administer the program at Annapolis in any way. It encompasses a great deal more than simply book-learning."

Tommy the Cork replied, "Well as a matter of fact, that's one of the main reasons I am proposing he go to the Naval Academy, because he has become a terrible thorn in the side of U.S. industry and a number of businessmen I represent. They are people who are doing business with the Navy, theoretically, but actually they are having to do business with Admiral Rickover, and they consider him an impossible problem in either getting or carrying out a contract with the Navy."

I asked him in what way. He responded, "Well, I'm sure you know that Admiral Rickover is very cantankerous, and when a businessman comes into his office to discuss a business proposal, he demands to know his qualifications and why he thinks he can produce the high quality of material demanded by the nuclear standards. Admiral, you must remember that these are experienced businessmen and they are not used to being talked to in this rough fashion or having their credentials doubted. And those who do have contracts find that Rickover puts one of his staff in their plant to monitor the way the contract is being administered—whether the specifications are being fully adhered to. As you know, his standards are very, very tight and sometimes a production line may fall off just a little bit, according to my sources. Not enough to cause a problem, but just not quite up to the standards established by Rickover. You've got to find a way to ease up on these businessmen or you're going to lose some of your contractors."

I pointed out that as long as two bidders were involved, there was always competition and that in many cases the pricing was determined not on the basis of the bid but from a fixed-priced contract. Rickover felt that to be fair to the producers who were building something they had never before undertaken, to higher standards than ever before, they should be helped rather than hindered by Rickover and his people providing advice and negotiating terms. Tommy the Cork said, "But Rickover's negotiating terms always end up to his advantage, and the established businessmen and their factories are not achieving the margins that they think are fair." I replied that they nevertheless accepted the contracts—which they didn't have to—and accepted the government inspectors in their plants.

With that, Tommy the Cork exploded in a controlled fashion and said, "Admiral, he is just rude and terribly demanding and my people are not used to that kind of treatment. They want to get in the nuclear business but it is just asking too much of them to have to deal with Admiral Rickover and constantly arguing about the quality of their product being up to government standards. Admiral Rickover won't give them any slack."

"Mr. Corcoran," I replied, "I think we might as well end our discussion right now for two reasons. First, I admit that Admiral Rickover is irascible, but he is in a very important job that requires for safety's sake very tight standards, and he is insisting on them because the lives of the sailors and people who would be affected by a nuclear accident must be protected. If your constituents want to get into the nuclear business that's what they're going to have to put up with. Rickover cannot be spared, and I would have no thought of moving him out of that position. Second, the very idea of using the young midshipmen at Annapolis as the recipients of this old man's cantankerous ways in order to spare American industrialists from the unpleasant task of working with Rickover, and pushing the hardship off on four thousand young college students, is absolutely preposterous. You really are treating the midshipmen at the Naval Academy with contempt when you suggest that it's okay for them to be picked on by Rickover but not appropriate that your financiers take the heat. Our session is ended."

Corcoran stormed out, taking the turndown with what I thought was perhaps an inevitability in his own mind. At least he could go back to his constituents and collect his fee, telling them he had gone to the mat with the Navy but that the CNO was just as arrogant as Rickover.

In 1999 a definitive biography was written about Corcoran, titled *Tommy the Cork, the Supreme Lobbyist.* Tommy the Cork was enough of a character in his own—compared to Rickover—to have his bio on the *New York Times* bestseller list.

I finished up with Rickover in June 1964, but command of the *Enterprise* would not turn over until October. So I was ordered to OpNav to assist in setting up a new directorate on the CNO staff—"the Office of Navy Program Planning" under Vice Adm. Horacio Rivero, a brilliant officer who had stood number one in his class at the Naval Academy and later served six years as a four-star admiral. After retiring, he became U.S. ambassador to Spain for four more years. Rivero became very supportive of nuclear power and exerted a strong influence in the retired community in mobilizing support for me among this normally truculent caucus of retired admirals when I was CNO.

In August of that year, the Holloways suffered a personal tragedy when our son was killed in an automobile accident. Young Jimmy was to begin his sophomore year at the University of Virginia, which he was attending on a Marshall Scholarship. The first expression of sympathy to my family was a call from Admiral Rickover, who had read of the accident that morning in the *Washington Post* early edition.

TWO-REACTOR CARRIER

Among my responsibilities as special assistant to Vice Admiral Rivero were nuclear propulsion and aircraft carriers. Rickover had planned that the follow-on carrier to the *Enterprise* would have a four-reactor power plant, cheaper to construct and considerably less expensive to operate than the *Enterprise*'s eight-reactor plant. But Secretary of Defense McNamara had vetoed the very idea of any more nuclear-powered surface ships on the basis that his special Office of Program Appraisal under Alain Enthoven had concluded that nuclear-powered aircraft carriers were not cost effective. The Navy was in a bind. Congress, by now strongly influenced by Rickover through the Sea Power Subcommittee of the House Armed Services Committee—created at Rickover's suggestion—would not consider authorizing a nonnuclear carrier, and McNamara would not approve a nuclear version. His refusal to change his position in the face of the Navy's positive studies and overwhelmingly favorable analysis concerned his assistant secretary of defense for research, development, testing, and evaluation (RDT&E), Harold Brown (later to become secretary of the Air Force and the secretary of defense under Carter). As Brown said, "Bob has dug himself a hole and now has to find a way out of it."

That opportunity arose in the fall of 1964, when McNamara, on a visit to the Bettis Nuclear Laboratory in Pittsburgh, was shown by Rickover the mock-up of a reactor capable of 70,000 shp and designed to serve as a single reactor propulsion plant for a destroyer. This reactor had twice the power of an *Enterprise* reactor. McNamara asked Rickover if two of them could power an aircraft carrier. The proper answer should have been, "It depends on the size of the carrier." The *Enterprise* was driven by 280,000 shp. But before anyone else could answer, Rickover responded with a loud yes, and McNamara then turned to Admiral McDonald, the CNO, and said, "Send me a memo on this on Monday." I was among the small party accompanying McDonald, Rickover, and McNamara on the Bettis trip, so I was aware of the exchange.

In my capacity as coordinator for both carriers and nuclear propulsion in Rivero's office, I was following up on the invitation from McNamara when I intercepted a draft memo going back up the chain of command to the CNO before it got to the Office of Program Planning, where it would come for staffing. The proposed response to SecDef McNamara, to be signed by CNO, was a shock. In essence, the memo read, "No. The Navy wants the four-reactor carrier we have been planning as the follow-on to the eight-reactor plant." This response would have ended the Navy's nuclear carrier program with the *Enterprise*.

The responsibility for preparing the reply to McNamara had been preempted by the Naval Material Command, whose four-star admiral had been bypassed regularly in Rickover's dealings with Rivero and the CNO. The Naval Material command's staff had not a single nuclear-trained person, yet they hadn't consulted the Office of Naval Reactors in drafting their reply. I immediately prepared a separate memo, without reference to the Material Command's draft, for Admiral Rivero to sign out to the CNO. This version stated, "Yes, Secretary McNamara, the Navy thinks your proposal of a two-reactor carrier is the way to go, and we stand ready to move ahead as soon as you give it the okay."

This, of course, was checked out with Dave Leighton, Rickover's carrier propulsion plant expert, and then taken to Vice Admiral Rivero, or "Rivets," as he was known to his friends. Rivets was a quick study, and he read the draft memo twice, made no changes, and initialed it on the spot. In his job Rivets had immediate access to the CNO, so he then took the memo in to Admiral Dave McDonald, who signed it as Rivero waited. Both Rivero and McDonald were aware of the pressing need to seize the moment. They wanted to get a commitment from SecDef before his staff could get to him to change his mind. Instead of an approval to go ahead with construction, the CNO felt sure that Enthoven's staff recommendation would be to conduct a new series of studies on a two-reactor carrier. Secretary of Defense McNamara did approve the two-reactor carrier, and promptly. It became the *Nimitz*, the first of a class of ten twin-reactor carriers of that design.

Leighton later confided to me that initially he had been concerned about the technical feasibility of the twin-reactor design. He would have preferred to go with a four-reactor version first, just because of the research and development involved. Each of the two reactors would have to produce 120,000 shp. One of the *Enterprise*'s reactors generated only

35,000 shp. That was an enormous jump in scale. There were possibilities of unforeseen radiation patterns with so much nuclear flux in such a confined environment. But when Rickover agreed to take it on, all doubts among the scientists and engineers in the Naval Reactors Branch evaporated. That was the faith they had in Rickover.

THE *ENTERPRISE*

In July 1964 I was ordered to the command of the *Enterprise*, which was then in the Newport News Shipbuilding and Dry Dock Company's yard for the refueling of its eight reactors. This was a fourteen-month job and had never been done before. Rickover wanted me there for the final buttoning-up of the ship and to be on board during the sea trials, but not to relieve as CO until the *Enterprise* had been pronounced by the yard and the Navy as ready for sea in all respects.

I moved on board the carrier while it was undergoing overhaul and refueling in the shipyard, leaving my family behind in our home in Arlington. It has been customary in the Navy for the oncoming CO not to arrive on the scene more than a week before the change of command. The idea is to let the outgoing commander savor the final days with his crew without having his successor on hand to confuse the issue of who is actually in command. Admiral Rickover, however, in his typically pragmatic approach, uncomplicated by such things as precedents and naval customs, insisted on a two-month turnover on board. I resolved the differences by holing up in the *Enterprise*'s flag cabin, working an eight-to-five day and taking all my meals ashore. I stayed completely away from the commanding officer and the running of the ship. The then-current CO, Capt. Mike Michaelis, had his hands full with the refueling operation and getting the ship ready to return to the operating fleet. In addition to reviewing the reactor technical manuals, I needed to study the current tactical publications and operational procedures that would govern the operation of the ship and air wing in the environment of a tactical unit in combat when the *Enterprise* rejoined the fleet. Rickover probably never knew such procedures existed. In any case, he would look upon that as my problem, not his.

Almost since the introduction of carriers into the U.S. Navy in the 1920s, and certainly since the beginning of World War II, the carrier commanding officers were limited to tours of about one year. There were two main reasons for this. The first, and probably the original, justification was that the intensity of the carrier operations, due to the dangerous nature of flying aircraft off of ships, was considered so stressful for a commander that the exposure to such stress should be limited. A second reason, and probably the most important, was that command of a carrier was the sine qua non of the naval aviator. It was absolutely essential for a Navy pilot to have command of an aircraft carrier in order to be eligible to even be considered for promotion to rear admiral.

So for career purposes, the carrier was essentially the turnstile for the advancement of naval aviation officers to flag rank. The same situation did not prevail in the case of other line officers, who could be selected for flag rank after command of a battleship, a cruiser, or a squadron of destroyers or submarines.

In the years following World War II, the force levels of attack carriers in the United States had stabilized at about fifteen. But there were, in addition, nine antisubmarine warfare carriers. That meant that if a carrier skipper were given a two-year tour as commanding officer, there would be only twelve naval aviator captains eligible for consideration for promotion to flag rank each year. By limiting the command tour to twelve months, that number was doubled. Of course, not all of the carrier commanding officers were promoted. One might not be selected on the basis of a poor performance in command of a carrier, such as a grounding, a collision, or, in fact, any tour of duty in which the carrier did not perform up to the very high standards established in the fleet. So it became well established after World War II that the tour of duty for a carrier captain would be one year. This policy seemed to be satisfactory until Admiral Rickover became involved in the selection of the commanding officer of the *Enterprise*.

Rickover was a pragmatist and a self-centered one, as well. He had put a great deal of his own time and a commitment of his organization's resources in the selection, training, and supervision of the captain of his nuclear-powered carrier, *Enterprise*.

Rickover personally had screened those officers recommended by the CNO and then had made his recommendation, which was tantamount to selection. For a year, the prospective commanding officers had been trained in his headquarters under his immediate supervision for a six-month period and then turned over to his staff in Washington and at the nuclear carrier land-based prototype in Arco, Idaho, for a rigorous hands-on course of nuclear-power engineering and reactor control.

Altogether, his organization had committed almost a year and a half of its time in selecting and training the officer to be the CO of the *Enterprise*. So Admiral Rickover had decreed that one year in command was not enough time to pay back the investment.

His theory was that if he found an officer whom he considered suitable for command of the *Enterprise*, he would be satisfied to leave him there indefinitely. But he knew of course that would never be acceptable to anyone in the Navy for many compelling reasons. So he settled on a two-year tour of duty for command of a nuclear carrier and prevailed upon his supporters in Congress to require the Navy to abide by this policy. These members of Congress were basically the congressmen on the Sea Power Subcommittee of the House Armed Services Committee and Senator "Scoop" Jackson in the Senate, who carried an enormous amount of weight as far as the Navy was concerned and was a great believer in Rickover.

The chief of naval operations and the chief of naval personnel fussed with the extended tour, but only mildly. They did not want to take on Rickover and his allies, knowing it would be a defeat for them in the long run. And then, there was only one nuclear carrier in the fleet and the impact on the promotion opportunities for aviation captains would not be too severe. There were many senior people in the Navy who believed that more than a one-year tour was needed in command of all ships and aircraft squadrons. They felt it was unfortunate that for reasons of providing command opportunity for naval officers, pressure from the career management system at BuPers had forced reduction to only one year, to the detriment of stability in the fleet.

In any case, the CNO believed the two-year tour was warranted in view of the nuclear carrier's radiological risk potential, which justified the policy that only the best and most experienced senior officers—commanding officer and executive officer—as well as those directly associated with the nuclear plant itself serve in these nuclear-powered ships.

10

The *Enterprise*

Full Speed Ahead

A dmiral Rickover said, "Let's see how fast she can really go." This didn't sound like Rickover, but it did sound like fun, pushing eighty-seven thousand tons of warship with new reactor cores and a clean bottom to its maximum speed. It was 2100, and we were both on the bridge of the *Enterprise* enjoying a cup of Navy coffee after a long day of drills and exercises and relishing the prospect of an equally active evening putting the power plant through a series of operational trials.

I had taken over the *Enterprise* the day before, 15 August 1965, at a change of command ceremony on the hangar deck with the carrier alongside the pier at Newport News Shipbuilding and Dry Dock Company. Both Admiral Rickover and Dabney had been in attendance, but my father, now a retired four-star admiral, was in the hospital, unable to see me take command of the world's largest warship.

The next day, the *Enterprise* got underway at 0800, standing out the channel with me on the bridge for the first time in command. Engineering acceptance trials had been successfully completed under the former commanding officer and the *Enterprise* had completed a year-long refueling of the eight nuclear reactors, which now had longer-life nuclear cores of a new design. Now Rickover wanted to see how well the ship performed. We had been building up to full power over a six-hour period and had arrived in our assigned operating area about fifty miles off the coast. Rickover was personally monitoring all vital signs in the propulsion plant. At about midnight, the speed run began with me at the conn and Rickover giving advice. He said not to use the ship's rudders—there were four of them—as any movement out of their fore and aft position would produce drag and reduce the ship's speed. I complied with this guidance for about ten minutes, until the eighty-seven-thousand-ton vessel began to wander all over the sea on its own. I told Rickover I could not avoid using some rudder but would apply only the minimum amount of helm necessary to keep the carrier on a safe course.

Rickover was increasing the engines' speed, revolution by revolution, until the *Enterprise*'s engines reached their maximum rpm. At this point the ship's speed indicator, as well as the special test devices, indicated that the carrier had attained a speed of more than thirty-seven knots—more than forty miles an hour. We sustained this speed for an hour before reducing the engine rpms and the reactor power slowly to preclude shocking the engineering plant with sudden transients.

The *Enterprise* returned to Norfolk, but this time it went alongside one of the carrier piers at the Naval Operating Base (NOB) Norfolk, the Navy's huge installation on the Hampton Roads waterfront. There the loadout began of the thousands of tons of supplies of all kinds, food, clothing, toiletries—everything needed to support more than six thousand sailors for six months without coming into port. Once deployed, the *Enterprise* would receive all of its resupply through replenishment vessels at sea.

In the 1950s Capt. Hyman G. Rickover and his Naval Reactors group in the Navy Department had developed a pressurized-water nuclear reactor that was sufficiently powerful and at the same time safe enough to be the propulsion plant in a U.S. submarine. Thus the USS *Nautilus* became the world's first nuclear-powered vehicle and a true submarine. That same pressurized-water nuclear-reactor design was then scaled up under the initiatives of President Dwight D. Eisenhower in his "Atoms for Peace" program, to be used for the design of the first civilian nuclear power plant at Shippingport, Pennsylvania, providing electricity to the commercial grid supplying the Pittsburgh area.

With the success of the USS *Nautilus*, Adm. Arleigh Burke, the chief of naval operations, quickly saw the potential for nuclear power in surface ships, especially aircraft carriers, and gave Rickover the go-ahead. This first nuclear-powered carrier, the USS *Enterprise* (CVAN-65), was commissioned at Newport News in 1962. In order to achieve a nuclear aircraft carrier operational capability with minimum design and development time, Rickover had selected a ship design layout similar in size and configuration to the *Forrestal* class of conventionally powered carriers. The engineering placement remained essentially the same, with eight nuclear reactors replacing eight boilers. Similar to the *Forrestal*, the *Enterprise* had four main engines to turn four propeller shafts driven through conventional reduction gearing. The steam plant was actually a technical regression from 1,200 to 600 psi steam, and Rickover had to design a special flexibility into this plant to accommodate the thermal transients caused by the use of the steam catapults for the ship's aircraft. The eight reactors were similar in design and capability to the pressurized-water reactors being used in the nuclear submarine program. In spite of the fact that virtually every component in the carrier's propulsion plant and steam system had to be a new and technically unique design, it all worked properly from the day the first reactor was scheduled to go critical.

Within a week the *Enterprise* had completed voyage preparations and the loadout of supplies and was underway for the U.S. Naval Station at Guantánamo Bay, Cuba. There the ship would report to the Naval Training Command under the command of the crusty Rear Adm. John Bulkeley, who had received the Medal of Honor in World War II as a PT boat squadron commander for evacuating General and Mrs. MacArthur and their son from the island of Corregidor in Manila Bay after the Japanese captured Manila.

Admiral Bulkeley was one of the most senior rear admirals in the Navy, and he was certainly the most crotchety. He was a perfectionist, demanding adherence to the basic Navy standards of maintaining a shipshape man-of-war. He was very tough on all of the people and units under his authority as the training officer for the Atlantic Fleet. He was especially focused on carriers and their squadron commanders. I believe this preoccupation was the result of his feeling that carrier commanding officers had spent little time in commanding ships but had simply flown airplanes from their decks, with little understanding of what made the big ships run. In a way he was correct, except that the quality of the officers who successfully screened for carrier command guaranteed that future carrier skippers would be bright, technically competent officers who clearly understood that the aviation aspects of their carrier command were the counterparts to the guns and torpedo tubes of the destroyers, cruisers, and battleships. They certainly understood their responsibilities for the safe navigation and most effective management of the ship and crew.

OFF TO WAR

The *Enterprise* had progressed well into her first four weeks of the programed six-week shakedown syllabus when there came a surprise message from commander, Air Force, Atlantic Fleet, relaying a message from the Pentagon, instructing the *Enterprise* to cut short its shakedown training and return immediately to Norfolk to prepare to deploy to Southeast Asia. This was understandable to those of us who had been following events through the classified intelligence briefings, but to 90 percent of the crew and their families, the change in plans came as a shock.

The U.S. government had committed its support to the fledgling democracy of South Vietnam in its defense against the North Vietnamese intrusion and Vietcong guerrillas, who were armed and supported by China and the Soviet Union. The North was determined to unite all of Vietnam under its Communist regime. By the fall of 1965, the situation in South Vietnam had deteriorated to the point where the Joint Chiefs of Staff had recommended to the president that substantial reinforcements be sent to assist our allies in Southeast Asia if they were to survive the threat. The Navy decided that the *Enterprise,* instead of going to the Sixth Fleet in the Mediterranean as a unit of the Atlantic Fleet based in Norfolk, needed to be where the action was, in the Gulf of Tonkin. The reason for this was obvious. The *Enterprise* at that time was the largest warship afloat and ostensibly the most powerful of all time. During the first refueling, nuclear cores with a three-year lifespan in fleet operations had been installed. She had been built under the fiscal year (FY) 1958 program and commissioned in November 1961, but subsequent carriers—the *America* (CVA-66) and *John F. Kennedy* (CVA-67), funded in FY 61 and FY 73, respectively—had reverted to oil fuel rather than nuclear power. The Navy had asked for a nuclear-powered carrier in each case, but Secretary of Defense Robert McNamara and his systems analysis staff had rejected nuclear power as not being cost effective. So the nuclear-powered carrier was on its way to extinction unless it could be demonstrated that nuclear power would so improve combat effectiveness that its additional cost was justified. The field of battle was obviously the test that could make or break the justification for nuclear power in carriers.

The JCS orders had directed the *Enterprise* to return to homeport and then proceed directly to the Gulf of Tonkin. Within twenty-four hours, refresher training in Guantánamo was terminated and *Enterprise* was en route to Norfolk at high speed to load combat stores and ammunition and to embark a special air wing for Southeast Asia, a combination of squadrons that had not yet even been determined.

The CNO, Adm. David L. McDonald, decided to take advantage of the ship's unique capabilities by adding two squadrons of attack aircraft from the West Coast to the carrier's normal air wing complement. The *Enterprise*'s ability to operate the additional aircraft was not so much because of the size of her flight deck, which was not appreciably larger than those of her conventional sister ships, but because of her enormously increased capacity for aviation fuel and ammunition. Without the need to carry black oil for her own propulsion, she could carry 90 percent more jet aircraft fuel and 50 percent more aviation ordnance than could the largest conventional carriers, in addition to carrying black oil fuel for escorting ships.

Carrier Air Wing 9, as the reinforced *Enterprise* wing was designated, consisted of two squadrons of F-4B Phantom IIs, the most advanced and capable tactical aircraft in the world at that time. Originally designed and produced by the Navy as its standard fighter, the Phantom II was eventually adopted by the U.S. Air Force, NATO, and most free-world air forces. With a ceiling of more than forty-five thousand feet and a maximum speed of Mach 2, the F-4 could outperform any other fighter in any air force. Added to the air wing were four squadrons of A-4C Skyhawks, the relatively small and easy to maintain attack bombers capable of nuclear as well as conventional weapons delivery. The Skyhawk's utility for carrier use lay not only in its small size but also in its large load-carrying capability. Empty, the Skyhawk weighed less than nine thousand pounds, but fully loaded with bombs and fuel on the catapult, it grossed more than twenty thousand pounds. These two Navy tactical combat planes were also favorites of U.S. allies. For example, on Armed Forces Day in Israel in 1969, the traditional "flyover" by the Israeli air force consisted exclusively of F-4 Phantom IIs and A-4 Skyhawks, both U.S. Navy–designed carrier planes sold to the Israelis to constitute the first line of their combat air force.

Also included in Air Wing 9 was a squadron of six RA-5C Vigilante reconnaissance aircraft, detachments of three A-3B Skywarrior tankers, E-1B Tracer radar surveillance aircraft, and UH-2A Seasprite rescue helicopters. Additional splinter groups of electronic countermeasures planes and a twin-engined passenger and cargo transport (carrier on-board delivery, or COD) would join the air wing when the *Enterprise* arrived in the South China Sea.

Only a one-week window was available to have the West Coast squadrons fly into the Naval Air Station Norfolk and be hoisted on board the carrier. Their personnel would be flown to Norfolk by U.S. Naval Reserve transport squadrons to walk on board with their personal gear. The support equipment for the air wing, much of it specialized for the type of plane assigned, had to be flown by Military Air Transport Service (MATS) planes from the air stations where the squadrons were based to Norfolk and then loaded on board ship. The biggest problem, however, was the change in personnel. It was the Navy's policy at that time to make every effort to assign its sailors and officers to the coast of their prefer-ence, East or West. The *Enterprise,* upon departure for shakedown, had been destined to remain in the Atlantic, homeported at Norfolk. As a consequence, most of the personnel now on board were men who preferred East Coast duty. When the homeport was changed to San Francisco, which was the case when the *Enterprise* was ordered to deploy to the Pacific Fleet for combat operations in the Gulf of Tonkin, the Navy was obligated to transfer the sailors in the crew who had an East Coast preference and replace them with sailors who had indicated a prefer-ence for the West Coast. The problem caused the most difficulty for BuPers and the Atlantic Fleet personnel offices, but it still resulted in headaches for the *Enterprise* when sailors had to be transferred from their duty assignments and divisions where they had several years of experience and replaced with new men, who, although competent, were moving into a new ship with new shipmates.

The *Enterprise* was underway on schedule on 26 October 1965, bound for Puerto Rico and two days of simulated Vietnam strike operations using live ordnance against the Vieques Island practice ranges. This was the first time the *Enterprise* and her aircraft had operated together since her refueling overhaul at Newport News Shipyard more than a year earlier. Remarkably, both the air wing and the carrier received an overall grade of excellent for the live-ammunition exercise. Then, without a port visit, the ship's bow swung southeast and headed for the Cape of Good Hope, the Indian Ocean, and the South China Sea. The first task was to top off combat consumables, jet fuel and ammunition. The carrier spent the entire first night alongside the oiler *Sabine* (AO-25) loading jet fuel, and an ammo ship, the *Shasta* (AE-6), from which more than four hundred tons of bombs and missiles were loaded.

With the nuclear-powered frigate *Bainbridge* (DLGN-25) in company, the *Enterprise* broke away from the replenishment ships, ringing up twenty-eight knots. The combat deployment of the first nuclear-powered carrier battle group had begun. Steaming at twenty-eight to thirty knots across the Atlantic and Indian Oceans, the carrier conducted full-scale flight operations for nine days of the three-week transit. Officers on board the *Enterprise* had been told the ship would be committed to combat immediately upon arrival in the Gulf of Tonkin. No warm-up period would be possible. So these flight operations en route were vital. In fact, it was not until reaching the Straits of Malacca that we found the solution to servicing a flight deck packed with ninety airplanes. Because of the sheer numbers of aircraft, we had to invent new procedures for aircraft handling and flight deck patterns never used before on U.S. carriers. In the final days before arriving in the western Pacific at the Straits of Malacca, I was on the flight deck convincing the aircraft handling officer that the only solution to the problem was the most unorthodox scheme of having the first planes to land taxi up to the bow on the portside then circle down the starboard side to park for refueling and rearming. Neither the pilots nor the aircraft handling crews liked taxiing aft on a flight deck with a steady wind of forty knots coming from the bow of the ship and other aircraft landing on the angled deck. But it turned out to be the basis of the new standard operating procedure, which allowed all forty aircraft in a single launch to be recovered, refueled, rearmed, and then launched an hour later.

When the *Enterprise* reached the Straits of Malacca, the ship's aviation fuel tanks were low because of the extensive flight operations en route. A U.S. Navy oiler was waiting in the approaches to the straits. At 1900 that evening, the *Enterprise* hooked up to the USS *Navasota* (AO-106) and remained alongside for eleven hours, taking on 1.3 million gallons of jet fuel as the tanker negotiated the turns in the narrow strait with the *Enterprise* maintaining station alongside—with only a seventy-foot gap— over which the fuel lines were pumping aviation fuel forward and black oil aft. The black oil was for the carrier's escorting destroyers, most of which would be conventionally powered.

The following day the *Enterprise* turned north to head for Vietnam at thirty knots. That morning a COD transport aircraft landed on board with members of the staff of Task Force 77 to brief the *Enterprise* crew on operations in Vietnam. The *Enterprise* was to commence combat operations immediately upon arrival. The air wing components were new to each other and to the ship, and the *Enterprise* had not completed a shakedown, but no one on board questioned our being ready. Training and work-up, though, would not be easy. More than 6,250 people were in the crew and their average age was under twenty-two. Most of the sailors, in fact, were on their first cruise. The brief time to prepare for the transfer from the Atlantic Fleet to the Pacific Fleet, the additional two squadrons in the wing, the special considerations of nuclear power, and the immediate requirement to handle maximum loads of live ammunition all added to the dimensions of the task.

The ship's officers, with the exception of the commanding officer, executive officer, reactor officer, chief engineers, and supply officer, all of whom were nuclear trained, had not been handpicked for the *Enterprise* assignment. All were individuals who were routinely qualified and due for a tour of duty on an aircraft carrier. The *Enterprise* was to be their duty station for the next three years.

In the air wing, all of the squadron commanders were veterans of previous combat tours in Korea or Vietnam. These were the hearts and minds of the ship's fighting capability, the combat leaders. Either the commanding officer or executive officer of each squadron led virtually

188   CHAPTER TEN

every combat flight. The leader was the plane first in on the attack. The professional and courageous leadership of these strike leaders in Vietnam was clearly a deciding factor in the effectiveness of the carrier air war, but the Navy paid dearly for it: Sixty-seven air wing commanders, squadron commanders, and executive officers were lost in combat during the conflict.

A profile of the squadron commanders who served on board the *Enterprise* on the 1965–66 deployment would be typical of that found in any naval air wing at that time. All were mature officers, in their early forties, with more than twenty years' experience as commissioned officers, most of it flying planes off carriers. About half were graduates of the United States Naval Academy, and the others were products of the Naval Aviation Cadet Program at Pensacola, Florida, and the "regular" NROTC program. More than 60 percent had advanced degrees, mainly master's degrees in personnel management, aviation ordnance engineering, and aeronautical engineering. Four of the squadron commanders went on to become rear admirals, and all of them made captain. Three were killed in action as squadron commanders, and one died as the result of an accident landing on the *Enterprise* at night. All were competent aviators and fine leaders. In the Navy, squadron commanders were not assigned on the basis of seniority alone. Each one was the product of a selection board convened in the Bureau of Naval Personnel that picked only the very best from those naval officers with the requisite qualifications and aviation experience and demonstrated competence. These officers were all exceptional leaders admired by their junior officers and crew and absolutely committed to their responsibilities.

Not all of the ship's officers were of the same caliber as the squadron commanders. Some, such as the ship's operations officer and air officers, in key department head spots, were former squadron commanders who were getting in their mandatory shipboard tour of duty. Others, such as the combat information center officer, aviation ordnance officer, and aircraft handling officer were Navy pilots who had failed to screen for a command but were hoping to recoup their chances with a good performance on board the *Enterprise* in combat. All of them were committed and, in fact, inspired. There were a couple who turned out to be incompetent, however. They were unable to run their divisions or organizations at the level of performance essential for the extraordinarily high tempo combat operations that would be encountered. In these cases, either the executive officer or captain stepped in to troubleshoot the problems and provide special guidance to the officers. That, in most cases, along with constant supervision and good assistants, sufficed to boost the division's or department's performance.

All in all, the *Enterprise* was ready for combat when the carrier arrived at Point Yankee and reported for duty to commander, TG 77.0 on 2 December 1965. The combat veterans among the ship's company were confident and the commander of the task force was hopeful. Not that any of that really mattered. We were there, committed to joining the battle. There was no other choice. It was our responsibility and ours alone to be ready.

11

The *Enterprise*

Vietnam

In a priority dispatch from the Gulf of Tonkin, South Vietnam, Rear Adm. Henry Miller, USN, the embarked task group commander, advised the secretary of the navy, "I have the distinct honor and pleasure to announce to you that on the second day of December 1965 at 0720H, the first nuclear-powered task group of your Pacific Fleet and the United States Navy engaged the enemy in South Vietnam."

The *Enterprise* had commenced air operations at 0700. The wire service covering the occasion reported that the "carrier's bridge and every available spot on the superstructure was covered with newsmen and military observers watching this unprecedented first in the history of war on the seas: the use of a nuclear-powered aircraft carrier in combat operations. With *Enterprise*'s entrance into combat, a new era was opened before the world."

The *Enterprise* marked her combat debut by launching twenty-one Phantoms and Skyhawks in a strike against Vietcong installations near Bien Hoa, South Vietnam. There were rough spots in that first day at war for the "Big E." A Phantom pilot, obviously shaken by his first exposure to combat, was forced to eject after making seven unsatisfactory landing approaches and then being unable to plug into an airborne tanker for emergency refueling. The pilot was picked up by the carrier's plane guard helicopter and returned to the *Enterprise*. He was uninjured in the parachuting but was flown off on the first available carrier on-board delivery transport for transfer back to the States and a naval career in an assignment that did not involve flying. A second Phantom was lost when a premature bomb explosion put holes in the fuel tank and the pilot and radar intercept officer (RIO) ejected over South Vietnam when the tanks ran dry. Soldiers of the Army Special Forces group at Hon Quan arrived thirty-five minutes later and brought in an Air Force rescue helicopter to evacuate the aircrew. By the afternoon, operations had smoothed out and the *Enterprise* and Air Wing 9 had completed every mission on the daily flight schedule. CVW-9 flew 125 strike sorties on that date, unloading 167 tons of bombs and rockets on the enemy.

THE WAR IN VIETNAM

The United States' involvement in the Vietnam War was a process of long gestation, quite unlike the immediacy of our sudden and complete immersion in Korea, where the decision to join in a full-blown war against a well-armed, veteran North Korean army was made by the president in a matter of hours.

Our interest in opposing communism in Vietnam began as early as September 1950, when President Truman decided to establish the small U.S. Military Assistance and Advisory Group (MAAG) in Saigon in tacit support of the French effort to suppress the Communist Viet Minh, who had gained control of the rural and mountainous areas in that part of French Indochina.

Then, early in his presidency, John F. Kennedy directed a major expansion of U.S. military presence in the country, which grew to seventeen thousand advisors in 1963 and included the use of U.S. Army helicopters for the tactical deployment of the South Vietnamese troops against the Vietcong and the invading North Vietnamese.

On 2 August 1964, North Vietnamese torpedo boats attempted to attack the U.S. destroyer *Maddox*, which was on patrol in the Gulf of Tonkin. With the intervention of aircraft from the carrier *Ticonderoga*, the torpedo boats were driven off. Two nights later the U.S. destroyers *Maddox* and *Turner Joy* reported being under attack again by hostile torpedo boats while conducting a patrol in the gulf. Radar targets were taken under fire by the destroyers, but darkness and bad weather hampered the search by aircraft dispatched from the *Ticonderoga* and led by the air wing commander, Cdr. Jim Stockdale. No visual sighting of enemy craft was made, raising the question of whether this night attack had actually taken place.

Based upon the initial reports of the "Gulf of Tonkin incident," President Johnson reacted immediately, ordering the Navy to retaliate. The next day, in Operation Pierce Arrow, the carriers *Constellation* and *Ticonderoga* launched sixty-four strike sorties against the torpedo boat bases of Hon Gai, Loi Choi, Quang Tri, and Ben Thuy and the oil storage depot at Vinh. This carrier task group was the only force immediately available for timely retaliation. Ninety percent of the oil storage facility at Vinh was destroyed, in addition to twenty-five P-4 type torpedo boats, more than half of the entire North Vietnamese operational inventory. Two A-4 Skyhawks were shot down by enemy AA fire, killing one pilot. The other, Ens. Everett Alvarez, became a prisoner of war (POW) and was repatriated after the Paris Accords in 1973. This was the start of offensive air combat operations over Vietnam, which included Flaming Dart in 1965, Rolling Thunder from 1965 to 1968, and Linebacker in 1972. It was Linebacker II in 1972 that forced Hanoi to sue for a cease-fire. The carriers participated in all of these campaigns and flew more than half of the combat sorties.

Concerned that an air campaign alone might be insufficient to stem the advance of the North Vietnamese military forces into South Vietnam, President Lyndon Johnson agreed to deploy U.S. combat ground forces into South Vietnam to prevent the imminent collapse of the army of South Vietnam. In July 1965 he ordered 175,000 combat troops— soldiers and Marines—into South Vietnam.

THE TWO WARS

The United States' concept of operations for military operations in Southeast Asia was perhaps most succinctly characterized by Gen. William Westmoreland, USA, as "fighting two separate wars." One war was the engagement in South Vietnam, in which U.S. ground forces, consisting of soldiers and Marines and supported by Marine Corps, Navy, and Air Force tactical air, joined the Army of the Republic of South

Vietnam (ARVN), their U.S. advisors, and the South Vietnamese air force and Australian and South Korean troops to battle Communist ground forces. Initially these were the Vietcong, best described as guerrillas: South Vietnamese farmers by day, soldiers by night. But early in this war the North Vietnamese began inserting regular North Vietnamese army troops, replete with heavy artillery and armor, into South Vietnam, where they directly engaged the U.S. and ARVN forces.

U.S. Naval Forces, Vietnam and U.S. ground forces had the additional mission of winning the "hearts and minds" of the South Vietnamese through pacification and nation-building measures that can be summed up as working with the rural South Vietnamese to rid their villages of the Communists and then providing advisors to organize the villages through their own governing hierarchy of local chiefs and headmen to defend themselves against the return of the Vietcong and the North Vietnamese army.

All of the U.S. and ARVN ground forces were limited to operations within the provisional borders of South Vietnam, except for a limited foray into the Laos sanctuaries to interdict the North Vietnamese army's supply lines to South Vietnam. The friendly forces engaged in this war in South Vietnam were never permitted to cross the DMZ into North Vietnam. The penetration of North Vietnam was the mission of Westmoreland's second war.

North Vietnam had maintained the charade that the North had no part in the fighting in the South but that the Vietcong were simply "agrarian reformers" in conflict with the local governments. The presence of regular North Vietnamese army troop units was categorically denied. So the United States found it difficult to justify, in terms of world opinion, an all-out military campaign into the sovereign territory of North Vietnam. Instead, the United States would rely on what were originally described as "surgical strikes" on military targets, where the chance of collateral damage to nonmilitary targets could be further minimized by stringent rules of engagement (ROE). Therefore, the forces involved in this second war included SAC B-52s flying from Guam, Air Force tactical fighter wings from bases in Thailand and South Vietnam, Marine Corps tactical aircraft from South Vietnamese bases, and naval aircraft flying from carriers at Yankee Station in the Gulf of

Tonkin. When practical, U.S. Navy surface combatants, cruisers, and destroyers conducted gun strikes against North Vietnamese logistics and military targets along the coasts that were within range of their guns. Routinely the surface warships were extensively committed in gunfire support of friendly troops ashore in South Vietnam.

The *Enterprise* and Air Wing 9 were initially assigned to conduct strike operations in support of our allied ground forces engaged "in country." During a major air effort on 5 December, while in support of an Army Green Beret unit beleaguered in a jungle outpost, the *Enterprise* topped its earlier operational sortie performance. The following message was from the commander, TF 77, to commander, Seventh Fleet: "I am pleased to advise that the pilots of Air Wing 9, operating from USS *Enterprise*, set a new one-day record for strike sorties flown. One hundred sixty-five strike sorties were flown today. This number is 34 greater than the record prior to Big *E*'s arrival on Dixie Station." Dixie Station was the euphemism describing carrier operations in South Vietnam. The *Enterprise* had flown 211 sorties that day, 177 of which were classified as combat sorties, including the 165 strike sorties. Unfortunately, this date also marked the loss of the first *Enterprise* pilot to enemy action when an A-4 was shot down on a recce flight. The pilot was killed.

After ten days of operations into South Vietnam, commander, Seventh Fleet ordered the ship to move north to Yankee Station, where she was to conduct special operations. Yankee Station was the reference point in the northern Gulf of Tonkin where strikes into North Vietnam originated. "Special operations" was the code name for strikes into North Vietnam against well-defended and important targets near Hanoi, Haiphong, and other strategic areas, all heavily guarded by Soviet surface-to-air missiles and Russian MiGs. Task Force 77 maintained a minimum of three carriers operating from Yankee Station, and on several occasions there were as many as five. This carrier force conducted strike operations twenty-four hours a day, regardless of the weather. One carrier flew from midnight to 1200, another from 0800 in the morning to 2000, and a third from 1200 until 2400. This way targets were covered around the clock with the full weight of two carriers during the daylight hours, when the attacks were most effective. Every five days the carriers' flying periods rotated, so that in thirty days on the line, each carrier had an equal share of night flying, which was hardest on the pilots.

When the twelve-hour flying period was over, the work was not done. During the nonflying hours, the carriers replenished their fuel, ammunition, and stores. When the last plane in the day's air plan had touched down on the carrier's deck, the *Enterprise* immediately swung out of the wind and headed for an underway replenishment (UnRep) group at twenty-five knots. The URG consisted of three or more support ships: an oiler, an ammo ship, and a general stores vessel steaming in a line-abreast formation. Usually these ships were about ten nautical miles away from the carrier formation, struggling at their maximum speed to follow the carrier group.

In February 1966, during a routine, post-flying day replenishment operation, the *Enterprise* took aviation fuel and ammunition from the *Sacramento* (AOE-1), the first of a new class of fifty-nine-thousand-ton combat support ships that carried great quantities of both of these combat consumables. The *Enterprise*'s performance this day elicited the following message from the *Sacramento:* "Yesterday's underway replenishment of USS *Enterprise* transferred a total of 465 short tons. Of this total, 196 short tons were transferred by VERTREP (vertical replenishment, that is, by helicopter). This is a new record for us for a single day's work and I believe it is a record for any replenishment ship." The commanding officer of the *Sacramento* was Capt. Harold Shear, later to be my vice chief of naval operations. This was a new high for carriers as well as the replenishment ship.

The *Sacramento* later sent the following message to commander, Seventh Fleet: "The Navy's first fast combat support ship, USS *Sacramento* (AOE-1), set a replenishment at sea transfer first while operating off the Vietnam coast with the attack carrier *Enterprise* on 2 June in the South China Sea. The nuclear-powered *Enterprise* eased alongside *Sacramento,* rigged four transfer stations, and began to receive the first of a total of 241 short tons of vital conventional ordnance items. The *Sacramento*'s two Boeing UH-46A helicopters were aloft to transfer simultaneously with the alongside stations and they 'bombarded' the flight deck elevator of the attack carrier with palletized ordnance until the completion of all deliveries. The total transfer evolution required 55 minutes, yielding a total transfer record of 258.9 short tons per hour. This is the highest transfer rate recorded for *Sacramento* to date, and it is believed to be an all time high for sustained replenishment of a significant quantity of ammunition." This, of course, then became a new record for carriers as well.

Each carrier at Yankee Station conducted replenishment operations almost every day and took four to six hours doing so. It was a matter of policy that all ships remained topped off in all categories to be prepared to respond immediately to any new crisis without having to take the time to load out supplies.

Two-thirds of all replenishments were done at night under "darken-ship conditions," with carriers, cruisers, destroyers, and Russian spy ships all over the place on different courses and at varying speeds. In addition to having command of his ship, a carrier captain in Task Force 77 was also in command of a task unit consisting of his carrier and two escorting destroyers. Making a rendezvous with the UnRep group and getting the carrier and destroyers alongside safely in the minimum elapsed time was a nice exercise in navigation, maneuvering, communications, and shiphandling. It was a matter of professional pride to accomplish the full sequence of an underway replenishment evolution without a waste of time and with a minimum of radio transmissions.

On 26 April 1966 the *Enterprise* launched her first sortie of the day as the sweep second hand on the bridge clock clicked past the vertical at precisely noon. The last plane of the flight schedule "trapped"—made the final arrested landing—at 0037 the following morning, 27 April. At that moment, before the last plane was unhooked from the arresting gear, CO, *Enterprise* assumed his role of commander, Task Unit 77.6.2, consisting of the *Enterprise* and two destroyers, and commenced a series of verbal orders in the clear—not encoded—over the voice radio on TBS to Task Unit 78.4.3, a URG made up of an oiler, an ammunition ship, and a general-stores ship escorted by two frigates (DEs). The initial orders were for the two units to come to new courses so that each group would head directly for the other, and increase speed. The URG was directed to increase speed to eighteen knots and the carrier unit to twenty-five knots.

The two task units were now closing directly toward each other at a speed of fifty miles an hour, with no lights showing, visible to one another only as greenish blips on the ship's radarscope. Taking position at the naval tactical data system (NTDS) console, I could see the entire tactical situation on a large cathode ray tube (CRT). By manipulating the controls of the NTDS console, intercept courses could be laid out, maneuvering board problems worked, and the course and direction of every ship on the screen monitored. Otherwise, all of these course and speed requirements had to be computed with pencil on a printed-paper maneuvering diagram.

From their initial positions, the two formations were maneuvered so that they would meet head-on in about ten minutes. That was the objective: to join up the carrier with the service force unit as quickly as possible and accomplish the replenishment of ammunition, aviation fuel, and dry stores. Speed tempered with safety was the important factor. Long overtaking tail chases were an anathema.

Five minutes before rendezvous, the URG was ordered to turn to the replenishment course, a heading selected to put the relative wind on the port bow of all of the ships—the optimum wind and sea conditions for maneuvering in this evolution—and to form a line abreast maintaining eighteen knots. The captains of the URG ships, with many replenishments in their logs, had anticipated this order, and as the URG ships completed their turn to the replenishment course, all three ended up in a line abreast, a thousand yards apart, at the prescribed replenishment speed. Meanwhile, by working the NTDS, the time to turn and a course were computed that would put the carrier one thousand yards on the port beam of the oiler, which was in the center of the UnRep formation on an opposite course at twenty-five knots.

All vessels of both groups were still in "darkened ship," that is, showing no lights at all, and only three radio voice transmissions had been made. As the carrier reached the point directly on the port beam of the oiler, which was now on the UnRep course at eighteen knots, the helmsman was ordered, "Left standard rudder." At twenty-five knots, the *Enterprise* answered the helm in a lively fashion, eighty-nine thousand tons of ship kicking up a wide phosphorescent wake and commencing to heel outboard as she entered the turn.

The air officer had announced on his flight deck bullhorn, "Stand by for a turn to port" to warn all the plane handlers on the flight and hangar decks to hold the brakes on their aircraft or insert chocks under the wheels of those planes that were not tied down or did not have a plane captain in the cockpit. The planes were being moved to respot the deck after the final plane recovery. The carrier's deck would take a five- to seven-degree list during this 180-degree turn, and unless properly secured, the aircraft, like the cannon on the frigates of old, would roll freely unless braked or tied down. As the carrier approached the 180-degrees of turn, the helmsman was ordered to "Steady up" on the formation replenishment course. If the maneuver was done correctly, from an accurate distance abeam using the prescribed rate of turn and the proper ship's speed, the *Enterprise* rolled out on the replenishment course exactly twelve hundred yards astern of the oiler, moving directly up the oiler's wake at an overtaking rate of seven knots.

Now the oiler's wake could be seen, delineated by the phosphorescent turbulence on even the darkest nights. The carrier's course was then adjusted to parallel the oiler's heading, 120 to 150 feet—an eyeball estimate—to the left of the oiler's track in the ocean. In a support operation, the carrier always makes the approach on the replenishment ship and always comes along its port side. The carrier's bridge is located on the right-hand edge of the flight deck, and that is where the conning officer conducts his approach, from the right wing of the carrier's bridge, about 150 feet above the waterline. As yet, the oiler was only a black blur in the night darkness, and a sailor stationed in the very prow of the carrier called out to the bridge over his sound-powered telephone when the *Enterprise*'s bow was even with the oiler's stern.

At this point the order was given—"All engines back full"—breaking the silence of the pilothouse. During the entire operation there was minimum talk. No conversation, only reports, orders, and acknowledgments. All the lights on the bridge were out or dimmed to preserve the night vision adaptation of the conning officer and his assistants.

The order to "back full" was executed simultaneously in all four engine rooms, slowing the propeller shafts from 139 rpm to zero in less than a minute by introducing steam to the turbines in a reverse direction and decelerating the propellers at a standard rate to keep all shafts in synchronization. In the ninety-eight-degree temperature and the earsplitting din of each engine room, the throttleman, a veteran first-class petty officer, closed his eighteen-inch throttle wheel with practiced skill, his eyes glued to the steam gauges in front of him to respond to the bridge's orders in exact accordance with a precise deceleration schedule. An error on his part could cause a collision, wipe out replenishment fuel lines, or dangerously stress the nuclear power plant.

As the carrier moved up the port side of the oiler, low-intensity floodlights came on at the replenishment stations on both ships to illuminate small groups of sailors in dungarees and bulky kapok life vests. All wore various colored plastic hardhats to identify their duties at that particular replenishment station. Again, there was total silence; no talk or movement except as was necessary in the pursuit of their duties.

As the carrier's bridge came into position, about one hundred feet from the left wing of the oiler's bridge, the order was given: "All engines ahead two thirds, make turns for 18 knots." I adjusted the timing of this order, based upon my shiphandling experience with the *Enterprise,* so that the *Enterprise's* relative movement stopped when the two bridges were directly abeam and both vessels were making a good eighteen knots through the water without any relative movement ahead or astern.

At this point the carrier's bullhorn, directed to the oiler, called out, "Stand by to receive the line firing gun. On the oiler, all topside personnel take cover." That meant to get behind a bulkhead, spray shield, or piece of machinery. A boatswain's mate from the carrier was now clear to fire the line-throwing gun to propel a projectile, a 6-inch-long, half-inch-diameter brass rod, across the upper decks of the oiler. This projectile had a lightweight line attached, the messenger to which heavier working lines were married. The boatswain with the line-throwing gun aimed at a forty-five-degree elevation over the bridge of the oiler and pulled the trigger. Out flew the bronze rod over the oiler, falling into the sea on the far side. At the sound of the report, the sailors on the oiler leaped out of their protected locations into their assigned positions for the replenishment evolution. On both ships, every sailor topside has a specific assignment in which he has been trained and become an expert. There are no spectators, no loafers or lollygaggers. Any sailor without a specific duty remains clear of the replenishment stations and operations.

Meanwhile, several sailors on the carrier had prepared messengers of light line with lead-weighted "monkey fists" attached, which they attempted to manually heave across the seventy-foot chasm separating the two ships. A monkey fist is made of twine or light line braided into a two-inch-diameter ball around a piece of lead or iron. Usually about half of these heaves successfully reached the oiler. When a throw was too short, the sailor would make up his line and try again.

In less than a minute there were half a dozen messengers across and the oiler's crew hauled them in to bring on board the heavier and stronger lines that were attached. These would carry the weight of the full hoses and pallets of ammunition.

One of the first messengers brought over was a sound-powered telephone line for bridge-to-bridge conversation. The carrier's captain was first on the phone, usually to determine the identity of the oiler's skipper, also a Navy captain. More than half the time it would be a friend or contemporary, often a naval aviator on his qualifying deep-draft ship. After a few brief remarks and greetings, the two COs relinquished their phones to their respective supply officers, who conferred with each other on the fuel, ammunition, supplies, and services to be transferred.

Exchanging movies throughout the fleet during replenishment was a sacred ritual at sea. Every ship had a "movie officer," usually a junior officer whose reputation would be based upon his skill in trading up for grade A movies in exchange for the class Bs in his temporary custody. Movies were shown in the wardroom, the chief petty officer (CPO) mess, the first-class mess, and on the sailors' mess decks every evening after dinner. But with a watch system of four hours on and eight hours off, the showings were not well attended and few sailors saw a movie from beginning to end. The movies were a modest diversion for a crew who only got ashore for four days for every thirty days at sea.

After several hours alongside the oiler, the *Enterprise*'s aviation fuel tanks were topped off with JP-5, which for safety reasons was the Navy's standard fuel. It was a little less volatile than the JP-4, which was used with shore-based jet aircraft and had a very slightly higher energy content. When the JP-5 replenishment had been completed, and without any waste of time, the rigs were sent back to the oiler, the lines cast off, and the *Enterprise* increased speed to twenty-five knots to pull up ahead of the formation, swing out to the side, and repeat the entire process, making an approach on the ammunition ship on the right wing of the formation.

Alongside the ammo ship, the bombs, rockets, and missiles were transferred in pallets by the high-line method. The individual loads were heavy—two 2,000-pounders or four 1,000-pounders to a pallet—and had to be swung across the seventy- to one-hundred-foot distance between the two ships and then gently put down on the hangar deck of the carrier. There the boatswain's mates turned over the payload to the ordnance-men who, with their bomb carts, moved the ordnance from the hangar deck to the ammunition hoist to strike down the explosives to the magazines. These were in the bowels of the central part of the ship, where they received the maximum armor protection.

At the completion of the ammunition reload, the *Enterprise* again increased speed to depart the formation out ahead and, if necessary, make an approach on the third replenishment ship in the UnRep formation, the general-stores ship. This was necessary only every second or third replenishment because the crew consumed a great deal less food, toothpaste, and candy than the air wing did bombs and jet fuel.

The captain usually remained on the bridge during the actual transfer of fuel and ammunition, often dozing in his comfortable armchair. The captain is the only person, through custom, who can be seated while on the bridge, and only those actually on watch are welcome to spend any time on the bridge for other than routine errands and visits.

As captain I normally took the conn for most approaches during the night and in periods of fog and low visibility. The senior department heads, however, were given the opportunity to take the conn during replenishment approaches in daytime and also scheduled for periods of conning the carrier while alongside the replenishment ship during both day and night operations, unless the weather was severe or the replenishment group was having to change course frequently. This experience was very important for the career of the department heads aboard carriers and was a useful qualification for boosting their chances for a carrier command.

In the small hours of 27 April, I had seen the last aircraft recovered at 0037, rendezvous with the URG, and receive replenishments from an ammunition ship and an oiler before leaving the bridge to turn in at about 0400. From 0400 to 0830 it was a quiet night. The captain of the ship retires when he can to the "sea cabin," a very small compartment just aft of the bridge on the carriers, spartanly equipped with a bunk over a built-in set of drawers, a desk, and a primitive head (toilet). One hundred feet below is the captain's inport cabin, which is a relatively elegant suite consisting of a sitting room/office, with a comfortable bedroom and head attached. But the commanding officer remains in his sea cabin when the ship is underway. He cannot afford to be that far away from the bridge, as it is his responsibility to take over if necessary as events arise during the watch of an officer of the deck.

At 0830 on the morning of 27 April, I climbed into my armchair on the port side of the pilothouse, which overlooked the flight deck, and after a cup of the quartermaster's "joe" from the small coffee mess on the bridge, I was brought a tray of breakfast: two eggs sunny side up on whole wheat toast. Normally, after a breakfast on the bridge, the captain will call for his dispatches, the message traffic that has come in during the night that he must necessarily review as soon as possible. The action copies of the important messages had already been routed directly to the department head with cognizance over the matter, but it was essential that I see virtually all of the messages addressed to the *Enterprise* for action and for confirmation, so that I was informed enough to make the proper decisions as events might arise.

On this particular morning, my phone call to the ship's office to bring up the messages resulted in a responding delegation consisting of the regular communications messenger, the executive officer, the communications officer, the captain's Filipino steward, his Marine orderly, and a few hangers-on. The communications officer said, "Please read the first message, captain," and with some trepidation I took the message folder, wondering whether the war had ended, the *Enterprise* was going home early, or what. Instead, the top message was from the secretary of the navy to AllNav (all Navy). The subject was the "results of the 1966 flag selection board."

At the bottom of the list of nineteen captains who had been selected for admiral was James L. Holloway III. What a surprise. I had been selected for promotion for admiral two years before becoming eligible for consideration within the zone. While still receiving congratulations from my personal staff, the boatswain's mate sang out, "The admiral is on the bridge" and up walked the carrier division commander, Rear Adm. "Mickey" Weisner, commander, Task Group 77.7, who with his staff was embarked in the *Enterprise* as his flagship. Mickey was a longtime friend of mine whom I held in highest esteem and admiration.

While it was nice to receive my first congratulations from such a congenial source, I said to Mickey that my first concern was that, having been selected for admiral, I hoped I would not be relieved of command of the *Enterprise* and sent to a flag billet right away. Mickey, who had served as director of naval officer detailing in Washington, set my mind at ease. "First," he said, "you are so far down on the list, you won't make your number [actually be promoted] for a least a year, and second, Admiral Rickover is not about to let you go before he has gotten his promised two years of service out of you."

At about this time, the emergency alarm on the flight deck sounded and the pleasant conversation and congratulations were instantly terminated as the admiral, captain, and XO rushed to the port wing of the bridge to see what was the problem on the flight deck. It turned out that in conducting the regular preflight tests of the number two catapult by firing a shuttle forward without a plane or load attached, one of the sailors in the catapult crew had been struck by the shuttle and had collapsed. He was now immobile on the catapult track on the flight deck. The young sailor was carried away in a Stokes stretcher with a Navy doctor at his side, and later, word came up from sickbay that he had suffered a concussion but swift first aid and the medical officer's response had stabilized his condition and it appeared he would recover quickly with no permanent damage.

By now the excitement of the promotion had dissipated and the XO and I were immersed in the details of the upcoming flight operations that were to commence at noon, and reviewing several of the messages that would clearly need attention by the ship's engineering department. As flight quarters sounded for the impending noon launch, the sailors put on their jerseys, each a distinctive color to identify the man's duties, and the elevator warning horns blew as first the fighters and then the bombers were shuffled to the flight deck to be spotted for launch. It was now just another day on Yankee Station.

Two years later, when I had returned to the Pentagon and was eventually promoted to rear admiral as I took over the directorate of Strike Warfare in OpNav, I was told by Vice Adm. Tom Connolly, who was then DCNO (Air), an interesting story relating to my selection for admiral. Connolly was a very distinguished member of the naval aviation community, having served in a succession of influential jobs in naval air, including the development and production of the F14 Tomcat. It has been said that the Tomcat received its nickname in recognition of "Tom" Connolly's contribution to its existence.

In 1965, the year before I was selected for admiral, Connolly had been a member of the Flag Selection Board. Connolly said that I had been selected for admiral by that 1965 board and that my name had actually appeared on the final list. However, Connolly and several other "friends" of mine felt that it would be best if I were not included that year. Their feeling was that I would certainly get selected the year following, but to pick me in 1965 would definitely cause me to be relieved of command of the *Enterprise* before its deployment to Vietnam. The naval aviators on the selection board, led by Connolly, felt that both I and the Navy would be better served by letting me complete my full tour of duty in the *Enterprise*. I told Connolly that I was very glad that he had waited until I was actually promoted before he told me I had been selected and then taken off the list.

Replenishment at sea was one of the most remarkable features of the carrier operations in the Gulf of Tonkin. Virtually all of the products transferred—fuel, ammunition, food, spare parts and toiletries—came directly from the United States; there was practically no transshipment through ports in the Far East. Although the carriers went into the naval base at Subic Bay in the Philippines after almost every period on the line, this was mainly for ship repairs, the offloading of dud aircraft (those that had received battle damage and were unable to be flown off), and crew rest and relaxation. More than 99 percent of all other logistical support— ammunition, ship and aircraft fuel, food and general supplies—was delivered to the carriers from logistic support ships during underway replenishments at sea.

In turn, most of the underway replenishment ships were loaded out in U.S. ports. The ammunition ships (AEs) would take on all kinds of ammunition at the ammunition depot in Concord, California, and then transit to the Gulf of Tonkin. The AE would transfer ammunition to the carriers several times a day for a month or so until their holds were getting low. Then they would join up with another ammunition ship in the forward area whose ammunition stocks were also depleted. The two ships would then consolidate. The AE that had been in Seventh Fleet the longest would transfer its remaining cargo to the other AE and then return to the United States for another loadout. The tankers and general cargo ships would conduct similar product consolidations as they rotated in and out of the Seventh Fleet. The same routine applied to the general store ships, which delivered fresh vegetables to the crews' mess directly out of the port of Oakland from California farms.

The oilers carried both aviation fuel and ship's fuel for the nonnuclear ships. Although much of the fuel came from the continental United States, some was also picked up from U.S. stocks at storage sites in the Pacific, such as Singapore, where it had been delivered by commercial tankers.

All of this provided significant efficiencies by not having to move these supplies through a port in the Philippines to a depot, then move them from the depot to the port again, having the carrier spend three or four days of premium in-port time loading ammunition or fuel. Each carrier replenished virtually every twenty-four hours from at least one of the ships in the URG. By this system of constant replenishment, the carriers did not wait for their fuel bunkers or magazines to become low. They were kept topped off so that the ship always had about ten days' supply of fuel and ammunition in the event that logistic support was interrupted or so that the carriers could be sent on an unsupported mission immediately, without taking time to load out.

The URGs were supplemented by COD aircraft. The COD was a twin-engined carrier-capable transport plane with a tailhook for landing on board. It was a modification of the very reliable S2F Tracker antisubmarine warfare plane being flown off the CVS carriers. It could be configured with seats for a dozen passengers or for general cargo. It was reserved for high-priority freight that could be efficiently air transported: people, lightweight electronics, replacement parts, and U.S. mail.

With the carriers conducting replenishment almost every day, the crews became very proficient at these operations. Replenishment could be conducted both day and night under weather conditions up to gale winds and a sea state of five and when the visibility was reduced to a quarter of a mile or less. During my time in the *Enterprise* there were several occasions when the fog was so thick the replenishment ship could not be seen from the bridge of the *Enterprise* until after the carrier's bow had passed the replenishment ship's stern.

This proficiency on the part of our captains in shiphandling while in the replenishment hookup enabled the carrier and the replenishment ship to maneuver—that is, change course and speed—without interrupting UnRep. This might be necessary for several reasons. Usually it was to change course to keep the wind properly off the bow of the replenishment ship. Often it was necessary to maneuver the URG formation to avoid the Soviet trawlers, which appeared to have a principal mission of getting in a position directly ahead of our replenishing carriers in an attempt to disrupt the process and slow down our operations. It was not unusual for a URG to change course 180-degrees without interrupting the transfer, simply to stay within the prescribed operating area.

While the carrier was transferring fuel, ammunition, or supplies aboard, other work in the ship did not stop. Aircraft handling was really a twenty-four-hours-a-day operation. First, the aircraft had to be spotted for the launch, then it had to be launched and then landed aboard and respotted for the next launch. After flight operations were terminated for the day, the aircraft had to be moved to various locations for repairs and maintenance. Dud aircraft were usually jammed up in the forward end of the hangar deck. Planes that required an engine adjustment or an engine change, which was done on the hangar deck, had to be moved to the stern where the engines could be run up to full power with the exhaust over the ship's fantail.

While flying for twelve hours, the air department had to use the balance of the twenty-four-hour day to maintain, repair, and get aircraft ready for the next launch and, at the same time, move ammunition from the magazines to the flight deck and load the weapons on the aircraft. This in itself was no easy task, considering the number of 1,000- and 2,000-pound bombs that required assembly, fusing, loading, and then a complete check to ensure that they would go off only when they were supposed to.

For the carriers in the Gulf of Tonkin, this tempo of operations—twelve hours flying, six to eight hours replenishing, and six hours getting ready for the next flying day, went on for thirty days without a day off.

On the thirty-first day, the *Enterprise* would leave the Gulf of Tonkin and proceed for a six-day port visit, usually at Subic Bay in the Philippines. Once during each cruise, the carriers were sent to Hong Kong as a special treat. There, the crew of the *Enterprise* was again "mentioned in dispatches" for its exemplary conduct ashore on liberty. The *Enterprise* completed five of these thirty-day line periods in her 1965–1966 deployment before returning to San Francisco, her new Pacific Fleet homeport, in July 1966. But on one occasion, the promised five days of R&R in Subic failed to materialize.

SPECIAL LIBERTY

In May 1966, the *Enterprise* had completed six months of its eight-month deployment to Task Force 77 in the Gulf of Tonkin. Unless a crisis occurred that required all available assets on the line, each carrier could plan on a port visit after thirty days of operations at Yankee Station. One day was consumed by the transit to Subic Bay and five days were spent at the Cubi Point Naval Air Station with the carrier moored to Alava Pier, which was reserved for carriers. Then one day was allowed for the transit back to the Gulf of Tonkin. So the carrier netted seven days off the line for every thirty days of combat operations. Of those seven days, five were in port and devoted to R&R. It was a meager reward for the hard work of the sailors and the flight crewmen, but they were grateful for it, and all the hands looked forward to the opportunity to break the routine at sea and get ashore for a beer or two.

May 1966 was typical of the *Enterprise*'s operating schedule in terms of activity. On the ninth, the *Enterprise* flew from nine in the morning to nine at night and then replenished stores from the *Pictor* (AF-54). On the tenth, the air wing flew from ten in the morning to ten at night and the ship replenished munitions from the *Pyro* (AE-24). On the next day, Wednesday, the *Enterprise* flew from eleven o'clock in the morning to eleven at night. At midnight the carrier replenished aviation fuel from the *Kawishiwi* (AO-146) and then went alongside the *Mars* (AFS-1) to take aboard general stores.

On the morning of 12 May, the *Enterprise* serviced two destroyers that had come alongside, passing them supplies by highline, and then conducted strikes between 1100 and 2300. The ship was at it again early on the morning of the thirteenth, conducting air operations from nine in the morning to nine at night and then, at 11 o'clock at night, going alongside the *Mazama* (AE-9) to load out bombs and rockets.

On the fourteenth the air wing turned out early for an 0845 deck load launch to strike targets in Hanoi and then continued cyclic flight operations until after 2000, at which time the *Enterprise* recovered her last aircraft and proceeded at high speed to rendezvous with the USS *Kawishiwi* again to replenish jet fuel. Then, at four in the morning, with a full load of jet fuel, the *Enterprise* broke away and headed for Subic Bay, her thirty days of combat operations on the line completed. The ship was scheduled for four days of R&R from 16 to 19 May in Subic Bay, followed by two days, the twentieth and twenty-first, in Manila to "show the flag." The ship would depart Manila on the twenty-second to be in position to commence flight operations at 1000 on Monday, 23 May.

The crew was, as always, looking forward to this break in the schedule. Forty to sixty sailors lived in a single compartment. Their bunks were stacked four high, and all of their possessions were stowed in a locker the size of a student in high school. They had to line up to shower, brush their teeth, and eat. There is no beer or liquor to relax them at the end of their sixteen- to eighteen-hour workday. Navy ships are totally dry; there is no alcohol allowed in any form on board, except for medicinal purposes. And then, of course, there was no femininity to soften the boredom of their all-male society. Liberty ashore was very important.

Shortly after the *Enterprise* disengaged from refueling with the *Kawishiwi*, the fleet received a typhoon warning from Fleet Weather Central in the Philippines that Typhoon Erma was roaring up from the south and would be in the vicinity of Subic Bay on the sixteenth, the day of the *Enterprise*'s scheduled arrival there.

Consequently, the *Enterprise* proposed to go into Subic on the seventeenth or eighteenth, after the typhoon had passed, and recommended canceling the Manila part of the visit in order to get some essential upkeep time for the ship and the air wing at Cubi Point Naval Air Station, where the carrier could go alongside a pier to have aircraft and equipment loaded directly on and off of the flight deck. Seventh Fleet quickly okayed the plans, but Mother Nature was operating with a different scheduler.

Instead of slicing through the Philippines and heading north, Erma slowly ground to a halt and interposed itself between the *Enterprise* and the Philippines so that the ship was unable to go to either Manila or Subic. As a result, the *Enterprise* did what ships do while evading typhoons: It maneuvered well clear of the storm, staying at least two hundred miles from the eye, and particularly avoided the northeast quadrant. Meanwhile, the crew cursed fate in every term that could be conjured up.

Every four hours the navigator would get a position report on Erma and a forecast of movement of the eye. To the dismay of everyone on board, the typhoon's projected track did nothing but drive the *Enterprise* back toward the Gulf of Tonkin. Finally, on 20 May, Erma blew through then curved toward the mainland and the path to Subic was opened.

Commander, Seventh Fleet directed by priority message that the *Enterprise* should proceed, at best possible speed, to arrive in Subic on 21 May, offload all dud and battle-damaged aircraft, and get underway at 1800 that same afternoon to recover a dozen or so replacement aircraft that would fly out from the Naval Air Station at Cubi Point to land onboard that night. Nothing was said about liberty.

As the *Enterprise* entered Subic Bay at first light on Saturday, 21 May, the weather conditions were ideal, with a clear sky and a light breeze. The tugs were waiting so the ship was able to make up to Alava Pier at 0630. As I stood on the starboard wing of the bridge watching the crew send over the heavy mooring lines to the pier, the XO, Capt. Sam Linder, joined me.

Sam, a fine officer who had stood close to the top of his class at the Naval Academy, had relieved Capt. Pete Peterson as XO three months earlier. Sam had gone through flight training before getting his master's and doctoral degrees in nuclear physics at the California Institute of Technology. He had been selected by Admiral Rickover for the nuclear program and been ordered as XO of the *Enterprise.* He had been selected for promotion a year early for captain, before his arrival on board the carrier. In addition to his being a doctor of nuclear physics, Sam was a fine naval officer who served his captain well and dealt harmoniously with the crew.

After lamenting the fickleness of fate that had deprived the crew of their five days of hard-earned R&R, Sam, ever the conscientious executive officer, proposed to me that officers be permitted to go ashore for lunch and the chief petty officers be allowed to do the same. Also, perhaps some especially deserving first-class crewmembers could go ashore for an hour or so to the PX. Because of our 1800 departure that night, nobody else would be permitted off the ship.

But I thought this through and said, "I think we should grant liberty to half the crew, sections 2 and 4, to commence at nine this morning and to expire at 5 o'clock this afternoon. We will keep sections 1 and 3 on board as the duty sections."

Like any solid, responsible XO, Sam stepped back a pace, obviously aghast, and said, "Captain, you're joking. Sections 2 and 4 are half the crew, three thousand men. We can't keep them from drinking once they are ashore, and we're bound to have some drunks and probably a number will miss the ship's sailing."

My rejoinder was, "You're absolutely right, Sam. That's why we're sending them ashore. They deserve to tie one on. They have been working their tails off and we owe it to this crew to give them every break when we can. Frankly, I trust these guys. I think that we can run this liberty in a way so that half the crew can have a real liberty and we'll still get the ship underway without any trouble." I recalled that when the *Enterprise* went through shakedown training in Guantánamo Bay, Cuba, the fleet training group insisted that we conduct an exercise that required the *Enterprise* to get underway with only two sections of the crew on board. This was to simulate a situation in which there was either a disaster at the naval base or a nuclear accident on the carrier during normal liberty hours that would require the carrier to be moved for the safety of either the base or the ship itself. The hard part was to have enough qualified reactor operators and engineers to run the propulsion plant safely while getting underway. At the time I thought this was a ridiculous drill and questioned whether we should actually try to get the carrier underway with only two duty sections. But it was a drill we had to perform in order to complete our shakedown training, and it turned out to be not that difficult. Now, with almost a year of fleet operations under our belt, the *Enterprise* crew was even more competent. I was confident that the engineering and reactor departments had enough trained and qualified people to handle all of the supervisory tasks in the nuclear operation.

Next I outlined my ideas on how the ship would handle the liberty. Sections 2 and 4 would go ashore for normal liberty, which would expire at 5:00 PM. This meant they could go do their shopping or sports on the Subic base or they could head for Olongapo to the bars and hot spots that would be open and ready for them—they operated on a twenty-four-hour basis. There would be sufficient members of the master-at-arms' force to meet the liberty party as they came on board, and sufficient numbers to make sure all of them went directly to their compartments. There they could shower, put on their clean skivvies (underwear; the sailors' pajamas) and get in their bunks and turn in. But no member of Sections 2 or 4 would be allowed out of their compartments until midnight, when they would be scheduled for their first underway watch. The sailors would have eight hours to rest or sleep it off and a big aluminum tray of midrats (midnight rations) under their belt to start off their new day. I called over the boatswain's mate of the watch and said, "Boats, I want you to pass the word to all hands, that liberty for sections 2 and 4 will commence at 0900 and will expire onboard at 1700 this afternoon."

"Boats," a first-class with twenty years of service, just stood there, bewildered. I repeated my instructions and made it clear that I fully intended that liberty be granted as had been indicated. Boats saluted, went over to the general announcing system microphone on the bridge, punched the "all hands" button, pushed the actuating lever down, blew his boatswain's call, and piped, "All hands."

Then he said in that raspy voice that all boatswain mates eventually develop, "Now hear this. Now hear this. Liberty will commence for sections 2 and 4, to commence at 0900 and to expire onboard at 1700 this afternoon." Then Boats said, "I repeat" and growled out his message again. The microphone lever snapped up, and for about five seconds there was absolute silence about the ship. The normal noises of klaxons blowing, hammers banging, and gangways creaking as the ship rigged its inport facilities were absent.

Then suddenly there was a tremendous cheer as the sailors realized that half of the crew would have liberty ashore, which was more than any of them had planned or even hoped for. The reaction of the men in sections 1 and 3, those who would stay onboard with the duty, was interesting. To their enormous credit, and probably characteristic of this crew, there were no complaints. They were just pleased for their shipmates who were getting to get off this iron lady even for just eight hours.

At 1630 Sam Linder and I took station on the starboard wing of the bridge overhanging the Alava pier and looked down the road toward the main gate. There wasn't a sailor in sight. Our liberty party had gone ashore in their whites with round hats and black neckerchiefs looking like a million bucks. They would be easily spotted among the numbers of base sailors and working parties, who were in their blue dungarees. At about 1645, one of the to-be-expected tropical cloudbursts occurred, a tremendous downpour that drenched the entire base.

Then in the rain they came in a crowd, filling up the entire road from curb to curb as they headed toward the ship at a fast walk. By ten minutes to five the liberty party had reached the brows and were pouring across the gangways to the ship. At two minutes before five, the last dozen arrived on the backs of their comrades, semiconscious or unconscious, but on time. They looked awful. Their once-spotless white uniforms were drenched with rain and soiled with mud. The only thing wonderful to see was the smiles on their faces.

The officer of the deck called from the quarterdeck to say that the men had all gotten to the main gate, which was equipped with turnstiles for security, at the same time. They were held up for fifteen minutes by the bottleneck or they would have gotten on board before the thunderstorm. Not a single sailor came on board after 1700, and by 1715 it was clear that every sailor of that more than three-thousand-man liberty party was back on board and accounted for. No one late, nobody missing ship.

By 1730 the eight base tugs had arrived and were making up their lines on *Enterprise*'s port side. The crew of the ammunition ship, which was moored astern, was on the pier to handle the carrier's lines, ready to cast them off the bollards when called upon to do so.

By 1755 the *Enterprise* was singled up with all systems tested. As the sweep second hand passed by 1800 on the bridge clock, the last line was cast off. There was a single long blast on the ship's whistle and the *Enterprise* was underway for the Gulf of Tonkin and back to war.

That evening at 2345, the ship, fully darkened, headed west toward the Gulf of Tonkin and Yankee Station, threading its way through the fleets of small native fishing craft. The midwatch arrived on the bridge, the young sailors who would man the helm and the engine-room telegraphs, operate the radars, and handle the communications until 0400. They chatted with the off-going watch about how much they had enjoyed their unexpected liberty. They were happy, and their shipmates in sections 1 and 2 were pleased for them.

We had done the right thing, showing the crew not only how much they deserved a break but also how much they were trusted. But the decision to grant liberty was made only after reassuring myself that it could be done safely and within the standard operating procedures.

The morale of the *Enterprise*'s crew had always been high, and it was events like this that demonstrated the officers' concern for the welfare of the crew and our willingness to stretch a point and, perhaps, invite criticism in order to give the crew the breaks they deserved. It made the sailors believe that theirs was the finest carrier afloat. And they continuously made every effort to live up to that conviction.

The *Enterprise* had started out well. The message from commander, Seventh Fleet, Vice Adm. J. J. Hyland, congratulating the *Enterprise* after their first thirty days on the line in 1966, said, "Well done. I am very favorably impressed with the Big 'E's' performance on your first tour on the line. Your effort of over 104 sorties on 26 April, 100 of which were attack sorties in North Vietnam, obviously represents the result of training, hard work, superior planning and esprit de corps. This record is far less a tribute to the advantages of nuclear power than to the organic fueled people serving in this fine ship."

Only in the U.S. Navy could six thousand average American twenty year olds come on board the largest and most complex ship in history—with eight nuclear reactors and ninety-eight of the world's most advanced aircraft—and in six months set records for combat operations that still stand.

12

The *Enterprise*

Fast Turnaround

The *Enterprise* returned from Vietnam to San Francisco in late June 1966 to a real hero's welcome. At that time the *Enterprise* had an impressive cachet. It was the largest ship in the world, it was the first and only nuclear carrier, and its eight reactors gave it a speed of more than forty miles an hour. Then, too, at that time the majority of the American people supported the war and believed we would win. The Bay Area had declared the day of return "*Enterprise* Day," and on that day, any sailor with an *Enterprise* shoulder patch could get a free drink in most of the bars in San Francisco. There was a feeling of patriotism in the atmosphere. All three of the Bay Area's main newspapers devoted their front pages on 21 June 1966 to the *Enterprise*'s return from Vietnam to its new homeport, Naval Air Station Alameda. The country was looking for a tangible hero to fuss over, and for now, the *Enterprise* was it.

One-inch headlines in the *Oakland Tribune* proclaimed, "*Enterprise* Home," and the article beneath it declared that "this nation's most powerful lady returned from war today, her nuclear power churning her through the Golden Gate as thousands of welcomers cheered her on." The *San Francisco Examiner*'s front-page headlines stated, "Wild Greeting for Carrier." The *Enterprise*, the article stated, "steamed through the Golden Gate with a fleet of more than 40 small craft—sailboats, yachts and fireboats spouting spray were on hand . . . with Major John F. Shelly leading them."

The *San Francisco Chronicle* also had a front-page picture of the *Enterprise,* and its one-inch headlines read, "*Enterprise* Homecoming Snarls Marin County Traffic." Not only did two thousand people "line the sidewalks of the Golden Gate Bridge to watch the homecoming," the article stated, but "traffic on Highway 101 was backed up from the Bridge to San Rafael [and] crowds gathered wherever they could get a view of the Bay. . . . All of the bridge's parking lots were jammed and the overflow spilled into the Presidio and they too were quickly filled. . . . Despite the traffic there were amazingly no reports of accidents. They were moving too slow for anything to happen." The *Oakland Tribune* summed it up: "The *Enterprise,* the largest warship in the world, had done her job. It is only fitting that her welcome should be the biggest in the Bay area since that accorded the battered cruiser *San Francisco* during World War II." The homecoming was later written up in *Life* magazine, which displayed a picture of the *Enterprise* on its cover. The article also compared the attitude of the crowds as reminiscent of World War II, welcoming a heroic ship of the U.S. Navy home from the wars.

It was all very exciting. When the *Enterprise* came alongside the pier at Alameda, my wife Dabney was waiting with our two children, Admiral Rickover standing next to her. As soon as the first gangway was over, Admiral Rickover took off at a fast pace to be the first aboard. A chief petty officer stepped in front of him to block his way and sent Dabney aboard ahead of him. The chiefs knew their priorities. Or at least they knew those of the ship's commanding officer. Surprisingly enough, Admiral Rickover was not at all upset. He was so thrilled by the *Enterprise's* successful cruise that he was in an unshakable good humor. The combat experience of the *Enterprise* as the only nuclear-powered carrier had resulted in a great deal of ongoing press interest, and coverage had been universally favorable. Rickover felt that his proposed program for a fleet of nuclear-powered aircraft carriers had been given a powerful boost and that the tactical advantages of nuclear propulsion had been vindicated. He was probably right.

Dabney was brought up to the bridge, but I was still involved in getting the ship tied up. After a hug and a kiss, she said, "You're busy, I'd better get out of your hair." I replied, "Why don't you go down to my cabin and I'll meet you when the lines are doubled up." Admiral Rickover had arrived with Dabney. He was bubbling over with the excitement of the homecoming. He congratulated me and then immediately launched into a discussion of how well the reactors had performed. He said his Naval Reactors staff had saved the day by coaching by satellite telephone the ship's reactor department in making repairs on board to the number 7 reactor. He said no other organization could have accomplished that feat. I agreed with him and then added, "Admiral, I'm trying to get this ship tied up and I really can't talk to you about those things now."

Rickover said, "That's okay. I'll tell you what we'll do. You pick a nice restaurant and we'll go out tonight and get a steak. You and I can sit there, enjoy our steak, and go over the whole cruise." My face must have fallen because Dave Leighton, who was Rickover's number one assistant and often traveled with him, spoke up and said, "Admiral Rickover, are you out of your goddamn mind? Holloway has been at sea away from his wife and family for eight months. He doesn't want to talk to you. He wants to see his family." Rickover replied, "I'm sure Holloway would like to talk to me about how the nuclear reactors performed." Dave Leighton said to the admiral, "Come with me," and he and Rickover departed without any more fuss. I invited Rickover to join me at breakfast in the commanding officer's cabin the next morning. Rickover had to catch a plane back to Washington at 0930 but could just make it. That breakfast was an enjoyable session. Rickover was still caught up in the excitement of the activity of homecoming and the national publicity that his nuclear carrier, the *Enterprise*, was attracting.

A word about Dave Leighton, Rickover's assistant for nuclear-powered surface ships. I had worked very closely with Leighton, and I depended upon him enormously throughout my relationship with Rickover and later sought his personal advice on nuclear programs when I became CNO. Leighton was very smart, a brilliant engineer, and impeccably loyal. On occasion Rickover would get furious with him, have a tantrum, and say to him, "That's the dumbest thing I ever heard. I don't know why I put up with your stupidity. You're not doing what I told you to do." Leighton would stand there, listen to Rickover, then continue his conversation as if Rickover hadn't even spoken. Rickover would always simmer down and eventually agree with Leighton, once Dave had explained himself. He was enormously patient and considerate of Admiral Rickover. I believe that he always felt that these outbursts were Rickover's way of testing him, making sure Leighton was willing to stand behind his words and not back down.

After the euphoria of homecoming, which lasted about seventy-two hours, the crew of the *Enterprise* got back to work. This ship was a community, a home for four thousand sailors, and had to continue to function in that capacity. It was not just a case of letting everybody off to be with their families.

Commencing on 24 June, half the crew would depart on twenty days' leave, and the balance of the officers and men would manage the housekeeping affairs for the *Enterprise.* When the first leave period ended, on 15 July, the first leave party would return and the second group would depart on three weeks' leave. Those crewmembers not on leave would put in a full day's work from 0800 to 1700 and be aboard for twenty-four-hours duty every fourth day to provide the security and continuity required in a major man of war. The nuclear reactors had been shut down, and the electrical power for the carrier was being provided by its own train of diesel generator cars. If the *Enterprise* had hooked up to commercial shore power, the city of Alameda would have been blacked out.

Although the work was reduced to a minimum so that it could be accomplished without too much strain by the 50 percent of the crew on board, there were still essential functions that had to be accomplished. About 25 percent of the men were due for transfer through expiration of enlistment or completion of a sea duty, which meant transfer to a shore station for two years. At the same time, the ship was receiving replacements for this 25 percent, coming from shore duty to begin their three-year sea tour. In addition, there were the normal administrative affairs dealing with the lives of fifteen hundred sailors living on board a carrier, which, even though moored at a pier, still had to be provided with three meals a day, hot water, electricity, and everything else necessary to make life as comfortable as possible on board. Not more than 30 percent of the crew was married and had dependents in the area, which meant that for the unmarried sailors and junior officers, the *Enterprise* would be their home and services for them had to be as complete as possible under the circumstances.

Hanging over all this planning and the activities of the port period was the realization that in November, less than six months away, the *Enterprise* would again depart the United States for a minimum of seven months on the line, conducting combat operations in the Gulf of Tonkin. The ship had to start, then, in July in order to prepare for that next deployment. Every week of the five months available had to be profitably employed in training the replacement crew members, getting the ship ready to take aboard its air wing, stocking supplies, installing new equipment, and loading out with fuel and ammunition. Many repairs and modifications had to be made to the ship and its embarked equipment. Advances in technology were constant, and these five months in port were an opportunity to install the latest radars and new aircraft test equipment, make upgrading and safety changes to the nuclear plant, and train all the sailors in how to use and maintain the new equipment.

First on the list of material work to be accomplished was the necessity for the *Enterprise* to be drydocked so that its bottom could be cleaned and repainted, and any work to the hull of the ship that was below the waterline had to be accomplished. So the *Enterprise* was scheduled to enter the Hunters Point Naval Shipyard, in San Francisco, for drydocking. One problem was that the reactor plant had been shut down and the ship would have to be moved "cold iron," a Navy term meaning that the ship would have no propulsive capability of its own but would have to depend entirely on tugs. Furthermore, when unplugged from its electrical support, the train of diesel generators on the pier at Alameda, the *Enterprise* would have to provide all of its electrical power through the emergency diesel generators installed in the ship. This meant that only about 30 percent of the normal electrical load could be provided.

Although technically on leave, I returned to be on the bridge when the *Enterprise* was moved from Alameda to Hunters Point. According to Navy regulations, the captain was not responsible for the safety of the ship in a cold-iron movement like this, with the power supplied by Navy tugs under the control of a civilian Navy harbor pilot. Traditionally, though, my place was on the bridge whenever the *Enterprise* was not securely moored. The day of the move, the pilot reported on board with a total of ten tugs to assist him, four large, powerful, oceangoing tugs to move the carrier across the bay, and six small "docking" tugs to maneuver the ship in the very tricky evolution of crossing the sill of the drydock without allowing the ship to get cocked as its 1,000-foot length entered the 1,200-foot drydock. Unfortunately, on the day of the move, the winds were at twenty knots, gusting occasionally to twenty-five, which is pretty much standard for San Francisco Bay. This made the operation especially difficult. But safety was the number one consideration, and on the sixth attempt, the pilot, with very smart maneuvering of his tugs, was able to get the bow of the *Enterprise* over the sill of the drydock and slip it in without the sides of the ship making contact with the drydock. Our main problem was that the tug power was inadequate for the wind conditions, and there were no more tugs available in the entire Bay Area on that day. Six of the tugs had been U.S. Navy boats and the others were contract vessels from the local towing companies.

With the *Enterprise* moving to Hunters Point, the four thousand men in the ship's crew moved with her. The *Enterprise* remained in the Hunters Point Naval Shipyard for about six weeks and was in drydock the entire time. The period was used profitably by sending the crew to school and training courses covering damage control, firefighting, and nuclear weapons, as well as sending them to special training courses on the new equipment being installed in the *Enterprise.* Many of these courses, such as firefighting and damage control, were mandatory for the entire crew. Sailors were sent in groups of fifty to three-day courses at the local training base, and those assigned to firefighting and damage-control parties at general quarters were required to complete a two-week course. This training was, of course, in addition to the specialized training that taught the sailors their jobs in the ship, such as the operation of the aircraft catapults on the flight deck or controlling the search radars in the Combat Information Center. The specially trained reactor technicians had a great deal of work to do with the reactor plant cold. It was the only time the reactor spaces were fully accessible. It was very time-consuming and demanding work, but then these were very capable people.

In September the yard work was completed and the eight reactors were taken critical. Now the *Enterprise* would return to its special pier at NAS Alameda under its own power. During that forty-five-minute trip across the Bay from San Francisco to Oakland, there were several hundred sailors on board the *Enterprise* who were underway for the first time on a U.S. Navy man-of-war. The last week in August, the main task in the *Enterprise* was to get the ship cleaned up after the experience in the shipyard, where, as always, there had been much acetylene cutting and welding. By now all of the crew had returned from postdeployment leave and were busy installing new equipment and refurbishing the old, as well as attending the mandatory training schools.

We knew the ship had to be kept especially clean, well-painted, and completely squared away, because the *Enterprise*, being the one-of-a-kind nuclear carrier, was host to many visitors, from both the local community and Washington, D.C. Rickover made several visits just to satisfy himself that the engineering and reactor departments were being competently run and that they would be ready for the Atomic Energy Commission inspection, which would be held in October before deployment. Rickover usually invited himself for breakfast or lunch with me. He had apparently learned a lesson about intruding upon the family life of officers of deploying warships. His mood was always upbeat and he was quite cordial when he came aboard ship, although he would raise his voice and shout imprecations when, on his tours of inspection through-out the nuclear spaces, he saw something he didn't like. That was not often, but it was inconceivable that Rickover could miss anything that was awry, even by the most limited margin. Among the many visitors who came to the ship were the Harlem Globetrotters, the professional basket-ball troupe. They demonstrated their remarkable ball-handling talent and clowned and performed with an amazing skill on the hangar deck, much to the delight of the crew. They then joined the sailors at their noonday meal.

The State Department regularly sent foreign dignitaries to visit the ship—I think just to get them away from Washington, D.C., and out of their hair. On board the *Enterprise* they would tour the ship and then be treated to a fine luncheon in the officers' mess, suitably dining on all-American fare, usually concluding with strawberry shortcake. That seemed to be a favorite of visitors from overseas. Two handsome young ladies, both competing candidates for Miss California of 1966, visited the ship with their entourages and had themselves photographed with sailors and with the distinctive *Enterprise* island in the background. At the opposite end of the spectrum, more than seventy members of the distinguished Bohemian Club, a historic fixture in the culture of San Francisco, visited the carrier and then were entertained at lunch in the officers' wardroom, an event that resulted in many of the ship's people being given a return invitation to dine in the sacrosanct halls of the Bohemian Club in Nob Hill.

In addition to duties on board ship, I had my hands full with the publicity that always attended the *Enterprise.* My tasks covered everything from receiving the keys to the city from the mayor to making lunchtime speeches at local civic clubs. On one occasion I traveled up to the University of California in Berkeley to present a model of the *Enterprise* to Mrs. Nimitz, the widow of Admiral Nimitz, the World War II hero, in the Nimitz Library at the NROTC Building on the University of California campus.

BACK TO SEA

In mid-September the *Enterprise* went to sea for two days of independent steaming exercises (ISE), during which the ship conducted drills in firefighting, damage control, and deck aircraft handling. A single F-4 Phantom II had been flown on board the first morning, and the new sailors assigned to the flight deck spent the next two days pushing the plane around, tying it down, chocking it, and otherwise learning how to maneuver and secure planes on the carrier's flight deck. It was almost amusing to see the awe with which these new sailors regarded the single Phantom II, not realizing that in a month there would be eighty aircraft onboard.

During two days of ISE, the *Enterprise* provided a ready deck for three days of refresher landings for a number of pilots from the West Coast airfields as well as qualification landings for our own pilots, newly assigned to F-4 Phantom, A-6 Intruder, and A-4 Skyhawk squadrons. For initial qualification, a pilot needed to make six good daytime landings and then two night landings. These night landings were terrifying at first, and they never got easy, but much of the flying into North Vietnam would be on night missions.

The *Enterprise* returned to port for a week, and much of that time was used in correcting material deficiencies disclosed in the ISE and shifting people around to different assignments to better accommodate their capabilities. Some individuals were simply accidents waiting to happen on the flight deck and had to be gotten to other duties to save their own lives and not risk the lives of others.

When the *Enterprise* returned to sea the first week in October for Third Fleet exercises, the crew was beginning to come together and looked like they would be ready to deploy for combat on time. The Third Fleet, based at San Diego, was the training fleet on the West Coast, which provided individual ships the work-up through multiship task force exercises to prepare them for Task Force 77. Almost all of these Third Fleet exercises, even if they were primarily for the benefit of destroyers, cruisers, or even amphibious ready groups, required the participation of a carrier. That was because tactical aviation was such an essential component of all naval combat operations that the surface combatants as well as the amphibious forces had to have experience in working with the carriers and their aircraft.

In mid-October 1966 the *Enterprise* was at sea again for two days of ISE, running down the coast to San Diego for Third Fleet exercises. The *Enterprise* had received special clearance from the AEC to anchor in San Diego Bay in a designated spot where the ocean tides would flush out any fission products, should the ship experience an untoward incident. This is defined as the release of fission products to the atmosphere—the surrounding air or sea. Avoiding an incident was an overriding concern for nuclear-powered ships. The future of nuclear power in the Navy would be in jeopardy if there were a nuclear incident of a magnitude approaching the Three Mile Island breakdown. But even the release of a measurable amount of radioactivity could cast doubts upon the safety of the nuclear-powered ship from ecological and public health aspects. Whenever the *Enterprise* was in port, small power boats flying the green flag of certain antinuclear activists would circle in the vicinity almost twenty-four hours a day, dipping for samples of the water around us, especially where cooling or flushing water was being discharged overboard. Never were any of these activists able to detect even a trace of radioactivity above the background radiation that is always present in our atmosphere.

The U.S. Navy has never had a nuclear incident, even of the minimum degree, which is defined as a detectable measurement above this ambient that is always present in the earth's atmosphere. That can be attributed to the stringency of the oversight of Admiral Rickover and his people. The following incident illustrates the effectiveness of the radiation control built into the U.S. naval reactors by Rickover's people. In 1967 the *Enterprise* was anchored in Hong Kong Harbor, and when the ambient radiation of the local atmosphere was measured—as was part of our routine safeguards practice—the background radiation measured at the flight deck was higher than the readings taken in the actual reactor compartment with the reactors operating. This ambient radiation, it was discovered, was due to the A-bomb tests being conducted in China.

At San Diego the *Enterprise* was assigned to training duty with the Pacific Fleet Training Group, similar to the organization at Naval Station Guantánamo Bay, which had assisted the *Enterprise's* training during shakedown. The purpose of the San Diego group was to measure the ship's readiness to conduct operations in Southeast Asia. Yankee Station would be the scenario for the Third Fleet exercise.

The air wing had flown on board the *Enterprise* during the carrier's transit from Alameda to San Diego. It was still Air Wing 9, but with a somewhat different composition. It consisted of two fighter squadrons of fourteen F-4B Phantom IIs, two light attack squadrons of fourteen A-4C Skyhawks, one nine-plane A-6A Intruder squadron (a new aircraft for the Enterprise), one reconnaissance squadron of five RA5-C Vigilantes, a squadron of four E-2A Hawkeyes for airborne CIC (also a vastly improved capability over the previous cruise), three A-3B Skywarrior tanker planes, and a detachment of UH-2 Seasprite helicopters, totaling about three thousand people and ninety aircraft. The planes had flown in from their bases around the country. The fighters from NAS Miramar in southern California, the A-4s from NAS Le Moore in northern California, the A-6s from NAS Whidbey Island in Washington state, and the RA5-Cs from NAS Orlando, Florida. Some of the planes had landed at the Alameda Naval Air Station and then taxied under their own power to the carrier pier, where the carrier's cranes loaded them on board. About half of the aircraft remained ashore and flew on board after we had gotten to sea. The three thousand men making up the maintenance and operating crews of the various squadrons were flown into NAS Alameda by Naval Reserve transport squadrons, embarked with their sea bags and bedded down in their assigned berthing compartments and bunk rooms on board the *Enterprise.*

For three days at sea west of California, the *Enterprise* was put through an operational readiness evaluation (ORE), a warm-up for the actual inspection, known as the operational readiness inspection, or ORI. The crew would be exercised at general quarters and then at flight quarters to conduct air operations, simulating a schedule that would be flown in Vietnam. The crew was drilled at handling simulated battle damage, such as fires on the hangar deck, underwater torpedo explosions, and various other casualty simulations that would demonstrate our ability to recover from both battle damage and self-imposed accidents.

By Friday morning the ORE had been completed and the *Enterprise* was heading back into San Diego Bay and its special berth at the carrier pier at North Island. I was informed by the chief inspector, an aviation rear admiral whose primary duties were to command a division of two large-deck carriers, that the ship had done excellent or better in all areas except two, the communications department and the CIC. Both had been graded by the evaluation team as unsatisfactory. The *Enterprise* would have Friday afternoon, the weekend, and all of Monday to rectify the deficiencies that had been noted by the ORE inspection team before the ORI would begin on Tuesday with three more days of at-sea operations.

One of my personal tenets governing a commanding officer's approach to leadership was "command attention." This had been passed on to me by my father, and it meant, among other things, that the commanding officer should be involved in correcting his unit's problems, first by identifying the problem, then by defining the corrective action, and finally by a hands-on supervision of these corrective actions. My rationale was that the commanding officer is the most experienced officer in his command, and an officer of demonstrated good judgment—or he would not have been ordered to the job. The XO and I had solved the deck-handling impasse of the four A-4 squadrons during the trip across the Indian Ocean on the first cruise, when after nine days of flight operations the deck handling officers of the Air Department, all commanders and lieutenant commanders, could not devise a flight deck-flow pattern that would enable a deck load launch to be turned around in the required forty-five minutes.

I felt I could not accept the *Enterprise*'s deployment for combat with an unsatisfactory or even a borderline grade in CIC operations. The CIC was the heart of the ship's command and control system, where the orders of the ship's commanding officer and flag officers over him were translated into action for the operations of the ship and the control of the air wing.

On Monday morning, as the *Enterprise* cleared the channel sea buoy outside San Diego Harbor, general quarters was sounded to get the crew to their battle stations. We would conduct damage-control and shiphandling evolutions in preparation for the ORI while proceeding at thirty knots to the operating area to launch the air wing.

With the ship at GQ and the air wing at flight quarters, I turned over the conn of the carrier to the navigator who had gained my confidence on the previous deployment. I believed that at least he would not have a collision or run us aground. I had assigned the XO responsibility to fix the Communications Department and headed him for the communications center, where he found the problem to be an internal one. The administrative handling and routing of messages to the embarked admiral and his staff was the issue. I surmised that the embarked flag officer had felt he was not getting the message traffic delivered to him in hard copy soon enough. If this were the case, that would be easy to rectify, by assigning more and smarter sailors—and perhaps junior officers—to hand carry message traffic to the flag bridge. Meanwhile, I went to the CIC, the other source of the unsatisfactory evaluation. It immediately became apparent what the problems were. Just as it had bothered the inspectors, it made an equally bad impression on me.

CIC was located in air-conditioned spaces so that the electronic equipment would be in a cool, dry environment for proper and efficient operation. Personal comfort was secondary. But it was one of the few air-conditioned spaces on the ship, and it appeared that sailors assigned to CIC were using the center as a living space. All of the available room behind the display boards and operating consoles was filled with the personal gear of the sailors in the CIC, mainly the unmarried men who had no home ashore to store their personal gear when they went to sea. It was also a repository for much of the shopping at the Navy exchanges and bazaars of the oriental ports visited by the *Enterprise*—electric guitars, amplifiers, tape decks, kimonos, and mechanical toys—all in their original packing. Also because of the air conditioning, the off-duty petty officers used the CIC for a hangout. They gathered around the coffee mess and flaked out and dozed in the many corners and cubby holes between the consoles, display boards, and equipment. It was impossible for me or the CIC evaluators to know who was on duty, responsible for the operation of the radar and the constant updating of the Plexiglas plots. When I queried the CIC officer about the large number of petty officers in CIC going around with a cigarette in their left hand and a mug of coffee in their right, I was informed by him that the policy was for nonrated strikers to actually operate the equipment, the status boards, and communications. The petty officers acted as "supervisory" personnel. If there was a problem, or the nonrated striker couldn't handle a situation, then the petty officer would step in and take his place. I explained that this was not what I had in mind in assigning petty officer and striker billets to the CIC.

There were three main problems to resolve. First, all the personal gear in the operating space had to be eliminated. Second, the supervisors had to get back to the actual operation of the equipment instead of standing around waiting for problems to develop. And third, the ranks of the off-duty personnel who were mainly engaged in keeping their coffee mugs filled had to be thinned out. The problems with the CIC were evident, and the solutions did not appear to be complex or difficult.

The chief master at arms was summoned and told to find an empty compartment among the many voids below the waterline. The purpose of these void compartments was to divide up the lower hull of the ship into watertight sections to limit the flooding that would occur from a collision or from battle damage that holed the underwater hull of the ship. These compartments were far below the main decks, but they were convenient for any kind of storage that did not require frequent access— perfect for our purposes. The crew's overseas purchases would be stowed in these compartments and not reissued until the *Enterprise* returned to homeport. A sturdy hasp for double locking was welded onto the access door, and the ship's supply officer was responsible for the storage, security, accountability and issue of the men's property. The *Enterprise*'s supply officer, Commander Creekman, immediately took charge and made our crew's personal-gear storage system the model for the Pacific Fleet carriers.

A Supply Corps lieutenant, with a first-class petty officer assistant, was assigned the administration of the storeroom, responsible for preventing any damage or pilferage to the articles stored there. The nooks and corners of the living spaces of the junior officers' bunkrooms and sailors' berthing compartments had been the only available space for storing their personal belongings and the loot from the bargaining sessions with Asian merchants.

At the new storage space, hasps were installed, the door locked securely, and the record and accounting books were all in place by eight o'clock that evening. By midnight, CIC had been sanitized of every item and piece of equipment other than those listed on the Bureau of Ships authorized allowance. The second action was to establish a firm policy that during general quarters and flight quarters, the petty officers assigned to CIC would be seated at the radar consoles and maintain the status boards and situation plots. They would be assisted by the seamen strikers. The coffee mess was shut down during general quarters. While underway, only those men on watch were permitted to use the coffee mess.

With the senior petty officers and the most experienced technicians wearing the earphones, operating the equipment, and maintaining the plots, the effectiveness and efficiency of the entire CIC operation took a giant step upward. Now the CIC spaces more resembled an operating room ready for open-heart surgery than a room full of sailors having a coffee klatch in a godown (Chinese warehouse).

At first I had some concern about the reaction of the first-class petty officers and chiefs being put back on the consoles and plots. But with the extraordinarily high levels of activity generated by the operations in Vietnam, they had their hands full dealing with the rapidly developing situations encountered in modern warfare. They were far from bored and took a renewed interest in their primary responsibilities. As the cruise progressed and the *Enterprise* CIC won top grades on the ORI and was awarded the "E" for the best CIC in the fleet, morale was never a problem among the CIC personnel.

Now I have to answer a question. How could the CIC operation have so deteriorated and why had I not learned about it? My explanation is that it could happen in any department, division, or section of a ship as large as a carrier. The CO and XO do not have the opportunity to oversee all of the ship's operations on a regular basis. This is especially true during operations at sea and at general quarters, when the CO must be on the bridge and the XO is at his battle station at the secondary conning station in the steering engine room at the stern of the ship.

A replacement CIC officer had reported on board the *Enterprise* in July and taken over in a single week to enable his predecessor to take twenty days' leave prior to reporting to his next duty station. This new officer, a lieutenant commander, was inexperienced in CICs, although he had held a responsible job in the patrol squadron from which he came. He had been through the CIC school and fighter director training, but these facilities can only teach the technical aspects of the equipment and the mandatory procedures that are established by fleet doctrine. For an officer who has never served on a ship, there is the temptation to follow the path of least resistance. What can happen in these situations is that the new officer is told by his senior petty officers, "This is the way it's always been done in this ship. By keeping the senior petty officers off the consoles and the plotting boards they can be available to step in and take over in case of an emergency or crisis." This makes life a lot easier for the senior petty officers and gives them lots of time for schmoozing. The problem with this approach is that when things get dicey and the petty officers have to get back on the consoles, they may not be ready to take over without an adequate briefing on the current situation to bring them up to speed.

READY FOR WAR AGAIN

The ORI was a formal affair, as I pointed out, conducted by a two-star admiral who was a carrier division commander, having two aircraft carriers under his administrative command. His staff of experienced aviators had returned only three months earlier from a seven-month tour in the Tonkin Gulf embarked in the *Enterprise*'s contemporary carriers, the large-deck carriers in Task Force 77. The carrier division staff was aided by fifty or sixty officers and petty officers of the Naval Training Group from San Diego who set up the battle problem and kept the statistical score, reporting the reaction of the *Enterprise*'s crew to the various incidents thrown at them.

The battle problem simulated a carrier conducting operations off Vietnam. The rear admiral played the role of a task group commander, with the *Enterprise* as his flagship. He and his staff physically moved on board the *Enterprise*, occupying the flag quarters, subsisting on board for the period of the ORI and using the flag plotting room as their command center. The admiral was the chief inspector for the ORI and would personally sign and forward the report of the inspection to the commander, Air Forces, Pacific Fleet, who would then report to the Office of the Chief of Naval Operations as to the readiness of the ship to deploy overseas and conduct high-tempo combat operations in the western Pacific.

The ORI required the *Enterprise* to conduct operations similar to those in Vietnam. The air wing flew from the carrier to attack targets at the El Centro, California, Bombing and Gunnery ranges with live 500-pound bombs, and firing their annual training allowance of guided missiles against radio-controlled drone aircraft.

The ORI is a very intensive, seventy-two-hour session with few members of the ship's company or the inspectors getting much sleep. The carrier is presented with battle damage as the inspectors deliberately disable items of equipment to simulate that damage, and the ship is required to continue its operations without a break utilizing emergency procedures and jury-rigged secondary systems.

Admiral Rickover's group in Washington had sent a special detachment from his training group, the *Enterprise* land-based prototype at Arco, Idaho, to simulate casualties to the engineering plant. That was the area with which I was most concerned. But the reactor officer and chief engineer each did their expected professional job of reacting to the problems imposed upon them by Rickover's crew. They even gained grudging praise from the inspection group.

On Friday afternoon the battle problem ended, damage was restored, and the inspection team briefed the admiral as the *Enterprise* headed back toward San Diego. Before reaching port, the admiral called me into his cabin and offered his congratulations on the fine performance of the ship. The admiral said he was particularly impressed by the improvement in the CIC, which had been unsatisfactory in the preliminary operational readiness evaluation but during the ORI had been given the highest mark awarded so far that year to a carrier CIC by inspectors from the Fleet Training Group.

The communications department, which had also received an unsatisfactory preliminary grade on the ORE, had similarly improved and also received a grade of outstanding. These evaluations turned out to be so superior that, when the competitive year ended, the *Enterprise* had the highest grade of any carrier CIC and Communications Department in the Pacific Fleet. This resulted in the ship winning the Efficiency Award, or "E," for all Combat Information Centers and Communications Departments among the Pacific Fleet carriers.

With the operational readiness inspection concluded, the *Enterprise* returned to San Francisco Bay and its pier at Alameda for ten final days in port before deploying again to the western Pacific. The predeployment availability is intended to be used to rectify any last-minute engineering or material problems and to load the ship with spare parts for the reactors and the ship's electronics gear. The most complicated aspect of the spare parts loadout was to ensure that we had the necessary test equipment and spare parts for the six different kinds of aircraft that would be included in the carrier's air wing.

The combat consumables, aviation fuel and ammunition, were only partially loaded in order to keep the carrier's draft from becoming too deep to safely enter Pearl Harbor, and also to defer the loading of some relatively dangerous munitions that were considered too sensitive to handle in large quantities on board the carrier berthed in the metropolitan area of San Francisco. The balance of the ammunition load would be taken on board in Pearl Harbor and the aviation fuel from oilers after the carrier had sortied from Hawaii.

On 19 November 1966 the *Enterprise* was underway from Alameda again to spend its second consecutive Christmas on the line in the Gulf of Tonkin flying combat missions against the enemy in Vietnam. Five days later, the *Enterprise* arrived off Diamond Head on the island of Oahu and received instructions from the Harbor Entry Control Post to proceed into Pearl Harbor and moor at the ammunition pier. This caused raised eyebrows among some experienced Pacific Fleet officers, as no carrier larger than a *Midway*-class ship had been berthed at the ammunition pier because of the limited depth of water and the restricted maneuvering room afforded by the approaches to the mooring.

My concern was compounded when the helicopter with the civilian harbor pilot, provided by the naval base to conn the carriers through the tricky channels of the Port of Pearl Harbor, landed on board. The pilot stumbled twice before getting to the bridge and had a whisky breath that could stun an ox at six feet. Also disembarking from the helo were two old friends of mine, then assigned to the CinCPac staff, both captains and former carrier skippers. They had ridden out on the helicopter for a social visit to welcome me to Hawaii. Both were full of conversation and gossip about what was going on in Hawaii and what was happening back on the mainland. I realized immediately that it would be impossible for the civilian pilot to take the conn because of his inebriated condition. I would have to take the ship into Pearl Harbor on my own.

It was politely suggested to the pilot that because this was a nuclear-powered ship it was policy that the captain retain the conn, but I invited him to stand next to me and provide any advice as we maneuvered around Ford Island to the other side of Pearl, where the ammunition pier was located. The pilot had no problem disengaging himself from the officers in the pilothouse, and he retreated to the starboard wing of the bridge, where he draped himself over the windshield. The quartermaster's greatest fear was that he was going to throw up on the admiral's bridge just below.

As far as my well meaning but garrulous friends were concerned, I gave them all of my attention until the *Enterprise* entered the channel to Pearl Harbor, and at this point I simply reminded them, as the former skippers they were, that I was going to be fully occupied bringing the *Enterprise* to its berth, considering the condition of the professional pilot.

When the *Enterprise* arrived at the ammo pier, a second pilot, with six tugs at his command to do the docking, came on board by Jacob's ladder to work the carrier into its berth. He was sober and competent and knew the capabilities of the tugs, which I did not. With the help of six harbor tugs, and the flexibility of eight reactors and four propellers, the *Enterprise* made the landing at the pier without any particular trouble. Fortunately the wind was almost calm. With the high hull sides of a carrier, a strong wind on the beam could create much difficulty in getting these big ships to go where they were supposed to go at slow speeds.

There were moments of concern when the fathometer registered zero depth, but the pilot explained that this was due to the soft bottom mud at the ammo pier, which had been stirred up by the carrier's screws, and that there was probably a foot of water under the keel and three more feet of thin mud before the ship would hit a hard-grounding bottom. This may have been an accurate observation situation, but it was not altogether comforting.

Two days later, having taken on board the explosive cargo at the ammunition pier, the *Enterprise* got underway and moved to the carrier pier at Ford Island without incident, which was fortunate. One year later the *Enterprise*, under the command of its next captain, ran aground attempting to moor at the ammunition pier. In his efforts to extricate the carrier, the ship's engines were used at a high-power setting that sucked mud from the bottom into the ship's condensers, fouling them to the extent that the exhaust steam from the engine was not condensed into feed water. This loss of feed water to the boilers resulted in seven of the eight reactors scramming. A scram occurs when a reactor automatically shuts itself down because the reactor instrumentation perceives an emergency situation that could cause a nuclear accident or do damage to the reactor core. After a scram, the entire reactor plant has to be shut down and carefully inspected to determine if any damage has occurred.

On 26 September 1966 the *Enterprise* was moored at the carrier pier on Ford Island by 1000. Immediately a stream of VIP visitors commenced a procession on board, even though the local command had announced that there would be no visiting, except for official business, because the ship would be involved in loading critical supplies. That did not slow down the local mayor and members of the city council, and a number of senior retired admirals living in the area whose curiosity could only be served by a trip onboard the world's only nuclear carrier.

The following day the ship was opened for general visiting from 1000 until 1500, and that information was published in the local newspaper. By 1000 the police estimated that there were ten thousand people on the pier patiently waiting to get on board. Throughout the day the crowds did not diminish, and at 1600, when visiting hours finally were closed down, twenty thousand people, according to the local newspaper, had visited the *Enterprise.*

The next morning, 28 November, the *Enterprise* was underway at 0800, bound for the western Pacific, Task Force 77, and Point Yankee. The *Enterprise* arrived at Subic Bay on 5 December 1966 for a stop of two days to load guided air munitions, which were in such short supply throughout the fleet that they were being retained in the combat theater for battle use only—no training. These were the latest versions of the Sidewinder, Sparrow III, the antiradiation missile (ARM), and Walleye, a television-guided air-to-ground missile that was in limited production. Also, the *Enterprise* embarked a small group of intelligence specialists, including Vietnamese and Chinese linguists. These teams were in high demand and were also in critically short supply, so they were shuffled from departing carriers to new arrivals. They turned out to be invaluable in providing real-time information and intelligence on enemy aircraft and missile deployments and movements.

13

The *Enterprise*

Vietnam Redux

S hortly before daylight on 10 December 1966, the *Enterprise* joined up with the carriers *Franklin D. Roosevelt, Ticonderoga, Kitty Hawk,* and *Constellation* in Task Force 77 at Yankee Station, and by 0700 that morning it was launching the first sorties into North Vietnam in five months. Not much had changed since the previous July, when the *Enterprise* had departed Yankee Station. For both ship's crew and the air wing it was déjà vu. The U.S. Air Force and U.S. Marine Corps land-based tactical air and the carriers were still engaged in the Rolling Thunder campaign. The target selection was still coming mainly from the White House, with some Pentagon input and a pro forma CinCPac screening.

The positive aspects of this "sameness" was that the operations and the procedures were familiar to the 70 percent of the ship's people and air wing aviators, who were on their second tour in the Tonkin Gulf. For the air wing pilots, this was useful. They would still be familiar with the order of battle of the Vietnamese aircraft and antiaircraft systems, the terrain over both South and North Vietnam, and the operational in-flight procedures.

For the flight crews, the downside was the apparent lack of progress. After two years of combat, the same targets were being attacked—the same bridges, airfields, car parks, missile sites, and power plants—and under the same rules of engagement (ROE) from a White House that severely limited the pilots' tactics. These were ROE designed to avoid "collateral damage"—unintended damage to adjacent nonmilitary targets. Most of these Washington-mandated rules imposed restrictions in the selection of directions for attack- and flak-suppression runs that very much disadvantaged the pilots' tactics and increased the aircrafts' vulnerability to enemy defenses.

By this time, there was growing concern over the evident limited effectiveness of Rolling Thunder because of the restrictions placed upon target selection and the limited options available to the attacking pilots. An official U.S. Air Force military analysis of the campaign published in 2004 had this to say:

> Operation Rolling Thunder was a frequently interrupted bombing campaign that began on 24 February 1965 and lasted until the end of October 1968. During this period, U.S. Air Force and Navy aircraft engaged in a bombing campaign designed to force Ho Chi Minh to abandon his ambition to take over South Vietnam. The operation began primarily as a diplomatic signal to impress Hanoi with the United States' determination, essentially a warning that the violence would escalate until Ho Chi Minh "blinked," and secondly, it was intended to bolster the sagging morale of the South Vietnamese.
>
> The Johnson administration also imposed strict limits on the targets that could be attacked, for China and the Soviet Union were seen as the defenders of Communism who might intervene if the North Vietnamese faced defeat. Consequently the administration tried to punish the North without provoking the two nations believed to be its protectors.

According to the U.S. Air Force's leadership, the campaign had no clear-cut objective. Nor did its authors have any real estimate of the cost of lives and aircraft. General LeMay and others argued that military targets, rather than the enemy's resolve, should be attacked, and that blows should be rapid and sharp, with the impact felt immediately on the battlefield as well as by the political leadership in Hanoi.

The principal change in this second cruise for the *Enterprise* was the new air wing composition. In 1965, the unique feature of the wing had been the four squadrons of A-4 Skyhawk light attack planes. For the 1966 deployment, two of these Skyhawk squadrons had been replaced by a nine-plane squadron of Grumman Intruders, designated the A-6E. The Intruder was the most advanced all-weather tactical aircraft in the free world and possessed an enormous load-carrying capability, enabling the plane to launch from a carrier with fifteen thousand pounds of bombs. With its modern radar and electronics navigation system operated by the bombardier/navigator sitting to the right of the pilot in a tandem cockpit, the A-6 was capable of penetrating hostile radar-defended territory at very low altitudes at night or in bad weather and limiting the effectiveness of surface-to-air missiles. The Intruder attacked specific objectives either using its mapping radar or by locking onto a radar-significant target, such as a power plant, bridge or steel mill, with its fire-control radar.

Because of the great load-carrying capacity and its tactical versatility, the Intruder also became the centerpiece of most of the major daylight strikes on well-defended targets. Carrying seven to eight tons of bombs, and delivering them in a glide- or dive-bombing run, the A-6 markedly increased the tonnage of TNT that could be accurately laid on a target over what had previously been possible using the A-4 Skyhawks and F-4 Phantom IIs. For this second deployment to Vietnam, the *Enterprise* air wing included the most advanced aircraft in the free world and well over half of the flight crews had at least one combat tour in Vietnam under their belts, yet that did not mean that there would be smooth sailing.

In 1967, the carriers continued to be involved in the two well-defined and separate air wars in Vietnam. The "in-country" war was that in which the U.S. Air Force, Navy, and Marine tactical aircraft operated in close support of U.S. and allied ground forces engaged in the fighting in South Vietnam. The Air Force and Marine tactical air operated from bases in both Vietnam and Thailand. The other air war, known as "special operations," involved strikes into the sovereign territory of the invading enemy, North Vietnam. These operations, conducted under the campaign code name Rolling Thunder, mainly utilized aircraft from the Seventh Fleet carriers and U.S. Air Force tactical air wings in Thailand. Marine A-6s from bases in South Vietnam also participated in Rolling Thunder.

There was a clear difference in the character of these two wars. In South Vietnam, the operations were less complex and markedly less hazardous. The AA fire was not as intense, and there were no surface-to-air missiles or fighter aircraft. As a consequence, the strike groups consisted principally of weapon carriers. There was no need for flak suppressors or fighter cover. If a friendly plane were shot down, it was highly probable that the crew would be rescued because of the presence of friendly ground forces in the vicinity, the absence of a generally hostile civilian populace, and the immediate availability of land-based rescue helicopters.

The air war in North Vietnam was a different story. Strike groups had to penetrate what at that time was the most intense and modern air defense environment in existence. The strike groups faced fighters, high- and medium-altitude surface-to-air missiles, and highly accurate automatic weapons fire at low altitudes. Strike groups had to be accompanied by fighter cover, "iron hand" anti-SAM pouncers, electronic jammer planes, antiradar missile shooters, and rescue units held in reserve for covering and rescuing downed aircraft crews. Most of the shootdowns of friendly aircraft occurred in the North, and although in many cases survivors were able to eject and land safely in their parachutes, only a small percentage of the surviving aircrews were rescued. The air defense environment encountered by rescue helicopters was simply too intense in most cases to allow them to penetrate any distance at their slow speeds and low altitudes into North Vietnam.

Except during the several bombing pauses that occurred during the war, the principal combat effort of the carriers was in the air war in the North. However, some tactical air effort from the carriers was still routinely scheduled for the in-country war in South Vietnam.

Carrier operations into North Vietnam were conducted from the vicinity of Point Yankee in the Gulf of Tonkin. Operations into South Vietnam were carried out from an area in the southern Gulf of Tonkin called Point Dixie, and carriers conducting the air war in the South were said to be at Dixie Station. Because a carrier at Dixie Station was covering an operating area entirely inside South Vietnam, which was more easily accessible by the South Vietnamese air force, the U.S. Air Force, and the Marine Corps squadrons based in-country, there was not a high priority for the carriers to operate on Dixie Station except during one of the White House–mandated bombing pauses in North Vietnam.

Dixie Station was a normal assignment for a carrier and its air wing newly deployed to the western Pacific, breaking in for a month under combat circumstances that were not as intensive as those encountered up north. It became Seventh Fleet policy to assign newly arrived carriers in Vietnam to thirty days at Dixie Station so they received their baptism of fire in a lower-intensity combat.

Normally, at least three carriers were on Yankee Station at all times. Sometimes the number went up to four or even five, as carrier arrivals and departures overlapped. On at least one occasion, late in the war, there were six carriers simultaneously conducting operations at Yankee Station. With the minimum of three carriers at Point Yankee, targets in North Vietnam could be covered twenty-four hours a day.

The large-deck carriers, *Forrestal* and subsequent classes including the *Enterprise*, normally carried a complement of eighty to ninety tactical aircraft, consisting of two squadrons of F-4 Phantoms, two squadrons of A-4 Skyhawks, and one squadron of A-6 all-weather Intruder bombers. In addition, the carrier operated helicopters, airborne tankers, reconnaissance aircraft, and early warning E-2 aircraft in its organic air wing.

The Phantom squadrons flew combat air patrol (CAP) armed with air-to-air missiles such as the Sidewinder and Sparrow III. On armed reconnaissance and strike missions, the F-4s carried bombs—500- or 250-pound low drag—or air-to-ground missiles. The Skyhawks also flew strike and air-to-ground support missions with bombs and air-to-ground missiles, visually locating their targets and aiming their weapons.

The A-6 Intruder squadrons had the only real capability for all-weather attack. In this role they proceeded individually to their targets, bombing by radar. The A-6 was also the main element in the major daylight strikes, known as Alpha strikes, because of its heavy load-carrying capability. The A-4s and F-4s also flew night missions using flares to locate and illuminate targets for visual attacks by bombs and rockets. The A-6s operated alone at night, while Skyhawks and Phantoms worked in pairs. Special missions such as radar busting used A-4s or F-4s with antiradiation guided missiles.

The carriers employed two modes of flight operations, cyclic operations and alpha strikes. During cyclic operations, the *Enterprise* would launch twenty-five to forty aircraft in a single "event" every hour and a half during its twelve-hour assigned period of flight operations, conducting eight cycles of these events during each flying day. The first event would launch, then the second event would launch an hour and a half later and the aircraft from the first event would immediately land. Planes from the first event would be refueled and rearmed, their pilots briefed, and the planes launched again as the third event—just before the second event landed. Launch and recovery times were staggered among the carriers during the day to keep planes over the target area at all times. The largest number of aircraft normally committed to a single target in one strike in cyclical mode was twenty to thirty.

Alpha strikes were used to put a very heavy weight of ordnance on a single target complex in a very short period of time, either for the shock effect or because of a need to penetrate very heavy defenses, as in the case of attacks in the vicinity of Haiphong and Hanoi. On the alpha strike, virtually all available aircraft on the carrier were organized into a single strike group. Alpha strikes were usually coordinated with the other carriers on the line and, often, with major U.S. Air Force strikes coming out of Thailand. On occasion as many as five or six carriers could be available on the line due to the overlapping of carriers arriving and departing. Then five alpha strikes could pound a single target complex within an hour, with the Air Force coming in before and after the Navy effort.

Alpha strikes were usually scheduled by the higher authorities in Saigon or Hawaii. Sometimes Washington would call for heavy effort against Hanoi or Haiphong for political reasons perhaps unknown to the commanders in the field. This could cause difficulty for both the Air Force and Navy air commanders because the headquarters in Washington did not have a feel for the weather conditions prevailing in the area to be attacked at that particular time or period of the year. With so many planes in a restricted air space at one time, bad weather could really cause problems.

In 1967, the weather conditions over North Vietnam had been exceptionally unfavorable for combat air operations through the entire winter and into the spring. The prevailing conditions were low visibility at the surface and multiple cloud layers up to twenty thousand feet, with cells of high turbulence and rain embedded randomly in the air mass. All echelons of command, from the White House to the flag officers at sea, were frustrated at the almost total lack of effectiveness of the air campaign because of the persistent bad weather. Washington wanted results, and the afloat commands were trying to respond. The all-weather capabilities of the Intruder were being taxed to the maximum, but most of the radar-significant targets were on the proscribed list—the commercial industrial plants near Hanoi or the port facilities at Haiphong, for example. The military targets that were eligible were either fleeting— such as trucks—or SAM sites and troop-marshaling areas that did not present significant radar targets. So it was natural that whenever there appeared a possible break in the weather, the squadrons launched as many sorties as possible. Only too often the conditions were dangerously unfavorable. A plane flying in the overcast is a sitting duck for a SAM. To avoid a missile, the pilot must be able to see it, because to evade a SAM that is homing requires that the pilot outmaneuver the missile by a hard five-G turn at the last minute.

On 19 May a flight of four A-6s had launched from the *Enterprise* to bomb a truck park in the suburbs of Hanoi, a complex well defended by SAMs and MiG fighters. A fighter escort of eight F-4 Phantom IIs provided high cover and flak suppression. The Intruders crossed the coastline at fifteen thousand feet and immediately got a continuous blinking red light from their missile warning systems, indicating that they were being tracked by multiple SAM sites. The Intruders descended to eight thousand feet as they approached the target area, and through a break in the overcast they sighted three MiG-21s. The North Vietnamese fighters pulled up in a climbing turn as the Intruders attempted to use the cloud cover for protection. At this point, the escorting F-4s joined the melee and, in driving off the MiGs, themselves became targeted by the SAM sites. As the Intruders broke left in a diving turn to attack their target, a barrage of missiles, more than fifteen by one crewman's count, was launched, most of them tracking the A-6 bombers. One Intruder was fatally damaged by a detonating SAM warhead, and both its crewmen ejected at four thousand feet behind a ridge line northeast of Hanoi known as "Banana Alley." The pilot, Lt. Cdr. Eugene "Red" McDaniel, the operations officer of Attack Squadron 35, the *Enterprise*'s A-6 squadron, was captured almost immediately. He was flying his eighty-first mission into Vietnam. His bombardier/navigator, badly injured in the ejection, managed to evade the enemy for three days before being captured. He, unfortunately, did not survive captivity.

Meanwhile, the Phantom II fighter cover was having problems from the continuing barrage of SAMs. The leader of a two-plane section had been driven down to low altitude by the successive diving turns required to evade the missiles, and the two Phantoms were now under intense automatic-weapons fire from the ground. The flight leader, the executive officer of VF-94, one of the two *Enterprise* fighter squadrons, flew into the ground, his plane on fire. It is not known whether it was due to a SAM hit or heavy automatic AAA fire. Both he and his rear seat radar intercept officer were killed.

In his book *Before Honor,* Lieutenant Commander McDaniel describes an exchange he had on the flight deck that morning:

> Captain Holloway was checking things on the flight deck as the pilots were manning planes for the big strike on Hanoi and he climbed up to the cockpit of my A-6 as I was strapping in. He asked me where my target was and I told him "downtown Hanoi." Captain Holloway said, "You'll be okay, we've scheduled a lot of MIG killers and flak suppressors for you today." I told him, "I hope you are right," and Holloway slapped me on the back and answered, "Good luck. I'll tell them to save lunch for you." . . . Six years later, when I got out of prison camp, I called Vice Admiral Holloway, who was then Commander Seventh Fleet and asked him, "Are you still saving lunch for me?" I carried the memories of his final sendoff remarks all though my POW years.

TARGETING

The targeting source for Task Force 77, in terms of general policy guidelines—but sometimes even specific objectives—came from Washington to CinCPac. The specificity in the Washington targeting directions varied, depending upon political circumstances in the White House and the degree of involvement on the part of key individuals in the Pentagon. From the Washington guidance provided through JCS channels, CinCPac prepared a target list, which was drawn on by the military assistance commander, Vietnam (MACV), Gen. William Westmoreland, and commander, Carrier Force, Seventh Fleet, who coordinated carefully to ensure that national and JCS priorities were followed, that all assigned targets were covered, and that Air Force and Navy units were given targets that best suited their special capabilities. Commander, Task Force 77; commander, Seventh Fleet (C7F); and MACV could also add targets, as long as the national requirements were fulfilled and the target eligibility criteria adhered to.

Commander, Task Force 77's target list and general guidance were provided to commander, Task Group 77.0, a rear admiral aviator who, with his staff, was embarked in one of the carriers actually on Yankee Station. Commander, TF 77.0 then assigned the daily strike responsibilities to each of the carriers, depending upon how many carriers were available at Yankee Station and the aircraft composition of their air wings. Upon receipt of the daily air plan, each carrier's operations department then made up a schedule assigning specific mission sorties to the squadrons. It was up to the squadrons to ensure that adequate planes were available and that pilots and strike leaders were detailed.

Mentioned previously was the particular concern to combat flight crews throughout the entire Vietnam War for the very ROE under which they had to fly. Originally, these required the aircraft overflying Vietnam not to shoot unless shot at first. This theoretically was to keep the planes from attacking suspected military sites that were in reality civilian installations. The direction of approach and pullout from bombing attacks were often mandated from Washington so that aircraft with bomb loads were not flying over the inhabited parts of Hanoi or Haiphong, where the inadvertent release of a bomb or weapon might fall in a nonmilitary area.

The sort of micromanagement from Washington that dictated altitudes to be flown and directions of attack could be infuriating to the pilots that had to fly the missions, because the rule-makers in Washington did not necessarily consider the height of the terrain in assigning altitudes, or the direction of a rising or setting sun when prescribing attack and recovery directions. These are but two examples of restrictions that could critically favor the defenders on the ground. The rules of engagement were only one of the many seemingly bureaucratic difficulties that the combatants on our side had to live with throughout the Vietnam War.

BATTLE EFFICIENCY PENNANT

In February 1967, the commander, Naval Air Forces, Pacific Fleet (ComAirPac) was making his annual visit to the operating units of his command—the carriers and squadrons on the West Coast and operating in the Pacific. The Seventh Fleet was an important stop on his itinerary, and the *Enterprise* was one of the carriers assigned to his command.

The *Enterprise* was informed that ComNavAirPac, Vice Adm. Al Shinn, would be flying aboard at Yankee Station by COD on 25 February for an informal visit with the air wing and the embarked staff. He had emphasized ahead of time that this was not an inspection and that no special preparations were to be made nor elaborate briefings prepared. Those of us that knew Admiral Shinn felt comfortable taking him at his word and we looked forward to a pleasant visit from the admiral who would be writing our fitness reports. Shinn and his small party of about a half a dozen officers from his staff landed on board the *Enterprise* about noon, just after the final event of the day's operational flying.

Admiral Shinn established himself in the ship captain's in-port cabin, which was unoccupied. It was always made available for visiting VIPs at sea when the captain was living in the sea cabin. Shinn invited me and the two rear admirals at Yankee Station, assigned as commander, TF 77 and commander, TF 77.0, to join him and his small staff aboard the *Enterprise* for a general discussion of the carrier operations.

Admiral Shinn opened our session with an almost emotional discussion of the competition for the Pacific Fleet Battle Efficiency Pennant for carriers in 1966. Shinn started by saying that he and his staff had done everything possible to prevent the USS *Enterprise* from winning the award. His reasons were, first, the *Enterprise* had joined the Pacific Fleet only in December 1965 at Yankee Station. Second, as the fleet's only nuclear-powered carrier, it had received plenty of public visibility and recognition. By virtue of that he saw no reason why further honors should not be spread around a little more in his carrier force.

Initially, when the competitive scores had been tallied and computed, the *Enterprise* had won the overall Battle Efficiency E (award for excellence) as well as Es in four of the six departmental areas. Shinn said he sent his staff back to their statistics and adding machines to find some way to keep the *Enterprise* from running away with all of the prizes. At this time I was not entirely sure whether or not Al Shinn was speaking entirely in jest. But everyone else in the room was still smiling.

Shinn then quickly concluded by saying that after several recomputations of the competitive scores in an attempt to eliminate the *Enterprise,* he gave up. There was nothing else to do but confirm that the *Enterprise* had won the E for top overall performance among the nine carriers and had also carried off departmental Es for the CIC and Communications Departments. With that, Shinn turned to the senior aide accompanying him, who pulled from his briefcase a large bronze shield with the "E" for excellence on it, the actual award plaque for the E. Shinn then mellowed a bit and explained that they all knew the *Enterprise* had really earned this award, but his staff had somehow hoped that an older, conventional ship with a long tenure in the Pacific Fleet could have won the award just for sentimental reasons.

The ceremony broke up with me heading for the bridge, the E award firmly in my custody, and the admirals, their staffs, and the *Enterprise* and I all got back to the business of fighting the war in Vietnam.

THE WAR COUNCIL MEETS

In the early spring of 1967, C7F proposed a conference of the U.S. principals in Vietnam along with their allied counterparts to be held on board the *Enterprise*. General Westmoreland was enthusiastic and the conference was laid on. But frankly, it was an awful burden to be imposed on a warship in the middle of an active military campaign. The *Enterprise* was pulled off the line for a day and took station thirty miles off Saigon. The U.S. ambassador, Henry Cabot Lodge; the overall U.S. military commander in the area, General Westmoreland; the U.S. Army commander, General Abrams; the South Vietnamese president, General Thieu, and Prime Minister Ky, plus their aides and staffs and all of the U.S. Navy flag officers in the Seventh Fleet, were flown on board. Most of the conferees arrived as passengers in the eight-seat C-1 COD aircraft.

Prime Minister Ky, as the air marshal of the South Vietnamese air force, insisted on flying on board in the copilot's seat of a COD and almost outwrestled the Navy pilot on the controls during the carrier landing. The U.S. ambassador, General Westmoreland, President Thieu, and the U.S. Navy aviation flag officers all requested to be flown aboard in the bombardier/navigator's seat of an A-6 Intruder. This was a real test of naval resourcefulness as each of these dignitaries had to be equipped in flight harnesses then checked out in combat jet safety procedures.

The guests landed between 1100 and 1130, and the conference took place in the *Enterprise*'s war room. At 1300 an elegant lunch was served in the senior officers' end of the wardroom, replete with speeches from the leaders of both nations and glasses of nonalcoholic champagne. After lunch there was an impressive ceremony on the hangar deck during which Thieu and Ky presented medals to Seventh Fleet flag officers and the CTF 77 carrier skippers. This was followed by departure honors for each of the principals as they were lifted to the flight deck on the ship's deck-edge elevator. They then climbed into their planes and were from off to the military airfield at Saigon.

Then, at 1800 that afternoon, the *Enterprise* launched sixteen A-4s and eight F-4 Phantom IIs to resume their schedule of air operations against the Vietcong.

SHOW OF SHOWS

Not all of the visits on board the *Enterprise* were on official business. In May 1966 a USO troupe visiting the ground troops in Vietnam agreed to come on board to put on a show in exchange for a freshwater shower, a hot meal, and a night between clean sheets. Carrier hangar decks provided excellent venues for a USO revue. The *Enterprise* was off Saigon, on the 0800 to 2000 flying shift with a relatively undemanding schedule typical of Dixie Station.

The USO group, which included Danny Kaye and Martha Raye, landed two carrier-capable passenger aircraft at about 1500. The show was put on at 2000 on the hangar deck after flight operations had been concluded. Virtually all members of the crew not actually on watch were in attendance, some literally hanging from the rafters. With troupers like Danny Kaye and Martha Raye, the routines were funny and the acts mostly musical. Because the shows had to fit into the carrier's schedule of operations, the timing required that the troupe spend the night on board ship. To fly from Point Dixie to Saigon at 2200 in the evening was considered too risky. So Martha Raye was put up in the commanding officer's in-port cabin—mine.

The next morning, before the USO group boarded their two CODs for the trip back to Saigon, they spent the morning visiting the sailors in their work spaces. Kaye, an experienced pilot himself and owner of a twin-engine personal plane, visited the pilots' ready rooms. Before departing, he collected phone numbers of the pilots' wives so he could call them, upon his return to Hollywood, to report that all was well on board the *Enterprise.* My wife Dabney confirmed that he carried out this offer in a very courteous and delightful way.

I had gone down to my cabin to escort Martha Raye to her plane on the flight deck, and in an aside, told the Filipino steward, "Don't remove those sheets." A week later, at a "smoker" on the hangar deck for the crew, the scented—according to the young sailor auctioneer—sheets slept on by Martha Raye, unwashed, were auctioned off, and after a round of hot bidding, sold for two hundred dollars. The money went to the *Enterprise* recreation fund, and the original buyer at the auction turned around and sold each of his two sheets to shipmates for $125 each. It is remarkable how much fun a group of sailors can extract from a single visit from home.

For the remainder of the cruise, the *Enterprise* was able to live up to the standards it had set for itself, as well as the fleet, by winning the Battle Efficiency award. Not only did the *Enterprise* continue its top perfor-mance in the area of combat air operations and replenishment, but the ship's crew was also "mentioned in dispatches" when in May the carrier visited Hong Kong and elicited from the senior officer present, a British vice admiral, the following message: "Your fine bluejackets have again earned my admiration for their exemplary conduct ashore on liberty during your recent visit to Hong Kong."

CARRIER- AND LAND-BASED TACTICAL AIR

The carriers of the Seventh Fleet, Task Force 77, played a major role in the war in Vietnam throughout its entire eight-year prosecution. More than half of all of the combat sorties flown into North Vietnam were flown by naval aircraft.

It is interesting to compare the Air Force and Navy tactical air operations during this war. The Air Force flew out of bases, mainly in Thailand. Because of the distances involved, the strike group would refuel in the air once or sometimes twice, en route to the target, and after the strike would fly east over the Gulf of Tonkin. Then, in an operation controlled by a Navy cruiser in the Gulf, "Red Crown," the strike group would be joined up with a group of Air Force 707 tankers from Guam and be refueled—their second or third in-flight refueling— to get the tactical fighter wings back to their bases in Thailand. Air Force tactical operations were basically a continuous series of alpha strikes. On the other hand, the Navy conducted mainly cyclic operations with occasional alpha strikes when targeting demanded. More targets were being covered on a continuous basis, but with a lower level of effort per individual target than was provided either by alpha strike or the Air Force system.

The carriers were able to move about within the Gulf of Tonkin to bring their aircraft closer to their targets, thereby eliminating or substantially limiting the amount of air-to-air refueling necessary. This was important because aerial refueling facilities from the carriers were limited. Carrier-based tankers were normally used only in emergency situations when planes became inadvertently low on fuel because of unplanned occurrences, such as rescue operations or ad hoc strikes on fleeting targets of opportunity. On one occasion, for example, during an alpha strike on Haiphong, the *Enterprise* moved to within thirty miles of that port city to launch its strike group, and the A-4s were able to remove their drop tanks and, in their place, carried three 1000-pound bombs into the target.

RECAPITULATION

In June 1967 the *Enterprise* completed her second combat tour in Vietnam and headed for her Pacific Fleet homeport, Alameda. The carrier had been 230 days out of homeport and had served five uninterrupted thirty-day stints at Point Yankee, flying a total of more than 14,000 sorties from her flight deck, 11,470 of which were combat sorties, and delivering a total of 14,023 tons of ordnance. This amounted to 114 tons of TNT per day against a well-defended enemy.

In the course of these operations, the *Enterprise* had refueled forty-seven times alongside an oiler, taking an average of 555,000 gallons of jet fuel per replenishment, and loaded ammunition on thirty-nine occasions from ammunition ships underway, receiving on board an average of three hundred tons of bombs and missiles during each one of these underway replenishments. As in all combat tours, the *Enterprise* and her air wing paid a price, losing twenty aircraft and eighteen air crewmen to hostile fire.

The finest recognition of the *Enterprise* and its gallant crew for the 1965–67 combat deployments to Vietnam was the award the coveted Navy Unit Commendation to the ship and the embarked Carrier Air Wing 9 on the occasion of the change of command ceremony in Alameda on 19 July 1967, when I departed the *Enterprise* after two full years as its captain.

Although I received American, South Vietnamese, and South Korean decorations for my command tour on board the *Enterprise*, perhaps my most satisfying recognition came across my desk thirty-five years later in the form of the following e-mail written by a former crewmember on the *Enterprise*. I must confess I was deeply touched by his words. Sadly for me, I was unable to connect with him by return mail. I would like to have thanked him as representative of the more than six thousand young sailors on board the *Enterprise*, whose dedication to duty is what made their ship great:

> Dear Sirs:
>
> While accessing the web I accidentally stumbled across your web-page. During the years of 1966 to 1968 I served on board the USS *Enterprise*. The first captain that I served under was Captain James Holloway III. In reading thru your webpage I noticed that he was the Chairman of your foundation. I have for the last few years searched to find out whatever happened to Admiral Holloway. I was extremely excited to hear that he is affiliated with your organization. I served aboard the *Enterprise* as a Boatswains mate in First Division. I was assigned watch duties on the bridge as a helmsman and was fortunate to have spent many hours under this great man, even during the few times that I would mistakenly allow the ship to drift a few degrees off course, only to hear the Captain yell to me to correct my heading. I left the ship in December of 1968 as a third class boatswain mate. I can not remember exactly when Admiral Holloway left as commander of the ship, but I believe it was around 1966 or 1967. The two captains that I served under that followed him could not fill his shoes.

They were good men but Admiral (Captain) Holloway was the one that everyone would remember as being the captain of the first nuclear-powered aircraft carrier that was part of the Vietnam conflict. I have always kept this man in a special part of my heart. This may sound corny but he has been an inspiration in my life. Many days and nights while I was on bridge watch at the helm during flight operations with the roar of the jets on the flight deck, with wings loaded with ordnance waiting to be dropped, I would watch this man do his job. In his face and his eyes you could see the determination that made anyone around him feel secure, and comfortable, that every decision he would make would be the right one. At the time I was only an 18 year old kid on his way to growing up fast. I feel that this man, without even knowing my name, was instrumental in the positive direction of my life. Recently I found out that a couple of years ago he was a guest speaker at one of the *Enterprise* Association's reunions. I would have given anything to have known, and to have been there. Can the Admiral be reached by E-mail or U.S. Mail or could this be forwarded to him? In the coming days I will enjoy going through your website and in the future hope to be able to visit the foundation. It sounds like you people do a lot of good work. It makes sense that the Admiral would be affiliated with your organization.

Edward Menard, BM3 Northbridge, Mass.

14

The Pentagon

Aircraft Carrier Program Manager

I n November 1967, as I was leaving a meeting of the Joint Navy–Air Force Technical Standards Committee in the OpNav conference room at the Pentagon, an Air Force general turned to me (I was in blue service uniform), pointed to a large photograph of a *Forrestal*-class aircraft carrier hanging on the wall, and said, "Nice picture. What kind of ship is that?" I answered, "That's an aircraft carrier." He paused, smiled smugly, and said, "Oh yes, I didn't recognize it. It isn't on fire!"

On 8 July of that year, the *Enterprise* had arrived at the Naval Air Station Alameda and moored at its own pier. Ten days later, two years after I had assumed command of the ship, Capt. Kent Lee, USN, relieved me as commanding officer at a stirring change-of-command ceremony on the hangar deck. I was detached with orders to report to the Office of the Chief of Naval Operations. Upon arrival in the Pentagon, I was immediately sent to call on the CNO, Adm. Tom Moorer. Although I had been selected for rear admiral, I had not yet "made my number"— actually been promoted. There were no vacancies yet available in the quota of flag officers allowed by law for the active-duty Navy. So I was still a captain, a four-striper, and this early summons from the front office had me a little giddy.

Admiral Moorer gave me a warm welcome and got right to the point. He quickly laid out his plans. Just weeks earlier, during flight operations off Vietnam, a serious fire on board the USS *Forrestal*—the most recent in a series of conflagrations—had destroyed much of the ship's air wing and severely damaged the large-deck carrier's flight and hangar decks, together with most of the installed aircraft servicing equipment. There was considerable loss of life, both in the embarked squadrons and in the ship's crew, in addition to the severe damage to the ship, which would take a year in the shipyard to repair. During that time, the U.S. Navy's carrier force levels would be reduced by one. There were no replacements when a carrier was withdrawn from the fleet.

Of deep concern to Admiral Moorer and the Navy's top leadership was the reaction in the press, which immediately asked, if the *Forrestal* could suffer such devastating damage from a noncombat accident, did that not reveal a carrier's vulnerability to enemy action? And, further, did not the inherent vulnerability of the carrier to even noncombat incidents bring to question the advisability of investing billions of dollars and advanced technology and skilled manpower in such a fragile weapon system? Moorer considered that no less than the future of the aircraft carrier in the U.S. Navy was at stake.

Moorer had planned for me to form a study group of the best talent available to review the entire issue of safety in carriers and propose measures to reduce the vulnerability of carriers to catastrophic fires, such as had occurred in *Forrestal.* I would then serve as executive director of the study and produce a program of actions that would significantly improve carrier safety and minimize the potential sources of carrier fires and explosive accidents at sea. A three-month deadline was established for submitting a comprehensive report and set of recommendations to the CNO. To highlight the importance he attached to this carrier study, Moorer had recalled to active duty a retired four-star naval aviator, a highly respected former vice chief of naval operations and one-time chief of the Bureau of Aeronautics, Adm. Jim Russell, who would be the honorary head of the study.

The chief of staff of the U.S. Air Force had turned up the burner under the whole issue of carrier vulnerability, and his criticism of the carriers was being echoed in the halls of Congress. The entire carrier building program, which included the *John F. Kennedy,* then under construction, and all of the follow-on carriers, were in jeopardy. Admiral Moorer was hoping the creation of a major study effort would defuse, at least initially, criticism of the Navy's carrier force and eventually bring about changes that would substantively reduce the vulnerability of carriers to the explosive potential of the thousands of tons of volatile fuel and ammunition handled routinely on board.

The fact that a highly visible study effort was in progress, with a senior four-star flag officer visibly in charge, would demonstrate the Navy's profound concern over the issue and the CNO's intention to do something about it. Although Admiral Russell was the nominal head of the study, he had been retired for some time and was out of touch, so it would fall to me, as executive director, to form the study group, recruit members and set up the support staff, arrange the working spaces, and, of course, find parking spaces.

Admiral Moorer had released the priority message I had drafted tasking the various offices in OpNav and the technical bureaus to detail personnel to the study group in response to requests by the executive director. All of this sounds routine. The problem, as always, in these extra staffing requests was that the offices and bureaus tasked were not going to give up their most experienced and talented people for three months' duty in a task force when their capabilities were very much needed in their permanent assignments. These facilities were staffed with just enough people to carry out assigned duties and there was little, if any, slack. As a consequence, the least-capable members of OpNav and technical bureau staffs would be sloughed off to the study group. This was simply a fact of life. At least the transfers to the group were done quickly. Within a week to ten days, the basic group had been assembled and organized in spaces made available in the offices of the Center for Naval Analyses.

Later, in a personal memo to Admiral Moorer, I was able to report that although there were no superstars among the officers detailed to the study group, all were good naval officers who rose to the occasion and did not shirk the hard work, long days, and weekend hours. The CNO could be proud of the quality of his officer corps as even average officers could rise to the occasion for above-average performance in critical situations.

There were half a dozen naval officers in the study group, mostly lieutenant commanders and commanders, and three or four civilian scientists and engineers from the Navy laboratories. The civilians were not in constant attendance but would always show up when summoned and were excellent conduits to the other talented people in their particular laboratories that could make a contribution. Moorer had assured Russell that his presence was not essential in Washington on a full-time basis. I laid out an organization for the study group and sketched out the plan of attack and assigned the various tasks that had to be accomplished. I felt comfortable in taking over this job because of my total immersion for the past two years in operations on board the *Enterprise*, which almost entirely involved aircraft operations with fuel-filled aircraft and explosive ordnance. There was, of course, much to be done. First, information on carrier accidents had to be collected and evaluated. Then the various munitions and refueling systems had to be analyzed for reliability and safety in every aspect of their employment on board ship. Next, necessary changes would have to be developed in the design, production, and delivery techniques that would eliminate most potentially dangerous sequences. Finally, we would have to determine whether the proposed safety measures would interfere with the mechanical functioning during the operational use of the weapon to the extent that the munitions or fueling systems would become ineffective for use in combat.

The week before the deadline date for the report to go to the CNO, the basic work was done and all that remained was to put the report in final draft and to provide, in response to a late request by the CNO, a list of actions the study group recommended be taken by the Navy, together with their approximate costs, and identify the congressional appropriations to which the projects or programs should be charged. The report of the study group was well received by Admiral Moorer, and the CNO instructed his staff to draft an endorsement to the secretary of the navy stating that the CNO agreed with all the group's recommendations and intended to implement them for remedial action, through Congress if necessary, for immediate consideration. He would authorize reprogramming existing funds to support the actions he considered imperative to correct the vulnerability of carriers to disastrous fire.

The Navy's technical bureaus and laboratories fully supported the rationale and findings of the study, largely because their people had participated in the effort and the CNO had seen fit to reprogram funds to carry out its recommendations rather than take the fixes out of Material Command's budget. Admiral Moorer's understanding of the technical aspects of the report, and his effective approach to rectifying the situation, was in no small part due to a two-year tour of duty he had at the Naval Aviation Ordnance Test Station at Chincoteague, Virginia, a billet in which I also served, six years after Tom Moorer's tour.

Based upon the many manifestations of management inefficiencies that had surfaced in the course of the carrier study, I sought a personal meeting with the CNO in the days following its release. I privately recommended to Admiral Moorer that a "Navy Carrier Program" be created under a single manager. My experience with the carrier study had revealed that authority and responsibility for the many and various aspects of carrier design, construction, operations, and overhaul were scattered throughout OpNav, the Navy Secretariat, the Naval Systems Commands, the Naval Laboratories, the Nuclear Power Directorate, and the Atomic Energy Commission. Moreover, the fleet commanders were beginning to weigh in on matters of carrier aircraft complements, ship deployments, and force levels.

Admiral Moorer confessed that he had harbored the idea for such a step for the past year and agreed that this was the time to make it happen. He accepted the recommendation on the condition that Admiral Rickover would concur. Rickover was contacted, and he not only agreed but enthusiastically supported the reorganization, recommending that I be assigned to set up the new program and function as its first incumbent. Rickover's main motive probably was that he would be getting his people in on the ground floor.

The rules for the organization of a weapons system "program" were explicitly defined in secretary of the navy instructions. The directives provided for a program manager in the Naval Material Command, then under the command of Vice Adm. I. J. Galantin, who reported directly to the secretary of the navy. This program manager would have a counterpart in OpNav, the program coordinator, who reported to the chief of naval operations.

Within days, I had drafted a directive for the CNO's signature that created the aircraft carrier program coordinator in OpNav (OP-03V) and the Aircraft Carrier Program Manager Office in the Naval Material Command. This was the format prescribed by the then-cognizant directives of the Navy. The CNO called the Bureau of Naval Personnel to order Rear Admiral Holloway into both positions.

Most of the substantive decisions in the carrier program would be made by the CNO and the OpNav staff in the operational area and by Admiral Rickover and his Naval Reactors for technical matters. Rickover was in the process of developing a two-reactor nuclear-propulsion plant to replace the eight-reactor propulsion plant that had been used in the *Enterprise.* Rickover, of course, wanted his part of the nuclear-power carrier program to be carefully tied in to the overall effort, so he made his own engineers available to OP-03V. They were the best in the world, and Rickover was willing to spend his own money—Congress ensured that he always had plenty—to be certain that components of carriers other than the nuclear propulsion plant, such as the catapults, ammunition elevators, and electrical systems, were properly engineered and manufactured and performed up to the standards Rickover had imposed for nuclear work.

It was not difficult with Moorer's backing to quickly have the new entity, program coordinator for aircraft carriers, organizationally located as a special assistant to the deputy chief of naval operations for fleet operations and readiness, with authority to report directly to CNO. The OP-03V principal would be supported by a staff, the size of which would be ultimately determined as the program took form. The initial authorization was for a rear admiral as OP-03V, with one captain, one commander, a lieutenant commander, and a GS-6 typist. Office space in an already overcrowded Pentagon was not easy to come by, but a broom closet, literally, on the fifth floor of the Pentagon was converted into a small office space with the promise that additional facilities more appropriate to the rank of the incumbents would become available in six months. With the files from the carrier vulnerability study in hand, the infant organization was able to start work. The next step was to ensure that all correspondence coming into OpNav carrying the words "aircraft carrier" or the letters "CV" in the subject title, would be routed to OP-03V for action. The uniformed members of the staff, the captain, commander, and lieutenant commander, all had been hijacked from the carrier study group. These individuals, experienced in the protocols of the Office of the Chief of Naval Operations, visited the deputies of the Offices for Air Warfare, Operations and Readiness, and Planning and Programming and made copies of their file correspondence relating to all aspects of aircraft carriers. At this time, the first Xerox machines were arriving in the Pentagon, and this made the task of duplicating the records much easier. Within weeks after Admiral Moorer had given the okay, OP-03V was up and in business. This was due largely to the fact that the CNO set the example. He himself was busy dealing exclusively with our office on carrier issues, and the rest of OpNav had to follow his lead or be left behind.

OP-03V IN BUSINESS

OP-03V had more clout than its assets would indicate. Four officers and a secretary sitting in two small rooms, one of which was still furnished with a large sink for cleaning mops, were putting their trademark on a lot of important correspondence. Our reputation was waxing. One day, leaving a conference in the office of the SecNav concerning contracts with Newport News, the sole shipbuilder capable of producing nuclear-powered carriers, I was walking down the E ring returning to my office and was joined by the assistant secretary of the navy for financial management, the very competent Barry Shillito. We chatted a few minutes about the recent decisions that had been made concerning the carrier program, and Shillito said, "I'm so glad to see that we have a program manager for this very important component of the Navy. One of these days I would like to come up to your spaces and take a look at the operation." I knew that what Shillito had in his mind's eye was a large loft with dozens of engineers and analysts in green eyeshades poring over drawings and spreadsheets concerning the design, construction, maintenance, and current operations of the Navy's aircraft carrier fleet. I had no objection to visitors coming up to the fifth floor premises and being exposed to our primitive environment. I had learned from Rickover that one's colleagues—who are always one's competitors—do not get covetous if your working spaces are as shabby as those of OP-03V. But people seldom visited the fifth floor of the Pentagon.

A major crisis and test for OP-03V occurred in the spring of 1970. The Senate Democrats, led by Senator Walter Mondale (later a Democratic Party candidate for vice president), mounted a determined campaign to cut the defense budget and reduce the size of the armed forces. Their initial targets were budget line items with high costs. The nuclear-powered carrier was their principal target. Also joining in this movement were a coalition of House and Senate members who were persuaded that the Navy should be limited to small (twenty-five-thousand-ton) carriers and light, inexpensive aircraft to "reduce fleet vulnerability" and reduce overall defense costs.

Senator Mondale introduced an amendment to the 1971 authorization bill to the effect that there be no further authorizations for the construction or advance procurement of another nuclear-powered attack carrier until a joint subcommittee of the House and Senate Armed Service Committees could conduct a comprehensive study of the past and projected costs and effectiveness of aircraft carriers and task forces and, through review of the need for the current force level of fifteen aircraft carriers, justify conclusively to Congress the nation's need for a fleet of large carriers. This amendment, of course, became the law.

Congress decided on joint hearings, chaired by Senator Stennis and including the following members: Senators Stewart Symington, Henry Jackson, Strom Thurmond, John Tower, and John Murphy and House members Charles Bennett, Sam Stratton, and Robert Stafford. From the executive branch, the Navy was designated the lead agency and the CNO appointed me as principal witness. My main responsibility was to draft and present the Navy's statement. Secretary of the Navy John Chafee, Admiral Moorer, Vice Admiral Rickover and Chairman of the Joint Chiefs of Staff General Wheeler would testify in support. Senator Mondale was the principal witness for the other side, and he was supported by his own staff, Armed Services Committee staff members, several senators and congressmen opposed to carriers, and a number of civilian consultant panelists from local think tanks such as Brookings and the Georgetown Center for Strategic and International Studies. I would be allowed by the rules of the committee to testify in rebuttal to their statements.

The hearings ran from 7 to 16 April 1970, and the report, dated 22 April 1970, amounted to 767 pages of testimony. The conclusions were to "strongly recommend that the Congress approve the request of the President for funding long lead time construction items for CVAN-70 in Fiscal Year '71." The decision was unanimous from all voting members, with Senator Symington (who had served as the first secretary of the Air Force after the establishment of the service by the Defense Department Reorganization Act of 1947) abstaining. This action was the watershed that firmly established a continuing congressional commitment for nuclear-powered carriers into the future. All of the negative provisions of the Mondale amendment against the future of the Navy's carrier program had been unanimously defeated.

The Navy considered that the Stennis hearings on the Mondale amendment were of such significance to the Navy and to the nuclear-powered carrier program that CVAN-74 was named the *John C. Stennis*. The OP-03V testimony in support of nuclear carriers became the basis of the justification for future carrier construction in the Navy's shipbuilding plan over the subsequent period of the nuclear carrier program, which in 2006 was still in business in OpNav, busy overseeing the fleet introduction of the *George H. W. Bush*. The OP-03V program has been the major factor in shaping today's carrier force, which includes ten *Nimitz*-class ships: the *Nimitz, Dwight D. Eisenhower, Carl Vinson, Theodore Roosevelt, Abraham Lincoln, George Washington, John C. Stennis, Harry S. Truman,* and *Ronald Reagan*. The keel for the *George H. W. Bush* was laid at Newport News in the summer of 2004.

The principal characteristics of the *Nimitz* class have remained constant for the life of the program: two 120,000-shp nuclear reactors driving four propeller shafts. The length overall is 1,092 feet, the flight deck width is 252 feet, the beam at the waterline is 134 feet, and it displaces approximately ninety-seven thousand tons fully loaded. These ships are capable of a speed of over thirty knots, which equates to more than thirty-four miles per hour. A normal complement of aircraft would be eighty-five combat planes, and a ship's crew with an embarked air wing consists of more than five thousand people. The current cost of the *George H. W. Bush* is about $4.5 billion.

Eight years later I again encountered Fritz Mondale. We found ourselves side by side in Arlington Cemetery, walking behind the caisson bearing the coffin of Gen. Chappie James, USAF, from the chapel to the grave. Mondale was President Jimmy Carter's vice president and I had just retired as CNO. We reminisced about the carrier hearings in 1970, and then Mondale said, "I still have your picture on the wall of my office." I reacted with surprise. "My picture?" I asked. "Well," he said, "the picture of the aircraft carrier inscribed, 'Senator Mondale, if you vote for the carrier in the authorization bill, we might name this one after you.'" I had forgotten all about that, but it was a friendly token of the courteous ways that at the time were the manner of the Senate no matter how rough the politics were.

THE CARRIER PAMPHLET

One of the projects undertaken in OP-03V was the preparation of a handbook-sized publication titled *All the Questions You Had About Aircraft Carriers but Were Afraid to Ask*. I had drafted the text in consultation with Dave Leighton of Admiral Rickover's staff and then arranged with the Newport News Shipbuilding and Dry Dock Company to publish the pamphlet in a very attractive but professionally businesslike format. I don't remember how many were printed, but there were a sufficient number to distribute one to every officer in OpNav, the Ship Systems Command, Air Systems Command, and the office of each member of Congress. Other copies went to advocacy organizations such as the Association of Naval Aviation and the Tailhook Association. The idea was to have a readable message in a handy-sized pamphlet, with two objectives: to inform those who needed to know and to make sure all of those responsible for promoting the program were consistent in their statements. This fact book of the Carrier Program Office was instrumental in marshaling support within the DoD and the Congress for the authorization and funding of the *Dwight D. Eisenhower* in 1977 and the *Carl Vinson* in 1979. The booklet remained in circulation for more than ten years with at least one reprinting. President Carter vetoed the 1979 DoD budget because it contained a *Nimitz*-class carrier, which would have been CVN-71. The pamphlet was dusted off and recirculated in Congress, along with another CNO document I had written called "The Case for the Nuclear Carrier." The following year, Congress included CVN-71 again in its FY 80 budget and President Carter again vetoed the defense authorization bill. This time Congress overrode Carter's veto, and the proposed CVN-71 became the USS *Theodore Roosevelt*.

THE CV CONCEPT

The secretary of defense controls the significant force levels of all the services: the number of divisions in the Army and Marine Corps, the number of carriers in the Navy, and the number of tactical fighter wings in the Air Force. Although OSD had been stuck on the number fifteen as the force level for attack carriers since the post–Korean War era, in 1967 the Navy was also operating nine antisubmarine warfare carriers (CVS). The CVSs were *Essex*-class ships that had done a full career of more than twenty years as attack carriers but, because of age and material condition (wear), had been transferred to ASW duties and redesignated CVS. As the new large-deck *Forrestal*-class carriers entered the fleet, *Essex*-class CVAs had to be dropped from the CVA category so as not to exceed the limit of fifteen CVAs The *Essex*-class attack carrier that was being replaced would undergo a short overhaul to correct the most debilitating deferred maintenance and to equip the carrier to operate the lower-performance propeller-driven ASW aircraft, the Grumman S-2 Tracker. Then, like dominoes, a CVS also had to be dropped from the ASW force to stay within the nine-ship CVS force level. Those deleted CVSs joined the amphibious force, in many cases as helicopter landing assault ships. If their material condition was too poor, the retired CVSs were sent to the scrap yards. This was an interesting example of the long-livedness and the great utility of carrier-type vessels. By 1968 most of the *Essex*-class ships constructed during World War II were twenty-five years old or more. Originally, the service life of an *Essex*-class ship was considered to be twenty years, but the exigencies of the Cold War had caused that figure to be extended to twenty-five through various applications of the Service Life Extension Programs (SLEP) and other remarkable feats of shipyard skill. The greatest problems were the engineering plants, which had been run hard and had even become unreliable in some cases. Further, in some of the CVSs, their hull plating had become so dangerously thin from years of continuous operation at sea, first as CV/CVAs and then as CVSs, that there was a real question of the vessels' seaworthiness under heavy sea conditions.

In 1967, after I had become the aircraft carrier program manager, it appeared as if the Navy would not be fiscally able to maintain a force level of nine CVSs along with fifteen CVAs. The input to the carrier force was only one new carrier every two years. This was the carrier construction program in the Navy's Five Year Defense Plan. By late 1968 the situation of carrier force levels—especially the ASW carriers—was going to become critical, and that had to be faced.

At the same time the carriers were growing old and leaving the active ship inventory for the scrap heaps, Naval Aviation was having problems with its aircraft inventory. The war in Vietnam had started with the F-8 as the standard fighter, and within a year this was replaced by the F-4 Phantom II. The A-6 began arriving in the fleet in numbers in 1967 as the all-weather attack plane in the carrier air wing. Neither the F-4 nor the A-6 could be operated from *Essex*-class carriers. Both required the larger catapults and additional deck space afforded by the *Forrestal* and later large-deck classes. As a consequence, the *Essex*-class carriers deploying to the Seventh Fleet for combat in Vietnam were equipped with F-8 squadrons for fighters and A-4s in the attack role. Both of these aircraft were still fine planes. The Chance Vought F-8 Crusader had a better air-to-air combat record against the MiG than any other aircraft, Navy or Air Force, in the free world. The A-4 had proved to be a tremendous workhorse for the fleet and was also capable of delivering nuclear weapons as well as six tons of conventional ammunition. Nevertheless, fighters with an all-weather capability as exemplified by the F-4s were required for fleet air defense in all theaters, under all conditions.

It had become the practice for all aircraft carriers, whether in the Atlantic Fleet, destined for deployment with the Sixth Fleet in the Mediterranean, or in the Pacific Fleet, headed for combat in the Gulf of Tonkin, to be equipped with a standard air wing for its class. By 1968 the standard air wing for the large-deck carriers was two F-4 Phantom II squadrons, two A-4 squadrons (the A-4s were beginning to be replaced by A-7s, the Corsair II), one squadron of A-6 all-weather medium bombers, five RA-5C Vigilante supersonic reconnaissance aircraft, four E-2C Hawkeye radar surveillance aircraft, plus detachments of A-3 Skywarrior bombers for in-flight refueling and several helicopters for air-sea rescue and utility purposes. The *Essex*-class CVA air wing consisted of two squadrons of F-8 fighters, two squadrons of A-4 light attack planes, F-8 photo planes for reconnaissance, A-3s for refueling, and utility helicopters for search and rescue.

The CVS air wing included two squadrons of Grumman S-2 Tracker ASW aircraft. These workhorses were twin-engine propeller-driven planes with a crew of four: pilot, copilot, and two radar and weapons operators. In addition, there was a detachment or squadron of ASW helicopters. Whenever the deployment dictated, there would also be a detachment of four A-4s, equipped to use Sidewinder missiles for air defense. These A-4s were added to the embarked air wing when the carrier was involved in operations beyond the normal fighter cover of a deployed CVA, such as independent CVS operations in the North Atlantic.

In 1968 the CVS situation became critical. Although the CVS force level remained at nine, there were no replacement carriers for those CVSs that would be dropping out of the inventory because of old age. To resolve the situation, the air antisubmarine warfare community proposed a new construction program of ASW carriers that would be of much simpler design than the large-deck *Forrestal*-class ships that were being built for the attack carrier mission. At this time, the Lockheed S-3, the twin-jet ASW aircraft with a crew of four, was entering the fleet to replace the S-2s. But the S-3's weight, recovery speed, and launching requirements were substantially less than the attack carrier air wing F-4s and A-5s. This meant that the new construction CVS could have smaller catapults and arresting gear of less capacity.

Unfortunately, it was at this time that the building program for the large-deck carriers was being seriously questioned. The opponents were a group of liberal congressmen motivated to cut defense spending and a determined cadre of systems analysts in the office of the SecDef, who favored increased expeditionary capability and mobility for the Air Force's tactical fighter wings as an alternative. Furthermore, the increased cost of the nuclear-powered attack carriers was, to some degree, complicating the large-deck carrier building program. The net impact of these potentially negative issues created a budget climate that clearly made the entire concept of a new ship construction program for CVS carriers totally unrealistic.

A solution suggested by the air ASW community with some support from the OSD and from within the CNO's staff, was to convert three or four of the fifteen attack carriers in the fleet to CVS duties. The pressure for such a step was the potential threat of the burgeoning Soviet submarine fleet. But the priority facts were that the war in Vietnam was real, and the naval aircraft in the theater were flying combat sorties into North Vietnam. These tactical air strikes against the North Vietnamese were the only offensive action on the part of U.S. forces in the war at that time. U.S. ground forces, both Army and Marine, were being withdrawn from the theater, so that U.S. combat involvement was mainly a matter of tactical aircraft of the Air Force and Marines operating out of land bases in the theater and naval aircraft flying from carriers in the Gulf of Tonkin. The requirement for carrier-based sorties to support the Rolling Thunder and Linebacker campaigns in the U.S. air offensive against the North Vietnamese was so overwhelming, in addition to the other worldwide commitments of the U.S. Navy, such as the demand by CubCUS-NavEur to keep two carriers at all times in the Mediterranean, that any thought of converting any big deck CVAs to a CVS mission became unreal. To the contrary, the Navy was requesting authority from OSD to deploy a CVS in the CVA role in the Gulf of Tonkin, replacing its S-2 and helicopter ASW aircraft with F-8s and A-4s, of which there were sufficient in the inventory to create an additional CVA air wing.

Because the CVA level in the Navy was so very closely controlled by the SecDef, being considered the key measure of U.S. naval power, there was considerable back and forth between OpNav and OSD in 1967. It mainly concerned which CVS to convert to a CVA. The SecDef eventually authorized the employment of a CVS (the *Intrepid*, later replaced by the *Shangri-La*) in the CVA role in 1967 but did not change the authorized force levels of CVAs from fifteen to sixteen.

It was at this point that I proposed a long-term solution, referred to as the "CV Concept," that could solve all of these carrier issues. I drafted a package of position papers and implementing dispatches and briefed them to the CNO. Admiral Moorer, as was often his style, ordered implementation of the proposal on the spot. The elements of the CV Concept were as follows:

1. All aircraft carriers in the U.S. Navy capable of operating fixed-wing aircraft with catapults and arresting gear would be designated "CV."
2. There would be no standard aircraft complement for a CV.
3. The aircraft assigned to the embarked air wing would be determined for each deployment. If the CV were deploying to combat in Vietnam, for example, the air wing would be tailored for that mission and consist mainly of fighter and attack planes.
4. If the CV were deploying to the Sixth Fleet where combat was not in progress, but where Soviet submarines would be routinely encountered in both the Atlantic and the Mediterranean, the

CV's air wing would be mainly ASW aircraft, the S-3 Viking and ASW-configured helicopters. The dollar cost to prepare a CVA of the *Forrestal* class to operate an ASW-oriented air wing was $925,000 for shops and support equipment, as opposed to the price tag of about $500 million for a new CVS.

5. The capability to change the carrier's air wing would normally take place prior to a carrier's deployment but could in an emergency be changed with the carrier deployed at sea.

This change in air wing composition while at sea did occur on two subsequent occasions within the next three years, and I was involved in both operations, first as the commander of the Carrier Striking Force, Sixth Fleet (CTF 60) in 1970 and in 1972 as the deputy commander, Atlantic Fleet, at which time the USS *Saratoga*'s air wing was changed from an attack type to an ASW wing, with the aircraft staging in both directions through the U.S. Naval Air Station in Bermuda.

The CV Concept exploited the arrangement of "base loading," instituted in conjunction with the introduction of NATOPS, whereby when the carrier squadrons were not embarked in a carrier between deployments, the individual squadrons were based at naval air stations segregated by type. Light attack planes (A-4s and A-7s) were consolidated at NAS Jacksonville and NAS Lemoore, fighters (F-4, and later F-14) at NAS Oceana and Lemoore, and all-weather attack planes (A-6) at NAS Whidbey Island and NAS Oceana. The replacement air wings, which provided both initial and refresher operational training by type air-craft, were located at the stations where the same type fleet squadrons were based.

Previously, the different kinds of squadrons assigned to an air wing would remain together at one air station under their shipboard wing commander. Now, each kind of aircraft would have its own type aircraft wing commander, a flag officer experienced in that particular type, to oversee the training and logistics of that branch of carrier aviation. Squadrons had become much more efficient when shore based between cruises, with the special supply support, training facilities, and target areas, concentrated in a single geographic area, readily available to the single-mission type aircraft based at the airfield.

This arrangement greatly improved the aviation maintenance situation, with the supply support and the overhaul facility located on the naval air station with the type of aircraft supported. These features of the CV Concept were phased in over 1968 to 1970 and are still in effect in naval aviation in 2007, a quarter of a century later.

Adm. Bud Zumwalt, Admiral Moorer's relief as CNO, also was impressed with the CV Concept. In his book *On Watch*, he states, "This idea [the CV Concept], originated by then Rear Admiral Jim Holloway, was to make all carriers which customarily had been designated as either attack carriers (CVAs) or antisubmarines (CVSs) into dual purpose vessels. . . . All that this involved was modifying the deck-loadings so that each ship carried both attack and anti-submarine planes instead of one or the other, adding some minor command and control apparatus, and of course installing the spare parts and the maintenance equipment that such a change in deck-loading necessitated. The cost of changing a carrier over was $975,000, a sum minuscule by comparison with what almost anything else in the DoD costs nowadays."

JUSTIFICATION FOR LARGE-DECK
NUCLEAR CARRIERS

It was the testimony of Senator Mondale's witnesses in 1970 that best identified the main arguments of the anticarrier groups, or at least the issues they considered to be the most vulnerable in the rationale for the aircraft carrier program. From this testimony, the basic justification and defense of the carrier in the debate were articulated in a point paper called "The Case for the Nuclear Carrier." This point paper was distributed through the Navy Department for the guidance of naval officers and senior civilians to prepare them for appearances before Congress, meetings with OSD officials, delivering prepared remarks, drafting magazine articles, and meetings with the press—in fact, for just about any occasion when the subject of aircraft carriers might be broached. This was not the sort of position paper that could be handed out to the public. The paper tried to cover all of the many aspects about carriers that needed to be known to appreciate their role as the principal ship in the U.S. Navy. Consequently, the paper became so lengthy that it began to lose its usefulness as a handy reference.

The one aspect of aircraft carriers that seemed to evoke the most criticism was vulnerability, which I attempted to recast as carrier "survivability." Because of the mindset on carrier vulnerability that had been established among the public, we worked hard on getting this message across. Our rationale ran along the following lines:

1. No U.S. Navy aircraft carrier has been damaged by enemy action since 1945, although the carriers have been in the forefront of every U.S. war since that time. The critics have attempted to downplay this evidence of carrier survivability because of the limited nature of these wars, but it is nearly certain that those are the kinds of wars we will encounter.

2. Carriers have demonstrated in the most intense levels of conventional naval warfare that they can survive concentrated and repeated attacks and still retain sufficient operational capability to carry out their mission. In World War II, the Japanese launched 2,314 aircraft in kamikaze attacks against the U.S. fleet, with the carriers as the main target. In spite of the fact that the kamikaze was for all practical purposes a guided missile with one of the most sophisticated guidance systems possible—a human being—not one U.S. fleet carrier was sunk in those attacks. In fact, not a single modern fleet carrier—*Essex*-class World War II design and subsequent—has ever been sunk. Some were hit and damaged in World War II, but all eventually survived.

3. Modern carriers are very durable ships, built to absorb considerable punishment as well as to deal it out. If a carrier does sustain hits from conventional bombs, torpedoes, or missiles, there will be damage, of course, but that doesn't mean the carrier will be destroyed or even put out of action. The hardness designed into modern attack carriers is illustrated by the accidental fire in 1969 aboard the nuclear-powered carrier *Enterprise*, when nine major-caliber bombs (750 to 1,000 pounds) exploded on its flight deck. The ship could have resumed air operations in four hours, as soon as the debris was cleared from the after end of the landing platform. Three of the multiple installations of arresting gear and two of the catapults were operational, and the holes in the flight deck were quickly covered with sheet steel by damage-control parties.

4. In contrast, during the Korean War, all friendly tactical airfields were overrun and captured by enemy ground forces at least once. In Vietnam, more than three hundred Army and Air Force

helicopters and fixed-wing aircraft were destroyed by enemy action on U.S. airfields, and about three thousand more aircraft were damaged. On the other hand, since World War II no naval aircraft has ever suffered enemy damage on board one of our aircraft carriers. These unique advantages of basing U.S. military forces and logistics in international waters, where they are available around the world to respond to trouble sites, have become the controlling considerations in the future military strategy of the United States.

5. Bases on foreign soil are extremely vulnerable to both military and political actions. Our extensive airbase structure in Southeast Asia—Cam-Rahn Bay, Tonsonut, and Da Nang—is today being used by the Vietnamese and is available to the Russian Pacific Fleet. Wheelus Air Force Base, which during the 1950s and 1960s was our major SAC base in North Africa, is now a Libyan air force base. Even if facilities are not seized outright by unilateral action by the host nation, they can be temporarily denied for political reasons.

6. It is a normal assumption that naval vessels are especially vulnerable in a nuclear war. That is true. No ship can survive a direct hit by a nuclear warhead. However, ships at sea are probably the least vulnerable units in the array of military and economic targets because they are moveable. The most vulnerable targets are our fixed command structures, such as the Pentagon, Offutt Air Force Base, the Norfolk Naval Station, the SAC air bases, and our industrial potential throughout the major cities of the United States. All of these could be targeted by ballistic missiles, and currently there is no way to protect fixed targets from ballistic missile attacks once the missile has left its silo. On the other hand, there does not currently exist any method of providing terminal guidance to an ICBM that would enable it to home in on a moving target. A carrier can move twelve miles during the time of flight of an ICBM, far enough so that the carrier would escape destruction.

7. Today the principal concern about the aircraft carrier's vulnerability centers on antiship missiles other than the ballistic variety. Carriers are certainly vulnerable to antiship missiles, as are all

surface ships. The Navy considers that antiship guided missiles, whether submarine-, surface ship-, or aircraft-launched, will constitute the principal threat to the carrier into the foreseeable future. So current fleet doctrine depends principally upon the aircraft carrier to defeat the cruise missile threat through the ability of the carrier's aircraft to intercept the enemy launching platforms before they reach their missile release points. These launching platforms would be enemy aircraft or hostile surface ships. In both cases the F/A-18 would use highly effective guided weapons for the destruction of both air and surface ship missile launchers.

THE ANTICARRIER BIAS

Since their beginnings, aircraft carriers have attracted detractors as well as proponents, and their detractors are a diverse group of activists.

Ever since the Reorganization Act of 1946, which established the Air Force as the military service with primary responsibility for all military aviation, the Air Force has been uncomfortable with naval aviation, and the carrier was not only the symbol but the sine qua non of naval aviation. Naval aviation was a competitor with the Air Force tactical fighter wings for resources, and that has been reflected in much of the defense debate in the OSD.

Then there are the antiwar activists. They want to reduce both defense expenditures and the nation's capacity to extend military influence, stances that, in fact, increase the chances of becoming involved in war. This group has been well represented in Congress, the White House, the media, and public organizations.

The carrier is a plump target. It is expensive, and that expense is represented in a single line item in the budget. By the extraction of that one carrier line item, billions of defense dollars can be excised in a single budget-cutting action. Antiwar activists point out that each carrier requires surface ship escorts. Originally it was four destroyers but today four destroyers, an Aegis cruiser, a nuclear submarine, and a fast combat store ship. The defense foes' logic is that if carriers are eliminated, these other ships are no longer needed and should similarly be cancelled.

The most difficult anticarrier group to deal with, however, is the rebels in our own camp. These are officers of the Navy in all warfare communities, disaffected for a number of almost obscure reasons.

In the 1960s, the generation of World War II carrier pilots was reaching the point in their careers when they were eligible by seniority and experience for a carrier command. The idea of a year with Rickover to study nuclear physics and learn ships' propulsion engineering was anathema to them. As one World War II ace told Vice Admiral Pirie, the DCNO (Air), "As a carrier skipper, I don't care what kind of power plant the ship has. It could be propelled by rubber bands, just so long as when I call for full power, I get it. That is the Chief Engineer's job." The membership of the "I was turned down by Admiral Rickover Club" continued to grow with the addition of a number of respected and competent aviation captains. This was all right when there were plenty of non-nuclear carriers for them to command, but the attitude of these World War II heroes had been imparted to a younger generation of admiring aviators who were reluctant to give up the emphasis on flying for the drudgery of textbooks. Rickover's irascible nature was legendary and many naval officers had, in one way or another, felt the lash of his tongue. Word got around. Rickover was unpopular to the point of being despised, especially by the old-school flag officers of the sixties. This dislike of Rickover, which extended to surface warfare officers, submariners, and aviators alike, translated into an animosity for the nuclear program itself. Then, of course, there was the interwarfare community rivalry, much of it stemming from the competition for dollars in the Navy budget.

Others disliked the idea of so much of the Navy being taken over by the "fly boys," who weren't really representative of the old Navy. And finally, there were those who simply did not understand why carriers had to be so big and planes so expensive. They promoted the idea of cheap, light, uncomplicated carriers. Money could be saved, they felt, by going the vertical/short takeoff and landing aircraft (V/STOL) route and eliminating catapults and arresting gear. There was little thought given to the lack of battleworthiness in a carrier without the speed, armor, protection, compartmentation, and redundancy required in a warship. Those are what make a carrier expensive.

The fact that the V/STOL tactical aircraft is by inherent design markedly inferior to its conventional contemporaries in combat operational capabilities—speed, range, bomb load, and safety—was neither realized nor considered. The expense, weight, and complexity have all been invested in the short takeoff capability. Today, for example, the V/STOL version of the F-35 Joint Strike Fighter (JSF) is 10 to 15 percent less capable than its conventional counterpart, although both use common parts and systems except those required for V/STOL operation. This 15 percent reduction in capability could be the difference between winning and losing air superiority.

On one occasion I was making a presentation to the secretary of the navy to justify a cost increase in the total price of the *Nimitz* due to the addition of an air control radar system, absolutely essential for all-weather and night air operations. The secretary had just approved the change and asked if any of his staff had comments. Graeme Bannerman, assistant secretary of the navy for installations and logistics, spoke up, saying, in effect, that the *Nimitz* was the wrong design from the keel up. Our error, he thought, was letting the uniformed naval aviators control the design. The ship was simply a reincarnation of all of the previous carriers. In his view, the Navy should have recruited a dozen recent Harvard School of Business graduates and let them design a carrier from a clean sheet of paper without interference from the aviators.

Feeling that I simply had to respond, I said it was hard to conceive of a carrier without a point at one end and propulsion devices at the other—and a flat place on top. Everything else on the *Nimitz* in fact—catapults, arresting gear, elevators, radars, a hangar deck—were there for two reasons: they were evolutionary products of what had been proven best from various alternatives and they had been proven in combat or operational experience in some way, enabling the ship to be a better fighting machine. Carriers had been in every fight since Pearl Harbor. I was going to continue, but Bannerman had walked out.

WAR GAMING THE CARRIER

It was my job as carrier program coordinator and director of strike warfare in OpNav to give an annual lecture on carrier air warfare to the student body at the Naval War College (NWC) in Newport, Rhode Island. Normally I flew from Anacostia Naval Air Station in D.C. to Providence, Rhode Island, to be picked up by Navy helicopter and taken to the helo pad at NWC. Then it was a quick sedan trip to the stately pillared front entrance of the main building. The auditorium was directly inside.

The president of the college at that time was a flag officer of acknowledged intellect, selected for the assignment by the secretary of the navy.
As my sedan pulled up, the president graciously came down the steps to
greet me. We shook hands cordially, and his very first words were—he
was not a naval aviator—"In our war game last week, all your carriers got
sunk." All *your* carriers. Not "the Navy's carriers," not "our carriers," or
even "the carriers," but *your* carriers. I don't think he realized he had
such an anticarrier bias, but it came through loud and clear. Of course,
the end result of a war game primarily depends on the assumptions made
in setting up the scenarios. This kind of prejudice against carriers could
not have been helpful in his position as president of the NWC. After all,
the role of the aircraft carrier in the U.S. Navy was no longer questionable as it was in the 1930s. The carrier was in 1971 the acknowledged
capital ship of the Navy. Naval aviation represented almost half of our
service in terms of investment and manpower. It seemed rather outlandish for the college to promote a debate on the carrier's viability in
the U.S. Fleet. In those days, as today, the aircraft carrier was the only
ship in the U.S. Navy that had its active force levels established annually
in the DoD's draft presidential memorandum, along with Army and
Marine divisions and U.S. Air Force tactical fighter wings. Clearly, the
National Command Authority considered the carrier the primary index
for measuring U.S. sea power.

15

The Syrian Invasion of Jordan

The USS *Saratoga* had been conducting air operations the night of 17 July 1970, and I had been observing the night flying from the flag bridge until the final trap at 0200. I was still asleep in the flag cabin at 0700 the next morning when there was a sharp rap at the door. Before I could react even with a "What is it?" the door burst open to admit Vice Adm. Isaac Campbell (Ike) Kidd, commander of the U.S. Navy's Sixth Fleet. Ike had a napkin over his arm and a steaming cup of black coffee in his hand, which he politely served to me as I sat up in bed.

This was most unusual. I was a rear admiral, and Vice Admiral Kidd was my immediate superior. It was hardly consistent with flag officer protocol. But Kidd was considered somewhat of a character by his Navy colleagues. He had adopted the manner of a gruff old salt, with the homespun wisdom and rolling gait of a true man-o'-warsman. This belied, to some degree, his matriculation from one of the United States' classiest prep schools, St. Georges, in Newport, Rhode Island. But he was a seagoing naval officer, and as competent a naval leader as could be found in the three-star ranks. He was a bit of an actor even as an admiral, having once given a lecture wearing the rented uniform of a Soviet navy captain. So he relished the opportunity to have some fun with his friend and principal subordinate—Jim Holloway.

CARRIER DIVISION 6

In June 1970 I had reported aboard the USS *Saratoga* as commander, Carrier Division 6. The *Saratoga* was deployed to Sixth Fleet and at that time was in port at Naples, Italy. As the senior carrier division (CarDiv) commander assigned to Sixth Fleet, I was also designated commander, Task Force 60, an operational command that carried the title of commander, Carrier Striking Force Sixth Fleet. In this operational role, the carrier division commander was supported by a staff of about fifteen officers and forty-five enlisted men. The CarDiv staff was structured specifically to conduct operations and oversee the support of two or more carrier task units, with their embarked air wings and accompanying cruisers and destroyers. Consequently, the commander, Carrier Division 6 staff included senior naval aviators for operations and plans, an experienced former destroyer CO as surface operations officer, and an intelligence section built around selected air intelligence specialists. This staff was further organized to work in conjunction with the operations and intelligence departments of the carrier in which the flag was embarked.

Vice Admiral Kidd, a surface warfare officer, had taken over as commander, Sixth Fleet only two days before I relieved as commander. Ike was a year senior to me. We had known each other since our Naval Academy days. He was an acknowledged comer in the surface warfare community. His father had been a rear admiral in command of Battle Ship Division 1 aboard the USS *Arizona* and had been killed during the Pearl Harbor attack and awarded a posthumous Medal of Honor.

Although Ike was installed with his staff in the designated Sixth Fleet flagship, the missile cruiser *Springfield*, he spent most of every day at sea aboard the Carrier Division 6 flagship, the *Saratoga*. In the *Saratoga* there was always a lot going on compared to his own flagship. Ike would observe air operations, visit the pilots' ready rooms, gain familiarity with the combat aircraft, and discuss carrier task force operations at length. He usually arrived on board the *Saratoga* by helicopter shortly after 0800, and his coming was announced well in advance on the carrier's general announcing (loudspeaker) system when his helicopter called in for landing instructions. I was usually on the flight deck to meet him, and I would then turn him over to Capt. Jack McQuary, the commander, Carrier Division 6 chief of staff.

Ike Kidd spent most of his time on board the carrier with Captain McQuary over innumerable cups of Navy coffee cooled with liberal infusions of Carnation condensed milk, a trademark of Ike's. Jack was an alumnus of the University of California at Los Angeles and had experienced a brief fling as an offensive lineman with the Los Angeles Rams pro football team. He was an ardent sports enthusiast. They could spend hours just talking football. As commander, Task Force 60, I was in tactical command of the ongoing air operations of the Sixth Fleet, and in addition to the current operations, there was always the need for the planning of impending training exercises and contingency operations. The latter included crisis management and general war plans. So there was always much going on, and it all needed the constant attention of the CarDiv commander.

In September 1970 two events that had a profound impact on the Sixth Fleet collided in the Mediterranean. The president of the United States, Richard Nixon, decided to pay an official state visit to Italy that would include an underway visit to a Sixth Fleet carrier, and Jordan was invaded by a Syrian armored column, a situation that threatened to destabilize the always delicate equilibrium of the Middle East.

CRISIS IN THE MIDDLE EAST

On 6 September 1970 an Arab group of Fedayeen representing the Palestine liberation movement, hijacked an American, British, and Swiss commercial airliner, blowing each of them up after offloading the passengers and flying them to Dawson Field, near Amman, the capital of Jordan. There were several hundred passengers involved, most of them European, along with a number of Americans and Israelis. The hijackers offered to release all of the captured passengers in a trade for the Fedayeen and Palestinian guerrillas held in Swiss, German, British, and Israeli jails. It was understood that negotiations with the terrorists would be difficult because of the multinational composition of the hostage group and the Israeli policy of not responding to blackmail. On 7 September the king of Jordan, King Hussein, who considered himself and his country friends of the United States, violently condemned these actions of the Fedayeen. He was deeply embarrassed by the open presence of the renegade Palestinians within the boundaries of Jordan. His condemnation was reflected in the reaction of his loyal army, who were near mutiny over the insulting disregard of the Fedayeen for the sovereignty of Jordan. Hussein appealed to the United States for help. In Washington, President Nixon, through his national security advisor Henry Kissinger, put the National Security Council (NSC) machinery in motion. The Washington Special Actions Group (WSAG), headed by Kissinger, was meeting frequently in prolonged sessions as the events unfolded. This was a serious matter that could eventually involve us in a military action in the Middle East, a particularly dangerous course of action in view of the Soviet political entanglements in the Arab world and the several hundred thousand Americans already fighting the ongoing war in Southeast Asia.

On 8 September, President Nixon ordered the carrier *Independence* to move with its task group to the eastern Mediterranean just off the coast of Lebanon. As a precautionary measure, Ike Kidd and I agreed that it would be useful and timely, in anticipation of any contingency, if we followed up by getting all of TF 60 to sea. Washington confirmed this decision by emphasizing that a sudden but well-ordered fleet movement would be sending the proper signal to all of the players in the Middle East. So there was no attempt to disguise our intentions, and on the ninth, the Soviet embassy in Washington reacted with a strongly worded message to the State Department questioning the intentions behind the redeployment of the Sixth Fleet assets.

When Commander, Sixth Fleet had ordered Carrier Striking Force (TF 60) to proceed without delay to the vicinity of Cyprus and to take up positions at sea under conditions of increased readiness, many TF 60 ships had been making port calls in Spain, CTF 60's flagship *Saratoga* among them. The carrier *Independence* and its task group were visiting ports in the Aegean. All got underway immediately, forming up their tactical dispositions as they steamed east.

The *Independence*'s air wing included a Marine A-4 Skyhawk squadron with a reinforced complement of twenty aircraft, six more than the normal fourteen planes in a Navy carrier squadron. I ordered six of the A-4s to be flown off and temporarily based at the NATO airfield at Souda Bay, Crete. Ostensibly this was for weapons training and carrier-landing refresher operations. The real purpose was to make room for additional F-4 fighters. It was obvious that in any Middle East contingency, control of the air would be the first priority. I wanted as many fighters as possible in the eastern Mediterranean as soon as we could get them there. The *Saratoga* and her task group (TG 60.2) of cruisers and destroyers were in the western Mediterranean when TF 60 was ordered to sortie, so they would be several days later than *Independence* in arriving on station. Four F-4 Phantom IIs from the *Saratoga* were flown off to land on board the *Independence*, replacing the six Marine A-4s detached to Souda Bay.

As they arrived in the eastern Mediterranean, the Task Force 60 ships were assigned stations in the vicinity of Cyprus to take advantage of the geography of the Levant and the location of friendly air bases. This disposition of TF 60 was termed a "dispersed randometric formation," an operational concept based upon my experience with Point Oboe in Korea and Yankee Station in Vietnam. The main reference point was Camel Station, a geographic point located between Crete and Cyprus. Ships would be assigned to positions referenced to Camel Station and selected for specific tactical or strategic reasons. The British had airfields and a long-range air search radar on Cyprus that would be available to support Sixth Fleet operations. The ships would operate within the radius of their stations specified by the operation plan.

For this randometric formation, the stations were selected to provide a coordinated and complete visual and radar surveillance of the entire eastern Mediterranean from Syria to Egypt. The distances between the cruisers and destroyers were as much as ten miles, with pickets extended even farther to the east of Cyprus. Continuous fighter combat air patrols were maintained over the force, and all non–U.S. Navy air and surface traffic was intercepted, identified, and, if appropriate, diverted. At the same time, the carriers were maintaining a constant antisubmarine patrol of the surveillance area with their embarked antisubmarine helicopters. Task Force 60 had, in effect, established an air defense and identification zone (ADIZ) in the eastern Mediterranean. This was another concept adapted from the Task Force 77 operating procedures for operations in the Gulf of Tonkin.

Meanwhile, the situation in Amman was deteriorating. With the large number of Palestinians in the capital egged on by the Fedayeen activists who were asserting that the movement of U.S. warships was an obvious precursor to U.S. intervention in Jordan, law and order in the city had collapsed. It was virtual civil war. Jordan was disintegrating. Through it all, the Kremlin remained enigmatic, silent since 9 September.

In Jordan the beleaguered king stiffened, and on 17 September, Hussein boldly ordered his loyal troops to enter Amman and restore order. Large-scale fighting ensued, and Hussein repeated his request for U.S. support, specifically, tactical air strikes. This request was received in Washington with a flurry of increased activity. The WSAG was meeting several times daily, and the National Security Council was torn on how far the United States could go in support of the Jordanians without embold-ening the Russians to become actively involved. The carrier *John F. Kennedy*, then in its predeployment work-up at Roosevelt Roads in Puerto Rico, had been ordered to deploy early to the Sixth Fleet but would not arrive in the Mediterranean for nine days.

By 17 September, Task Force 60, comprised of two carrier task groups, TG 60.1 (the *Saratoga*) and TG 60.2 (the *Independence*), was well established at Camel Station conducting surface and air surveillance of all shipping and airline traffic in the area. It was at this point that President Nixon called commander, Sixth Fleet on a secure voice communications setup. It was so secure that, although the system was installed in the Carrier Division 6 flagship, I had forgotten of its existence.

Ike Kidd had been alerted by conventional dispatch, and he helicoptered over to the *Saratoga*. Asking me to accompany him, the two of us descended to the very lowest decks of the carrier. There, in a small compartment, was an electronics technician with a telephone handset. He merely said, "The White House is on the other end," gave Ike the phone, and departed, leaving the two admirals alone with the "White House on the other end." I also started to go, but Ike motioned me to stay. I heard only one side of the conversation: Ike's "Yes Mr. President," "No, Mr. President, I am not alone. I have Admiral Holloway with me," and "Let me repeat this, Mr. President. You plan to make a public announcement to the effect that the United States stands by its friend, the King of Jordan. The Sixth Fleet is moving to the eastern Mediterranean to ensure the national integrity of Jordan, to protect U.S. citizens and interests in the area, and to militarily defeat any effort that might interfere with these objectives. And you want my assurance that all this is within the Sixth Fleet's immediate capability."

Ike put his hand over the mouthpiece and turned to me, saying, "Jim, can I assure him that the Sixth Fleet is capable of doing all this?" I replied that it was a hard question to answer with a simple yes or no without some qualification. Ike leaned toward me and said in his most commanding voice, "Admiral, I have the President of the United States on the other end of the phone, waiting for a yes or a no. *Yes or no?*" I answered with a vigorous yes.

Afterward, as we climbed back up to flag plot for a cup of coffee, Ike said, "I hope you're right. On what did you base your estimate of the situation?" I told him that it was based upon the experience of World War II, Korea, and Vietnam, reinforced by my arrival briefings and discussions with Cdr. Bob Dunn, the air wing commander aboard the *Independence.* I had asked Dunn essentially the same question the president had posed. He had reminded me that more than half of his pilots were Vietnam veterans who had faced MiGs and SAMs in Southeast Asia. From what the current intelligence tells us about the Arab tactical air capability, it is far below that of the North Vietnamese. The AA and SAM defenses at Hanoi and Haiphong had been much tougher than the current Syrian order of battle, even if reinforced by Iraq and Egypt.

There was good news from Jordan on 18 September. Hussein's loyal army troops had evicted the Fedayeen from Amman in hard fighting and generally had restored order in the capital.

But there was to be no slack. The next day our intelligence reported to the NSC that Syrian tanks had taken up positions some 250 yards inside the borders of Jordan. Then, on 20 September, the Syrian tanks pushed well into Jordanian territory, where they were met by the Jordanian army. In two engagements near Ramtha, thirty Syrian tanks were knocked out and the column was temporarily stalled. King Hussein again requested U.S. air strikes to drive out the Syrians.

In Washington, the tension of the growing crisis was consuming the national security apparatus. Resisting the king's request for U.S. armed intervention was difficult enough, but what was generating even deeper angst was the possible entry of Soviet and Israeli military forces into the fighting. The Israelis could justify their action as "survival"—with the collateral objective of doing grave damage to Arab military capabilities. The Russians would benefit by a substantial increase in their influence in the Arab world. The Americans would be pushed to the brink to avoid a new shooting conflict in addition to our ongoing war in Southeast Asia. The situation in Jordan could degenerate into a confrontation that carried the most dreadful potential for the escalation to World War III, with all of its nuclear connotations.

The WSAG under Kissinger, with Nixon in almost constant attendance, was meeting in marathon sessions. Israel seemed to be taking the
first steps in their mobilization process, a forty-eight-hour operation that
was almost a certain precursor to war.

The first good news with concrete implications broke on 22 September. The Jordanians, bolstered by the expression of U.S. support,
mounted air attacks on the Syrian forces. At Irbid, Syria lost 120 tanks,
mainly to air strikes, with perhaps a third to mechanical breakdowns.
Significantly, the Syrian air force was held out of the battle on the orders
of a field commander, a Syrian air force general named Hafez Assad,
who must have seen the wisdom in avoiding any excuse for the
Americans and Israelis to openly engage in Arab affairs.

This was the turning point. The Fedayeen were brought under
control, and the Syrians pulled out of Jordan. Events quickly returned to
the status quo ante. The Russians were again politically ambivalent. The
Israelis cancelled any activity that could be interpreted as mobilization.
In Washington, the WSAG sessions ground to a halt, and President
Nixon made the decision to go through with his trip to Italy and his visit
to the Sixth Fleet.

Commander, Sixth Fleet received firm information that President
Nixon would like to visit a carrier on 28 September to see air operations
and observe a live fire power demonstration during his official state visit
to Italy. Always considerate, Vice Admiral Kidd asked me if I would
"mind" staying at Camel Station in the *Independence* while he took the
Saratoga to Naples and hosted the president's visit. Ike was concerned
that I would miss the opportunity to meet the president and run the air
show. I agreed without any further discussion. There was really no other
alternative, and I was privately delighted to forego the protocol of a
presidential visit. The next day, I moved my flag to the *Independence*,
taking along four or five key members of the staff while the rest of
commander, Carrier Division 6 remained on board the *Saratoga* to
handle administrative duties.

CAMEL STATION

Camel Station operations continued, but at a reduced tempo, with the
Soviet Mediterranean Squadron looking on. That was a normal
occurrence. They always showed great interest in what the U.S. carriers

were doing, trailing the Americans and attempting to rationalize our movements and dispositions. This was only natural. The Sixth Fleet was doing something different, and the Soviets wanted to find out what and why. They were showing professional curiosity. Neither the Task Force 60 commander nor the intelligence people in TF 60 ever evaluated the Soviet motivations as other than that. I remain convinced that these Soviet naval operations in the Mediterranean were not, as has been suggested by some journalists and naval analysts, either threatening or provocative. The Soviets may have been an ally of Syria, but they were not about to tee off a nuclear war by an unprovoked surprise attack, conventional or nuclear, against a major U.S. Fleet unit. And that is what would have happened. An attack against a U.S. operating carrier would have elicited a general war response. U.S. policy was sensitive to the enormous advantage that accrues to the side conducting the first strike. With the anticipated rapidity of escalation to nuclear warfare in a general conflict with Russia, U.S. policy was designed to ensure little chance for the U.S. forces to be left at the gate by a surprise attack. The Russians understood this, and it was clear to both sides that a Soviet attack on the Sixth Fleet, even with conventional weapons, could result in a retaliatory preemptive nuclear strike. This would be a poor tradeoff for the Russians.

The Soviet squadron was meticulous in avoiding confrontation. On one memorable occasion, the Syrians announced that a Syrian navy submarine, a diesel boat, was being sent into the eastern Mediterranean. The next day, as if on signal, all eleven of the Soviet navy submarines known to be in the Mediterranean, came to the surface and operated on the surface in plain view of our forces. It was the Soviet's most positive way possible to show the Sixth Fleet what Russian submarines were deployed to the Mediterranean, and that they were not threatening the fleet. The Soviets well understood that the Sixth Fleet's rules of engagement were to initiate an attack on any non-U.S. submarine submerged in the vicinity of a U.S. warship. The Russians wanted to make sure we understood it wasn't one of theirs.

With the striking force of the Sixth Fleet deployed in a disposition for attack or containment around the littoral of the eastern Mediterranean, the other Sixth Fleet task forces had quickly moved into supporting roles. The Sixth Fleet's marine amphibious group had been moved eastward to be available for contingencies and had been augmented by the arrival of the helicopter carrier *Guam* with a deckload of large transport helicopters, CH-53 Sea Stallions, as well as additional troops. The underway replenishment forces continuously provided fuel and provisions to the ships on Camel Station. Navy P-3 patrol planes and submarines maintained surveillance on all non-U.S. vessels approaching or transiting the surveillance area.

By 1 October the Soviet Mediterranean Squadron had started returning to its normal pattern of operations with the seasonal transfer of ships and submarines to and from their Black Sea bases.

OPERATION FLAT PASS

The situation in the Mediterranean had stabilized, except for the remaining presence of a MASH in Jordan. This field hospital had been moved to a site near Amman, Jordan, during the early days of the Syrian crisis as a humanitarian gesture of U.S. friendship toward Jordan. However, in the absence of casualties with the ongoing withdrawal of the Syrian Army, the U.S. government wanted to bring out this exposed and undefended American unit of noncombatants, including nurses.

The MASH was located near Amman, where it could be extracted through the King Hussein International Airport by strategic airlift forces, using C-5 and C-141 aircraft. Commander in chief, U.S. Forces, Europe (CinCEur) in Germany was tasked by the JCS in Operation Flat Pass to carry out the evacuation, with Navy carriers providing air cover. The projected route of the aircraft, based in Germany, would be to fly out to the North Sea, through the English Channel, over the Bay of Biscay, through the Straits of Gibraltar, along the length of the Mediterranean, and then precisely along the Israeli-Egyptian border into Jordan. That meant the airlift would have to refuel at King Hussein Airport before returning. The airport was a single landing strip, nine thousand feet long and fairly narrow. Unfortunately, the situation in Jordan was still so unsettled that security at the airfield could not be guaranteed by friendly ground forces. The runway could be held, but interdiction from the surrounding area by rockets or mortar fire could not be prevented.

CinCEur was presented with the prospect of a stream of giant cargo planes arriving at King Hussein Airport and being unable to land because of a cratered runway, trucks blocking the landing strip or harassing fire from mortars or artillery. The arriving aircraft, unable to land, low on fuel, would have to divert to an alternative destination, an airfield with runways long enough and strong enough and adequately equipped to refuel a fleet of C-5s and C-141s. There was not such an airfield within the remaining range of the aircraft. CinCEur's initial plan was to airlift troops into Jordan and establish an airhead at King Hussein Airport, sufficiently well equipped and properly situated, and set up a defensive perimeter of sufficient circumference to prevent interdiction of the airport by rockets or mortars. When the possibility of hostile use of field howitzers was considered, the size of the required perimeter became prohibitive. The initial estimate of one airborne brigade from Germany to ensure airfield security grew to a possible multidivision force. The security had to be airtight. There could be no chance of losing even one giant cargo aircraft to enemy fire, and the thought of the entire force having to divert and land at a proscribed airport and risk being impounded was equally unthinkable. At the height of this dilemma, it was reported that the CinCEur computer system had failed. Fortunately, planning for the MASH evacuation by the TF 60 staff had continued in parallel with the European Command (EuCom) effort, and when the CinCEur plans became uncertain, the JCS cancelled Operation Flat Pass and Commander, Task Force 60 was ordered to execute our own concept of operations, which the JCS had dubbed "Fig Hill."

OPERATION FIG HILL

The Task Force 60 staff had been planning Fig Hill for about a week when the execute order came through. Working through the naval attaché at the U.S. embassy in Israel, a small group of Carrier Division 6 staff operations and intelligence officers was flown to Tel Aviv from the carrier in the USS *Independence*'s C-1 carrier transport aircraft (COD). By the terms of the agreement with the Israelis, all U.S. national markings on the COD were painted over and the crew and passengers wore civilian clothes. The U.S. naval officers met with Israeli Defense Force representatives and in a daylong meeting, arranged clearance for an overflight of Israel into Jordan by U.S. Marine helicopters from the Sixth Fleet Amphibious Force, which had been already prepositioned in international waters off the coast of Lebanon. The agreement was completely detailed, with routes, communication frequencies and necessary procedures to handle the most probable contingencies.

The actual evacuation was conducted on 24 and 25 September as soon as the plan of operation could be written and distributed and before the Israelis, Jordanians, or CinCEur could change their minds.

The Marine transport helicopters launched from the *Guam* and other ships of the Marine amphibious units off the coast of Israel, out of sight of any observers on shore. Following the prescribed flight path each way, the helicopters overflew Israel at its narrowest point at low altitude then headed directly for Amman over the West Bank.

On the first inbound trip, the helicopters carried a heavily armed contingent of Marines who established a defensive perimeter around the landing zone (LZ), which was next to the MASH site but away from the King Hussein Airport. With the LZ set up within the perimeter, the Marine helicopters lifted out the MASH people with most of their equipment. Some was left as a gift to the Jordanians. The Marine infantry remained behind to keep the LZ secure. The helicopters returned on a second cycle to pick up the Marine ground force, the LZ was collapsed, and the infantry returned to their amphibious force units. There were no casualties, and the MASH was fully evacuated with the exception of the pieces of medical support equipment that were transferred to the Jordanians. There was very little notice or publicity concerning the entire operation.

NAPLES

Following President Nixon's visit, the *Saratoga* departed the Naples area and returned to TF 60 in the eastern Mediterranean. I transferred my flag from the *Independence* and rejoined the commander, Carrier Division 6 staff in the *Saratoga*. In early October, commander, Sixth Fleet scheduled a "hot washup"—a preliminary critique—of the recent Mideast operations, to be hosted by commander, Fleet Air, Mediterranean, the logistics commander for U.S. naval aviation in the Mediterranean. The *Saratoga* was operating off Cypress, so I arranged to be flown to Naples in the right hand seat of an A-6 Intruder from the Saratoga air wing. That is the bombardier/navigator's station, and I had to be checked out on the radar in the case we encountered foul weather.

The hot washup was a mandatory chore for me, but it would only last a half a day. So with things quiet in the eastern Mediterranean, I planned to take two days of leave and meet my wife and daughter in Naples. Dabney had arrived in Europe with our oldest child, Lucy, via space-available military passenger airlift to Germany on 10 September, intending to rendezvous with me in Barcelona. But when she arrived in Spain, I was gone. Then she met the ship in Naples, where the *Saratoga* had a week in port, and I wasn't aboard. So this brief visit to Naples would be our only get-together the entire cruise, as Lucy was due back in school by mid-October.

I packed a ditty bag with a few civilian clothes, put on my flight suit, hard hat, and oxygen mask, climbed in the Intruder's cockpit, and strapped myself in the bombardier/navigator (BN) seat. We taxied forward onto the catapult. The Intruder went "down" on the catapult due to low rpm in the starboard engine. Another A-6 had to be broken out and preflighted.

It was an hour and a half wait for the next launch. This time my pilot was the squadron CO. Our launch and climb out to thirty thousand feet were routine. It was a clear day and at one point I could see land on both the north and south coasts of the Mediterranean. As we approached the airfield at Naples, which is situated virtually on the slopes of Mount Vesuvius, the weather turned sour, with rain coming out of several layers of solid overcast. As we let down from thirty thousand feet and entered the soup we were being controlled by Naples air traffic center. The controller should have been speaking English, prescribed for international air traffic. If he was, it was not intelligible, and the pilot couldn't speak Italian. So he decided to cancel his instrument flight plan and try to get in underneath. As we went out to sea to let down beneath the lowest cloud layer, I got a quick refresher on how to work the radar in the ground terrain avoidance mode. As we headed back into Cappodichino Airfield under the overcast, the visibility dropped to zero when we neared Vesuvius. To make matters worse, the rain was so dense that I could not tell from the radar return, whether we were approaching a heavy rainstorm or a mountain of lava. The pilot was trying to fly instruments, coach me on the radar "knobology," and interpret the picture on the radarscope. He was having no more luck than I. Suddenly, through a break in the overcast, I saw distinctly, although only partially, the slopes of Mount Vesuvius, close and more ahead of us than below. I slapped the pilot on the shoulder and shouted, "Pull up!" He yanked back on the stick, jammed on full power to both engines, and put the A-6 in a left turn at maximum climb rate. It was hairy. We had come very close to smearing ourselves all over the Italian landscape.

We broke out on top and headed south for the NATO field at Sigonella on the island of Sicily. The weather was clear. As we spotted Mount Etna, another volcano, we also made a visual sighting of the airfield. At that moment, the low fuel light on the cockpit dashboard glowed red. I would have declared an emergency and gone straight in to land—we were lined up with the duty runway—but my pilot, having recovered his composure after our close call, elected to make a normal Navy approach, breaking left over the control tower at one thousand feet and landing out of a racetrack pattern.

In an hour the A-6 was refueled and preflighted by the U.S. Navy detachment at Sigonella, and again we launched for Naples. By the time we had completed the three-hundred-mile trip, the bad weather had dissipated and our arrival was routine. The Navy duty officer found a sedan and the driver bulled our way through the Italian traffic to the Excelsior, a lovely old-fashioned five-star hotel on the Naples waterfront where Dabney had taken rooms while waiting for me to show.

Two days later, I headed for the *Saratoga*, eight hundred miles away in the eastern Mediterranean, and Dabney commenced the drive in our new Volkswagen to Frankfurt, Germany, where she would return to the United States by SPACE A. The Volkswagen Company would ship our VW station wagon to a port of entry in the United States. For her, more than a month of following the fleet had netted only two days together. That confirmed our notion that the role of a camp follower was not easy, even for an admiral's wife.

AFTERMATH

Commander, Carrier Division 6 was relieved in the Sixth Fleet by commander, Carrier Division 4 on 22 November 1970, and the staff and I returned to our homeport in Mayport, Florida, on board the *Saratoga*.

It had been a good cruise from an operational aspect. Ike Kidd had showered TF 60 with kudos for President Nixon's successful visit to the Sixth Fleet and awarded me the Navy's Distinguished Service Medal. Admiral Zumwalt, the CNO, was ecstatic over the Navy's role in the Jordanian crisis and the MASH evacuation, which had been recognized in the JCS and OSD as solo Navy performances because the other services were unable to contribute. The secretary of the navy awarded the entire Sixth Fleet the Navy's Meritorious Unit Commendation.

In his monumental work *The White House Years*, Henry Kissinger sums up the Jordanian crisis of 1970 with the following observation:

> There is something abstract and esoteric, at least for laymen, about a fleet at sea. It follows unheard commands in response to dangers rarely seen. It affects people who almost never get a glimpse of what protects or threatens them. Throughout recent crises the Sixth Fleet had been the principal extension of our military power in the Middle East. It had helped mold events without ever approaching closer to them than two hundred miles. Highly vulnerable to Soviet land-based planes, the Sixth Fleet nevertheless had a decisive impact because an attack on it would bring into play the full force of the United States. The dramatic reinforcement of our naval power had been a crucial signal of our determination to prevent the Jordan crisis from getting out of hand. The fleet's importance had been enhanced by the progressive loss of our land bases and by political restrictions on those remaining.

Within forty-eight hours after Carrier Division 6 had arrived in Mayport, Admiral Zumwalt sent his personal plane to Jacksonville to return me to Washington to present a program of briefings to OpNav and the navy secretariat on the details of the Navy role in Operation Fig Hill. Apparently, the CNO considered that operation a near perfect demonstration of the employment and capabilities of the forward-deployed Navy-Marine forces. Although the accounts were well received, especially by the CNO, Fig Hill never garnered media attention or made the history books.

16

Vietnam

I was just buckling on my sword when the flagship's forward 6-inch turrets started firing. My quarters were just aft of the barbette, so the concussion was palpable. I thought, What's going on? We have a change of command in a half hour and that's no saluting battery. It was May 1972, and I had only been on board the *Oklahoma City* for two days. Obviously I had a lot to get used to. The phone in the cabin rang, and it was the chief of staff. "Don't be overly concerned," he said. "The North Vietnamese are pushing hard on an ARVN salient near Quang Tri, and we have some Marine advisors with the South Vietnamese troops there. The Marines are calling for gunfire support, and they want our 6-inch guns." I did know enough to understand that this was very important. We could not let our U.S. Marine advisors be overrun. After ten minutes and thirty rounds or so, all was quiet again. The *Oklahoma City* headed downwind to be sure we would have only gentle breezes for our ceremony.

I headed back to the fantail, where the ceremony for the change of command of the Seventh Fleet would take place. Vice Adm. Bill Mack, whom I was relieving, and I wanted a simple but traditional naval change of command. The principals—Vice Adm. Bill Mack, commander, Seventh Fleet; Adm. Chick Clary, the Pacific Fleet commander; and I—would be in full dress (hence the sword), the sailors would be in whites, and the Marines would be in blue trousers and wearing field scarves (neckties).

Things had changed in Vietnam since my departure from the theater on board the *Enterprise* in the summer of 1967. On 31 January 1968, the first day of Tet, the principal religious holiday throughout Vietnam, Hanoi had launched a countrywide surprise offensive throughout South Vietnam, utilizing more than 120,000 Communist troops, Vietcong and NVA regulars, which had infiltrated South Vietnam. U.S. intelligence had not detected any indications that would prompt a warning, and the U.S. forces and the ARVN were unprepared for the well-organized operation. Initially the offensive was successful, penetrating into the U.S. embassy compound and almost overrunning the U.S. Air Force air base at Bien Hoa outside Saigon. However, friendly forces were rallied by the U.S. commanders, and led by U.S. Army and Marine units, they turned the situation around, blunting the offensive and administering what turned out to be a sound defeat to the Communists.

Unfortunately the damage had been done—politically in the United States—in spite of the outcome of the campaign, which resulted in heavy losses to Hanoi's interests. In the aggregate, the reversal of the Tet offensive ended up as a significant military victory for the allies in Vietnam. For Hanoi, it was a defeat of its clandestine forces in South Vietnam of major proportions, resulting in a virtual annihilation of the subversive Vietcong political organization in South Vietnam. After Tet, Hanoi had to rely almost entirely on its regular North Vietnamese army for the invasion and conquest of South Vietnam.

In the United States, Tet came as a surprise, a perceived failure of intelligence. It was erroneously compared to a repeat of Pearl Harbor. The psychological and political damage to the continued prosecution of the war in Vietnam was not reversible. It was at this point that President Lyndon B. Johnson, disappointed and dispirited in his failure to disengage and facing the prospect of a continuing war in Vietnam with its political repercussions, decided not to run for president in the coming election. In November 1968, Johnson, in a move calculated to convince the enemy of our desire for an end to hostilities, declared a complete halt of U.S. air attacks into NVN. This so-called bombing pause was initiated on the basis of shaky "understandings" with NVN negotiators, which were never clearly validated or accepted by either side.

With the inauguration of President Nixon there was little change in the strategy for fighting the war. The objective of our Southeast Asia policy continued to be disengagement. The U.S. ground forces would be incrementally withdrawn beginning in 1969, and by August 1972, only forty thousand troops—all advisory personnel—would remain in the country. The ARVN would be increased to more than a million men and equipped and trained by U.S. advisors to take over the defense of their country. This strategic approach was described by Secretary of Defense Melvin Laird as "Vietnamization." During the Vietnamization process, President Nixon continued the effort to negotiate an end to the hostilities, depending largely upon the diplomatic skills of his national security advisor, Henry Kissinger.

Then, on 30 March 1972, the Thursday before Easter, the minister of defense for North Vietnam, Vo Nguyen Giap, launched a major offensive, sending three divisions of infantry, two hundred tanks, and a corps of heavy artillery—guns up to 130mm—across the provisional borders into South Vietnam in a headlong attack against the Army of the Republic of Vietnam.

As the well-trained North Vietnamese regular army divisions poured south into South Vietnam, they more resembled the Blitzkrieg forces of World War II rolling across the plains of Europe than a traditional Asian army. The troops were in the open, their trucks and tanks moving in columns along the main roads, with heavy artillery in tow. The furtive tactics of black-clad guerrillas terrorizing hamlets from hidden bases in the jungle had been abandoned. The ARVN—caught off guard by the surprise and the scale of the attack—was sent reeling.

President Richard Nixon responded immediately to the Communist invasion by directing a dramatic increase in the U.S. air support of the ARVN and against the invading North Vietnamese forces in the South, as well as ordering the resumption of bombing in North Vietnam. As the U.S. air offensive gained momentum with the deployment of additional carriers and reinforcing land-based air units, a new air campaign, Linebacker I, was initiated. This new offensive was more comprehensive and less restrictive than that of Rolling Thunder. It commenced on 10 May 1972, coincident with the mining of Haiphong Harbor by Navy carrier aircraft, and incorporated Air Force tactical fighters, Navy carrier planes, and SAC B-52s. To supplement the air offensive, C7F was directed to commit a substantial segment of the cruiser and destroyer force to Linebacker I in shore bombardment missions against the North Vietnamese, targeting the invading army's lines of communication. In several situations the warships were able to take the North Vietnamese forces under direct fire as the troops moved down the coastal roads.

SEVENTH FLEET CHANGE OF COMMAND

On the scheduled day for the change of command ceremony, the *Oklahoma City* had been assigned a shore bombardment mission on an urgent basis in an area where the North-South highway ran fairly close to the coast and the enemy trucks, tanks, and troops could actually be seen as they proceeded south from North Vietnam to Quang Tri Province in South Vietnam. The *Oklahoma City* was scheduled for a pause in their fire support for one hour at 0900 for the change of command ceremony. At about 0910, Adm. Chick Clarey, commander in chief, U.S. Pacific Fleet, arrived by helicopter on the *Oklahoma City* with several members of his staff. After landing, he freshened up and donned full dress whites, and the entire group moved back to the fantail, where all of the officers and men of Seventh Fleet staff were assembling, with a contingent of Marines and sailors from the ship's company. The Seventh Fleet Band provided the military music that was so much a part of a shipboard change of command ceremony. The sailors were filing aft to fall in, and some of them were already in ranks on the fantail, when there were two splashes on either side of the cruiser. The flagship was being straddled by enemy shore battery fire.

With that, the general alarm rang, the crew departed the fantail area and went to battle stations, and the cruiser quickly added turns, heading for a spot five thousand yards farther away from the coast, where it definitely would be beyond the range of North Vietnamese artillery.

So we started over. The *Oklahoma City* took a course downwind to provide a comfortable five-knot breeze over the main deck, the sailors and Marines fell in again, the band resumed the martial music, and the principals took their places in the formation, made brief remarks, and read our orders. After a gun salute, the fantail was cleared. The crew went below to change back into dungarees, and half an hour later, a Navy helicopter arrived on the stern to pick up Admiral Clarey, his staff, and Vice Adm. Bill Mack to return them to Saigon and the long flight back to Hawaii.

Meanwhile, I changed to khakis, and when battle stations were called away to resume shore bombardment fire, I took station on the flag bridge to observe the *Oklahoma City*'s 6-inch shells impact enemy positions on the coastal highway.

Commander, Seventh Fleet and his staff were an entirely seagoing outfit. There were no offices ashore for the staff. The entire functioning of the commander, Seventh Fleet staff in carrying out the command responsibility of the fleet commander was all provided in the fleet flagship, which at this time was the USS *Oklahoma City*, built at the end of World War II as a standard 6-inch gun cruiser. Subsequent to the war she underwent modification to equip the ship with a Talos battery, making her a missile cruiser. Talos was a very long range surface-to-air defensive missile system that could reach out and shoot down aircraft at distances of one hundred miles or more. The flagship was semi-permanently deployed from the United States to the Yokosuka Naval Base in Japan, where she was homeported. The families of the crewmen and officers lived in quarters on the base, or in the case of some in specially built housing on the economy. Those officers and men without dependents lived on board ship in compartments and staterooms. The *Oklahoma City* was configured to have a good-sized flag mess, which could accommodate twelve to sixteen people at the one sitting for each meal. The seats in the mess were assigned on the basis of seniority. Those officers on the staff who were not members of the flag mess ate with the ship's officers in the officer's wardroom. There was also a flag bridge that was one level above the navigation bridge. It was not utilized extensively, as most of the tactical operations of the fleet were delegated to the various task force, task group, and task unit commanders. But it was good to have a comfortable area where the admiral and the staff could observe what was going on in the vicinity or on board the flagship. Most of the operational work of the staff was in the Plans Division, and much of that was accomplished in flag plot. This was a form of combat information center that was provided with displays to show the relative positions and status of units in the fleet. It was in flag plot that the daily briefings took place.

The fleet staff would normally be about twenty officers and thirty enlisted men, but when the activity in the western Pacific and Southeast Asia picked up, the staff had been augmented by a dozen or so junior officers to handle the increased workload. Actually this didn't fully materialize, and for the first month or so after the resumption of Linebacker I, these additional people were underemployed. That tends to be a normal phenomenon for fleet staffs I suppose.

Because the flagship was equipped with three triple 6-inch gun mounts forward, the *Oklahoma City* was a valuable asset for shore bombardment. There was only one 8-inch gun cruiser in the fleet at that time, the USS *Newport News*, and the largest-caliber gun on a destroyer—of which there were about seventy in the augmented Sixth Fleet—was a 5-inch gun with more limited range and explosive power than the 6-inch. As a consequence the flagship was required to take her turn on the "gun line" conducting shore bombardment, either prearranged fire or call-fire from the troops ashore. With the advent of the Linebacker I campaign, which included shore bombardment against targets in North Vietnam, there was seldom a day in which the flagship was not involved in a period of shooting lasting from four to six hours at a stretch. This could be disconcerting to the staff and to life onboard of the staff members when the big guns were going off all night long. In the dental spaces, for example, a tarpaulin was placed over the dental chairs, because when the guns fired, the ceiling insulation, which was old and in need of repair, would break loose with the shock of gunfire and without the tarpaulin would have fallen into the open mouths of the patients.

The flagship's schedule was similar to that of the other cruisers and destroyers deployed to the Seventh Fleet. It normally consisted of about a month in the Gulf of Tonkin, then a trip back to its homeport of Yokosuka for a week of in-port time. When the *Oklahoma City* was out of the gulf, headed for its homeport or visiting a foreign port, the command functions of Seventh Fleet remained with the staff, with very little if any diminution of effectiveness. Even in the Gulf of Tonkin, connectivity between the commander and his forces was maintained mainly by radio and electronic message traffic.

Part of the responsibility of commander, Seventh Fleet was to show the flag of the United States and the power of the U.S. Navy throughout the western Pacific. This meant periodic visits to other nations on the Pacific Rim. These visits were not curtailed even with the war in Vietnam, and the *Oklahoma City* routinely would travel to such ports as Sasebo in Japan, Taipei in Taiwan, Hong Kong in China, White Beach at Naha,

Okinawa, and ports in Malaysia and Thailand. Once a year or so the flagship would travel to Australia, but that was set aside during the Vietnam War because of the time involved in transit. When the flagship traveled to foreign ports, these were known as representational visits, and commander, Seventh Fleet called on the heads of military service and the local civic government leaders. This usually included an exchange of dinner parties at the headquarters or capital and a reception on board the *Oklahoma City*. For this reason it was considered important that the wife of commander, Seventh Fleet be available on these representational visits to foreign ports. Of course, the spouse could not travel on the flagship, but a flag jet transport was maintained at the Naval Air Station in Yokosuka to fly the spouse to the port of visit to rendezvous with her husband and provide representation on the distaff staff side. These VIP aircraft were T-39 Sabreliners and were comfortable if not loaded with more than four passengers. Usually Dabney traveled by herself, and it took a certain amount of spunk to make these trips. On one occasion she boarded the Sabreliner as the only passenger. There was a crew of two jaygees as pilot and copilot with no flight attendant. The plane was flying from NAS Atsugi to Taiwan for an official fleet visit in the capital of Taipei. About three hours out of Japan, the plane suddenly lost pressurization at forty thousand feet altitude. The pilots rolled the plane on its back and dove at high speed almost straight down to ten thousand feet, where the ambient pressure would provide enough oxygen for survival. The plane, then unable to fly at altitude for its best fuel economy needed to make it all the way to Taiwan, headed back for Japan with fortunately enough fuel to reach Atsugi. Dabney, who had been in the back with her seatbelt buckled, had heard enough about what can happen in aircraft not to be terrified, and when the plane had leveled off at ten thousand feet, one of the pilots told me later that he was amazed at her remarkable calm when they explained to her what had happened. Dabney, however, did not attempt to take a second flight to join me in Taiwan on that occasion.

When the flagship returned to its homeport in Yokosuka, once or twice a year the port visit would include a maintenance availability in which repairs or modification to the ship would be made in the shipyard. This could mean that the period in Yokosuka extended to as long as two weeks, especially if drydocking was involved. On these occasions I would fly back down to the Gulf of Tonkin and remain on board a carrier, visiting the various ships in the fleet by helicopter, going up and down to the decks of destroyers and frigates at the end of a cable hoist. To make these visits more efficient for the fleet commander, commander, Seventh Fleet was assigned a jet transport that was capable of landing on a carrier. This was an A-3 twin-engine jet bomber that had the bomb bay sealed to make an internal cabin in which an operational seat was installed with built-in parachute and solidly bolted to the airframe to enable the seat with a passenger to withstand the arresting force of a carrier landing. The procedure was for commander, Seventh Fleet to fly by helicopter from the helo pad at Yokosuka, land at NAS Atsugi, transfer to the A-3 attack plane, and fly to the Gulf of Tonkin, where the A-3 would land on board a carrier. Then from the carrier, the fleet commander could visit the various ships in the gulf by helicopter and hoist, or by landing on the decks of other carriers and large amphibious ships. Usually a trip to the Gulf of Tonkin also involved a visit to the South Vietnamese Naval Headquarters in Saigon. When this occurred, a special helicopter was flown out from the port at Tan Sinut Airfield operated by Marines with window machine-gunners and antimissile protective devices.

The Seventh Fleet staff's working day normally began at eight o'clock in flag plot with a briefing, a very important part of the staff's operations in my approach to the fleet command. My staff experience was based upon OpNav, where I attended a daily brief. I used the daily briefing to get to know the staff and for them to understand the way I did business. A large-scale map was installed in flag plot on the biggest piece of plywood that could be found in Japan. Cardboard cutouts of ships were made in various coded colors to represent the different types and were placed on the chart with thumbtacks to indicate whether they were operating or in port. Plastic grease pencil status boards were installed similar to those in air operations in a carrier, where all the ships and forces in the fleet could be listed with the status of their operational capability noting any casualties that might limit their warfighting ability. The front lines of the ARVN were plotted on the large chart and when available the positions of major North Vietnamese forces were also displayed.

Compared to today's electronic situation displays it was primitive, but at least it displayed virtually the entire situation in Southeast Asia in a single graphic presentation. The brief would consist first of an operations overview in which the young officer would not be permitted to read from a piece of paper. Using a pointer he would walk around the chart and with the pointer indicate the ships or units that he wished to discuss covering such events as downed aircraft, a crash at sea, or a ship with an engineering casualty. Initially the briefers were terrified at the thought of not having a piece of paper to read. But when they were required as part of their duty to maintain the graphic display through-out the day as changes occurred, they grew familiar with the status of the forces in the fleet and became articulate in describing the current situation. The operations brief was followed by an intelligence rundown, and for this purpose a large screen had been rigged with a viewgraph to be used as the intelligence briefer wished. This was also available for any of the briefers. I insisted that there be no fancy slides. My point was it was time-consuming and manpower-extravagant to make fancy graphics with photographs when they would be used only once or twice. Instead I required the briefer to either write or sketch out what he wanted presented with a grease pencil on a clear sheet of acetate. One of my main objections to prepared slides is that they usually took eighteen to twenty-four hours to prepare, and by that time, they were often out of date in the fast-moving panorama of the war.

COMMAND RELATIONSHIPS

The command relationships among all of the military components engaged in Southeast Asia were extraordinarily complex and had to be meticulously defined and observed. To the uninitiated it might seem to be a superficial hierarchy to protect the turf of the several services and the many flag commands involved. However, a detailed command and control concept had to be put in place because of the disparate com-ponents involved, some of which were not amenable to the military communications, command, and control doctrine. There were the White House, the State Department, the Defense Department, foreign allies (South Vietnam), the Army, the Navy, the Air Force, the Strategic Air Command (SAC was separate from the Air Force). Furthermore, we were engaged in more than a single war: the Cold War with the Soviet Union (involving NATO and nuclear readiness), the guerrilla war with the Vietcong, the limited war against North Vietnam, and the threat of a war with the People's Republic of China, which was shooting down U.S. military aircraft that strayed into Chinese airspace.

The operational chain of command for combat activities within the Republic of Vietnam emanated from the National Command Authority, the president and the secretary of defense; to commander in chief, Pacific, the theater commander; and then to commander, U.S. Military Command Vietnam, who further delegated operational authority to his subordinate service commanders. In the case of naval forces in country, these were under commander, U.S. Naval Forces Vietnam. They were mainly military assistance people and the riverine forces. There were no naval major combatants assigned to Naval Forces Vietnam.

CARRIER WARFARE

By far, the most important single contribution of the U.S. Navy to the conflict in Southeast Asia in 1972 was the carriers. Except for advisory people, U.S. ground troops were being or had been withdrawn from combat in Vietnam. U.S. combat involvement was now limited to the U.S. air components: the Air Force, Navy, Marines, and SAC. The predominant scope of the naval air effort can be measured by the fact that over the period of the conflict, more than half of the combat sorties against North Vietnam were flown by naval aircraft.

The aircraft carriers and their task forces came under a different chain of command, originating with the NCA through CinCPac but then via commander in chief, Pacific Fleet; commander, Seventh Fleet; and commander, Task Force 77, the commander, Carrier Striking Forces. The rationale for this separate chain of command was that commander, Seventh Fleet had broad area responsibilities throughout the western Pacific, which included the command of major naval forces in employment plans and war plans covering a wide array of contingencies outside of the Vietnam conflict, as well as the responsibility for the planning and the conduct of a general war with the Soviet Union, including the fleet's nuclear capability. The doctrine of the Joint Chiefs of Staff had for years included a provision for such a chain of command for naval forces, in consideration of their mobile character and the wide range of their responsibilities from contingency operations to general war plans. Under the JCS doctrine, naval forces in the Seventh Fleet operated "in support" of USMCV.

Task Force 77 included all of the carriers and major combatants assigned to the carriers in a support role. The major surface combatants—cruisers, destroyers, and frigates—were transferred from their administrative commands in the continental U.S. (Cruiser Force Atlantic or Pacific Fleet, e.g.) to Task Force 75, Surface Warfare Force, Seventh Fleet. These units were operationally assigned to Task Force 77 in order to constitute the carrier task groups that were the basic tactical entities for carrier strike operations. A typical carrier task group would consist of one carrier, several destroyers, and three or four frigates. Occasionally a cruiser would be assigned to a carrier task group when it was not committed to gunfire support or other independent operations.

The major surface combatants rotated in and out of the carrier task groups to other duties such as gunfire support (shore bombardment) and the escort of the underway replenishment groups. The carrier task groups always remained about the same in numbers and types, but the identity of the surface combatants in the group was constantly changing.

I had delegated operational control of the carrier task group to commander, Task Force 77 (an aviation vice admiral) and his staff, who did most of the tactical planning for the carrier air operations. In particular, commander, TF 77 was responsible for the coordination of carrier air operations with land-based tactical air operations of U.S. Air Force units based in both Vietnam and Thailand. For this purpose, commander, TF 77 had a permanent representative at the USMACV headquarters in Saigon, usually a senior Navy captain. Commander, TF 77 and his staff were always embarked in a carrier. There were no operational or administrative spaces ashore. As the carriers rotated in and out of the Seventh Fleet on six- or seven-month deployments, the commander was continually shifting his flag. This also meant that when the commander's carrier flagship went into port after thirty days on the line for a week of maintenance, replenishment, and R&R, the commander and his staff were absent from the Gulf of Tonkin.

To cover these absences, the position of commander, Task Group 77.0 was created. This was an aviation two-star flag officer, one of the several carrier division commanders constantly being rotated to the Seventh Fleet on six- or seven-month deployments from commander, Naval Air Forces Atlantic and Pacific, respectively, based in Norfolk, Virginia, and San Diego. AirLant and AirPac CTG 77.0 was always on the scene in the Gulf of Tonkin and was assigned operational control of all of the carrier task groups in the gulf. The carrier task groups in the Seventh Fleet—and there could be as many as six—were assigned designations of CTG 77.1 through CTG 77.6.

The tactics employed by the carrier task groups and their embarked air wings were the standard doctrines set forth in the U.S. Fleet tactical publications and the Naval Air Training and Operational Procedures. NATOPS by that time had largely eliminated the procedural differences that had crept in during and immediately after World War II between the Atlantic and Pacific Fleets. However, some modifications to the NATOPS were made specifically for "special operations," the euphemism used to describe combat operations in the Gulf of Tonkin against the Vietcong and North Vietnamese. The carriers and their air wings trained and exercised in these special doctrines during their work-up periods in preparation for deployment to the western Pacific.

The targeting, in terms of general policy, broad guidelines and sometimes even specific objectives, came from Washington to CinCPac. The specificity of the Washington targeting directions varied, depending upon political circumstances in the White House and the degree of involvement on the part of key individuals in the Pentagon at the time. From the Washington guidance provided through JCS channels, CinCPac prepared a target list, which was drawn on by MCV and TF 77, which coordinated carefully to ensure that national and JCS priorities were followed, that all assigned targets were covered, and that Air Force and the Navy units were given targets that best suited their special capabilities. Commander, TF 77 and USMCV could also add targets, as long as the national requirements were fulfilled.

Commander, TF 77's target list and general guidance were provided to commander, TF 77.0, who then assigned daily strike responsibilities to the individual carriers, depending upon how many carriers were on the line and the aircraft composition of their air wings. Upon receipt of the daily air plan, each carrier's operations department then assigned specific mission sorties to the squadrons. It was up to the squadrons to ensure that adequate planes were available and that pilots and strike leaders were detailed.

During the Vietnam War, the Navy carrier force level was stabilized at sixteen attack carriers, although this number included one CVS operating in the role of a CVA. Administratively, nine carriers were assigned to the Pacific Fleet and six to the Atlantic Fleet. However, all carriers, regardless of fleet assignment, shared in the combat deployments to special operations (SpecOps). This was different from practice in the Korean War, when Atlantic Fleet carriers largely continued to deploy to the Sixth Fleet in the Mediterranean, while the Pacific Fleet carriers made most of their deployments to Korea. For the Atlantic Fleet carriers deployed to Vietnam, CinCLant retained administrative command (AdCom) but the units were chopped (meaning that their operational control was changed) to CinCPac when the ships entered the geographical boundary of CinCPac's theater. In addition to keeping five or six carriers in the Seventh Fleet, the U.S. Navy also was committed to maintaining at all times two carriers in the Sixth Fleet. The pressure of maintaining half the carrier force deployed over the long period of the Vietnam War eventually caused severe deterioration in the material condition of the ships, from which the carrier force really didn't fully recover until the late seventies.

MUSCLE FOR THE SEVENTH FLEET

By the end of May 1972, the reinforcement of the Seventh Fleet had been largely completed, and the fleet now was at its largest size and capability since World War II. The complement was 73,275 Navy people, 27,443 Marines in the Seventh Fleet Marine Force, six aircraft carriers on a continuous basis, sixty destroyers and escort ships, thirty-one amphibious ships, and twelve submarines. In addition, there were thirty-four logistic-support vessels—tankers, ammunition ships, supply ships, tenders, and special types—all in the Gulf of Tonkin, underway, supporting the combatants.

The tempo of combat operations had risen fast. On 24 May 1972, the Seventh Fleet Amphibious Force, consisting of three ARGs—a total of about a dozen large ships—initiated Operation Lam Son 72. This was a combined amphibious and vertical envelopment supporting operation with South Vietnamese marines being inserted twenty miles northwest of the city of Hue. Three Seventh Fleet cruisers and seven destroyers provided naval gunfire support for this operation, including the flagship *Oklahoma City*, whose 6-inch guns were essential to reach to the landing zone. All U.S. ground forces had been withdrawn from combat, and U.S. troop participation was limited to advisory and logistics roles. The South

Vietnamese marines were transported by landing craft operated by U.S. bluejackets and in helicopters flown by Marine Corps pilots with Marine flight crews manning the waist guns. This airborne insertion in the rear of the North Vietnamese troops turned out to be very effective in seriously disrupting the North Vietnamese army's drive to the south, forcing Hanoi to halt their offensive and redeploy to the rear to deal with the threat from the ARVN marines, who were then extracted by the Seventh Fleet Marine helicopters.

This operation was so successful that, on 11 July, Phase II of Lam Son 72 was initiated with thirty-five helicopters from the USS *Okinawa* and USS *Tripoli* lifting 840 South Vietnamese marines to a landing zone southeast of Quang Tri City. The Marine helicopters ran into heavy defensive fire. One CH-53 was destroyed by an SA-7 shoulder-fired heat-seeking missile, and two more CH-46 helicopters were damaged.

This operation was quickly followed up by Phase III of Lam Son 72, when two waves of helicopters from the USS *Okinawa* lifted 689 Vietnamese marines into a landing zone behind enemy lines seven miles northeast of Quang Tri City, which had the effect of easing the North Vietnamese pressure on Quang Tri and contributing to the subsequent recapture of the city by the South Vietnamese army.

MARINE HUNTER-KILLERS

The port of Haiphong had been idled by the minefields laid by carrier aircraft. Twenty-three merchant ships had been trapped in Haiphong and were unable to leave the port. Cargo ships from other Communist countries such as China, Poland, and the USSR, carrying war material and supplies intended for North Vietnam, were unable to enter the port to discharge their cargoes. The blockade of North Vietnam from seaborne commerce was working at 100 percent effectiveness. Then, in June 1972, we discovered that the Communists had developed a new technique for resupply. Communist cargo ships would anchor in the lee of a small island in the approaches to Haiphong Harbor and unload cargo into small craft, such as junks and sampans. These would then slip into coves and creeks east of Haiphong to land their cargo over unimproved beaches with coolie labor. This operation was first noted by Seventh Fleet carrier aircraft ingressing to North Vietnam for strikes in the Hanoi area, and this information was quickly passed to the amphibious forces, which sent Marine helicopters to investigate. The density of the native small craft near Han La Island indicated that this was going to become a major operation. Large numbers of small craft were being assembled in the coves and small harbors along the coast and some were already proceeding to the vicinity of the merchant ships.

According to our rules of engagement, the cargo ships flying the flags of the USSR, Poland, China, and other Communist nations could not be attacked, even though they were unloading goods. But the small craft were not only fair game but also extremely vulnerable to the machine guns of the Marine helicopter gunships. Within hours, I initiated a new operation on a priority basis called Marine Hunter-Killer Operation Number 1, or MARHUK One. The amphibious helicopter carriers were directed to move northward from the Bien Hoa area in South Vietnam, to the Haiphong delta and launch AH-1 Cobra helicopter gunships, which were to proceed to Han La and attack the small craft as they were making the trip in from the cargo ships to the unloading areas on the coastline. The initial results were spectacular. Large numbers of small craft were destroyed, forcing the North Vietnamese to abandon this ferrying of war material. The North Vietnamese tried to move small craft out to the cargo ships after the Marine helicopters had departed the area following the first strikes, but this was foiled when the helicopter gunships returned unexpectedly in a second wave of attacks. The tactics for MARHUK One were then to hold the Cobras out of sight in the vicinity of the anchorage. Then, when South Vietnamese boatmen reported that the North Vietnamese small craft appeared to be getting underway from the cargo ships or their landing sites, the Cobra gunships would be called in to attack and destroy them.

The Communists then tried to operate at night, and Marine helicopters responded with flares and night attacks. In desperation, the Communists then bundled the goods in waterproof coverings and put them over the side in the water, when the tide was moving in, hoping the tide would carry these bundles to the beach. This was effective in moving ashore such things as foodstuffs—rice and so forth—but there apparently was no feasible way to move in ammunition or heavy equipment. Furthermore, several times when floatable bundles of food-stuffs were put into the water to be floated ashore, an offshore breeze came up and overcame the effect of the tide and blew the bundles out to sea. The Marine hunter-killer helicopters would routinely shoot up the bundles in the water or attack the beachheads where the North Vietnamese coolies were extracting the bundles from the surf. MARHUK One operations continued for a month or so until the Communists gave up in frustration at their complete failure to ferry or float their goods ashore.

VISIT TO THE ARVN FRONT

In July 1972 the commanding general of the ARVN field forces in the Quang Tri region invited me to visit his troops near the front lines. Accompanied only by an aide, I flew into Saigon in "Blackbeard 1," the helicopter assigned to the *Oklahoma City* for the use of the Seventh Fleet commander. The helo was refueled, and with an escort of several ARVN helicopter gunships we flew up to the headquarters of the ARVN group that had recently defeated the North Vietnamese troops and retaken Quang Tri Province. I was taken on a tour of the front lines, met with the battle-weary ARVN troops, witnessed the stacks of weapons captured from the enemy, and was able to see several Soviet-made tanks that had been destroyed by carrier aircraft or captured by ARVN ground forces. After a lunch of field rations, the group returned to the ARVN command bunker to receive a briefing on the battle and the role of the Marine helicopters in the deployment of the ARVN and South Vietnamese marine forces. At 1500 it was departure time for me, and my hosts were getting anxious because the general area of the ARVN headquarters in Quang Tri had been subject to long-range artillery fire from the 8-inch Chinese guns provided to the North Vietnamese. These had recently been firing into the ARVN headquarters area in the late afternoon. My host, the ARVN general, was anxious for me to depart at my scheduled time for this reason. I was equally anxious to get out of there. Upon arrival at Blackbeard 1, it was determined that there was not enough battery power to turn over the engine to start. The pilot said there was nothing to do except to replace a certain electrical component in the battery circuitry and that would have to come from the fleet. He arranged to get power plugged in to operate his radio and was able to call a Seventh Fleet unit to have a message relayed to the flagship that Blackbeard 1 was down—the term used for a nonoperable aircraft on the ground—in Quang Tri Province. He requested that arrangements be made to obtain the necessary part and have it flown into the ARVN headquarters with a mechanic for installation. The ARVN then provided one of their helicopters to return me to Saigon, where I would be picked up at the Tan Son Nhut Air Base by a helicopter from one of the carriers and returned to the *Oklahoma City*.

In the retransmission, the message became garbled, so it was passed to the flagship that commander, Seventh Fleet in his helicopter was down in Quang Tri Province. Operationally, as opposed to mechanically, an aircraft "down" in Vietnam meant that it was crashed, normally due to enemy action. The flagship unfortunately passed this information back to the Pentagon without confirmation, and there was a brief period of consternation until the Pentagon asked for further details and the matter was straightened out.

LIEUTENANT (JUNIOR GRADE) LEHMAN

In October 1972 I received a back-channel personal message from deputy chief of naval operations, Vice Adm. Tom Connolly, advising me that the president had directed Henry Kissinger, as national security advisor, to assess the effectiveness of naval operations in the war in Vietnam. This probably was brought on by Army or Air Force supporters, because all U.S. ground forces were being pulled out of Vietnam and the involvement of the Army and the Air Force had been substantially reduced. Admiral Connolly reported that Kissinger was sending his personal representative to visit the Seventh Fleet, and he was expected to arrive within a week. This member of his staff was Lt. (j.g.) John Lehman, USNR, who was being given carte-blanche authority to visit, question, and explore as he saw fit. There was apparently great nervousness on the part of senior naval officers in the Pentagon. They were concerned as to whether such a junior officer would be qualified to evaluate the performance of an entire fleet in this complex theater of operations. So it was suggested that Lehman be discouraged from traveling throughout the fleet or talking to anyone but senior officers who would be able to give him "the big picture."

However, I had decided to take a different approach. Having gained some useful experience with visitors from the DoD and the White House during my previous tours as captain of the *Enterprise* and commander,

Task Force 60 in the Mediterranean, I had come to the conclusion that the best solution was to push these representatives into the front lines— if they were willing to go. There they had a chance to see the action for themselves, rather than getting it second hand through flag plot briefings, which could be a real turnoff, especially for someone who was serious about finding out what was really going on. My plans were for Lehman to visit a destroyer on the gun line and observe at first hand naval gunfire support. Then he would ride in an A-6 Intruder to experience flight operations from a carrier and proceed with the strike group up to the coastline as it penetrated inland over North Vietnam. He would, for obvious reasons, observe from the relative security of an overwater position outside of SAM range.

Lehman arrived at about 1600 by helicopter from Saigon in blue service dress uniform, clutching his visored cap in the wind stream of the chopper. We moved him into a comfortable private state room, and the supply officer dug up a pair of khaki pants and a short-sleeve khaki shirt plus an overseas cap. This was the uniform of the day for the staff, and it was much more suitable for clambering into and out of helicopters hovering over destroyer decks. With the senior staff section heads, I presented a short overview of the mission and composition of the Seventh Fleet, which Lehman took on board without any difficulty and with few questions. Dinner there in the flag mess was, as usual, pleasant and productive. When I had relieved as commander, Seventh Fleet, the flag mess had been a sorry spectacle. It had been "decorated" by the wife of one of the staff officers to make it "not so severe and military looking," with ornate plywood paneling, reproductions of Van Gogh paintings on the walls, and a trellis with plastic flower blossoms. This all was quickly removed. First, because the vibration and shock of gunfire had loosened the fasteners so that the panels were coming loose and the trellis had broken. But mainly because these flammable decorations were, by fleet regulations, "strip ship" items in wartime. Then the flag mess was restored to the traditional appearance of an officer's mess on a warship, with haze gray bulkheads, the fire main pipes that ran across the overhead for damage-control purposes painted white, and the large valves with their massive brass wheel handles uncovered from their aesthetic plywood boxes, the paint removed, and the brass polished to a bright shine. Standard aluminum wardroom furniture was reinstalled, and all of the seats were covered in white duck, which had been the standard on board the ships on the Asiatic station, probably a holdover from the Royal Navy. The few pictures on the bulkheads were photographs of other Seventh Fleet flagships and previous naval ships that had borne the name *Oklahoma City*. All were historically significant and of some interest to Navy types. The staff did a lot of business in the wardroom, and we wanted it to look like a traditional place of business in a man-of-war's cabin.

After dinner, I laid out the plans for Lehman's visit. In the event that Lehman might have demurred at the thought of flying in an A-6 off a carrier—and I thought there was a good chance that he would not want to do so, based upon my previous experience with the civilians from the Pentagon—I didn't want Lehman to be embarrassed. However, John Lehman was of a different stripe. He was positively enthusiastic about flying from the carrier and asked if he could go on a strike. I pointed out that we were losing people daily to the heavy ground fire over North Vietnam, and because of his assignment in Kissinger's inner circle, it would certainly be embarrassing if he were captured and had his fingernails slowly pulled out with pliers. He reluctantly agreed that it would be wiser not to put him in a position where he could possibly fall into the hands of the enemy, but he certainly wanted to go along as a crewman just as far as was prudent.

The following day, Lehman was sent by helicopter over to the carrier *Saratoga*, which was the flagship of commander, Task Group 77.3, at that time the senior aviation flag officer in tactical command of the Seventh Fleet air operations. He was a colorful individual, a rear admiral, known to his friends as the "Big Coolie." With his six foot four inch, husky frame and square jaw, he somewhat resembled the character Big Stoop in the comic strip *Terry and the Pirates*. On a previous tour of duty serving in the Pentagon, the Big Coolie, who was an especially dedicated advocate for carrier aviation, had taken to visiting the offices of the staff of the secretary of defense on the third floor of the Pentagon, where he would attempt to educate these civilian analysts on the benefits of carriers. He was physically more persuasive than verbally, and the secretary of defense eventually had to call the SecNav and instruct him to forbid the Big Coolie from visiting the third floor offices of the SecDef. The reason given was that he was intimidating the civilians.

The Big Coolie was an aviator's aviator. When he commanded an F-8 fighter squadron as a thirty-six-year-old commander, he was the top pilot in the unit in air-to-air combat. He had also commanded an air wing in which he flew all of the different types of planes in the wing. He had then been in command of a carrier before taking over a carrier division. He was clearly the sort of person who would give the impression that the aviation leadership of the operating Navy was tough, experienced, and professional. It had also quickly become apparent to me that John Lehman was an exceptional young man with an enormous amount of common sense to go along with his sharp intellect, and that he could certainly differentiate between the truth and elaboration. I thought that he would find in the Big Coolie an interesting and well-qualified spokesman for Seventh Fleet air operations.

Calling the Big Coolie on the radio telephone, I explained to him exactly what I wanted him to do in furthering Lehman's education in matters of Seventh Fleet operations, especially the carrier operations, which at that time amounted to about 90 percent of the Navy's involvement in the war. Lehman was to be checked out as a bombardier/navigator in the right-hand seat of a Grumman A-6 Intruder and launched on an operational mission. The Intruder would accompany the strike flight up to the coastline, then fly along the coast and pick them up again as they came out. He would fly the entire mission with the exception of the portion that was overland. It was essential we avoid exposing him to the possibility of going down and being captured.

The Big Coolie called me the next afternoon to say that Lehman had done well on his A-6 flight. He had been an enthusiastic crewman and had learned to operate the Intruder's complicated radar after only fifteen minutes on the controls. As a consequence, he had gained an excellent appreciation of the electronic and weapons capabilities of the A-6. The education of John Lehman in naval matters had begun. At that time, few of us would have guessed that he would end up being one of the most active and productive secretaries of the navy in its long history of distinguished public servants.

Lehman did visit other units of the Seventh Fleet, including surface combatants conducting shore bombardment. He liked the fact that I was riding a 6-inch gun cruiser and could watch direct gunfire missions against hostile targets ashore, observing the fall of shot and an occasional secondary explosion when an ammunition dump was blown up. John Lehman later wrote to me saying that his report to Secretary Kissinger had been a positive one, and that he had found little to criticize in the Navy's operations. He felt that Kissinger had been persuaded of not only the essential nature of the Seventh Fleet forces in the conduct of the war but also of the fact that they were making a unique and major contribution.

As a footnote, when I returned to the Pentagon after the Seventh Fleet assignment, I got in touch with Lehman, who had joined Fred Ikle on the staff of the Arms Control and Disarmament Agency. The two of us continued to share our mutual interest in naval aviation and the role and the capability of carriers in future war plans and military strategies. When I became chief of naval operations in 1976, I hired John Lehman for the CNO's personal staff as a consultant, mainly to advise in matters concerning SALT but also in a host of other operational and political subjects involving the Navy and, especially, carriers and Naval Aviation. When John Lehman became secretary of the navy in the Reagan administration and I had retired from the Navy, he continued to keep in touch and share his views with me on naval matters.

In later years, a retired naval aviator who had flown off the *Saratoga* in 1972 told me that he had been on the strike with Lehman and implied that John had insisted to his pilot that they not linger at the shoreline but go on with the other A-6s to the target. My vehement response was, "Don't tell me another word!"

17

Vietnam

Battle of Haiphong Harbor

In spite of the furious barrage of salvoes from her 8-inch main battery, the USS *Newport News* (CA-148), flying the flag of commander, Seventh Fleet, appeared to be trapped in the approaches to Haiphong Harbor. It was almost midnight on 27 August 1972, and three North Vietnamese torpedo boats had used the cover of darkness and the karst islands of the Dao Cat Ba archipelago to ambush the heavy cruiser. The Russian-built P-6 fast attack craft were moving at top speed to close off the only escape route.

The *Newport News* had been radically maneuvering on easterly courses and would soon run out of sea room. To the east was the Île de Norway archipelago, to the northeast the coast of Cat Ba, and to the north the shoals and minefields of Haiphong. It wasn't known if the P-6s had torpedoes or missiles or both. Torpedoes could be trouble enough as the North Vietnamese craft continued to track along a course that would intercept the cruiser's retirement path. The situation could become messy.

Then CIC reported a fourth fast attack craft had been detected. How had we gotten ourselves into such a fix?

LION'S DEN

Back in mid-August, the Joint Chiefs of Staff had directed me to plan for a naval gunfire strike, to be identified as Lion's Den, against military facilities in the Haiphong–Cat Ba area. The targets would include the Cat Ba Airfield, military barracks, coastal defense guns, ammunition dumps, and radars. This operation would be more than the ordinary Linebacker gun strike. Haiphong was about three hundred miles north of the front lines, and as the major North Vietnamese port, it had always been heavily defended. The Seventh Fleet had laid extensive mine-fields in the channels and approaches to the port of Haiphong on 9 May 1972. Since the mining, the North Vietnamese had considerably strengthened the defenses in the Haiphong area, which now included search and detection radars, coast watcher networks, coastal defense guns, gun-control radar, surface-to-air missile sites, and fire-control direction centers.

The Seventh Fleet staff intelligence officer, in briefing the enemy defensive capabilities for Lion's Den, advised that there would be no air threat. The Vietnamese aircraft in the area were day fighters with no ability to attack ship targets at night. All intelligence sources seemed to agree that torpedo- or missile-equipped high-speed patrol craft would not be a factor. No fast patrol boats had been sighted or detected in the Haiphong area from overhead photography or communication intercept in several months. Coastal defense artillery would constitute the only real threat to the bombardment group.

As commander, Seventh Fleet, I had some special concerns about Operation Lion's Den. My personal experience with naval gunfire operations was not lacking. In World War II, as gunnery officer of the destroyer *Bennion* (DD-662), I had directed heavy preparatory bombard-ments as well as direct gunfire support for troops ashore at Saipan, Tinian, Guam, Palau, and in the Philippines. At Palau, the *Bennion* had emptied her magazines three times in one week during the assault on Peleliu. The *Bennion* had suffered casualties from shore battery fire at Samar and had been next to the *Ross* (DD-563) when that destroyer had been put out of action by mines during the shore bombardment phase of the battle for Leyte. Most of the guns and ammunition being used for shore bombardment in Vietnam in 1972 were the same as those the Navy had employed in World War II: the 5-inch/38, 6-inch/47, and 8-inch/55. At that time in Vietnam, all gun-armed major combatants were taking their turns on the gun line. Even the Seventh Fleet's flagship, the *Oklahoma City* (CLG-5), a missile cruiser, was being called upon to provide shore fire support with her 6-inch battery every three or four days. There had been no disabling hits and only minor casualties from enemy counter battery fire to the Seventh Fleet cruisers or destroyers so far in Vietnam, although many hostile rounds had been fired.

The Seventh Fleet cruisers and destroyers were conducting gunfire support on a daily basis and generally had a low regard for the danger posed by the North Vietnamese shore batteries. When the fall of shot came close, the ship simply moved or changed course and speed, and the shore battery gunners had to recompute their fire-control problem. The North Vietnamese guns being used for coastal defense were field artillery pieces and not designed to track moving targets. Against fixed targets, though, they had proved to be deadly. The bombardment of the Marine base during the siege of Khe San was convincing evidence. The technique of field artillery is to fire a few rounds at a fixed point, observe the fall of shot, and then adjust the fire in range and azimuth until the rounds consistently hit the desired point. The battery is then said to be registered on the target. When the guns fire again, the initial rounds are on target and the area can be saturated with a devastating effect.

I continued to harbor the nagging worry that if one of our ships were to become immobilized within range of a shore battery, it would take only a few minutes before the artillery would be hitting it consistently. This was the heart of my concern. To reach the targets at Haiphong and Cat Ba, the bombardment group would have to close the shoreline to well within range of the enemy's coastal artillery emplacements. Although their rounds might lack accuracy against the moving ships, the sheer volume of fire from the large number of coastal defense sites, identified in our intelligence photos, would increase the chances of a "lucky" hit on a bombarding ship. If the projectile were to penetrate a vital area such as a magazine or an engineering space, the ship could lose power and become dead in the water. Then it would become a sitting duck for coast artillery.

In World War II, when this did occur, tow lines would be passed to the stricken vessel from another warship or a fleet tug (fleet tugs were always on hand during the bombardment and landing phases of World War II amphibious operations), and the damaged ship would be towed out of range. To pass a towline in Haiphong Harbor, at night, under an intense artillery barrage, with no air cover, would be messy at best. The chances of losing the towing ship were good, too. Other than the bombardment group, the rest of the fleet would be at least a hundred miles away.

A military commander has to be prepared to accept losses during combat in wartime, but not to expose his forces to *unnecessary* losses. The possible gains should outweigh the probable losses. This brought up a less evident but more sensitive factor. In the worst case, if a U.S. destroyer were sunk in Haiphong Harbor within range of shore batteries, the survivors in the crew could probably be evacuated in the minutes after sinking, but even then at considerable risk to the rescuing vessel. We would not be able to salvage the stricken warship, however. The bombardment force would be making its firing run on a seven-mile leg in a water depth of forty to fifty feet. A destroyer sunk in this depth would be salvageable but, unfortunately in this location, not by friendly forces. It would just not be possible to conduct a salvage operation, difficult at best, under the barrels of the enemy's heavy guns. Even establishing local air superiority in the salvage area would probably be impossible, being within effective range of a host of surface-to-air missile sites. On the other hand, the wreck would be susceptible to exploitation by enemy divers who could retrieve sensitive equipment. Classified material could fall into the hands of the North Vietnamese and then migrate to their Communist allies, the Chinese and Soviets. The compromise of electronics, code machines, and secret documents would be very damaging.

My paramount worry was nuclear weapons. At that time, U.S. national policy was to neither confirm nor deny that U.S. Navy warships carried nuclear weapons. The effectiveness of this policy was essential to our nuclear deterrent posture. It allowed our nuclear-capable warships— submarines, cruisers, and carriers—to enter foreign ports, both neutrals and those of our Cold War allies. At the same time, our actual level of nuclear readiness remained uncertain to the Soviets. If an enemy were able to examine the internal spaces of one of our deployed warships, the "neither confirm nor deny" policy would be weakened regardless of what was—or was not—found in the ship's magazines.

This concern for the possibility of damage or loss to our bombardment force in a Haiphong strike was expressed in secure phone discussions between our staff and their counterparts at CinCPacFlt. The
response was that the Pentagon was very keen on this operation and
the threat from shore batteries was judged to be minimal, considering
the record of the North Vietnamese coastal defenses. The mission planning would go ahead.

On August 25, C7F received a message from the JCS, via CinCPac
and CinCPacFlt, directing that surface combatants attack selected targets
from the CinCPac/JCS target list in the Haiphong–Cat Ba Airfield
complex with naval gunfire on 27 August 1972.

The directive was immediately passed down to commander, Task
Group 77.1, Seventh Fleet Surface Warfare Group for action. Several of
the Seventh Fleet staff officers wanted our staff to run the operation and
simply ask CTG 77.1 for inputs, but I demurred. I had always been an
advocate of delegating authority down the line as far as the capabilities
of the subordinate commanders would permit, and in this case, CTG
77.1 was an experienced destroyer officer with a competent staff group,
and the Seventh Fleet surface operations had been well run. The only
guidance to be passed to CTG 77.1 was to include the USS *Newport News*
(CA 148), our only 8-inch gun cruiser, in the strike force, and not to use
the *Oklahoma City*. There was no point in risking the flagship's sophisticated but fragile command and control electronics suit to a stray shard
of shrapnel. Some of this one-of-a-kind equipment was so delicate that
the shock and blast of the cruiser's own gunfire could put it out of
commission. Commander, Seventh Fleet would embark in the *Newport
News* by helicopter on the afternoon of the twenty-seventh to lead the
operation but would not exercise local tactical command.

I had decided to go along for two reasons. First, after expressing the
view that the result might not justify the risks, it was important to reaffirm
my confidence in my superiors' overriding judgment. Second, an
evening of fireworks up north would be a chance to observe the North
Vietnamese capabilities.

Four ships were selected for Lion's Den, and the force was designated
Task Unit 71.1.2. The officer in tactical command for the operation (CTU
71.1.2) would be Capt. John Renn, commander of Destroyer Squadron
25, riding in the *Robison* (DDG-12), a guided-missile destroyer. The

Robison would team with the *Providence,* a 6-inch gun cruiser, as one task element, and the World War II *Gearing*-class destroyer *Rowan* (DD-782) would join the heavy cruiser *Newport News* as a second task element. The *Rowan* had been selected for the mission because of a one-of-a-kind field modification that had converted the Weapon Alfa ASW rocket launcher to a Shrike antiradiation missile launcher. Shrike had been designed as an air-to-ground missile and was being widely used by Task Force 77 carrier aircraft against the North Vietnamese gun and missile control radars. The Shrike homed on electronic signals emanating from the active hostile radar. The *Rowan* installation was experimental and would be getting its first test as a surface ship weapon against coastal-defense and fire-control radars in Operation Lion's Den.

The elements of Task Unit 77.1.2 were pulled from the gun line off Quang Tri Province and dispatched immediately to the URG in the Gulf of Tonkin to top off magazines and bunkers from the fleet oilers and ammunition ships. The *Newport News* loaded more than one thousand rounds of 8-inch ammunition from the *Mount Katmai* (AE-16), a record replenishment for the cruiser. Then all ships began to steam north independently at twenty-five knots to rendezvous about seventy miles southeast of Haiphong.

Chuck Packer was a young third-class electrician's mate on board the *Rowan* that night, and he has recorded his experience and the recollections of several of his shipmates in a reminiscence titled "A Dicey Night up North." Packer remembers 27 August 1972 as

> the night we went all the way up North. In midafternoon of that day, the skipper, Cdr. Robert Comer, came on the intercom telling us that the *Rowan* was awaiting word from commander, Seventh Fleet, Vice Adm. James Holloway III in the USS *Newport News* (CA-148), concerning a possible raid on the main North Vietnamese harbor of Haiphong. That announcement lit a brushfire of discussion, apprehension, and, of course, scuttlebutt. Succinctly: What did this mean for us? We had less than two hours to ponder this thunderstroke when the skipper came on the intercom again confirming that the *Rowan* was, indeed, going to raid Haiphong in a matter of hours, along with the *Newport News, Providence* (CLG-6), and *Robison.* While I'm sure he added words concerning his confidence in our abilities and in his intention to bring us through safely, they were

drowned in the cacophony of fear and panic that were beginning to invade my thoughts. However, I still vividly remember five more or less instantaneous, distinct thoughts and occurrences. I remember standing on the starboard weather deck just forward of amidships when the announcement was made. Then the *Rowan* changed course north and put on twenty-five knots while starting to light off the third and fourth boilers and bring them on line. I thought of the confused night surface battles of the Solomons campaign in 1942, where destroyers took tremendous punishment resulting in much loss of life, and the severely injured sailors that were left fighting for their lives in the choking fuel-oil fumes and flames, having abandoned their sinking ships. The *Preston, Monssen, Gwinn, Barton,* and too many other cans went down with their dead and trapped crews during these types of night battles—the sort for which the *Rowan* was now headed at her best speed. I remember thinking that I had to get a grip on my emotions because the green boots on board would be looking to us "old salts" for cues and examples. Perhaps "leadership" would be too strong a word. Lastly, I remember the peace I experienced when I accepted that I could quite possibly die that night.

During the night of 26 August, the *Oklahoma City* also left the gun line off Quang Tri Province and headed north to join the four carriers in Task Force 77, the carrier striking force of the Seventh Fleet, which was engaged in around-the-clock aircraft strike operations into North Vietnam as part of the Linebacker I operation. The surface combatants were regularly rotated between the gun line and escort duties with the other Seventh Fleet task units as a matter of operating routine. The steady gunfire was wearing out their gun barrels, requiring the replacement of the barrel liners, which had to be accomplished in a shipyard. So equalizing gun barrel wear was an important consideration in scheduling for the gun line.

At about 1400 on 27 August, with little more than a toothbrush and a change of underwear, I climbed in a helicopter on the *Oklahoma City*'s fantail and was launched for the USS *Newport News*, some hundred miles to the north. After landing us on board the *Newport News* at 1505, our helicopter was refueled and sent off to spend the night on board the *Kitty Hawk* (CVA-63). Capt. Walter F. Zartman, skipper of the *Newport*

News, did not want any fragile and fuel-loaded aircraft on his exposed weather decks for the evening's activity. Among his concerns was damage to the helicopter from the blast of the cruiser's own 8-inch guns.

Zartman and I went over the pertinent message traffic and he briefed me on the plans for the operation. The four ships would arrive individually in the rendezvous area and maneuver independently on random courses until after dark, when they would be unobservable by any local fishing craft that might be in the area. Then, at 2000, the four ships would form up in a column with *Rowan* in the van as guide and proceed at twenty-five knots on a course that headed for the Point Do Son light, some seventy miles away, which marks the entrance to the Haiphong Channel.

It was a remarkable anomaly that the Do Son light had remained operational as a navigational aid for the duration of the war. Its obvious purpose had been to guide the munitions-laden cargo ships from China, the Soviet Union, and other Communist bloc countries to the wharves of Haiphong. Because of their neutral flags, there they could lie, untouched by U.S. bombs, and be unloaded between the air raids on Haiphong. When the mining of the port occurred on 9 May 1972, the flow of war material by Communist bloc shipping through Haiphong ceased. Yet the light remained on, flashing its identifying signal beacon by which the carrier planes could double check their on-board navigation and which would prove to be an important asset to Task Unit 77.1.2 as it maneuvered around the shallows, shoals, and mined areas in the approaches to Haiphong.

About ten miles off the coast, the two task elements would separate, with the *Providence* and *Robison* peeling off to close their assigned targets, which were generally southwest of Cat Ba. The *Rowan* and *Newport News* would continue on a north-northeast course to the entrance of the Haiphong Channel and conduct a firing run on an easterly course just outside of the five-fathom curve.

The *Newport News*, as the heavy hitter of the force, had the most important targets, nine in total, which included the fuel dump and vehicle storage at Cat Ba Airfield, the Do San radar, Haiphong SAM sites, the Cat Ba military supply dump, fire-control radars and coastal gun batteries. Several of these targets were at the extreme range of her 8-inch guns, however, and this required the cruiser to penetrate the Haiphong Harbor approaches as far as her twenty-seven-foot draft would allow.

The *Rowan's* primary mission was to screen the *Newport News*, but it had two preassigned targets for her 5-inch guns, both coastal defense sites. Hopefully the presence of a significant force of U.S. warships in such close proximity to Haiphong would stimulate the coastal defense radar network to provide targets for the *Rowan's* Shrike ARMs. The designated targets were from the CinCPac-JCS target list, but all of the ships were authorized to respond to active coastal defense artillery with counterbattery fire without constraints. The ammunition allocation for the *Newport News'* preplanned targets was 285 8-inch high-capacity rounds and 191 5-inch rounds. Once within detection range of the coastal radars during the approach, the column would make random changes in course and speed to avoid presenting the enemy with a clear picture of intentions while still making good the scheduled arrival time.

The rendezvous of the four warships was accomplished on schedule, and the approach to the objective area was as planned with no evidence of detection by local fishing or commercial craft. At 2200 the *Newport News* went to general quarters in preparation for the night's mission. This was a prudent move, providing plenty of time to check out all gunnery and engineering systems and to conduct emergency drills.

For my battle station, I joined the captain on the bridge and reassured him that I would stay out of his hair. As captain of the carrier *Enterprise* five years earlier, I knew how annoying it could be to have a flag officer on your bridge offering gratuitous advice and comments. In general, Navy regulations and customs of the service do well in making it clear that a captain remains in command while maneuvering his ship regardless of the senior officers aboard. In World War II, I had seen Cdr. Joshua Cooper, skipper of the destroyer USS *Bennion*, order the embarked squadron commander off his bridge when the commodore gave orders directly to the officer of the deck, who happened to be Lieutenant Holloway. The commodore immediately left the bridge, and the skipper eventually went on to become an admiral.

The Do Son light appeared on schedule, in its proper place and emitting its prescribed signal. As we raced north at twenty-six knots to approach the turn point for the firing leg, the ship's speed suddenly slowed to twenty-five knots without any change in power settings, and her longitudinal pitch rocked forward several degrees. The ship had crossed the ten-fathom curve and, at a depth of less than fifty feet, was reacting to the bottom effect. This only served to further remind me that only five miles to the north was an extensive minefield that had been laid by our carrier aircraft nearly four months earlier. But it was too late to have any concerns about a stray mine that might have broken loose from its moorings. That possibility was infinitesimally small, or so we had been told.

At 2321 the *Newport News* rang up twenty-five knots and came right to a heading of 070 as the main battery of nine 8-inch guns and the port 5-inch mounts swung out. We were about two and a half miles southeast of Do Son light and on our firing course. Captain Zartman gave the order to commence firing.

With the first impact of the cruiser's rounds, the shore batteries opened fire in return. Their guns were not using flashless powder as we were, so their muzzle blasts could be clearly seen as aim points for the ship's counterbattery fire. The number of enemy guns was surprising, their flashes lighting up a full 45-degree arc of the horizon off the port bow. The enemy incoming shells were falling in our vicinity, too—not too close, but the splashes were clearly visible. The cruiser had stationed sailors in the rigging as spotters to record and report the enemy's fall of shot.

At 2330 we turned right to a course of 091 degrees to run parallel to the five-fathom curve, which was only a mile or two north. By now the battle was fully joined and all combatants were engaged. The *Providence* and *Robison*, on our starboard quarter, had commenced their firing runs. The *Rowan*, up ahead of us, was banging away with her 5-inch guns in rapid fire against the coastal defenses and had launched two Shrikes at active gun-laying radar sites. Our spotters reported several splashes close aboard, scattering shrapnel fragments on the weather decks. The cruiser increased speed to thirty knots.

Equipped with a steel helmet and earplugs, I stepped outside of the pilothouse to the port wing of the bridge. From this open area the full range of sensations and the panorama of the battle could be experienced—the rush of the wind, the hot blast of the guns, and the acrid smell of gun smoke. The open vista of the wing of the bridge afforded a clear view of the North Vietnamese coast with the muzzle flashes from the shore batteries and the explosions of our projectiles.

What really captured my attention were the incredible towering cones of brilliant tracers rising ten thousand feet into the sky. They were

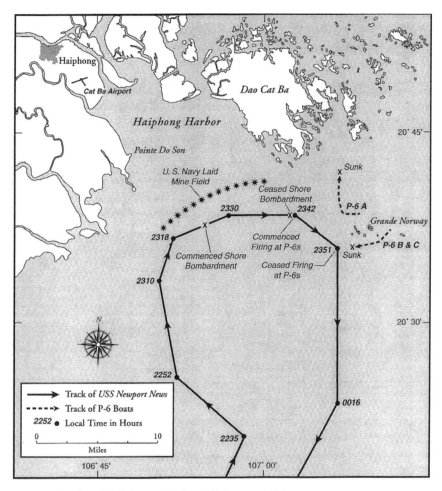

Battle of Haiphong Harbor, 27 August 1972. *Prepared by author.*

coming from the antiaircraft batteries at Cat Ba, Haiphong, and Hanoi, firing at Navy planes in the area. At the apex of each cone of tracers was a Navy plane attacking its assigned target or transiting the Haiphong-Hanoi area for an armed reconnaissance of one of the main supply routes from China, northwest of Hanoi. With the volume of this AA fire, it seemed inconceivable that an aircraft could penetrate those curtains of fiery tracers and survive. In spite of the torrent of gunfire, the pilots did not consider these defenses very effective against night attackers. The tracers were from automatic weapons, which are relatively small:

.50-caliber, 20mm, and 37mm guns. These weapons have a limited range and are normally not radar controlled. The gunner aims at where he thinks the enemy plane must be, based upon the engine's noise and the airbursts of the larger, radar-controlled AAA.

At 2333 the *Newport News* abruptly stopped firing. I could hear the klaxon's blare and the loudspeakers in the mounts call out, "Cease fire, cease fire." The shore-gunfire phase of Lion's Den had been completed. The *Rowan* had fired her preplanned missions and launched her Shrikes five minutes ago and had been detached and cleared to depart the objective area. The *Providence* and *Robison* had also finished up and were retiring to the south.

I stepped back inside the sound-proofed air-conditioned pilothouse. Captain Zartman came up to tell me that all the *Newport News'* assigned targets had been covered and that several secondary explosions had been noted at Cat Ba Airfield and the ammunition dump. As he was speaking, a dungaree-clad sailor with the outsized steel helmet of a battle telephone talker was tugging at the captain's sleeve. "Captain," he said in an even, clear voice, "Combat [CIC] reports a surface target, designated Skunk Alfa, at ten thousand yards bearing 088, heading for us at high speed."

It took no time at all for this to sink in. Without hesitating, the captain issued a stream of orders and the bridge reacted with an efficiency and a coolness that belied the sudden and ominous change in the tactical situation. Skunk Alfa was designated a hostile threat, all gun batteries were to take the target under fire, CTU 71.1.2 was informed, and the *Rowan* was directed to rejoin the *Newport News*.

I took a look at the navigation chart on the plotting table. Ten thousand yards at 088 degrees put Skunk Alfa, now visually identified with night observation devices (NOD) as a P-6 class Soviet-made fast attack craft, in the vicinity of Île de Norway, near a collection of small karst islands extending south of Cat Ba. This little archipelago was well suited for an ambush site. The rocks and pinnacles were already making it difficult for the fire-control radars to lock on to the patrol boat.

For what seemed an interminable time after the captain had given the order, the cruiser's guns were still not firing. Then the gunnery officer reported that the target's relative bearing was virtually dead ahead and the firing circuits for the 8-inch guns cut out at low angles of fire over the bow because of an electronics antenna that had recently been installed on the forecastle. The ship's heading was brought hard right to unmask the battery, and all of the cruiser's port-side guns opened up, firing as rapidly as they could be loaded.

Within minutes, the gunnery officer reported Skunk Alfa appeared to be on fire and seemed to be turning to escape on a northerly course. At almost that same instant, the intercom from CIC rang out with a report of two more skunks with the same characteristics as Alfa, sixteen thousand yards dead ahead, moving from left to right. They were apparently heading to cut across *Newport News*' southerly retirement route. As the cruiser's guns swung around to take this new threat under fire, again there was the problem of not being able to fire dead ahead. The quickest maneuver to unmask the batteries was a turn back to port, and this would put the *Newport News* again on an easterly course, headed for the shoals of Île de Norway rather than toward the retirement track to the south.

There was little choice. The P-6s were crossing the cruiser's bow with the bearing drifting to the right. Only a left turn would quickly bring the 8-inch guns to bear. As the ship came left in a tight heeling turn, the cruiser's guns swung out to the right giving the starboard 5- and 3-inch batteries their first crack at the enemy. Again the cruiser's guns banged in rapid continuous fire, and the twenty-one-thousand-ton hull was again shuddering from the recoil and concussion.

In spite of the hail of projectiles, the P-6s continued to come. Their zigzagging approach through the many ship-sized karst islands had confused the cruiser's radars. Tracking by optics was being hampered by the darkness of the night and the many islets. Worst of all, though, was the confusing effect of our own fire.

In the process of rejoining, the *Rowan* had been remanning battle stations and there was some confusion in the magazines. Several star shells had been fired by her 5-inch guns and had detonated prematurely, so that the flares hung at a low altitude between our ships and the enemy. Instead of silhouetting the P-6s, the patrol craft became effectively screened from us behind the glare.

There was one among the *Rowan's* crew that night who possibly had the best vantage point. Dana Perkins, a third-class signalman at the time, was manning his GQ station on the exposed signal bridge. Perkins relates:

I remember the night of the Haiphong Harbor pretty well. I don't think they passed the word of our objective until shortly before general quarters, as I'm sure the mission was of utmost importance and secret. Also I think that they didn't want us to have much time to think about what was about to unfold. As a signalman I was on the highest point on the ship and had a clear view of all the action. Myself and three other signalmen were manning the Redeye shoulder-fired missiles, loaded, armed, and ready to squeeze the trigger in the event the time should come. When we started to see the lit shoreline and lighted buoys of the harbor, make no mistake about it, the tension was high. All of a sudden the whole shoreline lit up with counterbattery, spewing bright fireballs as each round was fired at us. The North Vietnamese weren't using flashless powder like we had.

At one time I remember counting about twenty-two shore batteries rapid firing at the squadron. The shells were dropping all around us, leaving thunderous columns of white spray as they splashed into the ocean. Some of the shells were proximity and burst in the air. I remember one shell passed over the *Rowan* and burst in the air, causing the shrapnel to hit the side of the ship. I think it put some heavy-duty dents on the starboard side of the ship along the upper outer passageway. Luckily no one was hit! The whole time the ships in the squadron were firing on their intended targets with gun mounts and Shrike missiles. It was like the most intense Fourth of July display I'd ever seen. The *Newport News* was off our port side at about 270 relative position, rapid firing her 8-inch guns as fast as they could. All of a sudden the word came over the sound-powered phone that we had 2 torpedo boats (Russian *Osha* class, I believe), about eighty feet long, coming out to attack. The guys in the magazine were jamming whatever shells they could get their hands on into the hoist. The first round that we hit one of those boats with was actually a practice starburst round, and it tore right through it. The second round did explode.

To keep Skunks Bravo and Charlie under continuous fire with all batteries, the *Newport News* had been maneuvering on easterly and southeasterly courses and would soon run out of sea room. When a report was received from another ship, the *Providence*, that a fourth fast patrol boat had been detected, it became increasingly evident we needed to clear up the tactical situation and as quickly as possible.

I told Captain Zartman I was going to call for some help from tactical air. The pillars of AA fire had reminded me of the presence of carrier planes in the area, and that they would be loaded with flares and weapons for targets in Route Package Six. Commander, Task Unit 77.1.2 would not have been aware of their presence or capabilities. It was not an asset he would normally deal with. On the other hand, at the Seventh Fleet level I was informed on a daily basis of the operations of all fleet units.

The UHF radio handset was on the bulkhead of the *Newport News'* pilothouse. I pulled it from its cradle, punched the power button, and hit the guard channel switch. Now every operational Navy unit within a twenty-mile radius would hear my transmission in the blind: "Attention any Seventh Fleet Aircraft in the vicinity of Haiphong. This is Jehovah [commander, Seventh Fleet's personal call sign] on board *Newport News* with a shore bombardment force in Haiphong Harbor. We are engaged with several enemy surface units and need illumination to sort things out. Any aircraft in the area give me a call on guard. What we really need are high-power flares. Jehovah out."

Almost immediately an answering voice came up loud and clear on the guard channel: "Jehovah, this is Raven Four Four, inbound with a flight of two Corsairs [Corsair IIs, Chance Vought A-7s] for an armed recce in Package Six [the sector north of Hanoi]. We have flares and Rockeye on board. I can see all the shooting down there. I wondered what was going on. I am overhead and ready to help."

Staying on the guard channel so all friendly forces in the area would be aware of the tactical situation—and also to avoid any chance of losing communications—I instructed the flight leader, Raven 44, to light up the area with flares, report on what he could see, and stand by for further orders.

In less than thirty seconds, the entire seascape of the Haiphong Harbor approaches and the Île de Norway islands was suddenly, and almost blindingly, lit by a million-candlepower flare. Raven 44 reported he had the *Newport News* in sight with an accompanying destroyer and could see a cruiser—the *Providence*—and a destroyer to the east. He had also spotted two North Vietnamese fast attack boats closing the *Newport News* from the direction of Île de Norway. With a warning not to get too low because of friendly gunfire, Raven 44 was cleared to attack the hostile surface targets with Rockeye, a weapon that distributed a cluster of lethal bomblets in an oblong pattern over a large area.

The *Newport News'* guns increased their rate of fire to the maximum. The gunners could clearly see their targets now. While one Corsair dropped a flare, the other attacked with Rockeye. It was almost impossible to miss a ship with Rockeye, even a small craft moving at high speed, and a single bomblet could cause fatal damage to a P-6-sized boat. Under the continuing flare illumination, the Rockeye and ships' gunfire finished off three of the skunks (hostile surface contact), but not until the closest one had approached to within three thousand yards.

At 2342 the *Newport News* and *Rowan* ceased fire. There was nothing left to shoot at. The battle was over. The action had been intense while it lasted. In the seventeen-minute firefight, the two warships had fired 294 major-caliber rounds at the P-6s. Skunks Bravo, Charlie, and Delta had been sunk. Alfa was out of range, on fire, and limping north, about to be eliminated by the two Corsairs. The night was dark again as the last flare hit the ocean. The *Newport News*, only three miles southwest of Île of Norway, shaped a southerly course and increased speed to thirty knots to retire from the objective area and head for Yankee Station.

The Corsairs were from Attack Squadron 93 (VA-93). Lt. (j.g.) William W. Pickavance was the flight leader, and Lt. (j.g.) Pat Moneymaker was the wingman. (Both pilots retired from the Navy with flag rank.) Once Skunk Alfa was on the bottom, they were cleared to return to their carrier, the *Midway* (CVA-41), the evening's work done. With all flares and Rockeye expended on the patrol boats, their armed recce mission into Package Six was cancelled. For them the Battle of Haiphong Harbor had been far more productive.

Commander, Task Unit 77.1.2's after-action report submitted to CinCPac and the JCS was professionally brief and properly modest: All preplanned targets had been fully covered with the allotted rounds, three secondaries had been observed, and Shrikes had been fired at radiating radars but apparently with no permanent results. Counterbattery fire had been effective in silencing some coastal defense positions, but the Vietnamese gunfire had been heavy. The *Newport News* reported 75 rounds of very accurate hostile fire; the *Rowan* reported 50 rounds of accurate fire as close as twenty yards and straddling the ship. The *Robison* reported 140 rounds of very accurate fire, the closest being fifteen yards off the port beam. The *Providence* had counted incoming 60 rounds. Commander, TU 77.1.2 almost laconically went on to report, "While retiring, task unit was approached by several fast moving surface contacts. . . . *Newport News* and *Rowan* took contacts under fire resulting in their catching fire and breaking up. Aircraft took others under attack and appeared to sink same."

How successful was the operation? No photographic gun-damage assessment (GDA) was possible. Only three secondary explosions were observed. Yet the pumping of 710 rounds of 5-inch, 6-inch, and 8-inch high-explosive projectiles into a crowded area of lucrative military and logistics installations, all in a period of seventeen minutes, must have done psychological as well as military damage to the North Vietnamese war effort. All of this was accomplished with no friendly casualties, just shrapnel on the weather decks of two ships. Lion's Den was, as a front-page *New York Times* article reported, "a daring raid into strongly defended enemy territory. . . . The enemy has once again been reminded of the mobility of the fleet."

The next morning my helo arrived on board the *Newport News* from the *Kitty Hawk* to pick me up for the one-hour ride back to our flagship. Task Unit 77.1.2 was disestablished, and the *Newport News, Rowan, Providence* and *Robison* continued south to rendezvous with the ammo ships of the URG in the Gulf of Tonkin to top off powder and projectiles. The *Newport News* alone had expended 433 8-inch rounds, 556 5-inch rounds, and 33 3-inch rounds during the thirty-three-minute operation.

18

Vietnam

The U.S. Navy's mining of the navigational waters of North Vietnam and of its port areas had seriously impaired North Vietnam's ability to fight the war and had undermined the morale of its people. On 8 May 1972, in Operation Pocket Money, three A-6s and seven A-7s from the *Coral Sea* had dropped thirty-six MK-52 1,000-pound magnetic influence mines in Haiphong Harbor off Vietnam's largest port. The overall mining campaign had gone even further, with Navy aircraft dropping MK-36 Destructors and MK-52 mines in six other North Vietnamese harbors. The MK-36 Destructor was a 500-pound aircraft bomb converted into a magnetic influence mine by a special fuse. Naval carrier aircraft also mined some of North Vietnam's most heavily used coastal waters. The mines were programed to become active twenty-four hours after they were dropped. The existence, but not the location, of the minefields in the approaches to Haiphong Harbor was broadcast to the world so that foreign merchant ships would be reluctant to enter or leave the port of Haiphong. President Nixon had announced that the minefields would remain until all U.S. prisoners of war were released.

Militarily, the mining and the air interdiction campaign had made a serious inroad on North Vietnam's ability to continue the prosecution of its conventional invasion of South Vietnam by cutting off most of North

Vietnam's economic and military assistance from China and the Soviet Union. Air interdiction by tactical aircraft, including those from carriers, had reduced the enemy's overland imports from 160,000 tons to 30,000 tons per month. The mining of the North Vietnamese ports had cut seaborne imports from 250,000 tons per month to practically nothing. Unable to replace losses incurred during the fighting in the south, the North Vietnamese attack began to lose momentum after the capture of Quang Tri City.

The JCS, on the recommendation of the U.S. Navy's commander, Mine Force, had made the decision to employ only one type of influence mine—the magnetic. This was to facilitate later clearance operations. The Hague Convention of 1907 required that belligerents neutralize their minefields after hostilities cease. Planning for Operation "End Sweep," the name of the operation that would neutralize the minefields in North Vietnam, had begun well before the agreements reached by the Paris peace talks. Subsequently, U.S. intelligence had reported that the mining of Haiphong was having serious effects on the North Vietnamese economy and their ability to wage war. The U.S. negotiating team, under Henry Kissinger, had proposed removal of the mines as a bargaining point to obtain the release of the U.S. prisoners of war.

LINEBACKER II

Determined to apply whatever military force was necessary to convince the leadership in Hanoi that an end to the war in Southeast Asia was going to be in their best interests, President Nixon initiated Operation Linebacker II. This, for the first time, unleashed virtually unlimited air power against North Vietnamese industrial and military targets in the Hanoi-Haiphong area. Strategic Air Command B-52 bombers, carrying full payloads of conventional bombs, were the principal striking force, escorted by U.S. Air Force and Navy fighters for protection against the MiGs, and supported by tactical aircraft from the Seventh Fleet and Thai bases for flak suppression and electronic countermeasures.

The "Christmas Bombing," as it came to be known, commenced on 18 December 1972 and continued around the clock, day and night, for twelve days. At that point the North Vietnamese sued for an immediate truce to arrange a cease-fire and agreed to negotiations to end the war.

The United States had achieved a victory against Hanoi, yet not without costs. Fifteen B-52s were shot down by enemy fire. The SAC B-52 force was approaching the limit of its acceptable loss rate at the time Hanoi urgently appealed for a truce. The Seventh Fleet was heavily involved in Linebacker II and the Christmas bombings through the carrier aircraft of Task Force 77. By the eighteenth, seven carriers were in the western Pacific. From the flag bridge of the *Oklahoma City* I had the unique opportunity to watch six Task Force 77 carriers turn into the wind in a line abreast, stretching almost across the Gulf of Tonkin as they launched aircraft in the assaults on Hanoi.

The negotiators, meeting in France, signed the Paris Accords in January 1973. On the surface, the agreement seemed to provide both sides with legitimate reasons to conclude that the cease-fire was satisfactory to all the belligerents: In Vietnam the fighting would cease; for the United States, its military forces deployed in-theater would come home; the American POWs in North Vietnamese prison camps would be repatriated; and the U.S.-laid mines in Haiphong Harbor would be swept by mine countermeasure forces to neutralize the waterways and open the ports. The task of sweeping the mines to assure the safe passage of the approaches to the port areas of Haiphong and the other tributaries in North Vietnam fell to the Seventh Fleet. In anticipation of this requirement, Mine Countermeasures Force, Seventh Fleet was activated on 24 November 1972 for the planning and logistics of the minesweeping operation. "Mine Warfare Force, Seventh Fleet" was designated as Task Force 78. On 28 January 1973, the cease-fire went into effect in North and South Vietnam in compliance with the provisions of the Paris Accords.

OPERATION END SWEEP

Airborne Mine Countermeasures Squadron 1 comprised of CH-53M Sea Stallion helicopters, immediately commenced its deployment from the Norfolk Naval Base to the Gulf of Tonkin. This squadron had been stood up two years earlier at the Norfolk Naval Air Station, when I was deputy commander in chief, U.S. Atlantic Fleet. So I was quite familiar with the minesweeping techniques involved and the tactics that would be employed by these helicopters. Each of the CH-53M aircraft, the largest operational helicopters in the U.S. inventory, would tow a sled in the water, with the helicopter flying at an altitude of between three and six hundred feet. The sled carried a powerful electrical generator, which fed electromagnetic pulses to a wire, called the "tail," trailing from the sled into the water. These electronic pulses would be programed electronically to detonate the electromagnetic arming and explosive devices in the mines that had been laid by the TF 77 aircraft in the Haiphong estuary. Fuel to run the generators was carried in the helicopters and flowed from the helicopter tanks in a hose attached to the towline from the helicopter to the sled. At the completion of a mine countermeasures sortie, usually determined by fuel availability, the helicopter would return to a landing ship dock (LSD) and drop the towline in the water. The helicopter would then land on the LSD's. A small craft would pick up the tow lines to the sled and retrieve it, pulling the sled, with the towline and the two extended antennas, into the LSD's flooded dock for postflight inspection and set up for the next sortie. Meanwhile, the helicopter would be refueled and launched to pick up the towline and start again on another sweep pattern.

The helicopters had been transported from NAS Norfolk, Virginia, by C-5 transport, two CH-53s per aircraft with the rotor heads and the rotors removed. The Sea Stallions were flown to Subic Bay, Philippines, where they were offloaded at the Cubi Point Naval Air Station, their rotors were reassembled, the aircraft was checked out mechanically, and they were then flown to the helicopter carrier *Inchon*. When the entire component of squadron aircraft had been delivered, reassembled, and embarked on board the helicopter carrier, the Mine Countermeasures Force departed Subic Bay to rendezvous with the Seventh Fleet flagship off the coast of North Vietnam east of Haiphong.

Preparation for Operation End Sweep had commenced in September 1972, when commander, Mine Force, U.S. Atlantic Fleet reported to me as commander, Task Force 78, the Mine Countermeasures Task Force in the U.S. Seventh Fleet in the western Pacific. The TF 78 staff had been bolstered by the inclusion of the Navy's most knowledgeable and experienced mine warfare experts, including Capt. Felix S. Vecchione, who was virtually unmatched in his knowledge and experience regarding both the technical development and tactical application of naval mines.

Task Force 78 was officially activated in November 1972, and there was ample opportunity to collect assets for the operation and deploy them to the Seventh Fleet before 23 January 1973, when the "agreement on ending the war and restoring the peace in Vietnam" was signed in Paris. In accordance with the agreement, preparations for the return of the prisoners of war (Operation Homecoming) were made, the removal of mines from Haiphong Harbor (Operation End Sweep) was scheduled to commence within a month, and combat air operations over both North and South Vietnam were ended.

The day after the cease-fire was signed, the main elements of Task Force 78 deployed from Subic Bay to the Haiphong area. These forces included four ocean minesweepers (MSO), the helicopter carrier *Inchon*, and four amphibious ships, including two with docking capabilities to handle the minesweeping sleds towed by the CH-53Ms. During the six months of Operation End Sweep, ten ocean minesweepers, nine amphibious ships, six fleet tugs, three salvage ships, and nineteen destroyers operated in Task Force 78 in the vicinity of Haiphong.

In early February the Mine Force staff came on board the Seventh Fleet flagship, *Oklahoma City*, for a conference to prepare for final plans for the operation. Task Force 78 was well organized and had arrived in the Gulf of Tonkin with their gear in excellent shape. They would need, however, continuing logistical support with special attention to the spare parts and replacement units for their unique mine countermeasures equipment. Commander, TF 78 proposed that all material to be sent forward to the task force be given an "A Plus" priority, which means everything would be shipped by fastest means possible. That is the one area in which CTF 78 was overruled. My logistics mentor was Cdr. Charles T. Creekman, who had been my supply officer on the *Enterprise*. One of his fundamental logistics theorems was that priorities had to be assigned on realistic requirements based upon true need, not inflated to higher categories to provide "insurance" or to get ahead of the other guy. As he explained, that's the only way that the Navy supply system could run at its maximum effectiveness. If every item addressed to TF 78 were given one priority—the very highest—aftershave lotion would have the same priority with replacement transmission parts to repair grounded helicopters. Since all items being shipped to the forces afloat must compete for limited shipping space in aircraft and for special handling, there is no way for the outshipping activity to discriminate between aircraft parts and aftershave lotion, and what the ships in TF 78 would eventually have delivered on board would be pure pot luck. In 1970 I had seen this very thing happen. Commander, Sixth Fleet at the time of the Syrian-Jordan crisis had insisted that *all* material shipped forward to the Sixth Fleet units should have the highest priority, in spite of my protestations. As commander, Task Force 60, I had to keep the carriers' planes flying and the ships' radars working. Vice Adm. Ike Kidd, however, persisted, thinking that as an experienced line officer he was in a better position to judge how to "optimize" the system. The result was that the supply channels from the U.S. supply depots were clogged with junk that we really didn't need. Having been at the bitter end of the supply line in a squadron in Korea and on board the *Enterprise* in the Gulf of Tonkin, I had seen how well the supply system could work when run by the supply officers according to their system procedures. It turned out that there was never a crisis during Operation End Sweep due to a lapse in our logistics support.

The plan was for most of the initial minesweeping to be conducted by the CH-53M minesweepers of Helicopter Mine Countermeasures Squadron 12 (HM-12) supported by two additional Marine Corps helicopter squadrons of CH-53s. These large helicopters operated from the decks of the *New Orleans* (LPH-11) and *Inchon* (LPD-12), from which commander, Task Force 78 flew his flag. There were a total of thirty-one CH-53M Sea Stallion helicopters in all attached to the task force.

Because of the separated location of Task Force 78 in the approaches to the port of Haiphong in North Vietnam, more than 150 miles north of the provisional boundary between the two countries, I thought it was prudent to maintain an attack carrier task group in the vicinity to provide air cover for the mine logistics force. Over the period of End Sweep, the carriers *Coral Sea, Enterprise, Oriskany,* and *Ranger* were positioned to provide around the clock coverage in the event of any untoward actions or hostilities on the part of the North Vietnamese.

An important feature of the mine clearance operations was to provide an extremely precise navigation system that would enable the minesweepers, both airborne and ships, to ensure that the coverage of the mined area was complete and that there were no gaps in the lanes that were swept. Also, it would avoid redundancies in repeating operations over previously cleared areas. To provide this level of precise navigation, the

Navy had contracted for a civilian system RaDist, which used an array of electronic beacons fixed at known geographic locations on the ground. The small area covered by RaDist was a key to the precision that was required. But before the beacons could be erected on North Vietnamese soil in the vicinity of Haiphong Harbor and its approaches, we had to explain these devices to the North Vietnamese and get their approval for U.S. technicians to install them in their territory. I sent CTF 78 to Hanoi to negotiate this installation. The arrangements were conducted without incident between the CTF 78 staff, and Colonel Thai of the North Vietnamese army.

About mid-February, four ocean minesweepers were able to deploy their equipment and sweep the approaches to Haiphong to ensure the safety of ships operating in support of the helicopter sweep. Task Force 78 helicopters flew their first End Sweep mission on 27 February 1973 and continued their work during daylight hours, operating from the LPHs *New Orleans* and *Inchon*. The operation proceeded smoothly with flight operations taking place during daylight hours. The navigation system performed satisfactorily, although on several occasions civilian technicians were required to be put ashore to service the beacons. The sleds and ancillary gear used by the minesweeping helicopters suffered from wear and tear and required constant repair and basic maintenance. Considering that this was the first use of airborne mine countermeasures in a real tactical situation, 150 miles ahead of the front lines, the record of success reflects considerable credit on the people in Task Force 78.

During the clearance operations, only one MK-52 mine was detonated. All of the others had sanitized themselves at the end of their scheduled life, as programed, which occurred prior to the end of February. To fully test the safety of the channel, Task Force 78 had rigged an LST as a test vehicle. All loose equipment and unnecessary material had been removed and spaces filled with Styrofoam. A special shock-mounted deck was rigged for the conning and navigation of the ship, and forty volunteers were embarked. All precautions possible were taken to protect these crewmembers in the unlikely event of a detonation. A detonation was not anticipated, but there was always the chance of a stray mine or perhaps some sort of device planted by the North Vietnamese themselves. The test vessel, the *Waccamaw County*, made eight transits of the channel without setting off any mines, and I was able to report that the minesweeping operation had been completed. In retrospect this was a truly remarkable accomplishment.

Secretary of State Kissinger had proposed to the North Vietnamese negotiators that the U.S. Navy clear the minefields at the port of Haiphong and do it in thirty days. He made this proposal without the availability of any expert technical advice with him in his negotiating group. It is interesting how accurately Kissinger had predicted the time that would be required. It was on the thirtieth day of actual sweeping that the CTF 78 was able to signal that the mission had been accomplished.

After the North Vietnamese were notified that the ports of Haiphong, Hon Gai, and Cam Pha were free from the threat of U.S.-laid mines, Task Force 78 proceeded out to sea on 18 July 1973, officially ending Operation End Sweep. During the operation's period, the flagship *Oklahoma City* had remained in the Gulf of Tonkin, except for a brief return to Yokosuka for a five-day period of maintenance availability.

PEACETIME CRUISING

In February the *Oklahoma City* made a three-day protocol port visit to Kaohsiung in the Republic of China on Taiwan. The flagship also paid a three-day visit to the Japanese port of Sasebo, Japan. Then, on 22 January 1973, the flagship commenced a six-day visit to Hong Kong. Although referred to as a protocol visit, it was mainly for the R&R of the crew and the embarked staff. I exchanged calls with the British resident governor in Hong Kong, and in the course of our conversation, the governor asked me if I had ever served in the Seventh Fleet before taking over as its commander. I responded that I had been assigned to ships serving in the Seventh Fleet a total of seven times, beginning with service as the gunnery officer of a destroyer during World War II. The governor asked me if, at that time, I thought I would ever be commander of the Seventh Fleet. My response: At that time, I wasn't sure I was going to be promoted to lieutenant! My relations with the civic leaders and heads of state of the nations and major ports on the Pacific Rim were remarkably good at that time. I never encountered anything but a warm and cordial reception on any visit to the countries in the area.

With the war ended, and Operation End Sweep a success, Seventh Fleet focused on joint operations with Pacific allies in areas such as antisubmarine warfare and antiair warfare, which had not been extensively exercised during the period of Tonkin Gulf operations.

After the Linebacker II air campaign against Hanoi in the Christmas bombings, it appeared that the United States would be able to leave the field of battle in Southeast Asia in peace under honorable conditions. The defense of the South Vietnamese would now be their own responsibility, with the United States' assurance that the ARVN would be properly equipped and logistically supported. Base structures, logistics facilities, and communication networks, along with tanks, artillery and aircraft, were turned over to the Army of the Republic of Vietnam for the defense of their homeland.

However, the United States did not fulfill its agreement to provide South Vietnam with a realistic capability upon which to build a nation or to defend themselves, and military aid for South Vietnam was virtually forgotten during the confusion of the Watergate scandal.

Early in 1975, a veteran North Vietnamese army, equipped and supported by their Communist sponsors in China and the USSR, again invaded South Vietnam, rolling across the agreed cease-fire lines in the most brutal disregard of the accords the North Vietnamese had signed only two years earlier. They linked up with the thousands of Communist troops who had been left behind in South Vietnam by the 1972 agreement and were reinforced by North Vietnam army regulars prepositioned in the sanctuaries of Laos. The ARVN was smashed and overrun. In April 1975 victorious North Vietnamese troops entered Saigon. The long war was over. All Vietnam was surrendered to the Communists in Hanoi.

LOSS OF SOUTH VIETNAM

It can be rationalized that the South Vietnamese lost the war in 1975 after the United States had won it with a cease-fire in 1973. However, in retrospect, it is evident that our terms for the cease-fire were inadequate to eliminate the Communist threat inside South Vietnam, and the subsequent military aid and financial support were insufficient to preserve the required level of readiness needed for the self-defense of

South Vietnam. When the North Vietnamese violated the cease-fire agreement with their final invasion of the South in August 1975, the national leadership and the American people looked the other way while our former ally was overwhelmed and occupied by a veteran and professional North Vietnamese army, fully modernized with Communist bloc weapons and logistic support. Domestically, with the 1973 cease-fire in place, a war-weary United States had accepted legislation—the War Powers Act—that would make it difficult for a president to again involve the country in Southeast Asian hostilities. In 1975, when North Vietnam was on the march to Saigon, President Ford observed to the press that he could see no way for the United States to assist South Vietnam in its losing fight for survival.

For their part, the military leadership, the Joint Chiefs of Staff, and the in-theater commanders did push hard during the war for the authority to conduct bold decisive campaigns such as closing the Laotian supply route sanctuaries, and they argued in favor of budgets larger than the "guns and butter" policy would provide in order to better equip and train the armed forces engaged in Southeast Asia.

The operating forces in the field fought with courage and perseverance in spite of apathy and lack of moral support at home. Throughout the war, the military campaigns were generally successful and the battles hard-fought. In the invasion of Laos, which destroyed the North Vietnamese logistical sanctuaries, more than one hundred U.S. Army helicopters were lost in combat, with roughly the same number of Army pilots and crewmen killed or missing in action. These figures do not include the airborne troops who were being lifted into and out of the battle.

The tactical squadrons of the Air Force, Marines, and Navy provided essential close support to the ground forces in-country and were the only U.S. combat components engaged in the war in North Vietnam. With U.S. ground forces fully withdrawn from the conflict by the summer of 1972, the U.S. combat effort became almost entirely a matter of tactical air operations. About half the total sorties into North Vietnam were flown by naval aircraft. In the course of the war, 538 carrier planes were shot down, including 385 A-4 Skyhawks. In most cases the crews were not recovered. Among those lost in combat over the course of the conflict were sixty-seven air wing commanders, squadron commanders, and squadron XOs, all leading combat missions against the enemy. The total combat losses equated to about forty squadrons of tactical carrier aircraft.

A particular irritant to the forces engaged in Vietnam was the inhibiting rules of engagement. These restrictive ROE were to avoid unintentional "collateral damage" to civilians in the conduct of an attack on a military objective, but they forced strike groups to repeat predictable paths in approaching and departing target areas, eliminating the element of surprise and allowing the enemy to deploy surface-to-air missiles and MiG-21 fighters in concentrations along the entry and exit routes of the U.S. striking groups. The emphasis on avoiding collateral damage was an effort to demonstrate to the rest of the world the consideration of the U.S. toward limiting nonmilitary casualties. The extent to which this civilian control became micromanagement is evident by the fact that it was widely known that during the Rolling Thunder campaign, President Lyndon B. Johnson was personally selecting the targets to be attacked by the next day's sortie from the JSC-CinCPac target list.

A LONGER-TERM VIEW

The following is a personal view that has evolved from my contemporary involvement in headquarters planning and my association with so many of the decision makers during the Cold War, as well as a continuing postwar interest and study of its history. I will admit to what some may consider as an optimistic appraisal, but it is not a superficial "feel-good" emotion but the pragmatic product of a long-term and consuming period of reflection and analysis. During the 1950s and 1960s, the United States pursued a national strategy of containment against what was perceived as the Communist monolith of the Soviet Union and an even more hostile China. Holding the line in Korea, and then in Vietnam, was paramount in a long-term struggle that threatened national survival. For years we held to the domino theory—once one country falls to the Communists, it's only a matter of time before the next and then the next fall in succession.

In 1975 we turned our backs and allowed South Vietnam, Laos, and Cambodia to fall. Something had changed that made holding the line in Vietnam no longer critical. For years, the North Vietnamese had played the Soviets and the Red Chinese off each other as both vied for leadership as champions of "People's Liberation" movements in the third world. Despite both being Communist, the two nations distrusted each other. Ironically, the Soviets' massive effort to achieve nuclear parity with the United States had made it an enormous threat to China. Perceiving its own long-term survival now threatened, China sought to amend its relationship with the United States, a nation it once fought on the Korean peninsula. President Nixon's trip to China was a landmark diplomatic move that signaled to Hanoi that the sides were changing. Realizing that China's dependability as an ally was now questionable, Hanoi launched the Easter offensive to end the war on its terms. Fortunately, Nixon fought back and won—for the time being.

The Soviet Union, suddenly confronted by U.S-China rapprochement, saw that its global strategic position was weakened. Because Nixon and Kissinger had leveraged China, the Russians hedged. Expecting Soviet support when the U.S. Navy mined its harbors on 8 May 1972, Hanoi was shocked when the Soviets only issued a few protests and proceeded with plans to welcome Nixon to Moscow. Militarily, Hanoi now faced the might of the U.S. Seventh Fleet and U.S. Air Force in combination with the sudden loss of the dependable support of its longtime Chinese and Russian allies.

The U.S. strategy of detente, combined with the containment strategy of the 1970s, made holding South Vietnam no longer critical as the containment line of the Soviet Union had moved a thousand miles north to the Mongolian border. Circumstances had changed. The Americans fighting in Vietnam had held communism in check until the firmness of our military posture and the adroitness of our diplomacy had exploited the endemic fissures in the Communist hegemony and shifted the world's balance of power in our favor.

RETURNING TO WASHINGTON

In the spring of 1973, I heard rumors, through letters from friends in Washington, that I would be leaving the Seventh Fleet before long to become commander in chief, Pacific Fleet with a fourth star. This certainly would be a wonderful job, and if one had to leave Seventh Fleet, Hawaii was a great assignment in command of all of the Navy in the Pacific.

Therefore it was with something of a surprise and a bit of a shock when I received a personal message from the CNO, an electrically transmitted radio message known as "special category exclusive." This meant the message was exclusively for the addressee and was not to be distributed any further. In his message, Admiral Zumwalt said that he was recalling "Jimmy" back to Washington to be his vice chief of naval operations, with the implication that this was to position me for consideration as a potential candidate to relieve him when he retired in 1974. This particular comment could not have been a nicer gesture on the part of the CNO, and it did ease the disappointment in not getting a full two years in the Seventh Fleet.

19

Chief of Naval Operations

s I was ushered into the Oval Office, I saw President Nixon
sitting behind the famous desk. He seemed to be waiting for me
because there were no papers cluttering the top, as one might
expect. Nixon stood up and walked around in front of the desk, and
Secretary of the Navy John Warner, who had accompanied me into the
office, introduced me simply as "Admiral Holloway." The president
graciously asked me to sit down, pulled up a chair next to me, and
motioned for John Warner to join us. The president started the conversation by asking me my United States Naval Academy class and then
some other routine questions about my experience in World War II and
my more recent time in Vietnam. The conversation continued for five
minutes or so with the president asking me questions about my career
and family life and very politely listening to my responses. Then he
almost abruptly stood up and said to me, "Admiral, I know you will make
a good CNO, you have excellent recommendations." He took me by the
arm and we walked to the door, pausing for a moment so the photogra-
pher could catch the three of us in a photo opportunity. When we arrived
at the threshold of the Oval Office, the president paused again, turned
to face me directly, and said, "Admiral, get some discipline back in the
Navy. I'm an old Navy man and very proud of my service, and I don't like
what I see going on in the Navy today." With that he shook my hand and
we were ushered out by a Marine aide.

The president's comment concerning my qualifications for CNO was the first mention, on the part of any of my seniors, that I had been selected to relieve Admiral Zumwalt. When Secretary Warner had called me in the morning, I had been working at my standup desk in the office of the vice chief of naval operations. "Get your cap," he had said, "we're going to make a trip to the other side of the river. Meet me at the Mall entrance." Secretary Warner was waiting when I got to his car, and we drove to the White House, where I suspected that I might be meeting the president to have him pass judgment on me. But I did not expect a decision on anyone's part until President Nixon had had an opportunity to discuss the matter with SecNav and SecDef. As we left the meeting, Secretary Warner appeared to be delighted by the way things had gone. I sensed that he had been supporting my candidacy for CNO.

When we reached his official car he told the driver to take us to the Metropolitan Club, which is the premier watering hole for the power structure in Washington, D.C. As we headed for the dining room, John Warner said, "I think this calls for a celebration. They have the best shad and roe in town." It was the first time I had been inside this revered establishment, and I was suitably impressed. It was particularly thoughtful of John Warner to entertain me there as his guest. At the time, I was too overwhelmed to even imagine that in fifteen years I would be elected president of the Metropolitan Club.

VICE CHIEF OF NAVAL OPERATION

Admiral Zumwalt had brought me back to Washington from command of the Seventh Fleet to serve as his vice chief of naval operations with a promotion to four stars. Bud Zumwalt was a Naval Academy classmate of mine and we had also been together in the class of 1962 at the National War College. We had gotten to know each other very well during that year at NWC, and the four of us, the Zumwalts and Holloways, became close friends. And that is how Bud Zumwalt had treated me during his first three years as CNO. When I arrived in Washington in July 1973 for the vice chief of naval operations job, Bud and Mouza Zumwalt were effusive in their welcome to Dabney and me. Bud was particularly painstaking in his briefings to ensure that I understood the situation in the Pentagon and in Washington, and he was completely candid in discussing the personalities of the major players in town with whom we would be doing business.

For me, my role and my responsibility were clear. I was the CNO's alter ego, with no agenda or initiatives of my own. It was my job to see that his policies were forcefully implemented. I would adopt the classic approach, the same relationship as an executive officer toward his commanding officer. The CNO would consult with me on matters of Navy policy and management, giving me an opportunity for input and comment. It was understood that I should be very frank in my views, which would always be offered in private. When the CNO had arrived at a decision, I simply adopted his position as my own and did my very best to ensure its implementation in just the way Bud would want it done. This was not difficult for me: It was the Navy way. I had been in the same situation many times in my naval career, at both ends of the stick.

As it turned out, there was very little disagreement between us. Most of Bud's controversial decisions concerning Z-grams and the Navy's chain of command had been made the first three years of his tenure and at this point were established as part of the regime.

The two main issues in 1973 were the nuclear-powered carrier *Nimitz* and the F-14 fighter. As an aviator, I had a major interest in each of these projects, and Bud Zumwalt was solidly behind both programs. He had inherited both from his predecessor, Adm. Tom Moorer, so they were not his initiatives, but he very clearly appreciated the essentiality of these weapons systems and their fundamental contribution to the effectiveness of the Navy of the future. Admiral Zumwalt was not simply passive in his advocacy. He personally took the lead in generating support in the office of the SecDef and in Congress. In 1972 I was serving as deputy commander in chief, Atlantic, in Norfolk, Virginia. On three separate occasions Zumwalt had sent a helicopter to the CinCLant compound to airlift me to the helicopter pad at the Pentagon for lunch or for an afternoon briefing to help him persuade recalcitrant congressmen, assistant secretaries of defense, or systems analysts. I had been serving as the program coordinator of the CVN program when Bud had taken over in 1970 as CNO, and since then, Bud had always considered me the Navy's expert witness on nuclear carriers and air warfare.

Prior to that, as director of strike warfare under the previous CNO, Tom Moorer, I had originated the CV Concept, which had established as a matter of doctrine the principle of flexibility in a carrier's air wing in order to meet the operational requirements of the carrier's mission on its current deployment rather than try to maintain specialized antisubmarine warfare carriers and attack carriers. In his book *On Watch*, Zumwalt comments on his interest in the implementation of the CV Concept, which led him to order the Atlantic Fleet to actually conduct an exchange of air wings from an attack air group to an ASW air group on board an underway carrier off Bermuda.

There was really only one of Bud's initiatives, not yet brought to closure, that troubled me. Some time previous to my arrival as vice chief of naval operations, Zumwalt had asked the chief of staff of the Air Force, General Ryan, if he would like to have the Air Force operate from Navy carriers. When Bud briefed me on this proposal, he had expressed annoyance that Ryan had never gotten back to him with an answer. Zumwalt had pretty much given the Air Force a free hand on how they would implement such a plan: modify Air Force planes to make them carrier suitable or, more likely, equip Air Force squadrons with Navy carrier planes. But what would be the extent of the integration? As individual Air Force squadrons or as an entire tactical fighter wing replacing the carrier's air wing? I was bothered to learn that this proposal had been made in such broad terms and that it was still on the table. It seemed like a foot in the door to replace the naval aviation organization with the Air Force.

Such a plan had been implemented before, in the United Kingdom after World War I, when the Royal Naval Air Arm, in which the pilots were naval officers, was merged with the Royal Flying Corps to create a single air service, the Royal Air Force (RAF). RAF officers served as the pilots in the Naval Air Branch, a new component of the RAF established to take over the Royal Navy's aircraft squadrons. This did not work well, and in 1937 the Fleet Air Arm was reestablished under the Admiralty and carrier pilots again became officers in the Royal Navy.

In Bud's defense, he could cite the precedent of Marine fixed-wing squadrons being assigned to carriers. However, the Air Force situation was sufficiently different to introduce a host of new problems. Marine pilots go through Navy flight training and are designated naval aviators. Most Marine fixed-wing planes are Navy carrier aircraft, such as F-4 fighters and A-6 attack planes. Bud asked what I thought of his initiative.

In response, I pointed out the serious potential for the Air Force to restake its claim to all DoD aviation, possibly taking over naval aviation as an Air Force Specified Command, such as is SAC. Eventually, General Ryan did get back to Admiral Zumwalt, but declined the proposal without giving any specific reason.

The year with Bud was a good one for both of us. He mentioned several times that having a known quantity, like an old shipmate, as vice chief of naval operations gave him a chance to shift some of his workload so he could relax a little and savor his final year of running the Navy. Being Bud Zumwalt's vice chief was a pleasant experience. First, our professional careers complemented one another. His was strong in front-office administration, personnel, politico-military affairs, and systems analysis. Mine was mostly in fleet operations, aviation, and nuclear power. We both knew the Pentagon from previous tours of duty, and I understood how Bud liked to do things from our close association at the National War College and our previous tour together in the Pentagon in 1967–68. Bud was generous in his praise, which did much to keep morale up in the largely office-confined job of vice chief of naval operations. I still have in my files a handwritten note from Bud: "For 09 [vice chief of naval operations], Eyes Only: Jimmy, I want you to know how impressed I've been (but not surprised) to see how fast you have gotten up to speed and moved out. I'm going to enjoy my last 7 months. Bud."

One area in which the CNO and I had basic differences—and I think we handled it very well—was Admiral Rickover. Zumwalt considered Rickover an anathema, mainly because Rickover operated independently to a large degree and was rather careless—perhaps deliberately so—about keeping the CNO informed. This had been Rickover's style from his earliest days in the Navy. He considered himself the one person in the world who understood the technical side as well as the operational potential for nuclear power, and he did not want ordinary laymen, such as Navy line officers, getting in his way. This philosophy had been tolerated by Adm. Arleigh Burke, Admiral Dave MacDonald, and most recently Admiral Tom Moorer. These CNOs had recognized the benefits of nuclear power in submarines and aircraft carriers, and were content to let Admiral Rickover sell the program and manage it, as long as he didn't make mistakes. And Rickover didn't make mistakes.

Bud's problem with Rickover, and a legitimate concern, was that Zumwalt's programs for reform required major alterations in the Navy's way of doing things—its very culture—and he needed everyone in the Navy to accept these new philosophies if they were to be successful and retain a permanent place in the service's future. Rickover was really not a person who consulted with anyone on how he managed his programs on a daily basis. Furthermore, Bud's naval experience had not included much exposure to engineering or technical matters. He had served mainly in assignments involving policy and command. Consequently, Bud had never really cared to learn much about nuclear propulsion, either its capabilities or its limitations. He made that clear when he described his interview with Rickover for the nuclear-power program. His lack of rapport with Admiral Rickover meant that much of what Bud Zumwalt knew about nuclear reactors came from contractors' sales representatives. During the early 1970s these hustlers were making extravagant claims about what their companies could produce in terms of cheap, lightweight reactors. I sat through one office briefing with the CNO in which the contractor's representative said, holding up his briefcase, "I could fit a reactor powerful enough to run a destroyer in this briefcase." If that were true, it would be as safe as an armed hydrogen bomb in the back of a pickup truck. But because of his latent hostility toward Rickover, Bud wanted very much to believe the contractors who said that Rickover was much too conservative in his design philosophy to produce a reactor that could really exploit the full potential of the atom.

The one technology that was most frequently extolled by the charlatans of the science of nuclear power was the gas-cooled reactor, which had been under extensive development by the Airborne Nuclear Reactor Program (ANRP) sponsored by the U.S. Air Force. The program was cancelled after two decades of high-priority research by the government and the nuclear industry because of the lack of any real promise of a practical operational system.

Admiral Zumwalt seldom asked me, as vice chief, to comment on these contractor reactor proposals, largely because he did not want to put me on the spot of supporting the Rickover position vis-à-vis what Bud wanted to believe, that there could be a cheaper, lighter reactor system for naval ships as promised by the contractor's representatives. Frankly, it was very helpful of him, and it kept me out of a difficult position. On my part, I simply steered completely clear of Admiral Rickover during my days as vice chief, and the KOG was astute enough not to rock the boat. Actually, there were no material or compelling policy issues in the area of nuclear propulsion that required resolution at this time. The Navy and the CNO were fully committed to nuclear power in all carriers and submarines by this date.

On one occasion, Bud did discuss with me a proposal by his special staff group that the Navy program the construction of a fleet of catamaran troop transports that would be powered by gas-cooled reactors that could drive these vessels across the ocean at a speed of seventy knots. I was able to persuade Bud that the technology for a seventy-knot oceangoing catamaran or surface-effect ship was definitely not in hand in the immediate future (he didn't trust the advice of the Naval Ship Systems Command admirals, considering them too conservative and risk-averse) and that a nuclear reactor capable of generating the power that would enable any seagoing vehicle to attain such high speeds would be so heavy that there would be very little room left for troops.

As a matter of record, I have always held the view that Admiral Rickover has been unjustly accused of being overly conservative in his reactor design. Initially, he had gone forward with two basic engineering design concepts: the pressurized water reactor, which eventually came to be used in all nuclear submarines—ours, our allies, and the Soviets—and an alternative design, the liquid sodium reactor. This used sodium as the coolant and the energy transfer medium from the reactor to the steam plant. The sodium reactor was installed in the submarine *Seawolf* and in my opinion, as a line officer who happens to have a degree in nuclear design engineering, the sodium cooled reactor would have been almost impossibly complex to design and build and terribly complicated to operate. The fact that Admiral Rickover not only made it work, but that it was installed on an operating, fleet-deployed submarine for two years, is most remarkable. Fleet experience conclusively demonstrated that it was inferior to the pressurized water reactor. When *Seawolf* came in for its first nuclear refueling, the pressurized-water reactor replaced the liquid sodium reactor as the submarine's power plant. I have often used this as an example of why Rickover should not be accused of avoiding certain technologies because they were too difficult. Rickover was willing to take on all reasonable concepts, regardless of the technical and engineering difficulties, solve the problems, and make them work. He could then reject without criticism those concepts that were proven inferior from operational experience.

During this time, Secretary of Defense Jim Schlesinger was deciding who would take Bud's place as CNO that June. Zumwalt had brought me into the Pentagon hierarchy with four stars to make me eligible for consideration for the job of CNO and made it clear that I would be acceptable to him. I believe he favored as CNO Adm. Worth Bagley, who he felt would be better suited to continue the momentum of the Zumwalt reforms, but Bud was scrupulously fair to me as a candidate. Admiral Moorer, who was then chairman of the Joint Chiefs of Staff, made it clear that he supported me for CNO. Secretary Schlesinger went through a fairly exhaustive vetting process with all of the candidates. He would call me to his office about once a week, usually in the afternoon, for a cup of coffee and just talk. Normally these conversations were on matters of broad policy or somewhat abstract issues. One of his favorite topics was the possibility of employing nuclear weapons to demonstrate resolve without initiating a general nuclear war. He introduced matters of judgment, rather than subjects to determine where I stood on various issues. I found the exchanges stimulating and I very much enjoyed these sessions.

CHANGE OF COMMAND

I relieved Admiral Zumwalt as CNO at a splendid change-of-command ceremony held in Tecumseh Court in front of the main entrance to Bancroft Hall, the architectural as well as the sentimental focal point of the Naval Academy. Secretary of Defense Jim Schlesinger was the senior official presiding.

During my first interview with the press after becoming CNO, the obvious question was asked: "What changes are you going to make in the Navy?" My answer was, "There is a traditional expression from the sailing Navy that the oncoming officer of the deck should not change the set of the sails in the first fifteen minutes of his watch. I'm going to wait a while before I consider changing the set of the sails." This was more than just an adage; I considered it the only wise course. There was still a lot of post-Vietnam turmoil in the Navy at that time. Quite a few people, mostly within the retired, senior officer, and chief petty officer communities, still did not approved of Zumwalt's changes to the existing—and considered traditional—Navy way of doing things. There were also a lot of people who approved of Zumwalt's more liberal policies and were equally concerned that I would change things back to the way they had been. We had to get these differences under control, to heal and unify the Navy. The Navy didn't need more changes at that time.

Shortly after I relieved Admiral Zumwalt as CNO, Nixon resigned as president and was succeeded by Gerald Ford. For many years Ford had been chairman of the House Appropriations Committee and served on the Armed Forces Subcommittee. So he had an extensive exposure to the DoD budget and the character of the four services. Jerry Ford had a warm rapport with the people in uniform and well understood the correct relationships between flag officers and their civilian seniors.

Ford had served in the Navy during World War II, spending 18 months on the carrier *Monterey*, a cruiser hull converted to a light aircraft carrier. He remained on board until the carrier was returned to CONUS for repairs in 1944 after suffering severe damage in a typhoon. The CVLs had the speed and deck space to handle the high-performance aircraft that enabled them to steam with the fast carrier task forces of Admirals Spruance and Halsey, TF 38 and TF 58. Lieutenant gunnery Ford had reported on board the *Monterey* at its commissioning as an officer, and by the time he had been detached, he had earned nine battle stars on his Asiatic-Pacific campaign ribbon. He had earned the distinction among his fellow officers on board as being the designated officer of the deck during general quarters, an assignment of special responsibility that is indicative of the high professional respect he had earned as a young Navy Reserve officer. On several occasions Ford alluded to his days on board the *Monterey* and the great satisfaction that he had enjoyed in his brief but exciting tour of duty conning the carrier through the great carrier air battles against the Japanese in the Pacific.

One of the first of the foreign heads of state to pay an official visit to President Ford was the chancellor of the Federal Republic of Germany, Helmut Schmidt. The Fords entertained their German guests in Washington and Chancellor Schmidt responded with a cocktail party in Baltimore, Maryland, a comfortable drive for Washington guests and a nice change from the standard Washington venue of the visitor's national embassy.

The reception was held on the former U.S. Navy ship-of-war *Constellation*, a handsome feature of the newly restored Baltimore waterfront. It was late fall in 1974, but a lovely afternoon, and the guests were enjoying their drinks and canapés on the sloop's spar deck, the main deck open to the weather. I had been included in the guest list, probably because Schmidt was a naval history buff. I had been through the receiving line and was engaged in a superficial conversation with the German naval attaché, when I saw President Ford, with Chancellor Schmidt in tow, pushing his way through the crowd of congenial guests, obviously headed for me. Schmidt said to me, "Admiral, President Ford tells me you commanded the nuclear aircraft carrier *Enterprise*." I admitted that I had, and that it had been a memorable experience. Seeing my pilot's wings, he added that he had a great deal of admiration for the men who ran the carriers and those who flew off of them. I agreed and added, "Of course you know that President Ford served on board a carrier in the Pacific during World War II."

"No, I didn't realize that," answered Schmidt. Turning to the president, he asked, "Which one was that?"

"The USS *Monterey*," President Ford answered.

To my surprise, Schmidt said, "Oh, but that was one of the small escort carriers, not a big one." I was shocked at the chancellor's lack of tact. Clearly taken aback, Ford said, "*Monterey* was not a small carrier, was it Jim?"

I was speechless, being asked to settle a personal dispute between two heads of state on a very important aspect of the president's naval career. The *Monterey*'s designation was CVL-26, the CVL standing for "light aircraft carrier." She had been converted to a carrier from a cruiser hull laid down before the war. The CVL carriers at ten thousand tons were definitely smaller than the standard *Essex*-class carriers at twenty-seven thousand tons. I gulped and stammered, "The *Monterey*-class carriers were not the largest in the fleet, but they could steam at thirty-two knots and carried first-line fighters and bombers. They were classified as 'fleet' carriers, as opposed to escort carriers, and operated with the fast carrier groups in Halsey's and Spruance's task forces thirty-eight and fifty-eight." At that juncture the first lady, Betty Ford, joined the group and the chancellor shifted his attention to graciously greet her. I executed a quick and stealthy disengagement.

That afternoon I did a quick review of World War II carrier characteristics and force levels. During the war, the Navy had constructed sixty-nine carriers of the *Casablanca* and *Commencement Bay* classes, which because of their light displacement of less than eight thousand tons and limited speed of under twenty-five knots, were classified as "escort carriers" embarking the less capable FM-2 Wildcat fighters rather than *Monterey*'s newer and much higher-performance F6F Grumman Hellcats. President Ford had known what he was talking about.

FLEET READINESS

Less than two weeks after the change of command, the facts of life were driven home: Being CNO involved more than honors and ceremonies. The occasion was the hearings of the House Armed Services Committee on the material condition of the fleet. As CNO, I was the only witness to testify before the committee, which is the way it should have been. Force readiness is a "command responsibility," and I was sternly lectured by congressmen who had been congratulating me just weeks before. In their view, the material condition of the fleet was deplorable. I had to agree with them.

The committee staff had done their job well, collecting statistics on the steadily increasing number of material casualty reports per month, the growing percentage of ships not fully ready for war, for deployment, or even for getting underway. Even our own people were complaining. A retired three-star admiral on vacation in Bermuda put in a long-distance telephone call to me in the CNO's office to berate me about the awful appearance of two fairly new U.S. destroyers that had anchored in Bermuda Sound. According to the apoplectic admiral, they were rust-streaked, soot-begrimed, and peeling paint—all to such an extent that their lack of a man-of-war's smartness was clearly evident from as far away as the tourist-filled beaches in the resort areas.

The event that took the prize and caught the attention of the committee's chief counsel was the Atlantic transit the month before of a five-ship amphibious task group deploying from the amphibious base at Little Creek, Virginia, for duty with the Sixth Fleet in the Mediterranean. One ship, an LST, was unable to get underway and remained moored at the pier in Norfolk. Two more vessels, both LSDs, had feed-water problems and were forced to turn around shortly after leaving the

Chesapeake and return to Norfolk. A fourth broke down after leaving the Azores and was towed into port at the Spanish naval base at Cadiz. The one remaining ship, an amphibious transport, did make it all the way through the Straits of Gibraltar. Unfortunately, I could not assure the congressmen that such a miserable performance would not be an isolated episode, unless the Navy, with the help of Congress, turned around the awful downward trend.

The poor material condition of our naval vessels was a principal concern of the congressmen. I took a lot of heat, and it was well deserved. The committee's allegation was that the ships were in terrible condition. I agreed but added, "Yes, but Congress has to bear some of the responsibility. You haven't appropriated the necessary funds for overhauls, repairs, or spare parts. The Navy's budget is at the lowest point since 1948." My mention of Congressional responsibility annoyed some of the members even more, and their words were almost threatening. The committee responded that their staff was reporting that the crews were not doing the maintenance they should. I replied,

> There is some truth to that report, and there are two reasons. First, the work ethic in the fleet has eroded. We are working hard to correct that. But a more serious concern and a related cause is that we have a shortage of experienced petty officers, who are our real maintenance and repair technicians. The young sailors lack the training and experience to maintain, much less repair, this complex equipment. Our best sailors are not reenlisting. . . . They are frustrated in their jobs because they don't have the parts and equipment to maintain the ships and aircraft and they work long hours scavenging for temporary makeshift solutions. It is demoralizing for responsible, conscientious sailors. We are working on that problem, too, training our new people. But you've got to give us some time.

The committee chairman said, "We'll help you. We could legislate a policy that, for any ship that fails a readiness inspection, the captain will be relieved of his command." I said, "Please don't do that. The Navy is just as hard up for competent captains as experienced petty officers. And it's not necessarily the captain's fault. We've hit the point now where the more we push the crews, take their liberty away from them to work them after hours, the worse their morale becomes. Any more squeezing and they may give up altogether. It's a very delicate balance. We are routinely working them ten to twelve hours a day. But if it were to become sixteen hours a day, I'm afraid the men would become physically and psychologically exhausted." The committee's response? "We don't think you're being tough enough." So I had Congress on my back as well.

Actually the causes of the decline in the fleet's material readiness were several, and Congress was to blame for more than just a little. The main reasons for the decline were no secret. My predecessors in the Navy had been warning the Department of Defense and Congress for several years. The ships in the fleet had simply been run to death in Vietnam operations. Ship overhauls had been delayed, and then cancelled, to meet operating schedules or respond to emergency requirements. In-port periods were shortened. The crews were exhausted yet expected to perform deferred maintenance, in port, between cruises and during their postdeployment leave periods. Both crew morale and the program for much needed upgrades and repairs also suffered.

The carriers were particularly impacted because the catapults, arresting gear, and flight deck surfaces had not been designed for a tempo of operations that extended to twelve hours per day for thirty days without respite. Carrier aircraft were affected as well. Replacement planes for battle losses were rushed through overhaul and repair to get them back in the squadrons, and often deep preventive maintenance and essential upgrades to armament systems and safety improvements had to be left off lists of scheduled overhaul work.

With the end of the conflict in Vietnam, the pace of operations was slowed, but the program of repair, refurbishment, and improvement was only partially implemented. Now the problem was money. Funds intended for fleet maintenance and rehabilitation became part of the "peace dividend" and were largely diverted to federal social programs. There were many members of Congress who did not understand the relationship between the Fleet Operations and Maintenance (O&M) account in the Navy's budget and fleet readiness. To the uninitiated, as long as the Navy had enough sailors, the ships and aircraft ought to be properly maintained. The need for technical training schools to teach bluejackets the esoteric skills of maintaining modern weapons systems, the requirement for replacement spare parts for worn out as well as broken equipment, and the necessity to provide ships with dedicated periods in shipyards and naval bases where heavy equipment for big jobs was available were not recognized, or perhaps just not accepted. But there was also a pernicious problem that was especially bothersome. The Vietnam War had made serious inroads on the social mores of young Americans. There seemed to be a palpable diminution of the characteristic American work ethic in this postwar generation. To induce young people to enlist in the Navy, the recruiters had made promises of good pay, fun cruises, rapid promotion, and the opportunity to learn a marketable trade.

Unfortunately, the Navy couldn't deliver, especially to the young people who had been underachievers on the civilian side, both in high school education and in the job market. They could not understand why they had to start at the bottom of the ladder and how chipping paint and cleaning firesides were going to lead to promotion. They expected instant gratification, but they lacked the basic education for the more glamorous careers in electronics and computers. Their disenchantment became manifested in a lack of motivation for the menial tasks of keeping their vessel shipshape up to man-of-war standards.

I will confess that when I became CNO, I was not aware of the extent of the material problems in the operating forces. Many of our middle-grade officers, and flag officers as well, seemed willing to accept these lower standards, believing that they would be reflected only cosmetically in the external appearance of our ships. The failure and nonoperability of equipment, weapons, and systems due to neglected maintenance had not yet sunk in.

The carriers were the major fleet units most affected by this problem. As early as 1970, a three-star aviation admiral in the Pentagon had seriously questioned whether the Navy should continue to even try to hold the carrier crews to the higher, pre–Vietnam War material standards or simply accept "Band-Aids" as a way of life. Recovery seemed just too difficult. The harder the crews were worked, the more the reenlistment rates deteriorated. A climax of a sort had occurred when, during a firepower demonstration by a carrier at sea for a presidential visit, not one single air-launched missile hit its target. This was acutely embarrassing and a revelation to the flag officer conducting the exercise. He prompted a full investigation of the problem, catalogued in the exercise report, which resulted in a major overhaul of the Navy's air-launched weapons-system management.

Yet there seemed to be a general apathy and little sense of urgency in resolving the readiness problems in the operating forces. The excuse seemed to be, "That's the way it is on the outside. Our sailors are just reflecting the post-Vietnam counterculture." As vice chief, I had realized that we had problems, but I didn't have a solid appreciation of the extent. Maybe it was because as vice chief I had stayed in the Pentagon while Bud visited the fleet and field activities.

Then, in my first week as CNO, I was asked if I would inspect the new alcohol rehabilitation center that had recently been opened in NOB Norfolk. I had not realized that alcohol and drug rehab was a big issue in the fleet, so I was quite interested. I flew to Norfolk by helicopter, transferred to a car, and first drove around the naval base for a general overview. It was around 1130, and the car literally had to crawl because of the hundreds of sailors on the streets coming up from the waterfront. They were in dungarees. I asked the captain of the base, who was escorting me, where the sailors were going.

"They're going to the enlisted club," he replied. "We've got a great deal. Our E club is really making money. During the week, from 1130 to 1230, we offer a martini happy hour, two drinks for the price of one, and we have topless go-go dancers, too. It has really put this E club in the black."

"Are you in favor of this?" I asked.

"It's made the club solvent," he said. "We hardly need the slot machines anymore. The idea of a noon happy hour was proposed during our all-hands session at the base theater last year." This was a forum that had been established by an earlier Z-gram.

So I inspected the alcohol rehab center, which seemed underutilized, then went to the waterfront, where the fleet units—carriers, cruisers, destroyers, supply ships, and amphibious vessels—were tied up at the piers. On the waterfront, you expect to hear paint chipping and motors running, but it was dead quiet. I went on board a couple of ships and there was no work being done. I asked where the sailors were.

"Well, a lot of them have gone to the PX or are down in their berthing compartments," the captain said.

"If these sailors have been drinking at noon, you're not going to get any work out of them this afternoon," I said.

"Well, even though they have a couple of beers at lunch, they still ought to be able to do a day's work."

"Let me be realistic," I replied. "I'm a normal human being. If I had two double martinis in the middle of the day, I know I'd be through with any productive work. Physiologically, they're no different than I am. I can't believe they can be productive in the afternoon. I sure wouldn't want them working on my airplane."

I got a couple of the ship skippers together and they told me, "It's terrible, Admiral. These young teenage sailors go up to the club almost every day in their dungarees. They come back to the ship, but they don't work. They just sort of drift around going through the motions of doing their jobs, but nothing really gets done after the middle of the day." Here was an example of a lack of command attention all the way up the line that was really hurting the Navy. It was supposed to be good for the young seamen's morale, subsidized booze and topless dancers in the middle of the working day. But it was all wrong from every aspect and wasn't really legal. Most of the young sailors weren't twenty-one. Identification cards were never checked. The attitude seemed to be, if a kid is old enough to fight, he's old enough to drink.

I decided this middle-of-the-day bingeing had to be stopped. But it couldn't be limited to the enlisted clubs. When I got back to the Pentagon I personally drafted an order that in effect said, "There will be no alcohol served at any of the clubs on a naval base or station during working hours. Bar service will not open until 1700 and will close at midnight." The reaction was immediate. A fleet CinC called me and said he couldn't do this. "The retired officers and their wives in the local community will give me hell," he said. "They use the officers' club, and they like to have a cocktail or beer or wine with lunch." I replied, "I'm sorry that the retired got caught up in this thing, but the base clubs are primarily for active-duty people so they can dine without going off the base. If the retireds want to drink before 1700, they can have it at home or at a local bar or restaurant. Norfolk and Virginia Beach are full of them. We have to run these base facilities primarily for active duty fleet people." The Navy was actively overhauling its policies to reduce the unnecessary discrimination among ranks in the matter of social privileges, and any policy concerning alcohol had to be consistent for everybody. We had to be tough on this issue.

A week later a related problem surfaced. The chief petty officers' clubs asserted that it had been a long-term traditional privilege for them to remain open and serve liquor twenty-four hours per day. Their reasoning was that chiefs sometimes work unusual hours. And if a chief has the graveyard shift, and he gets off at eight in the morning, he ought to be able to go to his club and get a drink. My first reaction was that the Navy should not sponsor drinking at eight in the morning. There is no counterpart to this in civilian life. If they have to, the chiefs can get their drink at home or in a local bar. I held fast to my dictum of bar hours from five to midnight. So all of the base clubs had the same bar hours. There were sporadic complaints for a couple of weeks, and then it was accepted. After that, the issue of drinking during the working day went away.

The material readiness condition of the carrier force remained the principal concern of both the Atlantic and Pacific Fleets. The distribution of carriers between the two coasts was nine in the Pacific and seven or eight in the Atlantic, depending upon the often-fluctuating force level. The DoD established the Navy's authorized force level of attack carriers on an annual basis (carriers were the only ships in the Navy other than fleet ballistic missile submarines to have their number so tightly controlled by the National Command Authority). The Joint Chiefs of Staff further dictated the disposition of the carrier force by mandating that there should never be fewer than two CVs in the Sixth Fleet in the Mediterranean and that one carrier of the Seventh Fleet must always be deployed within one thousand miles of Taiwan. The Navy was not permitted to gap these deployments, which were essential to the nation's general war plans.

If a carrier were incapacitated by engineering difficulties that prevented it from getting underway, the schedules of all carriers in the fleet were affected, like dominoes. Carriers had to be extended on station, deployed months early from their maintenance availability in shipyards or crew training and work-up periods in their U.S. homeports in the assigned naval bases.

Although carrier material problems caused the major reverberations, there had to have been deep concern over the impact on overall operations and crew morale of the general deterioration of material readiness in the fleet, especially in the ships' engineering plants. If a radar did not work, a destroyer could fix it usually while deployed at sea. If a bad boiler prevented a destroyer from getting underway, the operating forces were deprived of its use. It was as if the number of ships in the Navy had been reduced by one.

It didn't take me long to identify the root cause of the problem. The entire professional area of naval engineering had been neglected since World War II. Command and control and weapons were the glamorous assignments in the surface ships. If a line office hoped to get ahead in the Navy, engineering duty was to be avoided at all costs. It was impossible to excel professionally in that department. The propulsion plants had been run hard and not well maintained. Engineering officers were, especially on the carriers, limited duty officers (LDOs), who, although very competent former enlisted men from the engineering rates, were nevertheless stuck in assignments in which they received little support and even less understanding from the ships' commanding officers, who had seldom served at sea in an engineering billet.

My own experience had been invaluable in reaching the solution to these deep-seated problems. During World War II, I had served in two *Fletcher*-class destroyers where the naval officers assigned as chief engineers had been graded by their fitness reports in their overall performance as naval officers in the top ten percentile of their year group. The engineering departments on those ships performed as well as the gunnery departments, and both were essential for the ultimate survival of both ships throughout four years of fleet deployments in combat. Professionalism and pride had to be restored to the engineering departments in our men-of-war.

The chief engineers of the *Essex*-class carriers in which I served as a pilot with an embarked squadron were LDOs, professionally competent but physically and emotionally exhausted from the succession of daily crises in the machinery and in their overworked troops. In these crises they received little sympathy or recognition from the captain and department heads, aviators who usually had no real appreciation of the chief engineer's problems. In fact, although the chief engineer was a department head and a member of the wardroom mess entitled to sit at the head table, he usually ate a sandwich of night rations while directing repairs in the engine room.

It became clear to me in the early weeks of my CNO tour that the first step in recovering from our crippling malaise in the material readiness of our ships was to restore professionalism and pride to the entire world of ships' engineering. Rickover's example of deep immersion of prospective commanding officers in engineering had impressed me. Further, my association with submarine officers through my nuclear training experience had been a valuable education. The lives of the crew depend upon a submariner's ability in safely conducting its primary maneuvers of diving and surfacing. This in turn depended upon 100 percent engineering reliability. Nothing less was acceptable.

My first step was to decree, as a matter of Navy personnel policy, that a prerequisite for assignment of a commanding officer of a commissioned ship would be service in the engineering department of a seagoing vessel. This caused cries of anguish to rise from the surface warfare community, but I had a full concurrence and support from my chief of naval personnel, Jim Watkins, a nuclear submariner who later became a CNO. When the younger officers realized the Navy meant business in this regard—no waivers—there was a scramble from the best and brightest to get to sea promptly as a ship's engineer.

The carriers represented a special problem. The challenges were of such magnitude that only the more able senior officers of special motivation could tackle the job and turn around a situation that was on the verge of coming apart. Again, it was Jim Watkins who, with a gutsy call, provided the solution. Senior top-performing commanders from the surface warfare community would be selected and ordered to the billet of chief engineer on a carrier for a normal head-of-department tour of two years. This was known as the Carrier Readiness Improvement Program. It could have been hard on the morale of the affected officers, who of course would have preferred to be a missile officer in an Aegis cruiser, but the program was part of a larger program to turn around an essential culture in the Navy that had gone awry. These officers responded magnificently, and the CNP made certain that they were professionally rewarded.

In the case of the nuclear-powered carriers—the first ship of the *Nimitz* class was just entering the fleet—top performing nuclear-trained submarine officers were to be ordered as CVN reactor officers and chief engineers. Again, the dedication and willingness to serve prevailed, and the operating record of the nuclear-powered carrier program, can only be praised and admired for its ongoing record of safety and reliability.

Innovation was required. The solution was a cram course in the practical aspects of steam engineering in Navy ship propulsion plants. Officially, it was the Prospective Commanding Officers Ships Engineering Course. Its genesis was interesting in that it was the result of an almost simultaneous confluence of ideas from Admiral Rickover and myself. I had long considered a concept, borrowed from the German army, of a two-week retreat in a remote but comfortable resort or lodge, under relaxed but not Spartan conditions, for newly selected flag officers. There would be a curriculum, including visits and seminars with senior naval flag officers, distinguished public servants, and respected pundits, with ample time provided for reflection, reading, studying, and discovering the personalities of one's professional contemporaries.

Rickover had developed a similar concept, but less of an unstructured retreat than a cram course in engineering, optimized for line officers of the rank of captain who already had orders to a major command—a deep draft, a cruiser, or carrier. Rickover had taken this concept to Jim Watkins to get his reaction, and the two of them came to see me.

They must have expected resistance, because Rickover offered to fund the project from some appropriated funds he had wheeled out of the Sea Power Subcommittee of the House Armed Services Committee for "professional education." Rickover also had a location selected. There were several unused buildings, actually "Baker huts," at the AEC reactor site near Arco, Idaho, where the initial training of the engineering crews and commanding officers of the nuclear surface ships, including the carrier *Enterprise*, was conducted.

I was all for it. Rick's approach gave substance and form to my idea of catching our line officers at a crucial point in their careers that would mark their debut as senior officers in the Navy. It would be a way of providing our future leadership with the opportunity of getting to know their counterparts in all the naval communities, surface warfare, aviation and submarines.

In an hour we had it conceptually ironed out. The location would be at the Arco site, and the duration would be about four weeks (although the course eventually grew to fourteen weeks as we looked at the results and gained experience). It would not be a pass-or-fail course but more like a war college. The attendees would be treated like senior officers. After all, this was the elite of the officer corps of the U.S. Navy, or at least two-thirds of the Navy: the aviators and surface warfare officers. The submarines got their practical engineering education at the nuclear training schools.

It was a very special group. All of the line officers of the surface and aviation Navy would come from these classes because they included all prospective ship commanding officers and a ship command was a prerequisite for selection to flag rank. Among the bonus benefits of these classes was that it gave the future leadership of the Navy a special opportunity to get to know one another in a uniquely Navy professional, but totally noncompetitive environment. There were no grades given, and there was much mutual support, such as tutoring by those officers who might have had much of the math and physics as undergraduates at the Naval Academy.

The accommodations were Spartan but adequate. Each officer had a private room with desk and well-stocked bookshelves in addition to the creature comforts of chairs and bedstead. One large room was set aside as a wardroom for socializing and dining. Accommodations were available in the town of Idaho Falls, but this involved a sixty-mile drive each way. Wives were discouraged from accompanying their husbands for the full course, so there would be adequate time to hit the books each evening. Radios and hi-fi sets were not allowed, but there was a television in the wardroom for "news." Some officers noted that for some reason the NBC channel was not available. It was observed that eliminating NBC also eliminated Monday Night pro football. The weekends were free, and in addition to staying in a hotel in Idaho Falls simply as an escape, most of the officers took advantage of the fishing, skiing, and hiking available at one of the many world class resorts in the local area.

The first class convened in November 1977 with twenty-five officers, and the numbers remained about the same for successive classes. The instructors were first rate, generally civilians and officers of the same caliber as the "facilitators" at the nuclear propulsion schools. Interestingly enough, there were a few officers who declined to accept orders to the school, and in doing so, gave up their opportunity to command a ship and qualify themselves for flag selection. The main reason was either an apprehension of the difficulty of the studies (although it was clearly indicated it would be a no-fail course). Others simply didn't want to work that hard or make the move and commitment of time. The quality of the Navy's cadre of commanding officers was not diminished by the removal of these officers from prospective command.

The influx of these new commanding officers, well trained and professionally competent in ship engineering, had an immediate impact in the fleet. Engineering proficiency improved markedly, and the material casualty rates in surface ships dropped noticeably, improving the morale in the engineering ratings and giving a further boost to material readiness. In two years, all ship commanding officers were qualified in engineering either through a tour of duty in a ship's engineering plant or through the Prospective Commanding Officers Engineering School.

SECRETARY MIDDENDORF

During my days as vice chief of naval operations in 1973 and 1974, the two principals in the Office of the Secretary of the Navy were Secretary John Warner and Under Secretary J. William Middendorf. Shortly after I had relieved Admiral Zumwalt as CNO, President Ford appointed John Warner to head the United States Bicentennial Commission, which was charged with planning, executing, and coordinating oversight of all of the government programs and activities concerned with the national observance of the two-hundredth anniversary of the founding of the Republic in 1776.

Bill Middendorf was moved up to take John Warner's place as secretary of the navy. This was not a disruptive move as far as I was concerned. As vice chief of naval operations, I had worked with the under secretary. Admiral Zumwalt had reserved the channels to Secretary Warner for the CNO's exclusive lines of communication.

Middendorf was a pleasure to work with. He was a bundle of energy, talent, and imagination, often described by his many friends in business and politics as a "renaissance man." Before coming to the Pentagon he had been the U.S. ambassador to the Netherlands. While there, he studied music and became a competent composer. As SecNav, he wrote music, mainly marches—over fifty—for the Navy and Marine Corps. He even composed the "Navy Wives March," which he dedicated to my wife, Dabney. Shortly after becoming secretary of the navy he had been invited to conduct the Navy Band in a Christmas concert for Navy families at Constitution Hall. Middendorf wore a rented teddy bear suit for the occasion. He was a great hit. As the secretary of defense observed, "Only Bill Middendorf has the talent to pull that one off."

Middendorf had gotten his commission as an ensign in the Navy Reserves from the NROTC program at Holy Cross University during World War II and served in the Pacific on an LCS(L), a small amphibious craft. After the war he returned to Harvard for a bachelor of arts degree, and he later got a master's in business administration and entered the field of finance. As an investment banker he met with substantial success. At the same time he entered political life, filling a number of prominent and influential positions in the Republican Party, including national treasurer.

Bill was, of course, a whiz at finance, which was of great benefit in the management of the Department of the Navy. More than that, however, Middendorf was endowed with great common sense, which he exercised to the substantial benefit of his office. As a former seagoing naval officer, he was anxious to be brought into the operational side of the Navy, which became, I think, a source of some frustration for him. But Secretary Middendorf, unlike many senior civilian political appointees in the Pentagon, understood his own limitations and quickly and wisely realized that he was not prepared by his recent background to render unconstrained judgments on the combat effectiveness of new technologies or to redesign tactical aircraft for carrier compatibility. (Reportedly, during the F-111 debate, in which OSD was attempting to adapt an Air Force fighter for carrier use and thus achieve the common all-service tactical plane, Secretary of Defense McNamara and Deputy Secretary of Defense Nitze designed a wing-folding mechanism to enhance the Air Force version of the F-111 for carrier suitability, using a rubber eraser and a pair of bent paper clips. The F-111 project was abandoned shortly thereafter.)

Middendorf was a great help in his strong and articulate support of the Navy's programs, especially with the Office of the Secretary of Defense and Congress during budget time. During those two years, the Navy was remarkably successful in gaining congressional support for our principal Navy programs, including the Trident Submarine, the Aegis

Cruisers, the F-18, and the CH53E Heavy Lift Helicopter program. During all of this time his interest in the seagoing Navy remained undiminished.

One day, in the spring of 1975, Bill Middendorf walked into the CNO's office, pulled up a chair, and began a conversation. "Jim," he said, "I am dedicated to this job and I love the Navy, but I don't feel I am making a real contribution in a leadership way. I have learned that the technical decisions are made through the material commands on the basis of extensive research and planning. Personnel matters are evolutionary and the products of years of service experience. Don't you have some area where I can put myself to work closer to the operating Navy? How can I be of more direct help to the people in the fleet?"

I didn't have to ponder that for very long. "You can help reverse the deteriorating material condition of the fleet," I said. Then I outlined our problems and what we were doing to try to turn the trend around. I mentioned our efforts to change the prevalent attitude in the fleet, that an engineering job was a dead end in a line officer's career. We needed to exercise "command attention" to reverse this perception, but I simply couldn't get out to the operating forces as much as I would like, especially with three JCS meetings per week and congressional committees in between. "Why don't you," I said, "as secretary of the navy, undertake a program of visiting ships in the operating forces?"

This in itself was not a new idea, but I thought we'd inject one major change. In the past, the SecNav or the CNO had been delivered on board, had received arrival honors, and then had been taken directly to the bridge or the captain's in-port cabin, where he called on the commanding officer and had a cup of coffee. Then, after a brief walk around topside, he moved on to the next ship. I suggested that he go directly to the engineering spaces after arrival honors and meet with the "snipes" of all ranks from the chief engineer to the lowest fireman. After just a couple of visits, I told him, you will know what to look for—in the bilges and firesides, for example—and will be able to speak knowledge-ably about what you see. Meanwhile, I continued, he should praise the dedication of the engineers and the importance of their jobs, and let them know that help is on the way in the form of full manning and brimming spare parts bins. Such a program, I thought, could do more to generate self-respect within the ships' engineering community than any other measure. It might put the skippers' noses out of joint at first, but they would welcome the results.

Bill was immediately enthusiastic about the program, and together we walked down to his office to get his executive assistant and the rest of the staff briefed on the project and started on the arrangements. The secretary charged into this program with his customary vigor, and the results were almost immediately evident. At first, when Middendorf would ask an engineering watchstander on the deck gratings when the commanding officer was last down in the fire room, the response was usually "Never." Word got around quickly, however, and the COs began regular visits to the boiler rooms to preclude any disappointment by the SecNav when he visited the ship's engineers.

The final upshot was that Secretary Middendorf made more than 350 ship visits in the fleet, for the express purpose of inspecting the engineering spaces and visiting the engineers, in nearly every case climbing into a boiler opened for cleaning. He established official plaques, one of which was to commemorate the visit of the secretary of the navy to the engineering spaces; the second was an inscribed award presented in the case of superior material condition or high morale in the engineering department. In his departure ceremony at the end of his tour as SecNav, I was able to say that he had visited more ships of our great Navy than any other in our history, including the legendary Vice Adm. John Bulkeley.

I was grateful to Secretary Middendorf for these efforts, and I considered that the program exemplified the partnership that we, the secretary and the CNO, shared in the Navy's leadership. I am convinced that our relationship amounted to a measurable benefit in the management as well as the morale of the Navy.

SECRETARY OF DEFENSE RUMSFELD

The ringing of the emergency telephone on the console behind the desk in the CNO's office startled me. Normally all phones rang in the outer office and were answered by a member of the CNO staff in order to screen and direct incoming calls. Of the three outside lines to the CNO's office, there always seemed to be at least one ringing or busy.

The bright red phone handset in the CNO's office was different. It was known simply as the "Red Phone" and it was a dedicated circuit that connected the CNO directly to the secretary of defense's desk. When it rang, it was because the SecDef wanted to talk to the CNO person to person, with no one else listening in or taking notes—at least not on my end. The ringing was unexpected because it was an otherwise quiet afternoon in October 1976. But on this day, I was not only the CNO but also acting chairman of the Joint Chiefs of Staff in the absence of Gen. George Brown, the appointed chairman. I picked up the handset and heard Rumsfeld's brusque voice saying, "Jim, get down to my office right away." I knew better than to ask Don why. As I went out the door of the CNO's office, I told Capt. John Poindexter, the CNO's executive aide, to make a couple of fast phone calls and see if he could find out what the critical situation was. If there was a catastrophe someplace in the world, he was to telephone the aide in the SecDef office, who would alert me before I went through the door into Rumsfeld's inner sanctum. That way I could avoid the appearance of being totally stupid.

There was no time, though. When I arrived at the SecDef's suite, his personal aide was standing at the door of Rumsfeld's private office. He said, "Admiral, please go right in." I entered the vast private office of the secretary of defense and was taken back by the scene. I could make out Don Rumsfeld sitting behind the famous Pershing desk, barely discernable through a cloud of blue smoke. Two tough-looking characters in their shirtsleeves were sitting next to him. All three had their feet up on the hallowed desk and were smoking huge black cigars. I was puzzled. Drawing closer, I recognized the two people on either side of Rumsfeld as Joe Henson and Joe Gattuso. Both were retired naval officers and both had been wrestlers at the Naval Academy. All three had been selected to try out for the U.S. wrestling team in the 1954 Olympics. Don Rumsfeld had been a championship wrestler at Princeton University. He had gotten to know Gattuso and Henson from that experience, and they had all remained friends. Henson had been in the Naval Academy class of 1946 and in 1954 had won an Olympic Bronze Medal for wrestling in the 138-pound class. Gattuso had not won a place on the Olympic team, but during the tryouts he had dislocated Don Rumsfeld's shoulder and broken his clavicle, causing Don to drop out of contention for the

Olympics. I had been a wrestler at the Naval Academy and had stayed in touch with top Navy wrestlers over the years, so I knew both Gattuso and Henson.

Don said, "Jim, come over here and say hello to your friends." As I approached the desk through the haze of smoke, Gattuso said, "We asked Don how long it would take for him to get you down here. It looks like he did it in less than three minutes." The two Joes then laughed uproariously.

Don motioned for me to take a chair and I joined them for about fifteen minutes. The talk was, of course, about wrestling, mostly great collegiate wrestlers we had encountered. When it was clear that it was time to go, I made my farewells, and as I was departing through the door I looked back and saw the two Joes putting on their coats and knotting up their neckties, still grabbing each other in exotic wrestling holds, laughing and scratching as they said goodbye.

When I got back to the office, John Poindexter was waiting for me and asked what had happened. I said that it was a personal affair rather than an international crisis and we could all relax. It is interesting that Don Rumsfeld, Joe Henson, and I were all three later inducted into the Wrestling Hall of Fame in Stillwater, Oklahoma.

I first met Don Rumsfeld in the spring of 1973. I had been selected to succeed Admiral Zumwalt as CNO, and before the change of command, the CNO asked me to represent him at a NATO conference in Brussels which all of the U.S. and NATO chiefs of service had been encouraged to attend. It was at this conference that I met the U.S. Ambassador to NATO, Don Rumsfeld, who was a naval reserve commander and a designated naval aviator He had gone through flight training in 1954. For his active duty, Rumsfeld had been assigned to the Naval Auxiliary Air Station at Corry Field outside of Pensacola, Florida, as a flight instructor, teaching student pilots basic Navy training, flying planes such as the SNJ, SNB, T-28, and T-34. Rumsfeld completed his active service in November 1957 but remained a selected Reservist. He flew out of the Naval Air Station Grosse Ile, Michigan, and in time became an aircraft commander in the S-2 Tracker, a carrier-based antisubmarine aircraft with twin reciprocating engines. During the three days of the conference, Don Rumsfeld and I, largely because of the ties of naval aviation, seemed to get along well. It also turned out that he had known my wife's brother, Lewis Rawlings, at Princeton. Rumsfeld had wrestled at Princeton in the same weight class in which I had wrestled at the Naval Academy some twelve years earlier.

When I next encountered Don Rumsfeld, he was the White House chief of staff to President Ford and I was CNO, spending considerable time at the White House working with the president's team briefing members of Congress on the need for a more robust defense budget. Then, in 1975, Rumsfeld succeeded Jim Schlesinger as secretary of defense. The prospect of a vigorous young Naval Reserves officer, who was also a naval aviator, as the SecDef seemed like a good break for naval aviation and the Navy.

The Joint Chiefs found out quickly that we were getting a different kind of boss. Secretary of Defense Rumsfeld had a decidedly personal style. Discussions were less structured, and Rumsfeld was much more aggressive in his approach to decision making. He did ask questions from his subordinates, but as a rule, he received the answers with an undisguised air of cynicism. It was as if he had made up his mind that he should assume that he could not believe what his chiefs were telling him. It soon became obvious that a response at odds with the secretary's preconceived position was to be avoided. This made it uninviting to speak up at one of his conferences. As a result, his decisions could often appear to be quite arbitrary.

In his early days as secretary, Rumsfeld was not always punctilious in his scheduled meetings. He was obviously diverted by his tight links to the White House and Chief of Staff Dick Cheney. President Ford was clearly in need of political advice during those critical days before the election. This gave rise to problems for the Joint Chiefs of Staff when Don was not readily accessible during these hours he was away at the White House. It was especially difficult for the service chiefs, who had real time operational responsibilities as well as pressing administrative and budget decisions to be cleared or approved. We could not always count on being able to contact him in a time-sensitive situation, and he did not characteristically afford us much latitude in delegated authority. This could make the working relationships quite uncomfortable, because it was not always clear what the secretary wanted done.

One of my first opportunities to talk to Don Rumsfeld after he had taken over as secretary of defense occurred in 1975, when I accompanied him to the White House to brief the president on our plans to meet with members of Congress in seeking support for the president's defense budget. We were the only passengers in the official car, and in the course of the conversation, Rumsfeld offered his views on civilian control of the military. He told me that he regarded the existing relationships to be far from what he thought the statutes intended them to be. He felt that the people in uniform were assuming too much authority vis-à-vis the civilian leadership. He had been unfavorably impressed by an incident shortly after he had arrived at the White House as chief of staff. Summoned to his first National Security Council meeting, his entrance to the cabinet room was blocked by a Marine lieutenant colonel in uniform. The officer said, "I'm sorry, Mr. Rumsfeld, but you can not go in." Rumsfeld asked why. The Marine responded, "Your security clearance for this level of classification has not yet come through and you are not on my list of those authorized to attend this meeting." Continuing the story, Rumsfeld said, "I didn't want a scene in front of the cabinet room on my first day in office, and I could see that this Marine lieutenant colonel was quite taken with his presumed responsibilities. My own reaction was that this was ridiculous. He knew I was the chief of staff to the president, and that regardless of whether or not the paperwork had been done to clear me to attend this meeting, it obviously was in process and was bound to happen. It was just a question of time. In my view he showed very poor judgment. Unfortunately, I believe that's the attitude that's becoming more and more a mindset among the uniformed people. Given a little authority, they are inclined to flaunt it without the flexibility that's necessary in many cases." He ended the conversation with a comment to the effect that he intended to address this issue early on during his days in the OSD.

Rumsfeld's personality had clearly stiffened from what I had seen in Europe when he was ambassador to NATO. This was perhaps inevitable, in that his responsibilities as SecDef were a great deal more abundant and substantive than his previous duties as ambassador. I must add, too, that after I had retired from active duty in the Navy and Don was no longer in government service, our relationship resumed its previous pleasant cordiality.

Captain Holloway, commanding officer of the USS *Enterprise*, looks through an old flight record book kept by Attack Squadron 34. Holloway flew with the squadron from the USS *Kearsarge* in 1948. *Naval Historical Center-NH 103853*

Chief of naval operations Adm. Thomas Moorer presents a second award of the Legion of Merit to Admiral Holloway for his 1967 service as commanding officer of the USS *Enterprise* as Adm. Hyman G. Rickover witnesses this testimonial to the effectiveness of the nuclear-powered aircraft carrier. *Admiral Holloway collection*

Adm. Elmo Zumwalt swears in Admiral Holloway as vice chief of naval operations, September 1973. *Admiral Holloway collection*

Admiral Holloway as chief of naval operations with his father, Adm. James L. Holloway Jr., USN (Ret.), in 1974. They were the only father and son to have attained four-star rank in the Navy while on active duty. *Naval Historical Center-NH 103854*

President Richard M. Nixon congratulates Admiral Holloway on his selection as chief of naval operations as Secretary of the Navy John Warner looks on. *Naval Historical Center-NH 103851*

As acting chairman of the Joint Chiefs of Staff, Admiral Holloway reports developments in the *Mayaguez* incident to the president and senior officials, May 1975. *Left to right:* Secretary of State Henry Kissinger; Admiral Holloway; William Colby, director of the CIA; President Gerald Ford; Secretary of Defense James Schlesinger; and Deputy Secretary of Defense William Clements. *Admiral Holloway collection*

Admiral Holloway with Naval Academy mascots during the Army-Navy football game at Philadelphia in December 1975. Navy won! *Admiral Holloway collection*

Chief Machinist's Mate Lilton Davis briefs Admiral Holloway on the work of the Diesel Laboratory at the Fleet Ballistic Missile Submarine Training Center at Charleston, South Carolina, on 18 March 1976. *Naval Historical Center-NH 103818*

Admiral Holloway speaks before a congressional committee while serving as chief of naval operations. In this role, he strongly and lucidly communicated the value of the Navy as an instrument of national policy and the ongoing need for readiness. *Naval Historical Center-NH 103811*

Admiral Holloway visits the destroyer *Spruance,* then one of the Atlantic Fleet's newest surface warships, at Charleston, South Carolina, on 18 March 1976. *Naval Historical Center-NH 103816*

Admiral Holloway attends a social function at Helsinki, Finland, in 1977. With him are (*left*) the commander in chief of the Soviet navy, Admiral of the Fleet N. I. Smirnov, and (*center*) the commander in chief of the Finnish navy, Rear Admiral S. O. Wikberg. *Naval Historical Center-NH 103855*

Admiral Holloway and Henry Kissinger confer with Vice President George H. W. Bush. *Admiral Holloway collection*

Admiral Holloway, as executive director of the President's Task Force on Combating Terrorism, briefs President Ronald Reagan and Vice President George H. W. Bush on the work of the task force, January 1986. *Admiral Holloway collection*

Vice Adm. John Ryan, superintendent of the Naval Academy, congratulates Admiral Holloway at a formal Naval Academy parade honoring those alumni who were presented the Distinguished Graduate Award by the Naval Academy Alumni Association, 20 October 2000. *Admiral Holloway collection*

Admiral Holloway shares a lighter moment with Secretary of Defense Donald H. Rumsfeld at a surprise birthday party for the admiral in 2002, after the Army-Navy wrestling match (Navy won). *Holloway collection*

Admiral Holloway as chairman of the Board of the Naval Historical Foundation, seated at the desk used by George Dewey as president of the General Board of the Navy (1899–1917) and Admiral of the Navy (1903–17). *Naval Historical Center-NH 103859-KN*

20

Chief of Naval Operations

Program Management

I n September 1974, Secretary of Defense James Schlesinger accepted the General Dynamics F-16 as the winner of the lightweight fighter competition and authorized production of the F-16 for the services. The Navy preferred the Northrop F-17 design and proceeded to upgrade the F-17 concept to satisfy its follow-on fighter attack plane (FAX) requirements. As chief of naval operations, I had approved a scaled-up version of the F-17 that was then designated the F-18. The F-18 included substantial improvements over the F-17 to make it carrier-suitable and all-weather capable with the Sparrow III air-to-air missile. Although I made this decision independently of the secretary of the navy, the decision was consistent with my statutory responsibility for military requirements.

Initially, a majority of the members of Congress wanted a single LWF to lower program costs. I had testified that "the Navy wasn't interested in a fighter that could only get on and off of a carrier by means of a crane, no matter how little it costs." Congressional opposition to a single LWF for both services—with probably the F-111 debacle of 1960 in mind— was neutralized. But the OSD was adamant that the Navy be forced to take the F-16. By spring this appeared to be a fait accompli to the extent that Secretary of the Air Force John McLucas, encountering me by chance in the E ring of the Pentagon, proclaimed in a loud voice to ensure that both I and the two Air Force four-stars in his company could clearly hear, "Admiral, the Air Force is the program manager for the F-16, and I can promise you we are not going to screw up the design and performance by adding a lot of stuff that the Navy wants. It's an Air Force lightweight fighter, and we are going to keep it that."

By April the situation had become critical. The Navy had not yet received the go-ahead from the DoD to go to contract for the F-18. The OSD was making plans for the Navy to procure a slightly modified version of the F-16. The main spokesman for this position was a civilian analyst in OSD, "Chuck" Myers, a member of the "Fighter Mafia" and a longtime watchdog of naval aviation.

I appealed to Secretary Schlesinger, and he agreed to hear out the issue "like a country judge," letting both sides argue their cases. The CNO was to represent the Navy, and Leonard Sullivan, another longtime carrier critic, would be the F-16 protagonist.

The meeting was held in April 1975 in Schlesinger's office. It was to begin at 1330 and go on until neither side "had anything more to say." Then Schlesinger would make the decision. The CNO was allowed to bring only two people "because of the size of the room." I selected Vice Adm. Tom Hayward, who headed Navy Programing, and Vice Adm. Kent Lee, the commander, Naval Air Systems Command. Both were experienced Navy fighter pilots. When the three of us arrived at the SecDef's office we were stunned to find more than a dozen OSD people assembled—Leonard Sullivan and Chuck Myers, plus analysts, engineers, and finance types. It looked like an attempt to overpower the Navy with sheer volume of testimony. The first part of the meeting involved lengthy discussions on the carrier suitability of the F-16. I advised that our naval test analyses indicated the F-16 would bang the tailpipe on the deck with unacceptable frequency. OSD claimed this could be solved by faster landing speeds and better pilot technique. Then came the discussion of the alternative program costs and the synergy of a single type of fighter for all services.

The CNO was to be the only witness to speak for the Navy side. When I complained that the short mission range of the F-16 would reduce the carrier air wing's striking radius by several hundred miles from even its current capabilities, Leonard Sullivan told SecDef that could be a plus; it would get the carriers back where they belonged, conducting antisubmarine warfare and covering amphibious landings.

I had saved my blockbuster until the SecDef's Office of Program Assessment and Evaluation (PA&E) had run through all of their arguments. I then advised that the F-16 was not acceptable as a carrier fighter because it lacked an all-weather capability. There was dead silence in the room. Schlesinger said, "Say that again and explain." I pointed out that the F-16 carried only AIM-9 Sidewinder air-to-air missiles and they were clear-air-mass missiles. In clouds, a radar missile like the AIM-7 Sparrow III was required. This capability, with the necessary radar guidance system and heavier pylons, had been incorporated in the F-18 design, but the F-16 would not accommodate an all-weather missile system without extensive redesign and added weight. Schlesinger was incredulous. He asked Sullivan to explain. There was silence and then confusion. Then Myers said, "Most of the time, maybe two thirds, the weather on the average would be suitable for Sidewinder. Why should we assume the enemy would attack in bad weather?"

I replied that if the enemy knew our air defense was no good in cloudy weather, that is precisely when they would choose to attack. The debate was over. There was another half an hour of perfunctory discussion, but the suggestion that Sparrow III be installed on the F-16 was never mentioned again.

Both sides had run out of discussion points, and SecDef adjourned the session. He called me into his inner office alone. "Admiral," he said, "you've got your F-18." After a pause, he added, "PA&E never pointed out to me the all-weather limitations of the F-16." On 2 May 1975, the OSD announced that the Navy had DoD approval to develop the F-18 for production.

The F/A-18 is still the Navy's premier aircraft. It has filled the carrier decks as a fighter-attack aircraft, replacing the A-7 attack plane and the F-14 fighter with a single plane that can perform both of its predecessors' functions. This gives the carrier enormous flexibility in its air wing, capable of launching more than fifty attack planes or fifty fighters, depending upon the tactical situation. With four squadrons of F/A-18s in each carrier's embarked airwing, the maintenance and supply support has been dramatically simplified, and the F/A-18 was designed for ease of maintenance, only needing a third of the man-hours required by the F-14. Early F/A-18 models performed admirably in Afghanistan and in 2003, during Operation Iraqi Freedom, and as the F/A-18E and F versions continue to enter the fleet, this will be another giant increase in air wing capability.

EDWARD TELLER AND THE SUBMARINE CARRIER

In the summer of 1976, I had been in the job of CNO for two years and had testified several times both years before the House and Senate Armed Services Committees and Appropriation Subcommittees on naval matters, extending from our strategy and military capabilities to the emerging weaponry of nuclear propulsion, ballistic missiles at sea, and satellite surveillance from space. Therefore, I was not completely surprised when Capt. John Poindexter, the executive assistant, said that Edward Teller, the father of the H-bomb, would like to discuss a highly classified subject. He indicated a preference for seeing me in a one-on-one situation without aides or other experts present. I told Poindexter to set up a luncheon in the office for the two of us and to give me an hour with Teller, whom I had not previously met.

Teller was a charming old gentleman, pleasant and polite, with a thick accent and all the other expected characteristics of a brilliant but perhaps absent-minded scientist. We had just been seated when he launched into the subject of our get-together, a proposal that he felt was terribly important to the future of the Navy. He said the Navy should construct a fleet of very large submarines that could serve as mother ships to small, high-speed submarines to operate below the surface of the water, in the same fashion that aircraft operate from a carrier on the surface. He proposed that the mother ship have an ample hangar to house the smaller submarines for rearming and crew replacement and that it be nuclear powered, as would the "fighter" submarines. The mother sub would proceed to a remote area of the ocean that was within the smaller submarine's range of the nation's strategic military objectives. From there, either resting on the bottom or at very slow speeds it would launch its small submarines, with their crews of only one or two operators. The miniature subs would then carry out the tasks that are normally the mission of the current *Los Angeles*–class boats, which have a crew of more than a hundred officers and men. These tactical submarines would, in Teller's words, be very fast, implying a speed of one hundred knots or more. These speeds astounded me, because my knowledge of hydrodynamics, which was not entirely primitive, told me that submerged objects, such as a fully submerged submarine, a partially submerged under-hull area of a larger ship, or even a smaller highly streamlined device such as a torpedo, were physically limited in their maximum velocity. To date the best speeds attained by a submerged body in our weapons tests was less than forty miles an hour in spite of extensive experimentation. Even theoretical studies conducted in an effort to improve the performance of underwater weapons, confirmed this limitation of the velocities of underwater bodies.

Teller continued to present his proposal, which depended upon a large number, twenty to thirty, of these tactical submarines, traveling at speeds of one hundred knots, for scouting, surveillance, attacking enemy submarines, destroying hostile warships, and sinking cargo ships. The analogy was obviously similar to that of an aircraft carrier, with the mother sub as the carrier and the small—even single-seat—tactical submarines as the aircraft. There was no discussion of what kinds of reactors would be used, the configuration of either of the categories of the submarines or the mode of propulsion. Teller had thought out the concept quite thoroughly but had given little or no thought to the feasibility of designing, constructing or operating the components. To him it was just a helluva good idea but the details of making it work he was leaving up to Rickover and the naval architects. I was surprised that Teller had never indicated why he felt that the present system would need to be replaced, or why his proposal would be any better. I am sure that it was the exciting idea of having fantastically fast "fighter" submarines zipping around underwater that appealed to him. But I was amazed that he as a physicist did not take into consideration that the current state of the art of hydrodynamic theory would limit the maximum speed of these underwater fighting subs to certainly less than fifty miles an hour.

After Teller departed, I concluded that I had learned a lesson: No matter how brilliant a genius may be in his field of study, that does not mean that he is equally knowledgeable in other fields, even those based largely on commonsense matters. I was to encounter this anomaly often in dealing with people throughout my career, and I reserved a caution when geniuses opined in sectors of know-how in which they had never previously demonstrated a competence.

However, as the technological clock ticks on, new developments occur to contest our conventional wisdom. Within a year after my conversation with Teller, Russian scientists developed a high-speed underwater body, a supercavitating missile, that was capable of much higher speeds than our hydrodynamic engineers had even thought was a remote possibility—over 250 knots! The Russian missile, given the Russian name for squall (Shkval), became operational in 1977, but was so shrouded in secrecy that it was only in the past two years that I have known of its existence.

Also, the essence of Teller's concept, a submarine mother ship carrying a flotilla of underwater craft that would be sent out to some distances from the "carrier" to explore or attack and then be recovered by the mother ship, is an ongoing research program in the U.S. Navy in 2006.

Today the underwater carrier can be an attack submarine or a strategic type, and the underwater craft are unmanned undersea vehicles (UUV). Currently their missions are mainly surveillance and reconnaissance into hostile areas of high danger to a nuclear submarine, or the shallow waters of a littoral shelf to explore for minefields or defensive devices in depths not deep enough for the mother ship.

The UUVs are unmanned now, but there are many parallels to Teller's concepts in both of these developmental programs that have made me conclude that Teller was wiser than I gave him credit for being.

PRESIDENT FORD AND THE CVAN-71

In the fall of 1976, I had been in the job of CNO for two years when President Ford called me to the White House. I was ushered into the Cabinet Room, where the president was in his shirt sleeves with members of his staff, several cabinet members, and the presidential budget people. President Ford was always gracious under any circumstances, and in spite of what was a tough, shirtsleeve working session, he politely offered me a seat at the table and got right to the point. "Admiral," he asked, "don't you think we should have an aircraft carrier in this year's budget?"

"Yes, sir," I replied.

"Don't you think it should be a big carrier?"

"Yes, sir."

"And don't you think it should be nuclear powered?"

"Yes, sir."

"What do you recommend?"

"A *Nimitz*-class carrier, Mr. President."

"I agree. It will be in this fiscal year's budget."

President Ford knew what he was talking about. He had been the speaker at the *Nimitz* commissioning ceremony in Norfolk, and sitting together on the dais, there had been a more than adequate opportunity to talk about the capabilities of the *Nimitz*, including comparisons with his own World War II carrier, the *Monterey*. Unfortunately, when Jimmy Carter won the election for president, his administration would not support the construction of any kind of carrier and, in fact, vigorously opposed Congress's move to include a large nuclear carrier in the FY 77 budget, vetoing the entire defense authorization bill because it contained an aircraft carrier.

JOHN McCAIN

Adm. John Sidney McCain Jr. had been the Navy's chief of legislative liaison at the time I was executive assistant to Vice Adm. Bob Pirie, the deputy chief of naval operations for air, in 1958. McCain, then a rear admiral, was famous as being enormously effective in this role, a persuasive proponent of naval forces who was instrumental in getting the Navy programs of the CNO, Adm. Arleigh Burke, through Congress. John Sidney McCain continued to rise in rank and correspondingly responsible positions, and he became commander in chief, Pacific, in 1972, during the war in Vietnam.

His son, John Sidney McCain III, had graduated from the Naval Academy in the class of 1958 and gone through flight training. He was a carrier pilot flying an A-4 Skyhawk when he was shot down on a combat mission in Vietnam. As a prisoner of war he inspired the admiration of all Americans when he rejected the offer of the North Vietnamese to send him home because of the severe injuries he had sustained in his crash. This was intended by the North Vietnamese as a gesture of goodwill because he was the son of the commander in chief in the Pacific, at that time the senior military commander in the field directing the efforts of the war in Vietnam. Lieutenant Commander McCain, in a public statement, said that he would not accept repatriation until all of his fellow POWs were released.

Dating back to my days in the Pentagon as an executive assistant to the DCNO (Air), I had developed an appreciation of the importance of the Office of Legislative Affairs, and the tremendous contribution that a competent chief could bring to the furtherance of the Navy's programs through the generation of congressional support. It took a very special sort of person—a diplomat, an officer of common sense and a broad intellect, and a strong operational naval background. It was important that the chief of Legislative Affairs be able to speak with personal authority about the programs that he was briefing to the members of Congress on behalf of the CNO. I had been very impressed with Rear Adm. John Sidney McCain Jr.'s competence in this assignment. He was effective in his ability to explain the Navy's need for the components that constituted the Navy's budget and he was convincingly persuasive in the logic of his presentations to the individual members. The most effective chiefs of Legislative Affairs were officers who had not only the fleet experience but also the brains to handle the complex matters of congressional relations. In this, the experience of having worked "on the Hill" as a junior officer in the office of Legislative Affairs, was important. It was for this reason that I had told my executive assistant, Captain Poindexter, to earmark young Lt. Cdr. John McCain III for assignment to legislative affairs upon his return to full-duty status after his rehabilitation from the injuries he had received in his crash and captivity.

I was therefore surprised to learn, when I happened to check with Poindexter concerning McCain's status, that he was reporting back to full duty and the Bureau of Naval Personnel had seen fit to assign him as the attack aircraft desk officer in the Naval Air Systems Command. I didn't know what had happened, nor did I really care at that instant. I wanted to get this back on track as quickly and smoothly as possible. I called Vice Adm. Jim Watkins, the chief of BuPers, but he was absent on a field trip. His deputy informed me that, in the detailing officer's judgment, this was the assignment that best suited McCain. Not feeling it necessary to justify my decision in this matter, I simply told the deputy chief of naval personnel to have McCain's orders changed, sending him to the Office of Legislative Affairs. The rear admiral said, "But, sir, we have already cut his orders and that means we'll have to do it all over again." Well, fortunately, this was a telephone discussion, for I would have found it difficult to restrain myself physically if we had been talking face to face. I simply said, "Get those new orders recut, reissued, and delivered by close of business tomorrow" and slammed the phone down. The rest of the story is that Lt. Cdr. John McCain III went to the office of the legislative liaison and earned a name for himself as a highly effective staffer. From there he left the Navy to become a member of the House of Representatives and, subsequently, a U.S. senator from Arizona and a potential candidate for the presidency. As a member of Congress in both Houses, his interest in, and support of, naval aviation—especially carriers—has never been wanting.

THE POLICY FOR NUCLEAR PROPULSION IN SURFACE SHIPS

My relationship with Admiral Rickover had always been a comfortable one from the day I completed my tour of training duty attached to his Naval Reactors Branch in the Bureau of Ships. Rickover had an excellent sense of humor, but not many people had an opportunity to experience his wit because he was usually too busy chewing someone out. For some reason, probably due to the nature of my duties after completing Rickover's course, I maintained a cordial relationship with the KOG and was able to exchange a bon mot and elicit a smile and a chuckle from his weather-beaten countenance. When I became CNO, our relationship did not really change perceptively. He didn't call me to his office as he had before I had gotten my fourth star, but he was just as forthright and down to earth as he had ever been. He did realize, of course, that I had power-making decision that I had not exercised before, but he also knew that he had access to me for briefing programs and explaining his recommendations. He felt that, being the first CNO who was nuclear qualified, I would have a better grasp of what he was telling me than would the average four-star, who was probably inherently not well disposed toward Admiral Rickover, whether they knew him personally or only by reputation.

It was customary for Rickover to have his office make an appointment with me and then he would arrive half an hour to forty-five minutes early, during which time he would sit on the aide's side of the CNO's outer office, where he kept the young aides, and especially the wave officers entertained by his stories and his usually corny sense of humor. When he entered the CNO's office, however, he was all business, and he usually had David Leighton, his senior engineering assistant for nuclear power in surface warships, with him.

Then, in May 1966, we had a major row. By then, no one was questioning nuclear power in carriers. The special and unique military capability of a nuclear-powered carrier is its ability to proceed at high speed to anywhere on the high seas without pausing to replenish or refuel, conducting defensive air operations en route to its objective area, and launching its initial offensive strikes during the approach, more than six hundred miles from the target, then continuing around-the-clock air operations while closing the target area—and with enough aviation fuel and ammunition in its capacious tanks and magazines to remain on station for ten days to two weeks, until the situation has been resolved or underway replenishment groups arrive. It is the fifteen years' fuel supply in the reactors that provide the ship's range and allow for very large stocks of fuel and ammunition to be stored in the carrier's hull, which normally would be reserved for fuel oil for the ship's propulsion. The issue was nuclear power in surface ships other than carriers, namely, destroyers and frigates, which had the mission of "escorting" the carrier in the operational task groups. The first of these nuclear-powered escorts had been the USS *Bainbridge,* which was part of the initial nuclear-powered surface warship program pushed by Adm. Arleigh Burke following the success of the submarine *Nautilus.* The *Bainbridge,* completed in 1962, was an eighty-six-hundred-ton missile frigate, as these large surface warships were then called. (They were later reclassified as cruisers, or CGN). It was followed by the construction of seven more nuclear-powered frigates. Now, fifteen years later, questions were arising over the usefulness of nuclear power in escorts. There were several problems, but the basic concern was the very high cost of a nuclear-powered destroyer in comparison to an oil-fired version. There also were questions as to what benefits were really gained by the nuclear propulsion plant, and there was deep concern that nuclear-powered escorts were proving to be a drag on the construction of the nuclear-powered aircraft carriers because of the political opportunity they afforded opponents of nuclear power, both in the OSD and Congress.

The specific problem was that, in justifying the construction of a nuclear-powered destroyer, Rickover and the Sea Power Subcommittee of the House Armed Services Committee were advocating all nuclear-powered task forces. These would consist of a nuclear-powered carrier, supported by a nuclear-powered cruiser and four nuclear-powered destroyers. Unfortunately, that was not the way that the fleet operators envisioned the employment of these ships. When the *Enterprise* deployed from Norfolk directly to the Gulf of Tonkin around Africa and through the Indian Ocean, she was accompanied by the one nuclear-powered surface ship then in the fleet, the *Bainbridge*. The two nuclear-powered ships were able to make the transit from the East Coast of the United States to Southeast Asia at a high speed, averaging almost thirty knots, because their nuclear power plants eliminated the requirement for having to refuel en route. However, when the *Enterprise* commenced combat air operations with Task Force 77, the situation changed. It was necessary to rotate gunships through the shore-bombardment assignments in Vietnam in order to equalize the wear on the ships' gun barrels. That meant that the *Bainbridge* would go on the gun line for fire support of the forces ashore with its 3-inch gun battery, and its place with the *Enterprise* would be taken by a conventionally powered destroyer. Essentially there was no notable difference in the efficiency of the *Enterprise* task group in the Gulf of Tonkin whether or not the escorts were nuclear powered. Also, many of the other carrier commanding officers and their embarked flags would ask to have the *Bainbridge* assigned to their task group—which was, of course, conventionally powered—simply for the unique experience or even the prestige of having a nuclear warship in their entourage.

The real difficulties then surfaced in Washington. When the testimony in behalf of the construction of the next nuclear-powered aircraft carrier was being presented to Congress, the opponents of nuclear power brought up the argument that if it was the Navy's policy to have nuclear-powered task groups, then it was not enough to build a carrier; it was necessary to build four nuclear-powered escorts for each carrier. At the time the Navy's plan was simply to use the nuclear-powered carriers to replace the nonnuclear versions in the fleet, and there were plenty of conventionally powered destroyers in the force levels to provide four escorts without the necessity of building another destroyer. Consequently, the cost of the nuclear carrier was represented by the opposition as being the cost of a nuclear-powered carrier plus the cost of four nuclear destroyers. This was clearly an extravagance, and I for one, having served for two years in command of the *Enterprise* and its task group in combat in Vietnam, simply could not justify the need to build additional nuclear-powered escorts at a cost of almost twice that of its oil-fired counterpart, which actually did not have to be constructed but was already available in the fleet. In May 1976 I issued an AllNav that defined the policy for nuclear power in new ship construction. The essence of this directive was that, one, all future submarines would be nuclear powered. And two, all future aircraft carriers would be nuclear powered. There would be no more nuclear surface combatants constructed in the future because the added expense could not be justified in the other classes in comparison to the benefits attained.

Rickover, whom I had kept informed during the formulation of this policy, was upset from the beginning, but when the AllNav was published, he went to his friends in Congress, and within twenty-four hours after the release of the message, I had congressmen of the Seapower Subcommittee calling me to find out why I had ignored Rickover's advice. Rickover had of course adopted the position that all future destroyers and cruisers should be nuclear powered. I explained to the members of Congress that we could not afford the nuclear-powered escorts, that a policy that required nuclear power in those ships was going to kill the nuclear-powered aircraft carrier program and there was nothing to be gained operationally from nuclear power in escorts. At this point the debate within the Navy hit the press. The news magazine *U.S. News and World Report*, in its 7 June 1976 issue, featured the disagreement between Rickover and the CNO in a cover article. The headlines reported that the CNO, working for a favorable vote in the Senate, had recently sent the following message to several key senators: "The issue is which advice should the Congress follow: the advice of the CNO, the senior uniformed official responsible for the readiness of naval forces now and in the future—whose views are supported by the Secretary of the Navy and the Secretary of Defense and Presidential decisions—or the advice of Admiral Rickover."

Rickover's influence could not be ignored. The vice chief of naval operations, a good friend and admired colleague, Adm. Bob Long, privately asked me if I would write a letter of apology to Rickover. My response was, "For what, doing my job as CNO?" But Rickover persuaded the House Armed Services Committee through the Seapower Subcommittee, which he had created and which was wont to do his bidding, to ask the full House to agree to voting $7.4 billion to build twenty-four ships, of which two were nuclear-powered guided-missile cruisers. However, the Senate eliminated the nuclear-powered cruisers and supported the start of a new class of conventionally powered destroyer, the DDG-47.

The differences in the two defense bills had to be resolved in conference, and the members heard testimony from both myself and Rickover. The conferees decided in support of the CNO. In denying the construction of two more nuclear-powered cruisers, the CNO's policy that nuclear power for naval ships would be limited to submarines and aircraft carriers only was firmly established.

REAR ADMIRAL STOCKDALE'S INTERVIEW

With the inauguration of a Democratic administration headed by President Jimmy Carter in 1977, the people at the head of the Department of Defense all changed. The secretary of defense was Harold Brown, who had served as secretary of the air force and then assistant secretary of defense for acquisition, in a previous Democratic administration. The deputy secretary of defense was a distinguished businessman from industry, the former president of Coca-Cola, Charles Duncan.

During the interim period between the election of President Carter and his inauguration, the Republican DoD team, headed by Secretary of Defense Donald Rumsfeld, did what was necessary to effect the proper turnover. Secretary Rumsfeld observed to several flag and general officers in an informal conversation that he was passing along to the incoming administration his conviction that the senior military officers in the Pentagon were exercising much more influence than was intended by the statutory policy of civilian control of the armed forces. It was his stated view that the senior officers in the services, the CNO, the commandant, and the chiefs of staff of the Army and the Air Force, did not adequately brief their civilian superiors—the service secretaries, the SecDef, and the senior civilians in the OSD—to the extent necessary to enable them to make the judgments and decisions for which they were responsible. Secretary Rumsfeld added that he was going to brief his relief, Harold Brown, of this concern. Rumsfeld believed that the first step in regaining civilian control of the DoD was to take over the assignments of flag and general officers.

It had been the custom, within the memory of all of the senior officers in the services, when I was vice chief of naval operations and CNO, that when filling a three- or four-star billet, the service chief would discuss the matter with his service secretary and recommend a specific officer. When a candidate acceptable to both the service chief and the service secretary was agreed upon, the secretary sent the nomination, along with appropriate justification and a color photograph, to the secretary of defense for his approval. Only in very rare cases did the CNO and secretary of the navy not agree on the service chief's recommendation, and even less often did the secretary of defense reject the service's nominee and ask for another nomination.

Shortly after assuming the position of secretary of defense, Brown informed the service chiefs that he was initiating a new procedure for the selection of officers for three- and four-star assignments. It should be noted that the only way in which a uniformed officer could be promoted to three or four stars was by assignment to a billet for which three- or four-star rank was prescribed. It was not a case of selecting an officer for three stars and then finding a billet for him, but quite the reverse. A three-star or four-star job would become open and the service would be told to nominate an officer to fill the position. It could be another three-star in a lateral move. Or it could be a two-star officer, in which case the appointment would carry with it a promotion in rank as well. A three-star officer, serving in a three-star billet, would be transferred when his tour of duty, normally two or three years, ran out. At which time the officer could be nominated to a four-star billet, to another three-star position, or offered a two-star billet. If none of those alternatives were selected by the secretary of defense, the officer would retire, normally at the highest rank held on active duty. Few officers would agree to revert to two stars after having served in a three-star or four-star assignment.

The new procedure initiated by Secretary Brown was that when a three- or four-star position opened up, the SecDef himself would, if it were a joint assignment, decide which service would be asked to fulfill the job. However, most of the three-star and four-star jobs were, through either job description or custom, an obvious selection within a particular service, such as the four-star vice chief of naval operations or the three-star commander, Atlantic Fleet Submarine Force. In joint billets, such as the deputy commander in chief, European Command, which could be filled by any of the services, the secretary would invite the services to make a nomination. All services might be invited or the secretary could limit nominates to the Army and Air Force, for example. In most cases the selection of a two-star or three-star officer was within a particular service, and the selection of senior officers within the organization of the services was normally left up to the uniformed chiefs of service with the service secretary's concurrence.

First, Brown said that he would make the selections from a larger group of candidates and would require the services to send down a minimum of four and, desirably, as many as six or eight candidates for a specific three-star or four-star job that came open. These nominations would include a detailed dossier with recommendations in each case, along with a color photograph of each individual. Then from these four or more nominations, the SecDef would select the officer for the position—such as commander, Submarine Force Atlantic Fleet—upon the basis of the dossiers.

The service chiefs were visibly upset at this approach, and were quite outspoken in objecting to this new plan. They pointed out that in most cases the SecDef would never have previously even met the candidates nominated, much less have a firsthand appreciation of their personalities or suitability for a particular job, such as their reputation within the service and their own warfare community. On the other hand, the CNO and the vice chief, between the two, would probably have known the candidates and their families for not less then ten years. As one of the chiefs said, we not only know their wives but their previous wives as well. But Brown remained firm. He stated that chiefs must understand that it was industry practice for the CEO to select his senior operating officers, and that over the years, the civilians in the Pentagon who had come in from business had developed the unique ability to size up an individual from a series of written reports, and would thus have an adequate appreciation of both the suitability and the potential competence of the various candidates for the duties of a new position. I was particularly vocal perhaps because the Navy, of all the services, by law had the smallest number of flag billets, roughly 250 compared to more than 400 each in the Army and Air Force. I told Brown that I could not think of a single case in which the Navy flag community could put forth four or five candidates for a three- or four-star position. I was limited by the special personal qualifications required for virtually every four-star and most of the three-star positions that came up. These qualifications were predicated on specific experience, training, background, and skills. In the case of four-star positions, there were relatively few officers in the

Navy at any one time who had the professional maturity, the extensive experience, and the respect from their service contemporaries that would qualify them for service in a four-star billet. Brown dismissed this thought with the comment that perhaps he and the assistant secretaries could perceive qualities in individuals that were not apparent to the officer's contemporaries because they were "too close to him." In any case, this session was ended with the secretary of defense's new selection process confirmed to be the Department of Defense policy.

The first test case came when the position of president of the Naval War College opened up. This was a three-star billet and required a very special kind of naval officer, one with both operational experience and a clearly intellectual cast of mind. The CNO and the SecNav quickly came up with their candidate, Rear Adm. James Stockdale, a hero of the Vietnam War who as prisoner of war had organized the prison camps to require the U.S. prisoners of war to resist any interrogation that exceeded the degree permitted by the Geneva Conventions. In retribution for his courageous leadership in defying his captors, he was so severely beaten that he suffered crippling injuries that personally affected his posture and his gait. His disabilities were clearly evident to anyone who met him. Furthermore, Stockdale had gained considerable public recognition because he had received the Medal of Honor, been featured in several television specials, and had written a book that was on the *New York Times'* bestseller list. All of these had emphasized the debilitating injuries he had suffered because of his leadership of the prisoners of war.

The names of four nominees were sent down to the OSD, but even then, the dossiers and the career summaries were clearly in favor of Stockdale, who had gained his reputation as an operator commanding a carrier air wing in combat in Vietnam flying from the USS *Intrepid,* as well as a reputation among his peers as an honest intellectual, based on his two years of postgraduate study after the Naval Academy, at Stanford University.

The secretary of defense informed me that his first choice for the position of Naval War College president was Rear Admiral Stockdale and that he would be interviewed by the secretary or assistant secretary for that position. Stockdale was duly scheduled, and he reported for his interview in blue service uniform with his full array of ribbons. The interview took about forty-five minutes, and at its conclusion, the gentle-man who had conducted the interview, who was not Secretary of Defense

Brown (he had been otherwise engaged), was thoughtful enough to call me to say that he had met with Admiral Stockdale, had been quite impressed by him, and thought he would be an excellent choice as the president of the NWC. The Navy should go ahead and write orders assigning him to that job. Then, as the conversation ended, the interviewer said, "Jim, one thing, though, why does he walk so funny and drag his arm that way?"

So much for a senior government executive being able to size up a stranger's suitability to fulfill a senior military flag assignment in a critical and demanding position.

SECRETARY OF DEFENSE BROWN AND NUCLEAR CARRIERS

In February 1977 I was in my third year as chief of naval operations, working for my third president, Jimmy Carter, and my third secretary of defense, Harold Brown. President Carter, who considered himself an expert in naval matters in spite of his very limited duty in the Navy, was not favorably disposed toward aircraft carriers. In getting ready for the FY 79 budget, I was scheduled to testify before the Military Subcommittee of the Appropriations Committee of the Senate, a very small but powerful committee on the Hill. The session was scheduled for 1000, and I was told that Secretary of the Navy Graham Claytor and Secretary of Defense Brown would accompany me to this hearing. I'm not sure if the three of us had been invited as a group, or it was their decision to appear with me to make sure I said the right thing.

I was told by the SecDef's office that the subject of an aircraft carrier probably would come up and that Brown wanted to reaffirm to me that the president's position was that there were no plans in the administration for the immediate construction of a new aircraft carrier, certainly not in the 1979 budget, and that the program in the future (at some unspecified time) would be for a small, nonnuclear carrier. If I were asked a question on aircraft carriers, that was to be the guidance for my response.

On the day of the hearing, Secretary Claytor, with whom I had a very pleasant and straightforward relationship, asked me to ride over to the Senate in his sedan. I knew it would be an opportunity for us to talk, and I was not keen on letting myself in for any additional instructions. True gentleman that he was, Graham Claytor on the trip over never brought up the subject of the testimony to be given at the hearings. We did talk about the state of the Navy in general, but there was no pressure from him for me to provide any set answers for the Committee.

In the course of the hearings, for which there had been only an innocuous statement prepared for submission for the record, one of the senior senators said, "Admiral, I do not see an aircraft carrier in this budget, aren't you concerned about this?" My response was that the budget I submitted to the SecNav included a nuclear-powered aircraft carrier, but it had been taken out during the budget review. The senator then said, "Well if you had your way, would you like to see a carrier in the president's budget?" I said yes.

Then the senator turned to the secretary of defense and said, "What are your feelings about including a carrier in this FY 79 budget?"

"We don't share Admiral Holloway's view," Secretary Brown said. "You must understand he is only the chief of naval operations and we have to look at the bigger picture. It is our position that we don't need another carrier now, but that we are not ruling out a carrier in the future."

"What kind of a carrier would that be?" the senator asked.

"We think it should be a much smaller carrier and without nuclear power and probably designed for V/STOL aircraft only," Brown responded.

"Admiral Holloway," the senator said, "how do you feel about Secretary Brown's position? Now I want the truth."

"Senator," I replied, "I can only repeat what I have consistently stated in my appearances before this committee for the past three years. I would without question prefer a new nuclear-powered carrier in this budget rather than a smaller, nonnuclear carrier some time in the indeterminate future."

When the hearing adjourned, Secretary Brown asked me to ride back to the Pentagon with him. Although Harold Brown was a very positive and somewhat didactic person, he was also a gentleman and did not become unpleasant in the car. He merely said, "Jim, you did not support the president's budget as we had intended you do." I said, "Mr. Secretary, there is a requirement for a chief of service when testifying before the Congress, that he is not just privileged, but that he is obligated to provide his own professional view when so requested by the Congress." Brown told me he had never heard of that before and would have to check with the General Counsel.

The following day, the *Washington Post* included the following article, which had been distributed by United Press International on 17 February 1977: "Defense Secretary Harold Brown said today the Administration endorses plans to end future construction of large deck aircraft carriers. He got cool backing from the nation's top naval officer. Admiral James Holloway III, Chief of Naval Operations, told a House Appropriations Subcommittee that while he supported the Administration's position, "I have to say my personal view is that I would rather see a nuclear carrier in this year's budget rather than two smaller carriers sometime downstream."

Secretary Brown never got back to me on the issue of the obligation of the uniformed head of service to express his own personal professional views before the Congress. I did, however, have the Navy's judge advocate general call the General Counsel's Office to reaffirm that this was the rule. The response was that I had been correct.

President Carter's position on carriers held firm. He cancelled the carrier in the FY 78 budget he inherited from President Ford and would not include any kind of carrier in FY 79. But Congress on its own initiative added a nuclear carrier in the 1979 budget, and Carter vetoed the entire defense budget to get rid of the carrier. The next year, Congress put a large nuclear-powered carrier in the 1980 budget, and Carter again vetoed it. But this time, Congress passed the appropriations and authorization bills, overriding Carter's veto, in order to include the nuclear-powered carrier. That ship became the *Theodore Roosevelt*, which in 2002 established an all-time record off Afghanistan for 241 consecutive operating days without a day in port.

In the final analysis it was a matter of personal integrity at stake. If after ten years of stating in my professional opinion that a large-deck nuclear carrier was the only acceptable carrier, what would the senators have thought of me as a professional officer if I suddenly said that a small, nonnuclear carrier was really better?

THE BATTLE GROUP ORGANIZATION

It was 1130 on Saturday, 14 September 1977, and I was in the CNO's office in the Pentagon at my normal Saturday morning routine of clearing the incoming box of thorny issues that needed a final decision by the chief of service. I had finished my work for the day and was about to head for the squash court for my regular Saturday match with the aide,

Cdr. Peter Booth, when John Poindexter, later to be national security advisor to President Reagan, came to my office. John told me that there was one more piece of business that should be wrapped up: a long-outstanding paper, actually left over from the Zumwalt days. It was a proposal that all seagoing staffs be structured identically as described by the term "mirror-image." In other words, a carrier division staff, responsible administratively and operationally for the control of two carriers and two air wings, would have the same structure as a destroyer squadron staff for eight destroyers. This would mean that because the carrier staff would be heavy with officers experienced in air warfare and air intelligence, these same positions and levels of skill would be reproduced on the destroyer staff. This was not a very commonsense solution. A carrier admiral then had a staff of thirty people on his carrier flagship, and the captain or rear admiral of a destroyer squadron or flotilla would have only a half dozen people, almost all of whom would be experts in destroyer operations. I had looked this over once before briefly, and it kept coming back. It needed to be settled once and for all time. I told John to put the folder in my briefcase and I would work on it over the weekend.

Sunday mornings I usually reserved some time to be available for original thought. So I started with a clean sheet of paper, and analyzed what we had in the way of operational staffs in the fleet now and what we really needed. Every time I pulled a thread, I found that the whole system tended to become unraveled. Our current fleet organization was patently outdated. It did not reflect the roles and missions to which the U.S. Navy was, by Title 10 of the U.S Code, committed to support: "to be prepared for prompt and sustained combat action at sea to gain and maintain maritime supremacy, and then to exploit this superiority by projecting power ashore in joint operations against the enemy." Instead, our fleet was organizationally structured in 1977 to reflect the administration of the Navy by types of ship—that is carriers, major surface combatants (cruisers and destroyers), escorts, submarines, amphibious ships, and logistics support vessels, rather than by groups of ships constituted to carry out a strategic or tactical mission.

The principal operational component of the fleet was still the fast carrier task force, made up of an attack carrier plus four to six major surface combatants to "defend" the carrier. This was not a valid representation of the functions of the task force components. Realistically, the carriers' aircraft, such as the F-14, were designed and deployed to defend the entire task force, including both the surface combatants and the carrier.

So I started with the National Strategy. We were then at the height of the Cold War with the Soviet Union. The main mission of the Navy was to gain and maintain maritime superiority in order to have control of the sea in those areas that were essential to the security of the United States, for example, in the Tonkin Gulf during the Vietnam War and the Sea of Japan during Korea. Control of the sea was absolutely essential for the Navy to project power ashore by carrier aircraft striking groups and with our amphibious forces, as well as to provide security for the lines of communication for both the Air Force and the Army deployed overseas. Yet our current fleet organization was very little different from what we had arrived at by the end of World War II, when the threat from Japan and Germany to the U.S. control of the sea had been largely eliminated. Now, in the 1970s, we were faced by a Russian navy twice the size of our own in numbers, if not in capabilities, but constructed and organized specifically for contesting U.S. maritime superiority.

What we required was a true warfighting organization to counter the military and political threat of our Cold War adversary, the USSR and its allies. To accomplish this, the Atlantic and Pacific Fleets would be structured into battle forces. These battle forces would further be organized into battle groups. Each battle group would include an aircraft carrier, two cruisers, four destroyers, and a nuclear submarine. The mission of the battle group would be, first, offensive operations to gain and maintain control of specific areas of the sea as required by our national military strategy. Those same battle groups would then be used for projecting power ashore.

When I returned to the office on Monday morning, I had the draft of a message in hand, addressed to the fleet commanders, explaining the battle force organization and asking for their comments. I showed it only to John Poindexter, who simply recommended that it go out as written. It was in the hands of the fleet commanders before the end of working hours on Monday. By Wednesday the concept had been circulated among the senior flag officers and I had answers from both fleets. It was accepted as the new fleet organization without change and with a personal urging from the two fleet commanders that it be implemented as soon as possible.

So the message was reformatted as an implementing policy directive and sent out before the weekend. It was not necessary to consult with the SecNav or SecDef, as it was the CNO's prerogative to establish the operating procedures of naval forces. The message conveyed the following philosophy:

1. The Battle Force organization of the fleet will reflect the mission, functions, roles, and employment of the U.S. Navy. Primary among these considerations is the maintenance of maritime superiority for the United States and its allies in the face of a growing threat at sea. The organization will be responsive to the changing balance of maritime power. It must reflect the current tactical and strategic concepts of the U.S. Navy.

2. To paraphrase the mission of the Navy as expressed in Title 10 of the U.S. Code, it is to conduct prompt and sustained combat operations at sea in support of national policies. In effect, it is to assure the continued maritime superiority for the United States. This requires that the Navy be able to defeat, in the aggregate, all potential threats to our continuing free use of the high seas. Thus the basic function of the U.S. Navy is sea control, which connotes control of designated sea areas and the associated airspace and underwater volume. It does not imply simultaneous control of all the earth's ocean area but is a selective function exercised only when and where needed. Sea control is achieved by the engagement and destruction of the hostile aircraft, ships, and submarines (or by the deterrence of hostile action through the threat of destruction) that threaten the seaborne forces and resources of the United States and its allies. Sea control is a prerequisite to all other naval operations and tasks, such as amphibious warfare or support of ground forces ashore.

3. The operating forces of the U.S. Navy are to be restructured through the operational organization of the fleet for the prompt and efficient accomplishment of the tasks imposed by the Navy's mission, functions, and roles as delineated by the national military strategy into battle groups.

4. The operation of the U.S. Navy will continue to be under the chain of command from the president and the secretary of defense

through the JCS to the commanders of the Unified and Specified Commands and be administered by the naval component commanders, who are the commanders in chief, Atlantic and Pacific Fleets. The component commanders' operating forces will be the numbered fleets, composed of operationally ready warships that represent a deployable capability to accomplish all general purpose naval warfare tasks. Within the numbered fleets, carriers, cruisers, destroyers, frigates, and submarines will constitute the afloat forces through which hostile naval forces will be engaged in battle at sea. In the numbered fleets these warships will be organized into battle forces and battle groups in the standing task organization.

5. A battle force is defined as the standing operational task force organization of carriers, surface combatants, and submarines assigned to numbered Fleets. A battle force is further subdivided into battle groups.

6. Battle groups are defined as integrated task groups capable of conducting offensive operations at sea against the combined spectrum of hostile maritime threats. A battle group would be a task group consisting of one carrier, two cruisers, four surface combatants, and one or two submarines, operating together in mutual support with the task of destroying hostile submarine, surface, and air forces within the group's assigned area of responsibility.

7. Then this same battle group, having gained control of the required sea space for maritime operations, exercises the versatility of its air wing to establish air superiority over the objective area to project power ashore to attack hostile targets with strike aircraft, long-range missiles and ships gunfire. Naval forces are now able to operate essentially free of enemy interference to accomplish other maritime tasks such as mine countermeasures, amphibious assault with Marines, or the administrative landing of Army and Air Force expeditionary units.

The battle force concept became immediately effective as the basis of the Navy's Fleet Operational Organization. It remained such without any modification or changes for twenty-six years, until 2004, when the Presidential Transformation Project resulted in a Navy reorganization of the fleet into striking groups formed around attack carriers and Marine helicopter carriers supported by destroyers, cruisers, and submarines in response to the 2002 Quadrennial Defense Review.

The Battle Force Fleet organization was probably my most significant contribution to the U.S. Navy in my tour as CNO. It accomplished two main goals within the Navy. First, it established a fleet organization that accurately reflected the Navy's roles and mission as established by the laws enacted by the Congress of the United States. In doing so, it used understandable nomenclature and language in the enabling governing instructions, which not only provided a succinct and common reference for all naval personnel but also clarified for Congress, the DoD, and the JCS an understanding of the Navy's implementation of its roles and mission to further the integration of the service into effective joint strategies, plans, and operations.

Second, the Battle Force Organization specifically provided that battle force and group commanders would be unrestricted line officers of any designation, selected on the basis of those flag officers best suited by virtue of their operational experience, warfare specialty qualification, and command maturity and judgment. In this way, a submariner, surface warfare officer, or aviator would be ordered to command a battle group. No longer would the commander of a task force, which included a carrier, be required to be a naval aviator. In broadening the command opportunities to all of the unrestricted line flag officers, it enabled the flag officers of designators other than aviation to fly their flags from aircraft carriers, and through this experience and exposure, to better understand the carriers capabilities and better appreciate the contribution of naval aviation to the Navy's mission.

I am fully convinced that the elimination of the parochial boundaries in the fleet operating forces has significantly expanded the support for the aircraft carrier's position as the capital ship of today's Navy throughout the entire professional unrestricted line corps.

NAVAL WARFARE INFORMATIONAL PUBLICATION NO. 1

In the early spring of 1978 I began to prepare myself, and the Office of the Chief of Naval Operations, for my successor in the job. The appointment for CNO is a four-year tour, with no extensions except during national emergencies or in time of war. I would be relieved of the job on the last working day of June, and among other responsibilities, I felt it necessary to come forward with a candidate for my relief. This was not meddling but was expected of me by the secretary of the navy, the secretary of defense, and the president, all of whom were involved in the selection process. Early on I had made my decision to support Adm. Thomas B. Hayward, who not only had the best qualifications of any active duty officer in terms of experience but also had the informal votes of the majority of the four star admirals in the Navy, according to a private opinion poll I personally conducted.

In my own case, I was told that I was in the running for selection for chairman of the Joint Chiefs of Staff, which would also become available on the first of July 1978. The secretary of the navy was lobbying for me, and the incumbent chairman, Gen. George Brown, told me I was his first, and only, choice. The chief of staff of the Army had declined to be considered, and the commandant of the Marine Corps was not eligible. This made it a choice between Gen. David Jones, chief of staff of the Air Force, and myself. Dave was running hard for the appointment.

Of course, I very much wanted to be chosen, but it became clear to me early in the selection process that I would not be acceptable to either President Carter or Secretary of Defense Harold Brown because of my uncompromising position on the large-deck carrier. When I testified before Congress and made my appeals to the SecDef in the defense budget process, I was conscious of the stigma of persona non grata I was creating for myself. But I did not see that I had any alternative either as CNO in support of an essential Navy program or in the pursuit of my own professional convictions.

Interestingly enough, two years before in 1976, during the Ford administration, I had been informally told to nominate my relief as CNO because I was shortly to be appointed chairman of the JCS to take Gen. George Brown's place. He was not being reappointed to a second two-year term because of some unfortunate political remarks he had made following a speech at the University of North Carolina. At the last minute, though, the White House decided it would be politically smarter to avoid the cause celebre that would be perceived by a decision not to renew a nonpolitical appointee for political reasons.

Essentially ruled out of consideration in the 1978 chairman appoint-ment, I applied myself to tidying up the programs and projects that I, as CNO, felt personally responsible for. In particular, I wanted to institu-tionalize certain processes within OpNav for the orderly translation of naval requirements into substance—the numbers and characteristics of ships and aircraft needed in the fleet to carry out the Navy's responsi-bilities within its roles and missions. The Battle Force Organization had been a first step, but more needed to be done.

After the experience of three wars and four years as CNO, it seemed almost a waste not to preserve as much as was reasonable in the form of lessons learned. As has been previously pointed out, such documents as the posture statement become personal trademarks of a CNO, and each new incumbent wants to put his particular cachet on the character of his administration. Yet there were doctrines and procedures, something like the NATOPS concept but at the CNO level, that were sterile and procedural but still essential underpinnings to the overall philosophy of a naval service.

The Battle Force Organization had been an opening gambit in this area, but it only went so far into fleet organization. The basic strategic concepts of the Navy needed, in my view, a relatively permanent documentation, and that would become the basis for my long-term legacy to the Navy as CNO.

To provide a professional character to this doctrine, I cast it in the format of a publication titled *Naval Warfare Publication No. 1: Strategic Concepts of the U.S. Navy* (NWP-1). Initially, I outlined the publication and turned it over to a young officer assigned to the immediate office of the CNO as a "CNO Fellow." He did an excellent job, but I soon found out that if I wanted to preserve the lore and lessons learned in thirty-five years of a naval career in my own style of expression, I would have to do it myself. And I did.

NWP-1 was written in longhand in pencil on ruled paper in the evenings at Quarters A in the Potomac Annex, the CNO's quarters. Others may have considered it a chore, but to me it was pure relaxation, disgorging the accumulated thoughts that I had sorted out in my mind over time but had never committed myself to transcribe. As the document progressed, I shared it with Capt. John Poindexter, and he was most helpful in his encouragement.

By the time June 1978 rolled around and I needed to involve myself with a turnover of my duties to Tom Hayward, I had finished really most of what I wanted to record for the guidance of future naval planners, *Part I: Generation of Naval Force Requirements*, and *Part II: Planning Employment and Readiness Doctrine for Naval Operating Forces.*

This material was enough to constitute a usable volume in the NWP series of warfare publications, so I turned it over to the deputy chief of naval operations for plans and policy, then Vice Adm. Bill Crowe, later to be chairman of the JCS and then U.S. ambassador to the United Kingdom under President Bill Clinton. His staff then had the document published in NWP format and distributed with the other naval warfare publications throughout the Navy.

Years later, in 1985, I received an official White House document titled "The National Security Strategy of the United States of America," prepared by the office of the national security advisor to President Ronald Reagan. The national security advisor at that time was Vice Adm. John Poindexter. He had inscribed the publication to me with the words "It all began with NWP-1."

As a final footnote, NWP-1 again came to light on 27 June 2006, during a symposium sponsored by the Center for Naval Analyses in Washington, D.C., on the subject of "U.S. Naval Strategy: Past, Present and Future." The symposium traced the history of those official publications that had, over the years, promulgated statements of the strategy of the U.S. Navy. Among the earliest documents in this series was NWIP-1(A), *Strategic Concepts of the U.S. Navy*, notable because it was the first of the official tactical doctrine publications in the Naval Warfare series to deal with strategy per se. I discovered it was the original 1978 publication, updated with some additions to the original. It was still being used as a reference in the curriculum of the Naval War College at Newport, Rhode Island.

21

The Joint Chiefs of Staff

In 1974 one of the two principal duties of the CNO was to serve as a member of the Joint Chiefs of Staff. It was generally agreed that the JCS responsibilities of the chiefs of service was their primary responsibility and being the uniformed head of their respective military service came second. This is indicative of the high regard in which the JCS, as a body, was held. The recorded histories of U.S. involvement in military affairs after the Armed Forces Unification Act of 1947 have generally emphasized the role of the Joint Chiefs as the principal military advisors to the president in virtually every critical national security decision.

The reasons for this are several. In his duties as a member of the JCS, the service chief was independent of the service secretary. As CNO, my operational chain of command to the president, the commander in chief, was directly to the National Command Authority—the president and the secretary of defense. The secretary of the navy was not in this chain of command. As CNO, I reported to the SecNav only in administrative matters concerning the Department of the Navy.

The Joint Chiefs of Staff were fully involved in national security policy matters at the very highest levels of government. We met three days a week on schedule, once each week in executive session with the secretary of defense. Both President Ford and President Carter held meetings with the JCS and the SecDef as a group in the White House, usually for lunch, at least once every three to six months. President Carter came to the Pentagon to meet with the JCS in their windowless conference room, known as the "tank," on one occasion, and again in the JCS Command Center in the Pentagon to participate in a JCS "Command Post" exercise involving a general war scenario.

When President Ford left office, the former president and former first lady, Betty Ford, entertained the Joint Chiefs of Staff and our wives at a private dinner party in the White House in which the only other guests were the secretary of defense and his wife. A particularly memorable part of that evening was when President Gerry Ford graciously danced with each of our wives, and we each had the opportunity to dance with Betty Ford.

In the 1970s the JCS was a far different organization than it became under Secretary Donald Rumsfeld. Under Rumsfeld's administration, the overall authority of the chiefs significantly diminished, to the point that they were no longer even in the chain of command with the National Command Authority in the decision-making process for the use of nuclear weapons and their release to the forces in the field. This very special and fundamental responsibility of the Joint Chiefs, for which they were especially well prepared and qualified through their background and around the clock staff support from the Joint Staff, was transferred in 2006 to civilians in the Department of Defense.

This comes in starkest contrast with previous years, when, for example, President Ford rejected Secretary Kissinger's proposal for a nuclear arms–limitation agreement with the USSR in which our side would give up cruise missiles in exchange for a reduction in the number of Soviet multimegaton ICBM war heads because the JCS had recommended against it. This was in spite of unanimous support of Kissinger's proposal from the rest of the National Security Council. Later, when President Carter planned a $9 billion cut in the 1978 defense budget, he would not move forward until a majority of the JCS was willing to agree with the president that the nation's defense would not have its capabilities reduced by a cut of this magnitude.

During my tenure as a member of the JCS, the chiefs met three times each week in the tank. Each chief was accompanied by his OPDEP, a designated three-star flag officer from the Plans, Policy or Operations branch of his staff. If the service chief could not attend a scheduled JCS meeting, his vice chief was required to be there. During my year as vice chief of naval operations under Admiral Zumwalt, I was a frequent participant in the meetings of the JCS as his representative. This proved quite useful in getting me ready for the JCS arena from the very beginning of my tour as CNO.

At each Friday meeting, the JCS were joined in the tank by the secretary of defense, and those meetings were usually, at least in part, conducted in executive session. The SecDef would always attend unaccompanied, which provided a particularly useful forum for frank discussion. This accomplished a great deal in clearing the air and promoting truly unified action within the Department of Defense.

Generally, the JCS did not become involved in intraservice force-level issues and usually avoided the discussion of roles and missions. They were considered the law, and as such they were not questioned or contested. This greatly facilitated our ability to operate with the immediacy demanded by emergent threats and instant crises. I cannot recall a single instance, in my four years, when failure of the chiefs to agree resulted in any delay in responding to an incident or managing a crisis.

There was one document, prepared by the chiefs on an annual basis, which dealt with force levels. That was a JCS plan at the secret level, referred to as the Joint Service Operations Plan, or JSOP. This JCS paper set forth all of the forces required to carry out the approved JCS war plans without risk. In other words, cataloging the assets that were required to assure the successful execution of our war plans, even if they had to be implemented simultaneously, as would probably be the case in a general war with the Soviet Union. The JSOP was prepared by the Joint Staff and really to determine what would be the forces needed if unconstrained by budgetary limitations. In 1978, for instance, the JSOP requirements showed a need for forty-six attack carriers.

Mainly, though, the JCS were involved with supervising the readiness of the theater commanders, such as CinCEur and CinCPac and ensuring that the individual services provided the field commanders the necessary and adequate resources in manpower, equipment, and logistical support to carry out their war plans. In the case of a crisis, the chiefs formulated courses of action, advised the National Command Authority of the alternatives, and then transmitted the NCA guidance and decisions to the Unified and Specified Commanders for implementation.

The JCS, in those days, consisted of the service chiefs—chief of staff of the Army, chief of naval operations, chief of staff of the Air Force, commandant of the Marine Corps (in matters affecting the Marine Corps and, later, as a full member)—and the chairman. There was no vice chairman, and the chairman's seniority was defined as the number one among equals. The chairman of the JCS was also a senior member of a number of allied combined military councils, such as NATO and the Southeast Asia Treaty Organization (SEATO). These responsibilities required the chairman to attend in person many of their regular and statutory meetings. His attendance was considered essential as a demonstration of the commitment of U.S. leadership and support.

When the chairman was away participating at these meetings for several days at a time in Europe or Southeast Asia, one of the service chiefs would function as acting chairman. This was in addition to continuing his own responsibilities as a service chief. It required that the acting chairman attend the daily JCS level intelligence and operational briefings by the Joint Staff and be available for access in his Pentagon office during normal working hours and in his quarters during the rest of the time of his acting JCS tenure. With the regularly appointed chairman away about 20 percent of the time, the system of acting chairman maintained an important Washington continuity in the National Command Authority chain of command and it made each service chief much better prepared to carry out his own responsibilities as a member of the JCS.

SEIZURE OF THE SS *MAYAGUEZ*

On 12 May 1975 the SS *Mayaguez*, a container ship in the Sea Land, Inc., commercial fleet, flying the U.S. flag and crewed by American civilian mariners, was steaming in a regular shipping lane in the Gulf of Siam about sixty miles from the coast of Cambodia. This lane passes within eight miles from Poulo Wai, an island claimed by Cambodia, Thailand, and Vietnam.

Without warning, a number of small gunboats, including three U.S.-made swift boats (PCF), headed from Poulo Wai toward the *Mayaguez* and fired a shot from a 76mm gun across the bow of the merchantman. The *Mayaguez*'s master was ordered to heave to, and heavily armed

Cambodians rapidly boarded the ship. The master just had time to call out on the international distress channel that his ship was being seized by pirates before he was held at gunpoint.

At the time of the *Mayaguez* seizure, Gen. George Brown, the chairman of the JCS, was in Europe attending a NATO meeting. Gen. David Jones, chief of staff of the Air Force, was in the scheduled rotation to be acting chairman if an emergency arose. When the *Mayaguez* seizure was reported, the Joint Staff immediately scheduled a meeting of the JCS with General Jones presiding. There were many questions as to what to do and how to respond because the available intelligence was so sketchy. Jones went over to the National Security Council meeting at the White House with the limited information the JCS had available.

At that point, I left Washington to fulfill a speaking engagement at a luncheon meeting of the Commonwealth Club in Boston. I flew to Logan Airport in a Navy A-3 jet bomber converted to a VIP transport and arrived early to visit a Soviet navy destroyer that was making a port call in Boston. Upon departing the Russian ship, I was met at the shore side of the gangway by a lieutenant from the staff of commander, Second Fleet, whose flagship was also paying a port call to Boston. The lieutenant said that there was a secure telephone call for me from the secretary of defense and that I was to take the call on board the Second Fleet flagship—the nearest secure telephone location.

I immediately went down the pier to the flagship, a heavy cruiser, and entered the secure command spaces. The call was put through to Deputy Secretary of Defense William Clements, and Clements, in his own direct fashion, told me to get the hell back to Washington as fast as I could. He said that the president had not been satisfied with General Jones's performance as acting chairman in handling the *Mayaguez* situation and they wanted me to take over as acting chairman. I persuaded the commander, Second Fleet to make my talk scheduled at the Commonwealth Club, and then, with an escort of Boston cops on Harley Hogs, I was transported to Logan Airport at high speed. From there I flew directly to Andrews Air Force Base in the A-3. I was met at the base operations office by Deputy Secretary Clements, who took me in his official car directly to the White House. On the way he filled me in.

Apparently the president had been frustrated to the point of dissatisfaction with Jones's handling of the crisis. First, Jones was late in getting to the White House to meet with the Security Council. His reason was that the stock photos he had wanted for his briefing were not "properly mounted." Then, according to Bill Clements, instead of proposing a course of action to President Ford, Jones asked the president what he wanted the chairman to do. Whatever the reason, Ford did not want to see Jones again as acting chairman and told Clements to have me take over.

Before leaving Washington to go to Boston, I had ordered, as a precautionary measure in my capacity as CNO, that the carrier *Coral Sea*, which was in transit from Japan to Australia, along with several other ships near the South China Sea, be diverted and proceed to the vicinity of Cambodia.

Driving in from Andrews, I was able to use the secure telephone from the car to talk to the National Military Command Center and get a quick update on the situation. There was little additional news and no fresh intelligence. Upon arrival at the White House, I went directly to the cabinet room, where President Ford was meeting with key members of his cabinet. I was asked for an input from the chiefs, and I explained that I had not stopped by to meet with the chiefs since returning but had been in touch with the Joint Staff, and that my recommendations were to start moving certain immediately available military forces into the area to have assets in place to provide multiple options. As intelligence developed and we learned more of the disposition of the crew of *Mayaguez*, we would put together the most effective task force to carry out the chosen course of action. We shouldn't wait for intelligence to trickle in before moving forces on to the scene. Speed was essential. The president quickly agreed with this approach and sent me back to the Pentagon to get things going. I had previously arranged for a meeting of the Joint Chiefs of Staff by telephone from the car, and I briefed them on the session at the White House. After a short discussion, I got their unanimous support for the proposed action. The Joint Staff, by this time, had put a plan together for the initial movement of available forces into the area. The chiefs further agreed that these deployments should be accelerated, and that the Joint Staff should immediately draw up several contingency plans to deal with the possible options the Cambodians might pursue in the disposition of the American crew.

The next day President Ford convened the National Security Council in the cabinet room of the White House. As acting chairman of the JCS, I accompanied Secretary Schlesinger, reporting to the president that the

JCS had met the night before and, in the absence of any definitive intelligence, had directed CinCPac to assemble forces in the vicinity, including the carrier *Coral Sea,* which was proceeding at high speed from its aborted trip to Australia; the first and second landing teams of the Third Marine Division, to be moved from Okinawa to Utapao Royal Thai Air Force Base (RTAFB); a special U.S. Air Force air police commando reaction force to Utapao; and the escort and destroyer *Harold E. Holt* (DE-1074) and *Harry B. Wilson* (DDG-7), which were in transit in the Indian Ocean, to proceed at flank speed to the location of *Mayaguez,* now anchored at Koh Tang Island, about thirty miles off Cambodia. This was not far from where the U.S. merchantman had been seized.

CinCPac was further directed to provide a continuous airborne presence of both combat and surveillance aircraft over the anchorage to "babysit" the *Mayaguez.* A Navy P-3 Orion was maintaining station as a command center in the area, with Air Force F-4 fighters and A-7 light attack planes relieving on station. There was a multitude of small craft— U.S.-made swift boats and local fishing craft—milling around in the vicinity. Whenever any of these boats attempted to approach the *Mayaguez,* they were driven off by machine-gun fire across their bows from the U.S. fighters. In the process, three swift boats were sunk.

The president reminded the NSC that the seizure of the *Mayaguez* had occurred at a very sensitive time. U.S. influence in Southeast Asia was at a low ebb. South Vietnam had been lost to the Communists, and Cambodia had just fallen on 25 April. Ford believed a strong and decisive reaction to the *Mayaguez* capture was essential, to both deter this threat to U.S. merchant shipping in the future and reassert U.S. influence and prestige in Southeast Asia. The ship had become a symbol of free U.S. presence in the sea lanes of the world. This interference was tantamount to piracy and could not be tolerated.

During the day, the president met with congressional leaders in small groups at the White House, where Secretary Schlesinger and I briefed them on the situation, and the president expressed his deep concern over the situation. Late that afternoon, the JCS, after reviewing the proposals from CinCPac and weighing the alternatives, came up with a plan for a three-pronged attack. Marines would board *Mayaguez* from the *Harold E. Holt,* which would pull up alongside. The use of a Marine force rapelling aboard from helicopters had been considered but then abandoned because it would expose the team to very high casualties. The boarding Marines would come from a specially trained unit at the Subic Bay base in the Philippines. A battalion-sized Marine landing force would assault Koh Tang Island in their heavy transport helicopters. The *Coral Sea* air wing would attack the main base of the Cambodian air force at Kompong Som Airfield in a punitive strike to deter any similar ambitions of other rebel groups in the now turbulent political atmosphere of Southeast Asia. The formal announcement of Ford's decision to take military action was made the next day, 14 May, at 1745, but the battle would not be joined for another twelve hours.

At first light on 15 May, the Marines landed on Koh Tang in a helicopter airborne assault. The reaction was deadly. The well-dug-in Khmer Rouge, firing rocket-propelled grenades and heavy machine guns from their reinforced bunkers in the jungle, knocked down one helicopter and forced a second to crash land.

Then, at 0800, the *Harold E. Holt* came alongside the anchored *Mayaguez*, and the Marines climbed aboard with scaling ladders to find the ship totally abandoned, with neither crew nor Cambodians on board. A small volunteer cadre of merchant mariners and engineers, boarding with the Marines, manned the ship's engine room and bridge. In five minutes the emergency generator was going. The anchor chain was cut with an acetylene torch, and the Marines had hoisted the U.S. flag by 0820. At 0845, the *Harold E. Holt* got underway again with the *Mayaguez* in tow.

Without any warning, at about 0900, a Thai fishing boat approached the destroyer *Henry B. Wilson*, which was providing gunfire support for the Marine assault, with the thirty-nine *Mayaguez* crewmembers aboard. The rescue of the ship and its crew was complete.

At Koh Tang Island, the action continued. The Marines were pinned down by the intense fire from the Khmer Rouge automatic-weapons fire, and only two-thirds of the first wave of Marines had gotten ashore. With one Sea Stallion CH-53 helicopter shot down, and a second CH-53 badly damaged by the heavy fire from machine guns and rocket-propelled grenade launchers, the second wave of CH-53 helicopter transports was driven off and had to return to Utapao to refuel and regroup. At 0730, only 109 of the planned 180 Marines were on the island, and they were scattered among three different locations. At 1130, 100 more Marines were landed. The plan called for 250 troops, but only four helicopter transports were available.

Before the additional marines could be lifted into the landing zones on Koh Tang, word was received that the *Mayaguez* had been recovered and that the civilian crew had been rescued. After consulting with the commander in chief of the Pacific Command via the Joint Staff, an exchange that took only minutes with the dedicated command communications, I recommended to the president that the Marines be pulled off the island as soon as tactically feasible. President Ford agreed, and the reverse airlift was completed by 2030 that evening.

The most important fallout from the *Mayaguez* incident was that, for the rest of the Ford administration, I was always acting chairman when George Brown was out of town. President Ford did not like the idea of rotating the position of acting chairman and having to deal with whoever happened to be around when the chairman was not available. So I needed to adapt my personal schedule so that I would always be in town and available for acting JCS duties whenever Brown was away. This amounted to about 20 percent of my time during the rest of the administration.

Perhaps the longer-term significance of this episode was that it was a forerunner to the provisions in the Goldwater-Nichols legislation, which required the establishment of the position of vice chairman of the Joint Chiefs of Staff in order to provide the desired operational continuity that had been missing with the acting chairman system.

OPERATION PAUL BUNYAN

On 18 August 1976, Washington, D.C., was preoccupied with political matters. President Gerald Ford, together with Henry Kissinger, secretary of state and national security advisor, was departing for Kansas City to attend the National Republican Convention. Ford was expected to be nominated as the Republican Party's candidate in the upcoming presidential elections. The secretary of defense, Don Rumsfeld, was in Michigan recovering from a thyroid operation. The chairman of the Joint Chiefs of Staff, Gen. George Brown, was in Europe attending one of the frequent and mandatory meetings of NATO. As chief of naval operations, I was acting chairman in the absence of George Brown.

Late that afternoon, the routine of the Pentagon, and subsequently all of official Washington, was shattered by a flash precedence message from Gen. Dick Stillwell, the commander, U.S. Forces in Korea and the commander in chief, United Nations Command, Korea. Stillwell reported that two U.S. Army officers had been brutally murdered by North Korean soldiers in the Demilitarized Zone in plain view of hundreds of troops on both sides. The intentions of the North Koreans in aggressively attacking a combined U.S. Army and South Korean (ROK) patrol without provocation were unknown. Stillwell had put all of his forces in South Korea on full alert. He was reporting this incident to Washington with the warning of a potential crisis that could widen to the dimensions of a full-scale attack on all UN forces in South Korea. At this point, Stillwell's intelligence people had not been able to judge the purpose of the attack or forecast the intentions of the North Koreans.

The full story of the incident came through quickly. The UN forces responsible for the surveillance of the DMZ had been concerned with the heavy growth of foliage that was obscuring their full view of the zone from the observation points on its southern boundary. The truce agreement that governed the DMZ clearly specified that both sides were to have unobstructed observation of all areas within the zone and consequently the right to remove any obstructions to this surveillance. In this particular case, a large poplar tree had grown to the extent that its branches were blocking the view of a sizable segment of the DMZ from two UN observation posts. As a matter of routine, the U.S. commander in Korea had deployed a force of engineers to chop down the offending tree to allow unobstructed observation. The North Korean representatives at Panmunjom had been properly advised as required that the U.S. would be sending out a patrol for this purpose that day and that the patrol would be unarmed. The soldiers would be provided only with axes and chain saws to do the necessary work. When the party of nine South Koreans, two U.S. officers, and four U.S. MPs walked out to cut down the tree, the DMZ was calm. A North Korean lieutenant and seven men entered the DMZ from their side and walked up to the two U.S. officers, who were lieutenants in the Army Corps of Engineers, and suddenly, without any explanation, demanded that work be halted. When the Americans said no, a North Korean guard trotted across the northern boundary into the North Korean side of the DMZ and returned with a truckload of troops. A North Korean officer suddenly shouted, "Kill them," and his soldiers jumped on the two U.S. officers and beat them to death. The remaining U.S. and South Korean members of the working party were shocked by the sudden attack and overwhelmed by the numbers of North Koreans. After a brief attempt to defend themselves they ran to the southern boundary and escaped through a gate in the fence. The U.S. Army routinely covered operations in the DMZ with combat photography and was able to get a complete film of the officers' skulls being crushed by the North Koreans with the very axes that they had carried.

When the details of the incident reached Washington, President Ford and Secretary Kissinger had already left town, and the only communications available to the president were nonsecure phone lines. A full discussion of the available intelligence and the U.S. options was not possible until a secure telephone could be gotten to the president. This was not an easy task, as the president was fulfilling a complex schedule of meetings and open sessions in Kansas City. Based upon what we could tell him in an unclassified phone conversation, President Ford directed Deputy Secretary of Defense William Clements to call a meeting of the Washington Special Action Group (WSAG) and to keep the president and Secretary Kissinger informed.

The WSAG was convened by the director of the CIA, then George H. W. Bush, and its principals consisted of Secretary Bill Clements for the DoD; myself as acting chairman of the JCS; Gen. Brent Scowcroft, Kissinger's deputy for the National Security Council; and Ambassador Philip Habib for the State Department.

Before heading for the WSAG, I had called a meeting of the Joint Chiefs of Staff in the JCS Secure Conference Room and briefed them of the situation. I also directed that the level of military readiness for war, the DefCon, be increased from the peacetime level of 5 to 3 in the Pacific Command and DefCon 4 worldwide. (On the DefCon scale, 1 is war and 5 is the normal peace time posture of the military.) I also asked that the JCS, through the Joint Staff, earmark all available forces that could be moved to Korea for a show of strength and be committed to the conflict if shooting started. No action was to be taken other than identifying and alerting units, until the National Command Authority (NCA) issued the execute orders.

The WSAG deliberated until late in the afternoon on the eighteenth without any decision being reached as to the probable intentions of the North Koreans. In the absence of a secure means of communication, the WSAG dispatched a White House aide to brief the president on the current situation and planned another meeting in the morning of the nineteenth.

On the way back to the Pentagon in the car, I told Bill Clements that the JCS wanted to send additional forces to Korea and needed his authority to do so. It would be justified on the basis that we were simply prepositioning forces to be in a better posture to respond to any eventuality. Bill was reluctant to "escalate the situation" but realized that he would have to rely on the judgment of the Joint Chiefs. So he authorized the JCS to redeploy forces as necessary to improve readiness, but we were instructed to avoid any actions that could be interpreted as being provocative.

On the evening of the eighteenth, the JCS met again. It was decided that, given the forces available, the most effective moves that could be undertaken immediately—without appearing to be provocative, which was now the clearly overriding concern of Clements and Habib—would be to reinforce the U.S. forces in Korea with a squadron of twenty-four Air Force F-4 Phantoms from Kadena Air Force base on Okinawa and twenty F-111s directly from the United States, refueling en route. B-52s based at Guam would also be scheduled to conduct training runs on the strategic bombing target range located just south of North Korea. These would be highly visible on the North Korean radar. The *Midway* and its accompanying destroyers and cruisers would be diverted from a port call in Yokosuka, Japan, and proceed at high speed to the east coast of Korea off the DMZ, bringing about fifty more fighters and attack planes into the theater. The level of readiness would be maintained at DefCon 3 in the entire Pacific theater.

On the next day, 19 August, the commander, U.S. Forces, Korea, Gen. Dick Stillwell, a tough, combat-hardened army general whom I personally knew and professionally admired, called me on a secure line from Korea to discuss the options available to the United States. He urged that he be given the authority to immediately go back into the DMZ with a heavily armed infantry patrol with engineers and cut down the offending tree as we had originally intended. We both agreed that there could be no other reasonable course of action to this incident. The United States had to go in and do what we had originally intended to do. To do anything less would be to demonstrate a lack of resolution and virtually invite North Korea to take further advantage of our perceived weakness with some further brazen incident. I had to explain to Stillwell, however, that I had assured the other members of the WSAG that the JCS would not make any preliminary moves that could be considered threatening or provocative without getting clearance from the president.

At noon on the nineteenth, the WSAG met in Secretary Clements's office in the Pentagon. Clements reiterated his position that the United States must avoid any provocative actions that might upset the North Koreans. He thought Stillwell's proposal, supported by the JCS, to send another patrol in to remove the offending foliage was too risky. We still did not know the underlying reason for the original North Korean reaction. So the discussion that afternoon examined other alternatives. Secretary Clements was being largely influenced by his aide, an Army lieutenant colonel who had served with the MPs in Panmunjom and therefore carried a great deal of weight. The lieutenant colonel suggested that we fill a body bag with napalm and have a helicopter drop it on the tree and then, using tracer ammunition, set it on fire and burn down the tree. The rationale was that we could eliminate the tree without having any U.S. ground forces enter the DMZ. The unorthodoxy of the scheme, the intrusion by a helicopter, and the use of napalm in the DMZ eventually caused his approach to be set aside by Clements, although it appealed to him as being "imaginative." As an alternative, Bill Clements turned to me and said, "Why don't we shoot one of your guided missiles from a ship at sea to take out the tree?" I explained to him that we didn't have a guided missile with the accuracy to take out a particular tree and there was just as good a chance it would take out a North Korean observation point as the offending poplar.

The meeting broke up late in the afternoon at an impasse. Supported by the JCS and Stillwell, I remained firm that our course of action, knowing only what we knew of North Korean intentions, should be to plan to reenter the DMZ with engineers and cut down the poplar tree with axes and chainsaws, providing a heavily armed escort of infantry, strong enough to protect the engineers long enough for them to do the job. That was our original intention and our right under the cease-fire agreement. We had previously gone in unarmed, and the North Koreans had chased us out and killed two U.S. Army officers in the process. To do anything less than our original plan would be a clear sign of lack of resolution bordering on irresponsibility. It would certainly be a capitulation to a blatant violation to the signed agreement and a crime of murder against the UN Forces by the North Koreans. Clements would not agree with this plan without further intelligence, feeling it was too risky. In his view, it invited an armed reaction by the North Koreans. In any case, he felt we should probably take no action until we could fathom the motivations and intentions of the North Koreans. Ambassador Habib, another distinguished public servant with whom I had worked successfully on many other occasions, had also taken the approach that we should do nothing until tempers had cooled off on both sides. He implied that his responsibility in the WASAG was to counsel restraint from rash decisions and precipitous action. I could only reply that unless the U.S. took action, and took it promptly, we would lose the initiative. To wait would give the North Koreans their desired opportunity to barrage us with rhetoric and threats that would somehow make it all our fault. We could not afford to lose this confrontation. Our reputation and our credibility depended upon our being resolute and unafraid to assert our rights.

On the morning of 20 August, I again had a long conversation with Dick Stillwell, who made an emotional appeal for immediate authority to send our troops into the DMZ to cut the tree down. He said the morale of his forces depended on it. They felt that, having been run out of the DMZ, where they had every right to be, it was a point of honor to return, prepared to fight if necessary, to carry out their mission. I reported to Stillwell the substance of yesterday's discussions at the WSAG, reassured him that the chiefs would do all they could to convince the National Command Authority that the only solution was to move quickly with our original plans. Stillwell was also convinced that there was little chance the North Koreans would react with armed force. It was only the unanticipated opportunity for a surprise attack with superior numbers that had led them to undertake the initial assault on the unarmed patrol. We both considered that the most dangerous course to follow was either to do nothing or to remove the tree by some other means than chopping it down with U.S. Army manpower. Any other action could demonstrate a weakness on the part of the United States, a lack of credibility in our willingness to fight in defense of our allies in South Korea.

Later in the morning of the twentieth, I again met again with Clements and Scowcroft. Ambassador Habib had essentially given his proxy to Clements and was attending the WSAG sessions only sporadically. As forcefully as possible I urged that he agree to propose to the president that we send an armed patrol in that afternoon (Korean time) and chop down the tree. To wait any longer would not only show weakness on our part but also surrender the initiative to the North Koreans, who might, in the absence of any reaction on our part, feel confident in taking some other outlandish action to further embarrass us. He again demurred making any firm recommendation to President Ford until we had better intelligence and a firmer appreciation of the North Koreans' intentions. I then asked him to allow us to present this alternative to the president as soon as we could arrange secure communications. We would explain to the president the division of the WSAG into two distinctly different views. Bill was perfectly agreeable to go forward with the two alternatives and to get presidential guidance as soon as possible.

Late that afternoon of the twentieth, the breakthrough occurred. Henry Kissinger called the JCS war room—where I was meeting with the Joint Staff—on a secure phone. He was sitting next to the president in the Convention Hall in Kansas City and wanted to hear the WSAG recommendations. He would then brief the president and we could expect an early decision. I explained the two different approaches that had divided the WSAG between the JCS and the theater commander on one side and the position of the acting secretaries of defense and state on the other. Secretary Kissinger responded immediately by saying, "I will recommend to the president that a heavily armed patrol be sent into the DMZ to cut down those trees with axes and chain saws. Hold the line while I get the president's answer."

Less than a minute later Kissinger was on the secure line again. "The President directs the Joint Chiefs of Staff to order the Theater Commander to proceed with his plan of going into the DMZ with the necessary protective force, and remove those trees," he said. "In doing so, he wants to be assured that all U.S. and UN forces in Korea will be alerted to respond to any reaction that the North Koreans might take in response to our operation."

I immediately informed the other chiefs and called Stillwell. It was agreed that the operation would take place at 1000 (2100 Washington time), which was then about four hours away. Stillwell said his people would be ready in every respect for any eventuality. I advised him that the JCS would be meeting in the war room with the acting secretary of defense present to monitor the operation, which had been nicknamed Paul Bunyan.

By 2100 on the evening of 20 August, the Joint Chiefs of Staff, plus the members of the Joint Staff who were associated with operations, had gathered in the war room. Acting Secretary of Defense Clements joined us, along with certain selected civilian members of the Office of the Secretary of Defense. We had General Stillwell on the loudspeaker telephone, and the large electronic charts in the war room were displaying the situation throughout the Pacific Command, Korea, and the DMZ. General Stillwell was airborne in his helicopter, which was to be his command post while directing the operation. He had put all of the military units in the UN command in DefCon 2, the highest condition of readiness short of general war. Ammunition had been broken out and distributed to the troops, all of whom were in full battle gear with helmets, armored vests, and weapons at the ready. A U.S. Army infantry division, backed up by an ROK division, had been moved into fighting positions just south of the DMZ so that if any enemy troops broke through the DMZ they would be covered by heavy weapons fire. Spotting planes and command helicopter were overhead and communications had been tested and contact established among all units. The combat units in the reserve marshaling areas were equally ready.

Dick Stillwell reported that his troops were ready to go, and morale could not be higher. He reassured the chiefs that he was still firm in his conviction that there would be no belligerent action on the part of the North Koreans but that he was also fully prepared to respond appropriately to any hostile reactions by the North Koreans. As H-hour approached, the tension in the JCS war room was tangible. The North Koreans had given no hint of what their reaction might be. We were presuming they wouldn't start shooting, but we were also aware of the unpredictability of these strange people, and the possibility that a nervous trigger finger might start a firefight. On the dot of H-hour, 1000 Korean time, the engineers, along with their protective patrol of about three hundred American soldiers in armored vests and with heavy automatic weapons, entered the DMZ. They went directly to the poplar tree, and as the infantrymen set up in a defensive perimeter, the engineers turned to with their chainsaws and cut down the tree in about twenty minutes. Then the group marched out of the DMZ.

How did the North Koreans react when out patrol entered the DMZ? A large number of North Korean troops had gathered along the fence on their side of the DMZ and in their observation posts. However, they were not in military formation, nor did any of them display a weapon. They were all obviously unarmed. It was clear that the North Koreans did not want to start an incident and were being careful not to be misunderstood as being aggressive.

Secretary Clements was pleased with the outcome. He was impressed with how smoothly the Joint Staff had worked and with the close coordination between the JCS Command Center in Washington and the forces in the field. It was a good lesson, too, for the number of civilians from the OSD staff who were present to see how a military operation works in the U.S. Military Command system. The force commanders in the field conduct the operations and the JCS is kept informed. If help is needed, or if events go awry, the full support of the Department of Defense is available to the theater commander. In a matter of two hours the business was all wrapped up: The F-111s were prepared to fly back across the Pacific to their U.S. bases, the squadron of F-4 Phantoms would leave the next morning for Okinawa, the B-52s would have completed their training flights on the South Korean bombing range, and the *Midway* and its cruisers and destroyers would return to Japan for a port visit in Yokosuka and liberty in Tokyo.

By the next day there were no tag ends in Washington. The president and Secretary Kissinger had been informed of the resolution of the incident. There was little left to do except to write a report and be prepared to brief the president in detail upon their return to the White House.

As a footnote, twenty-five years later, the Korean national television corporation in Seoul contacted me to request an interview on my role in the " tree chopping" incident. The producer explained that the Korean people still considered this episode the major crisis in their post–Korean War history. Gen. Dick Stillwell had very generously attributed much of the credit for the favorable outcome of the event to the steadfastness of the JCS and the acting chairman. The producer for the program came from Korea to the U.S. with his staff to film a two hour segment in my living room. Their deep appreciation for the strong support of their U.S. allies was openly evident and unmistakably sincere.

KISSINGER AND THE CRUISE MISSILE

In early 1976, President Gerald Ford was running hard for renomination and facing a very strong challenge from Ronald Reagan. He was very anxious to consummate some sort of a SALT II agreement to show progress in his administration for arms limitation. At that time, Henry Kissinger was in Europe negotiating with the Soviets on these issues and Kissinger cabled back from Vienna the outlines of a new treaty to which he had tentatively agreed. This agreement would ban the deployment of the U.S. Tomahawk missile on submarines and limit its deployment on surface ships to only ten cruisers with ten Tomahawks each.

Kissinger had previously sent the outline of this agreement to the Pentagon for comment. Secretary of Defense Donald Rumsfeld and Chairman of the JCS Gen. George S. Brown both indicated their agreement by initialing the draft. General Brown had previously shared this information with me, aware that the Navy was the principal service affected. I told him that the Navy would definitely oppose such an agreement, as Tomahawk was very important in the future plans of the Navy. It was essential to provide our submarines, cruisers, and destroyers with standoff weapons. This was absolutely necessary to provide them with an offensive capability into the twenty-first century and thus extend their useful life in the fleet.

I told General Brown—and this was in my authority as a member of the JCS—that I wanted a meeting of the chiefs to review this proposal and to develop a formal position for the JCS, with all of the members participating. Brown agreed to call a meeting of the chiefs to get a JCS position on the cruise missile before the proposal went to the NSC for a final decision.

However, before that meeting could occur, both General Brown and Secretary Rumsfeld left Washington to attend a NATO ministerial meeting in Oslo, Norway. It was at that juncture that the president called a meeting of the National Security Council (NSC) to formally review Kissinger's proposed agreement. In the absence of the secretary of defense and the chairman of the JCS, Deputy Secretary of Defense Bill Clements and I, as acting chairman, attended.

The announcement of the NSC meeting came on very short notice, and I had less than an hour to prepare myself before going to the White House. I immediately tried to call all the chiefs, but I could locate only Gen. Lou Wilson, the commandant of the Marine Corps. He felt we should not agree to treaty without a formal review by the Joint Staff and a meeting of the JCS. Armed with this backing, I went off to represent the Joint Chiefs of Staff in a NSC meeting chaired by the president.

President Ford first spoke to the council very much in favor of the proposal, remarking on the fortunate political timing of the agreement. Then the president went around the table, asking each representative for his position. I was under tremendous pressure. All of the other members of the National Security Council, as they were queried, were voting in favor of the Kissinger agreement. I was one of the last members the president called on, and he probably expected me to echo General Brown's position. But George Brown had not brought the matter before the Joint Chiefs of Staff, so by initialing the proposal, he was only expressing his personal position, not that of the chiefs. I replied that I was aware of the president's desire for a SALT agreement, and how important it was to the nation that we have one. But in representing the chiefs, I had to say that our responsibility was to secure the SALT agreement that was best for the security of the nation, both now and in the future, and that I was persuaded that this was an unbalanced agreement in that we were giving up a tremendous military capability in the cruise missile for a transient reduction in throw-weight on the part of the Soviets. I was convinced that the potential for the cruise missile in the U.S. Navy was virtually unlimited. We saw it as the principal weapon of the future for our cruisers, destroyers, and submarines and were considering an airborne version for use by carrier aircraft. I added that, given an opportunity to review the treaty, the JCS would not recommend it be accepted.

The president was obviously upset. But he was honest and in his reply said, "Admiral, I asked for your view and you gave it to me, but I want you to think about it very carefully, because this is a vitally important decision we are making today." I replied that there was no question in my mind that the chiefs would not be in favor of it, but I pointed out that he, the president, had to weigh the considerations from all aspects, including domestic politics, the views of our allies, and the reaction of the USSR. "You can certainly make the decision to go with this agreement with the chiefs registering their disagreement," I said. "It is a presidential decision. If you say it will be done, the treaty will be approved by the NSC. But in the ratification of the treaty in Congress, the chiefs will be called upon for their views. It is the responsibility of each member of the Joint Chiefs of Staff to give his personal opinion, and the chiefs will have to say we disagree, and that we advised the president of our disagreement."

The president then said, "We have everybody in the room voting for it, except for the Joint Chiefs of Staff. But I have to say, I will not go against the judgment of the JCS in matters such as this. Jim, will you go back and meet with your colleagues and discuss this with them again, and make sure you are accurately representing their position. We will reconvene the NSC meeting at four o'clock this afternoon."

When I arrived at the Pentagon, the other chiefs were standing on the front steps of the River Entrance to meet me, and we immediately went into executive session in the tank. The chiefs, to a man, were very positive in their position that we should not give up the cruise missile for the tradeoff that was offered in the proposal. I also believe that they were equally glad that they were not the messenger who had to convey this position personally to the president of the United States and his assembled National Security Council.

At the 1600 White House NSC meeting, I reiterated the fact that the chiefs were unanimous in recommending in the strongest terms that the president not agree to this proposal. So the NSC meeting was adjourned and the NSC staff was directed to send a message to Secretary Kissinger that the Joint Chiefs of Staff were opposed to the agreement, and that the president had decided he could not agree to the proposal without JCS support.

As you can imagine, I was not very popular at that time. The only people who told me that I did the right thing were Fred Ikle, who was the head of the Arms Control and Disarmament Agency, and his deputy, John Lehman, who was eventually to become the secretary of the navy. Lehman discusses this incident in some detail in his book, *Command of the Sea.*

As a sequel to this story, many years later, in 1988, I was a member of the Commission for a Long Term Integrated Strategy, along with Henry Kissinger, among others. During one of our meetings, Kissinger said to me privately, "Admiral, at one time I was very mad at you." And I knew he was referring to the cruise missile incident. I said, "Mr. Secretary, I know you were, but we all have to do what we have to do." He chuckled and said, "Well I'm not sure the decision wasn't the right one."

The Tomahawk cruise missile has become the most important weapon in the arsenal of the U.S. Navy's surface combatants, destroyers, and cruisers as well as in all attack submarines. Ballistic missile submarines are being modified to remove their Trident missiles and replace them with Tomahawks. It is effective against ship and land targets. Modern warships carry up to eighty of these missiles in vertical launchers. During the U.S. campaign in Afghanistan, the submarines, destroyers, and cruisers of the Fifth Fleet, operating off the coast of Pakistan in the Arabian Sea, fired 176 Tomahawks in the first hour of the war against targets in Afghanistan with 90 percent effectiveness, paving the way for the carrier strikes and the airborne assault. In the "shock and awe" phase of Operation Iraqi Freedom, 250 cruise missiles were fired into Iraq from the Fifth Fleet submarines and surface warships.

PRESIDENT CARTER AND NUKES

In 1977 Jimmy Carter won a closely contested election for the presidency, defeating Gerald Ford for reelection. After the election but before the inauguration, President-elect Carter came to Washington and stayed in Blair House, the guest house for the White House, for briefings preparatory to taking over. From the moment of swearing the oath of office, a new president is immediately responsible for the most important national security authority the president holds, the release authority for nuclear weapons. Jimmy Carter had not served in the federal government prior to this election and was not entirely familiar with the national security structure and the details of the lines of authority. Further, although many considered him knowledgeable in military matters because of his graduation from the Naval Academy and his service on active duty, his assignments had been at such a low echelon that Carter was limited in his knowledge of how the military command and control functioned—or even the Navy beyond the hull of a submarine.

Carter had attended the U.S. Naval Academy in Annapolis during the war years, from 1943 to 1946. After graduation he served aboard two obsolete battleships, the *Wyoming* and the *Mississippi*, which had been converted to training ships and operated generally within the Chesapeake Bay. After his obligatory two years in surface ships, Carter applied for and was accepted for Naval Submarine School in New London, Connecticut, where he graduated number two in his class after the six-month course. In December 1948 he was assigned to the diesel submarine *Pomfret* operating with the Pacific Fleet. In 1951 Lieutenant (j.g.) Carter was transferred to the USS *K-1*, a small, experimental training submarine (as distinguished from a "fleet boat"), where he served as XO and chief engineer. In 1952 he was selected by Rear Adm. Hyman G. Rickover for the Navy's nuclear-power program and reported to Washington to assist in the design and development of nuclear propulsion plants for naval vessels. He had been routinely promoted to the rank of lieutenant and was setting up a training program for the enlisted men of the nuclear submarine *Seawolf*, when, in October 1953, he resigned from the Navy to manage the family's farm in Plains, Georgia. So although he had served seven years as a commissioned officer in the regular Navy, his sea duty in an operational fleet assignment lasted less than a year.

Consequently, the Ford administration felt that it was important that Carter be briefed and instructed in high-level matters of national military command and control before he took over as president and would be responsible for exercising the decisions on the release of nuclear weapons in the event of a nuclear threat to the United States. At the same time, President-elect Carter had expressed a desire to have a meeting with the Joint Chiefs of Staff after having been briefed on the National Command and Control System and presidential responsibilities by a member of the National Security Council.

The meeting took place on a Tuesday morning in the conference room at Blair House. Accompanying Carter were his prospective secretary of defense, Harold Brown, an experienced defense public servant who had served as secretary of the air force and director of defense research and engineering under a previous Democratic administration. Also with Carter was Zbigniew Brzezinski, who would be President Carter's national security advisor. On the other side of the table were Gen. George Brown, chairman of the JCS; the chief of staff of the Air Force, Gen. David C. Jones; the vice chief of staff of the Army, Gen. Dutch Kerwin; the CNO (myself); and the commandant of the Marine Corps, Gen. Lou Wilson.

Carter lost no time in getting to the reason for our meeting. He explained that he had been very concerned when governor of Georgia over the confrontation between the Soviet Union and the United States, particularly over the possibility of a nuclear exchange between the two superpowers, which potentially could destroy both nations. He believed that something had to be done to reduce the possibility of an inadvertent release of weapons by one side that would then immediately trigger a massive response by the other. He considered that the only way to improve the safety of our two nations in this regard was if the national leadership took immediate initiatives to reduce the possibilities of nuclear warfare.

To that end, President-elect Carter said he had "called up Soviet premier Leonid Brezhnev on a pay phone to discuss this matter with him in a citizen-to-citizen relationship." Brezhnev had returned the call, and a dialog between the two ensued. Both Carter and Brezhnev had agreed that the only solution was the total elimination of nuclear weapons from the inventories of the two superpowers, and they further agreed that such an action could be initiated if Carter won the presidential election. Consequently, Carter had informed Brezhnev that if elected he would take steps to eliminate all nuclear weapons in United States' arsenal by the end of his first four-year term, if Brezhnev would undertake to do the same thing with the Russian stockpile. Apparently Brezhnev had agreed and President Carter was informing the members of the Joint Chiefs of Staff that this would be an early initiative of the new administration's national security agenda. Of course, the chiefs would be involved in the reductions, but also he expected the JCS to revise their war planning to be able to conduct the necessary operations to defend the United States and carry out our military war plans without the same reliance on nuclear weapons in the deployment of forces and resources. Clearly, Jimmy Carter was not aware of the degree to which the use of nuclear weapons or, more important, the threatened use of nuclear weapons was in our national security planning contingencies with the Soviet Union and its Warsaw Pact allies.

President Carter then asked me about the status of the ballistic missile submarine force and its security, and the detectability of Soviet strategic submarines. I presented the picture in general terms, pointing out that we believed that our missile boats were usually undetected on patrol by the Soviets, whereas we had gotten to the point that we were able to covertly trail the Soviet submarines but not on a regular basis. Nor were we confident that we had detected and knew the location of all of their deployed ballistic missile subs. After some rather desultory and profoundly technical discussion of underwater sound propagation, during which Carter made extensive computations in pencil on his lined pad, none of which any of the chiefs understood, the meeting broke up at 1115. Carter had done most of the talking, mainly briefing the JCS on his plans concerning nuclear weapons. Throughout the meeting Carter was most cordial and took the advantage of several opportunities to tell the chiefs that he intended to work very closely with the JCS in all matters of national security, would like to meet with us at least monthly. Among other things, he would like to conduct drills exercising the release of nuclear weapons, something that we should practice, he said, until they had all been removed. After the session ended, George Brown asked the chiefs to meet in the "tank" when we returned to the Pentagon to discuss the president's comments.

There was not much to say, except we believed that Jimmy Carter could not have realized how extensively our war plans were permeated with both the use of nuclear weapons and, more important, the threat of the use of nuclear weapons in our confrontations with the Soviet Union and its Warsaw Pact allies. In retrospect, I don't believe any of the uniformed people at that session felt overly critical of Carter for his compelling desire to eliminate nuclear weapons. I am sure we all agreed that the world would be better without them. But how to get the genie back in the bottle? It was too late. Both we and the Russians were far too deeply committed to completely disarm without inviting an unthinkable catastrophe if the Soviets cheated. I must admit that at the time I considered Carter rather naive in his simplistic approach to an impossibly complex issue. The experience was simply an example of what career military officers must often face in their dealings with senior civilians, elected or appointed from civilian life to exercise "civilian control" over the military establishment. After the initial shock at some impracticality proposed by the civilian leadership, there is usually a period of education and reflection, and then more reasonable courses of action evolve, usually without any further reference to the bizarre opening postulation.

President Carter was quick to learn in the area of nuclear weapons, and he became heavily involved in the command and control of their release. He set up briefings with the JCS in the White House and attended command post exercises in the Pentagon to rehearse the procedures for the control of nuclear weapons. It is worth noting that in June 1979, President Carter sat down in Vienna with Leonid Brezhnev to sign the treaty that resulted from the second round of Strategic Arms Limitation Talks (SALT II) between the United States and the Soviet Union. SALT II, which lasted from 1972 to 1979, sought to curtail the deployment of nuclear weapons and was a continuation of the SALT I talks initiated in Helsinki, Finland, in 1969.

22

Elder Statesman

On 30 June 1974 I turned over my duties as chief of naval operations of the U.S. Navy to Admiral Hayward in a traditional ceremony at the United States Naval Academy. The proceedings were right out of the *Landing Force Manual,* which both Tom and I wanted, rather than one of the choreographed affairs that are more like family reunions than a military evolution.

Secretary of the Navy Graham Claytor was the senior official present, and the participation of this distinguished gentleman and very much admired public servant brought dignity to the ceremony. Secretary Claytor had been selected for secretary of the navy on the basis of his distinction as a railroad utilities executive. I considered Claytor a good friend, and we enjoyed a warm and understanding relationship. He had served as a line officer in the Navy in World War II in destroyer escorts and had come away from his active-duty days with a feeling of respect for the officers with whom he had served and an appreciation of the character of the U.S. Navy. I sometimes felt that he was disturbed by some of President Carter's eccentricities as far as the military was concerned, but he was a loyal team player and saw to it that Carter's and Secretary Harold Brown's policies were properly administered. As a result, the good relationship between the uniformed Navy and its secretariat remained both correct and cordial.

Following the ceremony, Dabney and I drove to Arlington in our "privately owned vehicle" to our home on Ridge Road, which my father had built as a commander in the Navy in 1936 on his first assignment in the Navy Department. I took a month off to "unwind without unraveling"—a phrase that Admiral Rickover in particular enjoyed. I purchased a thirty-eight-foot sailboat through my daughter, who was a yacht broker in Annapolis—a fancy deal that involved putting the boat in the charter service in the Virgin Islands with no money down. The added benefit was that the law allowed me to use the boat in the Caribbean for thirty days each year for cruising. That was the introduction to a hobby that was to provide enormous satisfaction for the next thirty-five years.

I was fifty-six years old when I retired, and I fully intended to have a second career in a full-time job, but in the acrid atmosphere of the post-Vietnam era, and the restrictive policies on military retirees "double-dipping" (employment in any sector of the defense industry during the next two years) or any semblance of lobbying, opportunities for a second career in an employment that I would consider appropriate and personally satisfying were pretty much eliminated. So in the first month after retirement my wife and I enjoyed a quiet, comfortable sojourn, enjoying the sailboat and building a new home in the woods and on the water in Annapolis, Maryland. Then came the time for public service.

THE NAVAL HISTORICAL FOUNDATION

In August 1978, I received a phone call from former CNO Adm. George Anderson, who was on the board of the Naval Historical Foundation (NHF), asking if I would serve as president of the organization under Adm. Arleigh Burke, who had agreed to take the chairmanship of the board. I demurred on the basis of being too busy, but when George asked, "Too busy doing what?" and pointed out that all retired senior officers were busy, I agreed to take the job. It turned out to be a truly satisfying experience, and I am still there as chairman to this day. The close association with the Naval Historical Center, the Navy Museum, and the Navy's historians reopened an old interest in history that I had largely set aside during my last ten years of active duty. With the NHF I found both the work and the people with whom I was associated to be most enjoyable.

ASSOCIATION OF NAVAL AVIATION

Less than a week later, Adm. Tom Moorer, former CNO and chairman of the Joint Chiefs of Staff, called to ask if I would relieve Adm. Mike Michaelis as president of the Association of Naval Aviation (ANA) under Moorer, who was then serving as chairman. Again my attempt to evade the draft was fruitless and again I committed myself to an organization to which I was deeply committed—and still enjoy in my role as chairman of the board emeritus.

The Association of Naval Aviation had been established in the early 1970s by Vice Admiral Pirie, under whom I had served in 1958 as executive assistant. Later Admiral Moorer as CNO, had been wholly supportive in ensuring that the ANA was on solid ground and created a fulfilling, well-defined need for an advocate's voice for naval aviation in the nonmilitary environment.

The association was effectively organized and professionally managed, with offices in the Hilltop section of Falls Church, Virginia, and a full-time compensated executive director, a very able retired naval aviation captain who was responsible, in a large way, for the successful inauguration of this organization. In those days, the Association of Naval Aviation was remarkably productive, with a slick bimonthly magazine published by ANA with important material concerning naval aviation provided by the Pentagon in each issue, plus extensive news of the activities of the more than fifty local ANA "squadrons" around the country. Additionally, the foundation published an annual yearbook of naval aviation which was the compendium of facts and information about the state of naval aviation in the Navy that year, with individual articles prepared by senior active-duty and retired naval officers, including the CNO. The annual convention of ANA included a dinner that featured speakers of special significance, including President George H. W. Bush, who had been a charter member of ANA on the basis of his experience as a TBM carrier pilot in World War II. For more than two decades, the association has maintained a display in the Smithsonian Air and Space Museum that replicated a pilots' ready room on board an aircraft carrier. This was one of the more popular exhibits at the museum because of its concomitant utility as a theater.

Among the more spectacular projects of ANA was the association's sponsorship of the premiere of the movie *Top Gun* in 1985, a black-tie affair at the Kennedy Center in Washington, D.C., with the stars of the film (Tom Cruise and Kelly McGillis) in attendance, followed by a lavish reception in one of the hangars at National Airport (now Reagan International Airport). Drinks and a complete buffet dinner were served in the milieu of Navy planes—Tomcats, Intruders, and Hornets—on display.

I had played a substantive role in the creation, production, and premiering of this film. A Washington lawyer who represented Paramount Pictures in the capital, and a friend of mine through the Metropolitan Club, had given me a copy of the original script proposal for a movie about the Navy's air-to-air gunnery school, taken from an article in *Sunset* magazine. I wrote up a brief critique of the scenario, listing all of its inaccuracies and explaining why the Navy would never approve the script.

My comments got to the producers, Jerry Bruckheimer and Don Simpson, who after several iterations of my recommendations, decided to come to Washington to talk to me. For our initial session, I rounded up some especially impressive young naval aviators—including several former Vietnam prisoners of war and Vice President Bush's naval aide, a tall, clean cut, well-decorated F-14 pilot. He was known among his contemporaries as naval aviation's "Poster Boy." After a couple of sessions, the producers actually got excited about the idea of a movie featuring carrier aviation and the Navy's fighter school. When I brought Secretary of the Navy (SecNav) John Lehman into the discussions and captured his enthusiastic support, full cooperation of the U.S. Navy was assured.

Top Gun was the story of carrier fighter pilots going through the Navy's fighter tactics school in southern California, and it included a mini-air war with an unnamed Middle Eastern dictatorship, an interesting preview of real-life things to come. It was one of Tom Cruise's earliest hits and helped him on his way to stardom. In addition to the torrid plot and incredible aerial photography, the movie also produced several memorable popular songs, including "Take My Breath Away."

Top Gun was the number-one box office moneymaker in 1986, and the film's impact on the public was remarkable. Following the movie's release, the interest in Navy flight training virtually exploded. Applications from fully qualified candidates exceeded the available training quotas by 300 percent. SecNav John Lehman was able to get DoD authority to "bank" these applications and spread the input out over the next three years to assure a full input of top quality aviation candidates well into the future. My reward was a full-screen credit as "Technical Advisor" at the film's end.

In addition to this semiglamorous side of the Association of Naval Aviation, the organization was very effective in generating congressional action in 1980 to overturn President Carter's veto of the defense authorization bill, an action Carter had taken because it contained a *Nimitz*-class nuclear carrier. Congress overturned the veto, added a *Nimitz*-class carrier in their version of the authorization bill, and enacted that legislation over President Carter's objections. The Navy Office of Legislative Affairs largely credited that favorable congressional action to the briefings and written justifications prepared by the Association of Naval Aviation and distributed throughout the Congress to the members and their staffs.

THE DEFENSE SCIENCE BOARD ON V/STOL AIRCRAFT

In November 1979 Eugene Fubini, the chairman of the Defense Science Board, at the request of Secretary of Defense Harold Brown, established a task force to look into the potential for V/STOL aircraft in each of the military services. Of the twelve members on the task force, I was the only military officer, active or retired, in the group. This was obviously because of my interest in V/STOL demonstrated during the last two years of my active duty as CNO and several editorials on the subject that I had written in the Naval Institute *Proceedings* and other aerospace journals after retirement.

The final V/STOL task force report included only three significant conclusions. First, the services should continue with their ongoing helicopter development programs, which were providing state-of-the-art operational aircraft for the Army and Marine ground support missions and naval ASW platforms. Second, tilt-rotor technology for high-speed assault troop transport and search and rescue should be vigorously pursued. Third, the Marines should continue to develop a follow-on V/STOL tactical fighter to the Harrier. The report further suggested that V/STOL not be prosecuted on a broader, all-inclusive front to conserve resources and avoid the high-risk, low-payoff systems.

I was quite satisfied with these conclusions, because they would serve to dampen what I had considered, when I was CNO, the misguided enthusiasm in the Navy secretariat to promote V/STOL to replace all conventional aviation in the Navy. I believed the task force conclusions, which would restore the proper balance between naval requirements and the technological facts of life, were the best outcome that the Navy could hope for.

One remarkable comment was made in a minority view by one of our most distinguished task force members from academia. "The Navy," he said, "is putting the burden of safe landings on a pitching deck of a ship at sea on the aeronautical engineers by demanding the most delicate aeronautical responsiveness on the part of the airplane and engine at the most difficult part of the plane's flight regime—when it is slowed almost to the stall point. I recommend that the burden should be shifted to the ship designers and have a movable landing platform on the ship, that compensates for the motion of the sea!"

THE IRANIAN HOSTAGE RESCUE OPERATION

On the morning of 24 April 1980, Americans collectively picked up their morning newspapers to see a shocking headline: A U.S. military operation to free the diplomatic hostages confined in the U.S. Embassy in Teheran, Iran, had collapsed in a fiery debacle in the remote deserts of Southwest Asia. The news was especially stunning because only a handful of people, Iranian as well as American, were aware that such an operation had even been planned. I, for one, certainly did not, yet within weeks I would be recalled to active duty and report to the Joint Chiefs of Staff to conduct the investigation of the failed operation for the Department of Defense.

The U.S. Embassy in Teheran, Iran, had been seized on 4 November 1979. The JCS immediately started work on contingency planning to rescue the hostages. There was no readily apparent solution other then declaring war and launching a major military operation that could penetrate to the heart of Iran, rescue the hostages, and then try to get out. The chances of the hostages still being alive when—and if—we found them, were minuscule.

A total of fifty-three Americans were incarcerated in the embassy, and three, including the U.S. chargé d'affaires, were being held in the Iranian Ministry. It was not until March 1980 that a feasible plan with some reasonable chance of success was put together. The plan was based on the use of a dedicated aircraft carrier, the USS *Nimitz*. Eight CH-53 helicopters would launch from the Navy carrier in the Indian Ocean at night in radio silence. With no lights, they could fly below Iranian radar to a remote spot in the Iranian desert south of Teheran, about six hundred miles away. At the same time, six C-130s would fly from Masirah Island off Oman to this desert rendezvous spot designated Desert One.

Three C-130s would carry the 130 members of the ground force, about 90 Delta Force (specialized operations troops) and about 40 support personnel. The other three C-130s would carry fuel for the CH-53 helicopters. During the hours of darkness on 24 April, the C-130s would refuel the helicopters and the Delta Force would embark in them. Eight helicopters were prepositioned aboard the carrier *Nimitz* (a minimum of six were required to accomplish the mission). After refueling and loading the troops, the helicopter contingent would proceed north to a "Hide Site" near Garmsar, about sixty-five miles southeast of Teheran, where the troops would be landed. The helicopters would then move on to a second hiding place nearby. The helicopters and the ground forces would remain hidden during the day of the twenty-fifth, and the C-130s would fly from Desert One back to Masirah that night.

During the predawn and morning of the twenty-sixth, the Delta Force would be picked up at the Hide Site and transported in closed trucks chartered by secret agents in Teheran and driven to the vicinity of the embassy compound. There the Delta Force would assault the compound, rescue the hostages, and move on foot to a nearby soccer field. Then the CH-53 helicopters, flying from the Hide Site, would pick up the Delta Force and freed hostages and take them to Manyariyeh, an abandoned Iranian airstrip to the west of Tehran. Meanwhile, a force of U.S. Army Rangers, transported in C-141 aircraft, would have seized the abandoned airstrip. The Delta Force and hostages would transfer to the C-141s and be evacuated with the Rangers. The CH-53 helicopters would be abandoned and destroyed.

Unfortunately, things didn't work out that way. Two helicopters were forced to turn back due to mechanical difficulties between the carrier and Desert One. A third helicopter was found to have a total hydraulic failure at Desert One. An ad hoc decision was made to reembark the troops, return to Masirah, and have the helicopters return to the *Nimitz* and reprogram the effort for the following evening. While refueling one of the helicopters, a collision occurred resulting in a fire and explosion, and all of the helicopters and one C-130 were destroyed or badly damaged and had to be abandoned.

Although U.S. citizens had to presume that a rescue attempt was being planned, there had been no leaks of this expedition, and the first news of a military operation into Iran hit the morning papers on the twenty-fourth. The news reports accurately reported that a major rescue attempt had failed because of a breakdown in helicopters and a crash in the desert. They made it clear that the mission had been aborted with some loss of life after the fiery collision in the desert between a troop helicopter and a C-130 tanker.

With an operation of this size, under the direction of the chairman of the JCS and the personal oversight of the president, the prestige of the nation was at stake. Such a disaster was bound to ignite a firestorm of public indignation and demand for an explanation by the White House of the cause of the failure. However, the answers were not forthcoming. It was difficult to pinpoint the real cause of the abort and the ensuing disaster at Desert One. To analyze the operation and to determine the causes of the failures, the DoD ordered formation of the Special Operations Review Group, to be supported by the Joint Staff. With typical efficiency, the JS had put together an organization for the review group, appointed a chairman—myself—named the six principal members of the group, and ordered in a supporting staff from the JS organization. There would be minimum time in which to conduct the review and produce a report as there was great pressure from the White House to move rapidly. The report of the Special Operations Review Group would be the first official statement made concerning what had really occurred during the operation. The public, stimulated by the media, were pressing for answers on a daily basis. I agreed with the Joint Staff that by working our group six days a week plus overtime, and with open-ended support from the JS, we could produce a comprehensive report for the JCS in two months.

The review group itself consisted of six senior officers, with myself and two retired lieutenant generals from the Army and the Air Force—both with extensive experience in intelligence and special operations—

and three active-duty general officers assigned to represent the three services. They were Maj. Gen. James C. Smith, USA; Maj. Gen. John L. Piotrowski, USAF; and Maj. Gen. Alfred M. Gray Jr., USMC. All of these were absolutely topnotch officers. The Joint Chiefs of Staff had fulfilled their obligation to give us the finest support available.

By late July the investigation had been completed and a comprehensive analysis performed. I had assumed for myself the responsibility of drafting the conclusions, based upon the recommendations of the other officers in the review group. There were two general conclusions. The principal conclusion was frankly critical of the planning process, specifically the chairman's decision to conduct the planning with an ad hoc organization outside of the JCS structure. The conclusion also faulted the secretary of defense for not exercising the adequate oversight expected of the National Command Authority in allowing this faulty planning process to go on for several months before the JCS and the Joint Staff were brought in—as should have been from the beginning. Although this lapse in judgment concerning the planning process did not have a direct impact on the aborted helicopter extraction and the crash on the desert, it did delay the entire operation, and it demonstrated that too much secrecy in the guise of OpSec (Operational Security) would exclude certain very senior and experienced officers in the military structure with key responsibilities—such as the theater commanders—who would be involved in the execution of such an operation. The Operations Review Group considered that this failure to utilize the organization within the DoD and the JCS, and an attempt to plan such a complex operation with grossly inadequate planning resources, was a dangerous precedent and should be highlighted to prevent, insofar as possible, such a lapse from being repeated in a future situation.

In drafting this conclusion, I did not try to soften the criticism but was straightforward as to exactly what the faulty actions were, the problems they caused, and who was responsible for those decisions. I knew that the press in these cases was prone to accuse military officers investigating their comrades in uniform of a "whitewash." I felt we owed it to our colleagues to be scrupulously honest.

The draft conclusions were circulated to the members of the review group for their concurrence or comments. One of the retired officers initially declined to sign because of the critical nature of the conclusions. But he eventually came around when he became aware of the positive attitude of the three active-duty major generals.

Al Gray, John Piotrowski, and Jim Smith, as a group, had come to see me privately in my office. Gen. Al Gray acted as their spokesman. His words went something like this: "We fully agree with the recommendations found by our group and the way you have expressed these views in your draft. We are all ready to sign this report, but we want you to know that we do it knowing that this will probably be the end of our military careers. We are criticizing the chairman of the JCS and the secretary of defense, and although it is important to make the point clear in the general conclusion, we recognize that this could make life very difficult for us in the future. But we are all ready to sign the smooth copy of the conclusions and recommendations as soon as they are ready, and we do it on our own free will, without any reservation and in full agreement with the wording." With that, the three generals left the office without giving me a chance to say anything. This was probably for the best. It would have been hard for me to know what I could have said to adequately express my appreciation for their integrity.

There was, however, a happy ending. The generals' fears did not materialize. Al Gray went on to become a distinguished commandant of the Marine Corps. John Piotrowski's career included promotion to four stars and service both as head of the Air Force Materiel Command and as commander of the Space Command in a position of joint responsibility. Jim Smith also continued his illustrious career as an Army aviator.

THE PRESIDENT'S TASK FORCE ON COMBATING TERRORISM

The night of 10 October was black and moonless, as the Egypt Air Boeing jet 737 cruised along the coast of Crete at thirty-six thousand feet, en route from Cairo to Tunis. Suddenly the navigation running lights of seven U.S. Navy F-14 fighters blinked on in a circle around the airliner. The Egyptian pilots, who had thought they were alone in the sky, were startled and confused—until the F-14s rocked their wings, the international signal to "follow me and land." The Egypt Air 737 was escorted to the U.S. Naval Air Station at Sigonella, Italy, and forced to land. As the passengers were disembarked, among them were the Arab terrorists who had hijacked the cruise ship *Achille Lauro* and killed an American passenger. They were immediately taken into custody. They had expected to be landing in Tunis, where they would have disappeared in the Casbah and escaped arrest and trial for their hijacking and murder. The entire action had taken seven hours from the Tomcats' launch from the carrier *Saratoga* to their landing back on board, without at any time leaving international waters or airspace.

The mastermind of the coup had been Vice Adm. John Poindexter, the national security advisor to President Reagan. At that time, I was also attached to the White House staff as executive director of the President's Task Force on Combating Terrorism. John and I had discussed in very general terms the feasibility of such an operation just several days earlier. The essence of the plan was to conduct the entire mission in international waters and airspace to eliminate any requirement to obtain permission from a host nation to preclude a turndown or a leak that would have alerted the airliner.

The Tomcats were from Fighter Squadrons VF-74 and VF-103 assigned to the USS *Saratoga*, which was on a routine forward deployment to the Sixth Fleet in the Mediterranean. The intercept of the airliner had been run by an E-2C radar aircraft also launched from the *Saratoga*, as were the two A-6 tankers that refueled the flights during their seven-hour mission. As a footnote, Poindexter's son Alan, a naval aviator and now an astronaut in Houston, won the all-Navy award as best F-14 pilot in the fleet as a lieutenant (j.g.).

This extremely complicated operation, conducted on short notice, with assets available in the fleet on a routine forward deployment, and using regular fleet pilots—as opposed to special operations specialists—was the perfect example of the broad capabilities of the Navy. It illustrated how effective naval forces can be at all levels of conflict from general war to the twilight campaigns of terrorism.

This would be an important lesson for the President's Task Force on Combating Terrorism. The task force had been created in the summer of 1985 by President Reagan, largely as the result of the frustrations growing out of our efforts to respond to the hijacking of TWA Flight 847.

To be certain that all appropriate government resources were properly focused on combating the threat of terrorism, President Reagan had appointed Vice President George H. W. Bush to chair a government-wide task force to review and evaluate the effectiveness of U.S. policies and programs in this area. Terrorism was a relatively new threat to Americans, and until this time our response had largely been one of reacting on a step-by-step basis as incidents occurred. The creation of the task force provided the opportunity to review and shake down the system in an orderly and controlled fashion, without in any way interfering with ongoing capabilities to deal with the threat strategically or tactically.

The task force was made up entirely of officials actively serving within the administration with responsibilities for terrorism programs—with one exception, and that was myself. The task force proper—I refer to these members as the principals—was chaired by the Vice President Bush and included the secretaries of state, treasury, defense, and transportation; the attorney general; the director of the FBI; the director of the CIA; the director of the Office of Management and Budget (OMB); the assistant to the president for national security affairs; the chairman of the JCS; the chief of staff to the president; and myself as the executive director.

Policy statements, recommendations to the president, and the final written report would be deliberated upon, reviewed, and ultimately approved by the principals. The investigative work was largely carried out by a staff working group made up of eight or nine middle-grade officers from the State Department, the CIA, and the military services.

The task force submitted its report to President Reagan before the end of calendar year 1985, as required by the president's instructions, and from it an unclassified report was subsequently published for public distribution. The original report to the president was classified top secret and had a very limited distribution.

Terrorism at that time was not out of control, at least insofar as the United States was concerned. However, even then, the threat of terrorism was of very deep concern to the president. We had to take steps then to develop the programs, forces, and intelligence systems that could prevent or eliminate the threat. If we wanted to keep terrorism under control, we had to stay ahead of the threat, which we saw as growing in both sophistication and intensity. Even at that time, trends indicated that Americans, both in this country and abroad, would be increasingly targeted in the future. There were several reasons for this, the most important of which is that terrorism is really warfare on the cheap. Ideological groups that want to do harm to the United States and its friends but cannot afford a formal war realize that they can hurt and embarrass the United States through terrorist acts.

The task force, early on, concluded that the best solution to the problem lay in having such good intelligence, and such effective reaction forces, that potential terrorist actions could be preempted before they could occur in such a quick and effective fashion that the damage is limited. We needed to improve our capabilities for dealing with terrorists to minimize the effectiveness of terrorism. There could be problems, however, in reacting to intelligence. To make public the fact that a terrorist plot had been discovered and preempted would, at best, expose our intelligence apparatus and, at worst, cause the loss of agents or capability. Intelligence sources need to be protected if success is to be sustained.

The task force also concluded that the new breed of terrorist was totally dedicated, absolutely ruthless, possessed of great animal cunning, and in many cases received the technical and financial support of a sovereign government. We decided that it should be the nation's objective to prevent terrorist acts and eliminate terrorism. But we also had to be realistic. We had to expect that regardless of how proficient we might become in a technical sense, the other side was going to score an occasional success. When this happened, we wanted to ensure that the American public knew the facts—that we had an effective system, that it worked most of the time, and that it was the best this country could have while still preserving our individual freedoms.

The task force felt very strongly that America had to work continually toward an international environment that largely eliminated—or at least reduced—the root causes of terrorism: intense hatred of the United States and its allies. Then we had to develop a reliable intelligence system that could penetrate the milieu of the terrorists to give us forewarning of their activities. Third, we had to have a command and control system that would enable us to take advantage of our intelligence to preempt or abort planned terrorist actions. And we had to have the trained reaction forces that could respond immediately and effectively to an incident after it occurred. Finally, we needed the international agreements and cooperation that would permit this country to use its assets and those of our friends for the preemption or the resolution of an international terrorist incident.

The interception of the Egyptian airliner was one of the most spectacular and effective counterterrorist measures in this ongoing contest with terrorism. The ability of carrier-based F-14s to single out and identify the target airliner from a stream of air traffic crossing the black Mediterranean skies borders on the unbelievable. It took enormous skill and discipline to accomplish it.

It is apparent that U.S. naval forces will continue to have a major role in reacting to terrorist incidents of the international category. The main reason is that the U.S. Navy can operate in, and over, international waters. The U.S. can intercept and seize both ships and aircraft in international waters without getting anyone's permission. The problem of getting permission of a third party, even a friendly government, has been a repeated stumbling block in attempting to react to international terrorist incidents with our own forces. Sovereign governments in general are simply not going to permit the use of U.S. armed forces or paramilitary forces on their soil. They are going to try to resolve the issue with their own units. Quite often these units are far less proficient than our own. In the case of the 1985 hijacking of TWA Flight 847, which precipitated the terrorism task force, there were several locations where the hijacked aircraft was vulnerable to a take-down, but the United States was unable to get permission from the airfield's host government to inject our own forces for that purpose. The same would apply for a port in which a hijacked ship was located. However, when ships or aircraft are on or over the high seas, the United States may employ its forces without having to get permission from any third party. Similarly, rescue or assault forces operating from afloat bases such as an aircraft carrier in international waters are much more liable to be committed by the U.S. government than those forced to base from foreign soil. It is very doubtful that any other nation, friendly or unfriendly, would agree to allow the U.S. military to fly from that other nation's military bases to conduct a punitive strike against a nation that had indulged in state-sponsored terrorism against the United States. On the other hand, a carrier-based strike from U.S. vessels located in international waters or a helicopter assault with Marines or commandos from floating bases in international waters is quite thinkable.

"DISCRIMINATE DETERRENCE"

In 1986, the secretary of defense asked the Honorable Fred Ikle to convene a commission of private citizens to develop a long-term integrated strategy for the period from 1990 to 2010. John Lehman, who was secretary of the Navy at that time, was instrumental in having me named a member of this commission. It would be within the context of this strategic philosophy and the world of the future it would forecast that our nuclear-powered carriers would be employed. Both the proposed strategy and the evolving politico-military environment envisioned over the next twenty years could forcefully argue for a maritime strategy. The collapse of our overseas basing structure, the emergence of militarily powerful Third World nations, and the proliferation of nuclear powers would all tend to drive the United States toward an increasing reliance on sea-based forces.

The commission itself, which was sponsored jointly by the secretary of defense and the national security advisor to the president, numbered only a dozen members. It contained no members active in the government except for Dr. Fred Ikle, the undersecretary of defense for policy, who served as the official link between the commission and the administration. The commissioners themselves were an unusually balanced representation. They included the Republican secretary of state and former presidential national security advisor Dr. Henry Kissinger, as well as his Democratic counterpart, Dr. Zbigniew Brzezinski. Other commissioners were distinguished non-defense civilians such as the Honorable Anne Armstrong and intellectuals such as Dr. Joshua Letterberg, a Nobel chemist. And then there were retired military officers like Gen. Jack Vessey, a former chairman of the Joint Chiefs of Staff, and myself, a former service chief.

Most strategic policy documents had dealt with a very limited time frame—the secretary of defense's annual posture statement, for example—

and seldom extended beyond the four years of a presidential term. "Discriminate Deterrence," the title of the commission's report, looked at a much longer time period—the next twenty years.

The strategy proposed by the commission was all-inclusive. It covered the spectrum of warfare, from low-intensity conflict to the general nuclear exchange. It explored the geopolitical and technological trends for twenty years into the future. It dealt with arms control as well as war fighting and proposed that both be considered together in an integrated approach to arms limitation policies.

"Discriminate Deterrence" received mixed reviews from the press. The *New York Times* conceded that the approach was sound and the principles valid. An extensive commentary by Public Broadcasting TV characterized the report as having the potential to be one of the most important strategic guideposts over the next decade. The European press was almost without exception supportive of the commission's report. The basis for the general acceptance appears to be not so much any revolutionary ideas—there were few of these—but the fact that it was a single, all-inclusive, coherent national security policy statement developed by a bipartisan group of diverse background but extensive experience in top-level national policy positions.

It was time for a new look at our national strategy, in spite of the fact that many critics of our defense establishment continued to allege that the United States had no coherent strategy. The truth is that we did have an established and operating strategy and that it had been successful and enduring. This strategy had been installed more than forty years before, and over that period there had been no Soviet military aggression against our NATO partners or our Korean or Japanese allies. It is interesting that this basic strategy had existed since the end of the Korean War essentially intact, with the only adjustments being made at the margins. This strategy had worked and worked well. All of our original alliance partners were still free nations.

Nevertheless, it was time for a reexamination of our basic strategic concepts. Some circumstances had changed. The United States had lost its nuclear advantage over the Soviet Union. The overseas base structure upon which our forward deployments had been so dependent had progressively eroded to become only a small fraction of our basing system that existed after World War II.

It is important to understand that the commission was developing a strategy and not programs—that is, a philosophy rather than a shopping list. In principle, the commission's recommended strategy emphasized this nation's strengths. It proposed that the United States place more emphasis on forces that are versatile, are provided with the most technologically advanced equipment, have the mobility to respond to crises around the globe without reliance on overseas bases, and are still be capable of military operations across the spectrum of warfare, from low-intensity conflict to nuclear operations. This thinking was reflected in remarkably similar terms in the most recent Defense Policy Guidance (DPG) that was issued in 2004.

"Discriminate Deterrence" developed broad concepts in the formulation of the overall strategy at the different levels of warfare intensity. In dealing with wars on the periphery, the commission recommended that the United States emphasize mobile forces, which would require making major improvements in our strategic lift capability, mainly sealift. The continuing decline of our overseas base structure was exerting increasing pressure to revise our strategy. The loss of land bases had to be compensated for, and the exploitation of strategic sea- and airlift was urged. Again, this concern has proved accurate, and DPG 2004 has as a primary focus the naval forces to compensate for these reversals through sea basing.

The commission was particularly sensitive to the need of a wider public recognition that the Persian Gulf is crucial to the free world's economy and security. It had to be made clear to the world that the United States' leadership as a matter of national policy considered the Persian Gulf critical to our most sensitive and important security interests and that the United States would be prepared to fight to maintain access to this vital area. Current international events have certainly been responsive to this recommendation.

Technologically, the United States must exploit its strength in the field of accurate long-range guided weapons. In this way, important economies could be achieved by improving existing platforms through equipping them with better arms. This concept was not new; it is really a refurbishment of the philosophy that has been around for some time: put the performance in the weapon rather than in the platform. However, our report did not intend to imply that the development of currently programmed ships and aircraft such as the CVN-21 class of carrier and the advanced tactical fighter should not proceed. The emphasis should be on reaching a reasonable balance between platform and missile performance. The very word "discriminate" in the title of the commission's report emphasized a continued reliance on manned systems. Even with the greatly expanded availability of long-range guided missiles, manned aircraft will continue to be essential in a future world of many powerful antagonists with complex alliances, where the rules of engagement will demand positive target identification to avoid starting bloody conflicts through error or miscalculation.

The recommendations of the commission were rational, workable, and therefore useful. Most of the conclusions subsequently found their way into the ever-evolving strategy of the Cold War and have endured as fundamental precepts in the current strategic philosophies. I considered this to be a testimonial to the commissioners themselves. Successful and distinguished public servants such as Kissinger and Brzezinski were not tempted by easy, cheap, sensational solutions. From their experience they could judge what would work and what was pie in the sky. Their views, and the experience of the retired military commissioners, largely prevailed. On the other hand, the professional staff sometimes appeared to be a preoccupation of the public's expectations of exciting new ideas rather than realistic, attainable solutions that would have a higher probability of success in providing security for the United States over the next twenty years.

Midway through our studies, a five-day retreat was scheduled to assess the progress achieved thus far and to adjust the compass for the remaining deliberations and final conclusions. When I made the observation that our conclusions could suggest a defense establishment and a strategic concept that was largely an extension of what we had in 1986, there was a reaction of disbelief and disappointment on the part of most of the professional staff and several of the commissioners. The reaction was, "We will have labored for two years and have nothing to show for it!" I was impelled at that juncture to point out that in the absence of a fundamental technological or political change, such as the invention of the atomic bomb or the collapse of the Soviet Union, any new strategic philosophy produced by a commission such as ours would have to be evolutionary rather than revolutionary. It was totally unreasonable to assume that the existing strategy would be found to be completely invalid. After all, it was the product of the constant updating, based upon real warfare and actual events, of a strategy that had served us well for forty years. As a government commission, could we invent an entirely new concept for our national security? No. Could we enhance the integration of science and international affairs into our national security planning? Yes. And I think we did.

I learned from studying nuclear power under Rickover that if it is cheap, easy, and painless it hasn't been invented yet and probably never will be.

23

The Future

For more than six decades, since the earliest days of World War II, the aircraft carrier has been the principal warship of the U.S. Navy, the fighting ship around which the U.S. Fleet has been constructed and organized. Over this time the carrier forces of our Navy have consistently demonstrated their invaluable worth as an instrument of national power, through which the military strategy of our country has been exercised in direct support of the nation's most vital security objectives.

In 2006 the United States was experiencing an epochal juncture in its history. A fresh concept of transformation in our armed forces had been installed, a new strategy of preemptive war introduced, the advanced technology of precision guided munitions was in our inventories and a revolutionary DPG, *From the Sea*, had been adopted. The aircraft carrier is an essential component in all of these seminal developments in a continuation of its central role in our defense planning and military operations. More important, however, the modern aircraft carrier brings a unique and singular array of new military capabilities to add to our national security planning options across the spectrum of future warfare.

The importance of the aircraft carrier in our nation's defense lies in the fact that the carrier is the only weapon system that can provide air power at sea; and the free use of the world's international waters will be in the future, as it has been for the past sixty years, an absolute essential to our national security strategies. World War II unequivocally established—and the campaigns of the Cold War fully substantiated—that in modern warfare, military success cannot be attained without general air supremacy and local air superiority in the area of potential engagement. It is the aircraft carrier's embarked air wings, along with the tactical fighter wings of the U.S. Air Force and Marine fixed-wing tactical squadrons, that are the warfighting components in the U.S. Order of Battle which are in our defense planning, responsible for insuring that in any conflicts, air supremacy will reside on the side of the United States and its allies.

More specifically, the aircraft carriers of the U.S. Navy are responsible for assuring that during military operations at sea and in littoral environments, the United States has local air superiority in the objective areas to enable other specialized fleet elements to carry out their assigned naval warfare tasks, such as projecting seaborne troops ashore in a hostile environment, clearing mines, and supplying gunfire support and antisubmarine defense. The naval ships that are engaged in these missions—cruisers, destroyers, mine hunters, and amphibious assault ships—must be defended against enemy air attacks. The carrier's aircraft must also silence hostile fire from the enemy forces ashore defending the lodgment area and then provide deep interdiction air strikes and close air support for our own assault forces fighting to seize a beachhead. In the forward areas where these operations take place, friendly, land-based air is not available. It must be assumed that the territory under assault is under enemy control. It is only after the Navy and Marines have established secure lodgment ashore that friendly, land-based air can be employed.

The essentiality of a capable-carrier force in the U.S. Navy is mandated by our national security philosophy, a forward strategy that

1. Uses the oceans as barriers in our defense and avenues for extending our influence abroad. In case of war, we intend to engage the enemy on his homeland rather than ours. Not since the Civil War have the American people suffered the depredation of enemy troops or even hostile bombardments of our homeland.
2. Rationalizes the geographic situation of the United States on the North American continent. We have only two international

borders, with Canada and Mexico. Neither of these nations represents a threat to our security. Yet two of our states, several of our territories, and all but two allies lie overseas.

3. Relies upon overseas allies such as NATO and Japan and forward-deployed forces such as Navy carrier and expeditionary strike groups in the international waters of the Mediterranean, Pacific, and Indian Oceans.

4. Exploits the inherent mobility of naval forces and the "ready on arrival" capability of predeployed carrier strike groups to react to an overseas crisis immediately with the desired option, across the full range of politico-military actions, from a show of force to all-out war.

5. Uses the freedom of international waters for the transit of naval forces and military logistics and to provide naval and air operating areas in the vicinity of potentially hostile situations without the need to request the penetration of the territory, or territorial waters, of another nation. Two-thirds of the surface of the earth is covered by international waters, and 90 percent of the world's population lives within the radius of tactical aircraft from carriers operating in international waters.

The United States' recent history of modern warfare clearly demonstrates the capabilities of our aircraft carriers through their record of achievement, ever since their emergence as the principal force in our Navy.

WORLD WAR II, KOREA, AND VIETNAM

In 1942 it was the fast carrier striking forces that led the Allied forces across the Pacific, defeating the Japanese in the Battle of Midway and in every subsequent engagement involving carriers. It was these victories, in which the surface combatants of the two navies never engaged one another, that provided the environment of air and naval supremacy to allow the amphibious seizure of the network of fortified islands upon which the Japanese had based their defense of the homeland.

The forward strategy of the Cold War proved its effectiveness, as the first significant air support for beleaguered U.S. and South Korean forces was provided by U.S. Navy carriers during the initial days of the North

Korean invasion, when all of the friendly, tactical airfields in South Korea were overrun by the enemy. In the course of the war, Navy and Marine aircraft flew almost 40 percent of the ground support missions—275,912 of the total 737,436 sorties in support of the ground forces. Of these, 106,494 were flown from the carriers in TF 77. Military historians are in overall agreement that allied air power could not alone have won the war in Korea, but without the almost total air superiority provided by U.S. tactical aircraft, the conflict would have been lost to the Chinese. The evacuation of the 1st Marine Division from the Chosin Reservoir could not have been possible without tactical air support. Most of that support came from naval aircraft of TF 77 off the East Coast and Marines from escort carriers of TG 98.6 off the west coast of Korea.

In 1964 the initial strikes against military targets in North Vietnam were by aircraft from U.S. carriers, which had been routinely deployed in theater in accordance with the forward strategy of the Cold War. These were the only U.S. tactical aircraft available to carry out the retaliatory attacks directed by President Johnson in response to the Tonkin Gulf incident. After 1972, when President Johnson decided to take all U.S. combatant ground troops, except for advisors, out of Vietnam, the only U.S. military forces in combat in Southeast Asia were Navy and Marine aviation and the U.S. Air Force. It was the overpowering, round-the-clock air assault against previously proscribed targets in the Hanoi-Haiphong area in Operation Linebacker II, the "Christmas Bombing," that forced the Communists to sue for peace and sign the Paris Accords to end America's war in Southeast Asia. Over the eight years of that conflict, naval carrier aircraft flew more than half of all the strike sorties against targets in North Vietnam.

LIBYA

Operation El Dorado Canyon, the U.S. air strike against terrorism-related targets in Gaddafi's Libyan dictatorship on 15 April 1986, was a textbook example of the effectiveness of the U.S. strategic policy of routinely deploying aircraft carriers to international waters around the world in the vicinity of potential trouble spots. Since the end of World War II, it had been a key element of our Defense Planning Guidance to maintain two aircraft carriers on station in the Mediterranean Sea. As a retaliatory preemptive attack in response to a blatant act of state sponsored terrorism, Operation El Dorado Canyon had to be prompt, powerful, and directed at the core of the Libyan leadership. Given this presidential concept of operations, El Dorado Canyon could only be implemented with the immediate availability of aircraft carriers in the objective area. Only carriers had the full complement of all-weather attack aircraft, air superiority fighters, antimissile attack planes, electronic warfare planes, airborne radar command and control aircraft, and combat SAR helicopters, all of which were required for a major strike operation against a variety of well-defended and dispersed target sets. Air Force F-111s based in the United Kingdom joined the carrier planes in the mission. When the government of France denied overflight clearances for the UK-based F-111s, their ingress path required the Air Force component to fly down the English Channel, access the Bay of Biscay, through the Straits of Gibraltar, and along the Mediterranean littoral before turning south to Libya. This added thirteen hundred additional miles to the F-111 track and about four hours additional flight time and required a total of 28 KC-10 and KC-135 tankers. The carrier aircraft had a distance of less than two hundred miles to their targets. The operation was executed as planned. The time over target was less than twelve minutes to deliver sixty tons of munitions. No Navy planes were lost. In Washington, Operation El Dorado Canyon was considered a complete success.

OPERATION DESERT STORM

Since the Cold War, carriers have been prominent in their contributions to U.S. combat operations in the Middle East. Operation Desert Shield began on 2 August 1990, when Saddam Hussein sent three divisions of his elite Republican Guard across the border to invade Kuwait; two U.S. carrier strike groups were on routine forward deployment in the vicinity, one in the Mediterranean Sea and another in the Indian Ocean. Three days later the *Independence* was in position to launch her air wing against the Iraqi combat division in Kuwait and moved unopposed into range of Iraqi dispositions threatening Saudi Arabia. On 7 August, when President Bush committed U.S. forces to the protection of Saudi Arabia, the effective U.S. combat presence in the theater consisted of two carrier battle groups with more than one hundred fighter and attack aircraft, fully ready to launch an armed strike against the Iraqi air and ground forces. The two air wings were, in themselves, capable of gaining air superiority over Kuwait. The movement of land-based aircraft into theater had begun immediately, with two squadrons of Air Force F-15 Eagles ferried from the U.S. directly to Saudi Arabia supported by Air Force tankers. The initial readiness of these units was delayed by the limited availability of air and sealift to bring logistics and ground support personnel into the Saudi airfields. On 6 August, Saddam paused at the Kuwaiti border, although the Saudi opposition would not be much more than the Iraqis had experienced in Kuwait. Hussein was probably deterred by the implied threat of opposition from the United States, with its two carrier battle groups in the area.

Desert Storm was the offensive military campaign of the coalition forces. During the campaign, the Iraqis were driven out of Kuwait and allied forces then entered Iraq to defeat the Iraqi army and force Saddam's surrender. The Desert Shield phase of the operation was the buildup of coalition forces in theater to levels of "overpowering military force." The air campaign preceding Desert Storm has been given much credit for the relatively easy victories on the ground and the minimum number of friendly casualties. Navy and Marine Corps aviators flew from carriers and amphibious ships in the Red Sea and Persian Gulf for the entire forty-three-day period of the war. A total of six carriers were engaged, four in the Persian Gulf and two in the Red Sea. Carrier planes struck targets up to seven hundred miles distant. Navy and Marine Corps planes flew more than thirty thousand of the ninety-four thousand U.S. sorties in the overall campaign, or about 35 percent, which closely matched the percentage of Navy and Marine aircraft in the combat forces participating in Desert Storm. This clearly established the capability of carriers to generate combat sorties at the same rate as land-based air, in addition to an ability to attain maximum sortie generation rates immediately upon arrival in the theater. From the beginning, the Navy concept of force multiplying through the concept of the F/A-18 strike fighter began to pay off. On "D day" of Operation Desert Storm, four Navy Hornets from VFA-81, embarked in the *Saratoga*, were on a bombing mission against an Iraqi airfield when they detected two Iraqi MiG-21s seven miles away. They switched their F/A-18 strike fighters from bombing profile to air-to-air and downed both Iraqi aircraft using

Sidewinder missiles. They then continued their mission and scored direct hits on the enemy airfield. That encounter demonstrated the versatile Hornet's dual-role capabilities.

KOSOVO

In March 1999 the battle group on routine forward deployment to the Sixth Fleet in the Mediterranean joined with NATO forces and mobilized for Operation Allied Force, attacking usurping Serb forces in Kosovo. Facing an arsenal of antiaircraft artillery, air-to-air missiles, and tactical fighters, all representative of first-line Russian weapons technology, the carrier *Theodore Roosevelt*'s air wing of F-18s, F-14s, and A-6s flew more than thirty-one hundred combat sorties for more than half of the campaign's total without the loss of a single aircraft.

OPERATION ENDURING FREEDOM

In the reaction of the United States to the September 11, 2001, Al Qaeda attack on the World Trade Center in New York City, the indispensable value of the aircraft carrier as a principal instrument of national power reached its height. It was only because of the readiness and flexibility of the carriers, which were on station, routinely deployed to the western Pacific and Indian Oceans, that the swift and powerful military reaction to this act of terrorism was possible. The nation's response to this surprise attack had to be immediate, forceful, and punitive to those responsible, with a minimum of collateral casualties. At stake was the United States' reputation as the world's superpower as well as deterrence of future terrorist attacks on the U.S. homeland.

To put conventional ground forces into Afghanistan to pursue and destroy these rebels would require fully developed port facilities and a buildup of major staging bases. This would take much too long for a swift and incisive reprisal. That meant an attack directly from bases at sea.

On 21 September President George W. Bush approved the concept of Operation Enduring Freedom, a campaign that would use Special Operations Forces on the ground supported by U.S. air power. That those aviation assets would have to be primarily carrier-based was clear. Fighters would be needed to gain control of the airspace in the battlefield area. The enemy was known to have Soviet-made fighters and surface-to-air missiles. These had to be destroyed before the vulnerable transport helicopters, carrying the SOF troops, could be committed. The first requirement of the campaign was to "remove the threat from air defenses and from Taliban aircraft." The ground campaign would not proceed until air superiority had been achieved. There were no land bases in the theater available to U.S. fighters. Only Navy carrier-based F-14s and F/A-18s could be placed within range of the intended battlefields.

How to deliver the Special Operations Forces with their helicopters and equipment into the theater remained a pressing concern. The normal procedure would have been to use commercial sealift ships. This, though, would require modern port facilities, but there were none with access to land-locked Afghanistan. So the Navy carrier *Kitty Hawk* was used as a transport and operating base for the invading forces. In fourteen days, the SOF component, Task Force Sword, consisting of twenty helicopters, six hundred troops, and 860,000 pounds of ammo and equipment, was loaded on board, and the *Kitty Hawk* was underway at flank speed for the Arabian Sea.

After the first two days of combat, most of the fixed targets suitable for cruise missiles had been eliminated. The Air Operations Center's highest priorities became the Navy strike fighters, backed up by small contingents of B-1s and B-52s based in-theater. The ready availability of the F/A-18s, and their ability to attack emergent targets assigned after arrival on station, made them particularly useful in the fluid ground situation. A total of six carriers and four Marine expeditionary groups formed the core of the Navy's contribution to Enduring Freedom. It was the Navy's carriers, with their special military capabilities, that actually enabled the National Command Authority to employ the concept of operations that proved to be so successful in Enduring Freedom. By March 2002, the Taliban had been defeated.

OPERATION IRAQI FREEDOM

Operation Iraqi Freedom began on March 21, 2003, when Naval Aviators flying from carriers helped to usher in a new era in tactical warfare, an increase in military capabilities ranking with the introduction of jet aircraft or stealth technology. Contributing to the "shock and awe" of the initial air strikes of the Iraqi Freedom campaign deep into Iraq were five aircraft carriers operating in the Mediterranean and Arabian seas, launching air wing–sized formations into the night to deliver bombs and missiles against key military targets in the Arab capital with a precision and effectiveness never before achieved by tactical combat aircraft.

This was history being made. It would be the first battle of a campaign in which precision guided bombs and missiles would be used by aircraft against the enemy to the virtual exclusion of unguided bombs. The attack on Saddam Hussein's sprawling capital deep in the heart of Iraq, defended by rings of surface-to-air missile batteries and waves of protective fighters, was the first battle of Iraqi Freedom. Nine out of every ten of the munitions carried by U.S. Navy and Air Force aircraft during this war were precision guided.

This was not the first time that airborne guided weapons had been used by American tactical aviation, but it was the first time that they had been employed almost exclusively in such a massive aerial bombardment campaign. The second historic aspect of this air campaign was the use of carrier aircraft at night, in numbers, formations, and tactics that previously could have been employed only in daylight operations. This was a significant breakthrough. Until now, the night had belonged to the unconventional forces, the irregulars, the guerrillas, and the terrorists. That is where their small numbers and furtive tactics gave them the advantage. It was American technology that reversed this situation with the Night Observation Device, or NOD, goggles worn by the pilot or infantryman, which turn night into day.

In the 1992 Gulf War the planners figured on flights of aircraft carrying *multiple* loads of unguided munitions to ensure the destruction of *single* enemy targets. In Iraqi Freedom, one tactical fighter had the capacity to destroy multiple targets, one target per guided bomb dropped. In Iraqi Freedom, when night vision goggles could be made available to most of the engaged troops on the ground and all of the tactical pilots in the air, a real breakthrough in close air support was realized. The ground observers not only could detect the movement of personnel in their area but also were able to identify them as fighters or civilians and locate their presence with an accuracy that was usable for the guidance of airborne guided weapons.

Airborne guided munitions, combined with night vision–equipped observers on the ground, have made the tactical fighters of the Navy, Marines, and Air Force, along with Army and Marine helicopters, weapons of choice in combating insurgents and terrorists. With a thirty-foot accuracy and three-hundred-foot destructive radius, seldom is more than one guided bomb needed to eliminate the enemy. In these cases the target is fleeting rather than fixed, and only air-launched weapons are truly effective. It would take an hour for a cruise missile to arrive from a ship at sea, and by then an enemy raiding force could have made their attack and dispersed. The aircraft-delivered bomb, however, arrives with no warning and collateral damage to homes in the neighborhood is a minimum.

THE NATIONAL MILITARY STRATEGY
FOR THE FUTURE

The military strategy for the United States that was promulgated in the 2001 Quadrennial Review came to be known as the "1-4-2-1 strategy" because it called for the Department of Defense to defend the homeland against external aggression as the number one priority (1); deter aggression and coercion in four critical regions—Europe, the Middle East, Southeast Asia, and Northeast Asia (4); swiftly defeat the efforts of adversaries in two overlapping wars while preserving the president's option to call for a decisive victory in one of those conflicts, including the possibility of regime change or occupation (2); and conduct a limited number of lesser contingency operations (1).

In DPG 2004 for the years 2005–9, the secretary of defense introduced the concept of "Sea Basing" as the planning guidance for the implementation of the 1-4-2-1 strategy. In planning forces for this strategy, the DPG sets forth three conditions:

1. Assume that there will be no logistic sites or other forms of land bases in the combat theater. The Navy will establish a sea base.
2. Logistic support for all U.S. military forces committed ashore will be supplied and supported from the Navy sea-base.
3. These sea-bases are intended to give the U.S. an independent, sovereign, and sustaining capability overseas, and they must be able to perform this function two thousand miles from the nearest land base under U.S. control.

To carry out the requirements of DPG 2004, the Navy has reorganized its operating forces through the Global Concept of Operations, which will depend upon two main combatant forces:

1. Eleven carrier strike groups, each organized around a large-deck carrier as its centerpiece.
2. Eight expeditionary strike groups, each with a large amphibious helicopter carrier as the main component, with embarked Marine infantry and their organic strike and transport aircraft.

The Navy additionally established the sea-basing capability around a fleet of thirty-eight modified commercial cargo ships organized into four prepositioned support squadrons, based at sea in international waters adjacent to the four sensitive areas set forth in the 1-4-2-1 strategy.

On 7 February 2006, the secretary of defense published the administration's 2007 defense budget. It totaled $439 billion, a 7 percent increase over the 2006 defense budget, without including an additional $120 million provided separately for the war in Iraq. The budget was accompanied by the 2006 Quadrennial Defense Review, issued by the SecDef as a philosophical perspective to illustrate the DoD's view of the world situation and the relationship of that perspective to the budget programs. QDR 2006 did alter the 2001 national military strategy. It established the "Global War on Terrorism" as the number-one priority of the strategy and it eliminated the requirement that we end one of the "two overlapping wars" rapidly. Otherwise, QDR largely reaffirmed the 2001 strategy and the 2004 DPG. In fact, the DPG specifically called for enlarging the fleet and maintaining the carrier force level at eleven carriers. This was the only force-level guidance provided for naval forces. The QDR also noted, with approval, the Navy's acquisition of twelve new prepositioning ships for the future sea basing support fleet.

CARRIER FORCE LEVELS

The aircraft carrier force level in the fleet today consists of eleven large-deck carriers. Ten carriers are nuclear: one *Enterprise* class and nine *Nimitz* class. An additional nuclear carrier, the *George H. W. Bush* (CVN-77), is under construction, scheduled to join the fleet in 2008. No further aircraft carriers are fully funded. CVN-78 is planned for authorization and full funding for construction in 2007. It will be a large-deck nuclear-powered carrier of the CVN-21 class, essentially an improved *Nimitz* design. It will replace the *Enterprise*, the Navy's first nuclear carrier, in

2014, when the *Enterprise* is fifty-three years old. This will maintain the force level of nuclear carriers at eleven. Northrop Grumman at Newport News is the only facility capable of constructing a large nuclear carrier. The projected life span of a nuclear carrier can be extended to more than fifty years through appropriate rebuilding and modernization.

With the long useful service life projected for the nuclear carrier, there has been occasional concern expressed from some long-range planning analysts who have suggested that the aircraft carrier, like the dreadnought battleship, could become obsolescent. The response to this perception is that the aircraft carrier, like an airfield, can only become obsolete when tactical aircraft become obsolete and are no longer of use in warfare. Should this occur, there will then be no need for a U.S. Air Force or for Army aviation. The only function of these organizations, like that of the carrier, is to operate military aircraft in the defense of the nation. There is no suggestion, even in the longest-range plans of the DoD, that aircraft will become obsolete in the foreseeable future.

The concern that carriers may become more vulnerable in future wars is misplaced. The aircraft carrier is no more vulnerable than any of our fleet units. The carrier is, in fact, the primary source of protection for the conduct of virtually all other naval warfare functions. For example, strike operations by Marine expeditionary forces would be unthinkable without the level of air superiority and general naval supremacy provided by the large-deck aircraft carriers. And the land operations conducted by the Navy-Marine carrier and expeditionary forces is the only opposed entry capability available to the U.S. armed forces today. In all recent conflicts, World War II and afterward, more tactical aircraft on both sides were destroyed on the ground than on the decks of aircraft carriers.

The number of carriers, and their associated carrier strike groups, in the order of battle of the United States exerts a critical influence on this nation's foreign policy. Today, and into the future, the country will go to war with no more than the carrier force in being when the shooting starts. In the Korean War, when the successful outcome of the conflict was dependent upon the available air power that could be brought to bear against the North Korean and Chinese invaders, the Navy was able to triple the size of its carrier fleet by bringing World War II *Essex*-class ships out of mothballs and manning them with World War II veterans from the Navy Reserve. Today there are no carriers in mothballs available for mobilization. It would take five years to construct a large carrier, even with the highest priority. Therefore, the carrier force in being today, and its sustaining shipbuilding program, must be capable of supporting the nation's foreign policy in the most critical areas.

THE FUTURE THREAT FROM CHINA

It has been our policy to support the independence of Taiwan, and the U.S. government has been quick and positive to react when the status quo of that country has been threatened. In October 1958 the U.S. Seventh Fleet was reinforced to seven fleet carriers and deployed to the Taiwan Straits to deter the mainland Chinese from their threat to occupy two Taiwan-affiliated offshore islands, Quemoy and Matsu. The Chinese Communists backed down as the result of this confrontation and ceased all threatening gestures toward the offshore islands.

The George W. Bush administration has repeated the pledge to protect Taiwan against an attack from mainland China. In March 2005, Chinese leaders in Beijing introduced legislation that would authorize military action if Taiwan took concrete steps toward formal independence. This is a direct challenge to the president of Taiwan, who has made the island's defacto independent status a paramount goal of his administration.

If the United States were to reduce its carrier levels to eight or nine CVNs in the next several years, there would be a question of whether the nation could prevail in a military showdown over Taiwan with the Chinese navy of the future. Intelligence analysts from multiple sources agree that China is building a modern navy of nuclear submarines, missile ships, and supersonic maritime strike aircraft on an accelerated basis. Considering the long land border with Russia and India, and the lack of any Japanese navy (only a maritime self defense force), China's new navy can only be for the purpose of confronting the U.S. Navy on the Pacific Rim. In any Sino-U.S. confrontation over Taiwan, the U.S. carriers would be our main source of military power. Our surface navy could not survive in the Taiwan Straits against Chinese land-based air without the cover of carrier-based strike fighters to establish local zones of air and maritime superiority in which to engage Chinese amphibious forces. Basing U.S. Air Force aircraft on Taiwan airfields would not appear to be an option, because they would be within range of the new Chinese missiles launched from mainland sites.

Such a conflict, or even a confrontation, with the People's Republic of China over Taiwan may not occur. But to dissuade the mainland Chinese from threatening Taiwan, the United States must maintain a *credible* deterrence, a realistic *capability* to interpose in the event of a threatened PRC invasion. This capability only resides in the carriers of the U.S. Navy. It is unreasonable to think of even a threat to resort to nuclear weapons. The potential of a miscalculation on the part of the Chinese or ourselves could lead to an attempt at preemption resulting in a nuclear exchange. The defense of Taiwan is clearly not worth the risk of a nuclear war with the Chinese, with the attendant destruction of American cities and industry. Taiwan can be best defended through deterring a PRC invasion or conflict by maintaining the threat of intervention from a force of large-deck aircraft carriers in sufficient numbers to achieve maritime air superiority in the Taiwan Straits with squadrons of embarked fighter-attack aircraft representative of the most advanced aerospace and weapons technology.

.

Envoi

This has been a book about aircraft carriers. The subject cannot be considered completed without reemphasizing that, without the people to operate and maintain them, aircraft carriers and the planes they fly are immobile, inanimate objects. The skill, dedication, and courage of these young American men and women, which have enabled naval aviation to sustain the preeminent role of the aircraft carrier as the centerpiece of U.S. sea power, are perhaps singularly well exemplified by a young George Herbert Walker Bush, who at the age of seventeen, and not yet out of high school, walked into a Navy recruiting office the day after the attack on Pearl Harbor to sign up as a Navy pilot. He had to wait until he became eighteen, and then, with his father's permission, he joined up and began a career of public service that carried him to the White House as our forty-first president.

His selfless courage, which marked him as a hero among heroes, was commemorated in remarks I made at the keel-laying ceremony for the *George H. W. Bush* (CVN-77), on 6 September 2003 in Newport News, Virginia:

> George Herbert Walker Bush, the forty-first president of the United States, is a living hero to many people for many different reasons. To one very special group, the community of naval aviators, he is a hero

among heroes. To the carrier pilots of the U.S. Navy, George Bush is one of them. They are proud and possessive of their special relationship with this great American.

These naval aviators have a keen appreciation for the patriotism of George Bush. He was just out of high school, setting aside his plans to attend the college (where he was already accepted) in order to take his place in the front lines of the conflict as a carrier pilot. When he got his wings and commission, just days before his nineteenth birthday, he was the youngest naval aviator on record.

Navy carrier pilots remember with a vicarious satisfaction that Lieutenant Bush accumulated more than twelve hundred flight hours and flew fifty-eight combat missions. He also made 126 carrier landings during his service in the Navy, most of them in a large, fast torpedo plane on the small, pitching deck of a converted cruiser. Naval aviators give his pilot skills high marks. They remember that after his TBM suffered complete engine failure on a carrier takeoff, he ditched the depth charge–laden Avenger in a smooth crash landing that enabled his two crewmen to escape the sinking plane without injury.

But especially, naval aviators remember with an admiration born of their own experience his personal courage at Chi-Chi Jima Island in Japan. We should let the simple but compelling phrases of Lieutenant Bush's citation for the Distinguished Flying Cross tell the story: "For heroism and extraordinary achievement as pilot of a torpedo plane leading a two-plane section in a strike against a radio station, LTJG Bush pressed home his attacks in the face of intense anti-aircraft fire. Although his plane was hit and set afire at the beginning of his dive, he continued his plunge toward the target and scored damaging bomb hits before bailing out of his craft."

For the combat Navy pilot, the sentence that earns the highest level of admiration is the last one: "Although his plane was hit and set afire at the beginning of his dive, he continued his plunge toward the target and scored damaging bomb hits before bailing out of his craft." No one would ever disagree with the decision of a pilot in combat to bail out of a powerless, blazing aircraft at high altitude, where the getting out was good. But Lt. George Bush stayed with his fatally crippled plane to complete his attack. In doing this, he drastically reduced his chances of surviving. Bailing out at minimum altitude, he struck the plane's horizontal stabilizer and his parachute canopy was torn. George Bush was a hero in the definitive sense of the word, but his Distinguished Flying Cross came close to being a posthumous award.

After a dramatic pickup by the rescue submarine USS *Finback*, he remained on board for a month while the sub completed its war patrol. When the *Finback* finally returned to Hawaii, where he could disembark, George Bush asked to be returned to his old squadron, VT-51, still aboard the *San Jacinto* in the western Pacific. For the second time in his brief naval career, Lieutenant Bush had risen above and beyond the normal call of duty. In his status as a survivor separated from his squadron, he could have returned to the United States where his combat experience would be put to use training fleet replacement pilots. This was, in fact, standard practice. Naval aviators will always remember with undisguised approbation George Bush's decision to rejoin his comrades in arms in VT-51 and continue flying TBMs in combat at the forefront of the intensifying battle for the Japanese home islands.

For a nineteen-year-old Navy Reserve lieutenant (j.g.), this was the epitome of commitment. He remained with his squadron mates until VT-51 was disbanded in 1945, having suffered more than 50 percent casualties.

Within an hour, the keel will be emplaced and the *George H. W. Bush* will begin its existence as the most modern of the U.S. Navy's *Nimitz*-class carriers. It is comforting to reflect that when the USS *George H. W. Bush* joins its sister ships, the *George Washington* and *Abraham Lincoln*, in the battle line of our fleet, its entire military capability will be vested in the young Navy flyers of a later generation, who will have as their inspiration the example of the skill, commitment, and courage of that carrier's namesake, George Herbert Walker Bush.

Abbreviations and Acronyms

AA	antiaircraft
AAA	antiaircraft artillery
ACDA	Arms Control and Disarmament Agency
AdCom	administrative command
ADIZ	air defense identification zone
AE	ammunition ship
AEC	Atomic Energy Commission
AF	store ship
AFS	combat store ship
AG	miscellaneous support ship
AIM	air intercept missile
AirLant	commander, Naval Air Force, Atlantic
AirPac	commander, Naval Air Force, Pacific
ALNAV	all Navy message
ANA	Association of Naval Aviation
ANRP	Airborne Nuclear Reactor Program
AO	oiler
AOE	fast combat support ship
AP	armor-piercing
APC	armored personnel carrier
ARB	aircraft rearming boat

ARG	Amphibious Ready Group
ARM	antiradiation missile
ARVN	Army of the Republic of North Vietnam
ASW	antisubmarine warfare
ATAR	antitank aircraft rocket
AvGas	aviation gasoline
BB	battleship
BDA	bomb-damage assessment
BM	boatswain's mate
BN	bombardier/navigator
BuPers	Bureau of Naval Personnel
BuShips	Bureau of Ships
C6F	commander, Sixth Fleet
C7F	commander, Seventh Fleet
CA	heavy (8-inch) gun cruiser
CAP	combat air patrol
CarDiv	carrier division
CAS	close air support
CCDG	commander, Cruiser-Destroyer Group
CentCom	Central Command
CEO	chief executive officer
CGN	nuclear-powered guided missile cruiser
CIA	Central Intelligence Agency
CIC	Combat Information Center
CinC	commander in chief
CinCEur	commander in chief, European Command
CinCLant	commander in chief, Atlantic Command
CinCLantFlt	commander in chief, Atlantic Fleet
CinCPac	commander in chief, Pacific Command
CinCPacFlt	commander in chief, Pacific Fleet
CinccUSNavEur	commander in chief, U.S. Naval Forces, Europe
CLG	guided missile light cruiser
CNO	chief of naval operations
CNP	chief of naval personnel
CO	commanding officer
COD	carrier on-board delivery
ComNavAirPac	commander, Naval Air Forces, Pacific

ComNavAirPac	commander, Naval Air Force Pacific Fleet
CONUS	continental United States
CPO	chief petty officer
CPX	command post exercise
CRT	cathode ray tube
CTF	commander, task force
CTG	commander, task group
CTU	commander, task unit
CV	multipurpose aircraft carrier
CVA	attack aircraft carrier
CVAN	attack aircraft carrier, nuclear powered
CVE	escort aircraft carrier
CVL	light aircraft carrier
CVN	aircraft carrier, nuclear powered
CVS	support (ASW) aircraft carrier
CVT	aircraft carrier, training
CVW	carrier air wing
DCNO	deputy chief of naval operations
DD	destroyer
DDG	guided-missile destroyer
DE	escort ship
DefCon	defense readiness condition
DLGN	guided-missile frigate, nuclear powered
DMZ	Demilitarized Zone
DoD	Department of Defense
DPG	Defense Planning Guidance
EuCom	European Command
FAC	forward air controller
FAFIK	Fifth Air Force in Korea
FAGU	fleet air gunnery unit
FASRon	fleet aircraft service squadron
FAX	fighter attack plane, experimental
FEAF	Far East Air Force
FEBA	forward edge of the battle area
FFAR	forward-firing aircraft rocket
FY	fiscal year
GCA	ground-controlled approach

GDA	gun-damage assessment
GI	enlisted person or veteran
GP	general purpose
GQ	general quarters
GS	general service
HC	high-capacity
HM	helicopter mine countermeasures squadron
hp	horsepower
HVAR	high-velocity aircraft rocket
ICBM	intercontinental ballistic missile
ID	identification
ISE	independent steaming exercises
JCS	Joint Chiefs of Staff
j.g.	junior grade
JOC	Joint Operations Center
JP	jet fuel
JS	Joint Staff
JSF	joint strike fighter
JSOP	Joint Strategic Objective Plan
KOG	kindly old gentleman (Admiral Rickover's nickname)
LABS	low-altitude bombing system
LCS(L)	landing craft, support (large)
LDO	limited duty officer
LOC	line(s) of communication
LPD	amphibious transport, dock
LPH	amphibious assault ship
LSD	landing ship, dock
LSO	landing signal officer
LST	landing ship, tank
LWF	lightweight fighter
LZ	landing zone
MAAG	Military Assistance Advisory Group
MACV	military assistance commander, Vietnam
MARHUK	Marine hunter-killer
MASH	mobile army surgical hospital
MATS	Military Air Transport Service

MC	multichannel
MP	Military Police
MPQ	radar-controlled bombing system
MSO	minesweeper, ocean
MSR	main supply route
NAS	Naval Air Station
NATO	North Atlantic Treaty Organization
NATOPS	Naval Air Training and Operating Procedures Standardization
NAVFOR	naval forces
NCA	National Command Authority
NHF	Naval Historical Foundation
NOB	Naval Operating Base
NOD	night observation device
NROTC	Naval Reserve Officer Training Corps
NSA	National Security Agency
NSC	National Security Council
NTDS	naval tactical data system
NVA	North Vietnamese Army
NVN	North Vietnam
NWC	Naval War College
NWIP	Naval Warfare Informational Publication
NWP	Naval Warfare Publication
O&M	Operations and Maintenance
OMB	Office of Management and Budget
OpCon	Operational Control
OPDEP	operations deputy
OpNav	Office of the Chief of Naval Operations
OpSec	operations security
ORE	operational readiness evaluation
ORI	operational readiness inspection
OSD	Office of the Secretary of Defense
PA&E	program analyses and evaluation
PCF	patrol craft (fast)
PCO	prospective commanding officer
POW	prisoner of war
PRC	People's Republic of China

PSI	pounds per square inch
PT	motor torpedo boat
PX	post exchange
QDR	Quadrennial Defense Review
R&R	rest and relaxation
RAF	Royal Air Force
RDF	radio direction finder
RDT&E	research, development, testing, and evaluation
recce	reconnaissance
RIO	radar intercept officer
ROE	Rules of Engagement
ROK	Republic of Korea
ROKAF	Republic of Korea air force
ROTC	Reserve Officers' Training Corps
rpm	revolutions per minute
RTAFB	Royal Thai Air Force Base
RVN	Republic of Vietnam
SAC	Strategic Air Command
SAM	surface-to-air missile
SAR	search and rescue
SCRAM	emergency shutdown of a nuclear reactor
SEATO	Southeast Asia Treaty Organization
SecDef	secretary of defense
SecNav	secretary of the Navy
shp	shaft horsepower
SLEP	Service Life Extension Program
SOF	Special Operations Force(s)
SOP	standard operating procedure
SPACE A	space available
SpecOps	special operations
SSBN	ballistic missile submarine, nuclear
TAC	Tactical Air Control
TACC	Tactical Air Control Center
TACP	Tactical Air Control Party
TADC	Tactical Air Direction Center
TBM	Grumman Avenger torpedo bomber
TBS	talk between ships radio

TF	task force
TG	task group
TNT	trinitrotoluene
TOT	time on target
TWA	Trans World Airlines
UCLA	University of California, Los Angeles
UHF	ultra high frequency
UK	United Kingdom
UN	United Nations
UnRep	underway replenishment
UPI	United Press International
URG	underway replenishment group
US	United States
USAF	U.S. Air Force
USMACV	U.S. Military Assistance Command, Vietnam
USMC	U.S. Marine Corps
USN	U.S. Navy
USNR	U.S. Naval Reserve (Ready)
USO	United Service Organization
USSR	Union of Soviet Socialist Republics
UUV	unmanned undersea vehicle
V/STOL	vertical/short takeoff and landing aircraft
VA	attack squadron
VB	bombing squadron
VCNO	vice chief of naval operations
VERTREP	vertical replenishment
VF	fighter squadron
VHF	very high frequency
VIP	very important person
WSAG	Washington Special Actions Group
XO	executive officer

INDEX

The Naval Institute Press is the book-publishing arm of the U.S. Naval Institute, a private, nonprofit, membership society for sea service professionals and others who share an interest in naval and maritime affairs. Established in 1873 at the U.S. Naval Academy in Annapolis, Maryland, where its offices remain today, the Naval Institute has members worldwide.

Members of the Naval Institute support the education programs of the society and receive the influential monthly magazine *Proceedings* and discounts on fine nautical prints and on ship and aircraft photos. They also have access to the transcripts of the Institute's Oral History Program and get discounted admission to any of the Institute-sponsored seminars offered around the country. Discounts are also available to the colorful bimonthly magazine *Naval History*.

The Naval Institute's book-publishing program, begun in 1898 with basic guides to naval practices, has broadened its scope to include books of more general interest. Now the Naval Institute Press publishes about seventy titles each year, ranging from how-to books on boating and navigation to battle histories, biographies, ship and aircraft guides, and novels. Institute members receive significant discounts on the Press's more than eight hundred books in print.

Full-time students are eligible for special half-price membership rates. Life memberships are also available.

For a free catalog describing Naval Institute Press books currently available, and for further information about joining the U.S. Naval Institute, please write to:
Member Services

U.S. Naval Institute
291 Wood Road
Annapolis, MD 21402-5034
Telephone: (800) 233-8764
Fax: (410) 571-1703
Web address: www.navalinstitute.org